MULTICULTURAL ASPECTS
OF DISABILITIES

ABOUT THE AUTHOR

Willie V. Bryan is Professor Emeritus, Health Promotion Sciences, University of Oklahoma, Health Sciences Center. Dr. Bryan was an administrator and professor at the Health Sciences Center for 32 years. In 1985, he received the President's Committee on Employment of the Handicapped Book Award for *Psychosocial Aspects of Disability*, which he co-authored. Before his services at The University of Oklahoma Health Sciences Center he served as a Vocational Rehabilitation counselor for the state of Oklahoma, and also served as Director of Rehabilitation and Personnel for Goodwill Industries of Oklahoma City. Dr. Bryan has a masters degree in psychology, emphasis on rehabilitation counseling, another masters degree in education and a doctorate in counseling. He currently teaches courses on cultural diversity, helping relationships, and family counseling for the Colleges of Liberal Studies and Advanced Programs, University of Oklahoma, Norman Campus.

Second Edition

MULTICULTURAL ASPECTS OF DISABILITIES

A Guide to Understanding and Assisting
Minorities in the Rehabilitation Process

By

WILLIE V. BRYAN, Ed.D.

CHARLES C THOMAS • PUBLISHER, LTD.
Springfield • Illinois • U.S.A.

Published and Distributed Throughout the World by

CHARLES C THOMAS • PUBLISHER, LTD.
2600 South First Street
Springfield, Illinois 62704

©2007 by CHARLES C THOMAS • PUBLISHER, LTD.

ISBN 978-0-398-07708-2 (hard)
ISBN 978-0-398-07709-9 (paper)

Library of Congress Catalog Card Number: 2006050190

With THOMAS BOOKS *careful attention is given to all details of man-
ufacturing and design. It is the Publisher's desire to present books that are satisfactory as to their physical qualities and artistic possibilities and appropriate for their particular use.* THOMAS BOOKS *will be true to those laws
of quality that assure a good name and good will.*

*Printed in the United States of America
CR-R-3*

Library of Congress Cataloging-in-Publication Data

Bryan, Willie V.
    Multicultural aspects of disabilities : a guide to understanding and
assisting minorities in the rehabilitation process / by Willie V.
Bryan. -- 2nd ed.
    Includes bibliographical references and index.
    ISBN 978-0-398-07708-2 -- ISBN 978-0-398-07709-9 (pbk.)
    1. Minority people with disabilities--Services for--United States.
2. Minority people with disabilities--Rehabilitation--United States.
3. Social work with minorities--United States. 4. Social work with
people disabilities--United States. 5. Multiculturalism--United States.
I. Title.

HV1569.3.M55B79 2007
362.4089'00973--dc22

2006050190

This edition is dedicated to the Bryan, Lowe and Vickers families, who are not only my extended family, but also they have made significant contributions to my cultural composition.

PREFACE

Through the collaboration of a variety of individuals and organizations, the disability rights movement was given life and because of this partnership, the movement was able to accomplish some remarkable things that have benefited persons with disabilities. Until these various forces joined together, very little outside of U. S. Congressional action was being done to enable persons with disabilities to do anything other than dream about the American dream. Today, although not where we should be, American society is more accessible to persons with disabilities.

The disability rights movement borrowed many of its concepts and techniques from the civil rights movement of the 1950s and 1960s and was successful in adapting them to their needs and forged the previously mentioned partnerships which helped produce remarkable results. It is ironic that the movement that provided the foundation for the disability rights revolution has not been used by the disability community to emphasize and broadcast the needs of racial/ethnic minorities with disabilities. The fact that a significant number of persons with disabilities are persons of color seems to be of very little concern to organizations and agencies working with persons with disabilities. Little, if any, attention is given to the association of race/ethnicity, disability, and socioeconomic status. Stated in more succinct terms, very little attention is given to one's cultures. Unfortunately, helping professionals continue to concentrate on disability to the exclusion of culture. This book is an effort to bring to the attention of helping professionals the need to give significant consideration to cultural factors in their efforts to develop effective rehabilitation plans for persons of color with disabilities. This book goes beyond increasing awareness by offering information with regard to intervention strategies.

Disabilities are as old as humankind and those who possess a disability experience ambiguous attitudes and confusing treatment. Part of the reason for confusing treatments received from helping professionals can be attributed to the fact they have failed to consider one valuable variable–the cultural factors influencing the person's behavior. It is hoped that this book will assist helping professionals become better acquainted with the impact that culture has on the client and the impact it will have in the helping process.

W.V.B.

ABOUT THE SECOND EDITION

This second edition continues the theme of providing information with regard to factors that impact the lives of racial/ethnic minorities as well as women and the elderly in America. The information provided helps define cultures of the previously mentioned groups.

The book is divided into four parts: Culture and Multiculturalism, Disability, Disabilities and Multiculturalism, and Helping. In addition to updating information that was presented in the first edition, a new section—Helping—has been added. Part four—Helping provides considerable new information with regard to methods of assisting minorities with disabilities. Chapter 13, The Helping Relationship, is designed to assist the helper become more culturally sensitive with regard to better understanding one's own belief systems and motivation. Additionally, the chapter deals with understanding human behavior. Chapters 14 and 15, Individual Therapies and Family Counseling, provide a discussion of established contemporary therapies; the addition of these chapters reinforces the concept that new therapies do not have to be developed to work with multicultural persons with disabilities. The discussion of these chapters further emphasizes the fact that the helping professional must be aware of the variable of culture in implementing these helping tools.

Another addition is Chapter 3, Religion. It is this author's contention that religion for many persons of color is as important, in some cases more important, as any of the cultural variables that impact behavior. Unfortunately, too often clients' religious beliefs are not considered when assisting them. Therefore, it is vitally important that the helping professional be aware of this fact.

The updates and addition of new chapters will make the text a more complete discussion of cultural information needed by professional helpers in their efforts to assist multicultural persons in the rehabilitation process.

CONTENTS

MULTICULTURAL ASPECTS OF DISABILITIES

Part One

CULTURE AND MULTICULTURALISM

Chapter 1

CULTURE

Chapter Outline
- Introduction
- What Is Culture?
- Is there a Disability Culture?
- The Nature of Culture
- Understanding Cultural Diversity
- Multiculturalism
- Cultural Accommodation
- Acculturation
- Conclusion

Chapter Objectives
- Provide an analysis of the concept of culture
- Provide an understanding of cultural diversity
- Provide an analysis of the concept of multiculturalism
- Provide a discussion of acculturation

Introduction

Humans create culture: As discussed in this chapter, culture is not inherited but is developed through a socialization process; therefore, the premise that by classifying persons into ethnic, racial, and religious groups (to mention only three groups) and declaring that they have the same culture, we can explain their existence is false. There are several facts about culture that makes this belief untrue: (1) culture is influenced by proximity; (2) culture is not restricted by race or ethnicity; and (3) culture is mobile.

Regardless of ethnicity or racial background, the local social and environmental atmosphere will have an influence on the person's cultural development. This is not to say that racial or ethnic factors do not impact one's cultural development. However, what is being stated is the local culture, in which the person is involved, will have a profound impact upon one's cultural development. Offered as examples is the fact that native New Yorkers, who are African American, have similar mannerisms, such as speech patterns, as well as beliefs and attitudes, as native New Yorkers who are Caucasians. Whereas, African Americans in the southwestern part of the United States have similar speech patterns and attitudes as Caucasian counterparts in the southwest and these cultural differences often are strikingly different than African Americans in the northeast part of the United States. If a person moves, he takes with him many aspects of his current culture; however, over time, being influenced by the new cultural environment, he will gradually adopt the new prevailing culture.

Each group develops its own culture: Each individual is part of many cultures and if she intends to be accepted by those cultures, she incorporates many of that group's cultural values. If the group's values are contrary to the person's values, hopefully she removes herself from the group and associates with a group that has values, beliefs, and attitudes that are congruent with her cultural beliefs. Unfortunately, this does not always happen, in too many instances, to be accepted by the majority, some people compromise their standards.

Everyone has some degree of ethnocentrism: Ethnocentrism is the belief that one's culture is superior to all other cultures. At first glance, to some, this statement my seem absurd; however, as we give closer and deeper thought to what is being said the truth of this statement is revealed. As Americans, most of us, out of pride in our country and belief in our system of laws and government, think that the American culture is superior to other cultures. Harmful ethnocentrism occurs when a group is told they are better than other groups and this message is constantly reinforced through various forms of propaganda. For example, if the group with which one associates his cultural identity is constantly referred to as being gifted athletically and academically then over a period of time, one begins to believe the message. Pride in one's group is not bad; however, when we act upon our feelings of superiority, then our actions go beyond pride and become prejudice.

Because we decide to ignore cultural conflict, this does not make the same disappear: Avoidance and burying our heads in the sand does not solve many problems. Confronting and dealing with a problem is usually the best and most appropriate solution. Often conflict and tension are increased when confronting prejudice and bigotry; however, the alternative is usually worse, which is unfair and unjust treatment continues unchecked. In the case of disability discrimination when unproductive beliefs are held, such as persons with disabilities prefer charity rather than employment, if these and other similar beliefs are not challenged, not only does the discrimination continue, also the erroneous belief also continues to be held and perhaps grows stronger in that others adopt similar beliefs.

No one knows all things about all cultures: In an age where most helping professionals are sincerely concerned about being nonoffensive to any person or group of people, much concern exists with regard to how much professionals should know about cultures other than their own. Unless a helping professional has a very limited practice, it is impossible to know about every aspect of a person's culture. Honesty is the key word in discussing cultural awareness. Being honest with one's self that one does not know and will not know all aspects of a client/patient's culture and being honest by explaining that he does not know but is willing and interested in learning is not only important but essential.

What Is Culture?

The collective wisdom of anthropologists and others who attempt to explain human behavior and existence have failed to produce a clear-cut definition of culture. In all probability, because of the very subjective nature of what we consider as culture, a definition which is universally accepted will continue to allude its seekers. A comparison of some accepted cultural definitions tends to verify this point. Herskovits (1955) identifies culture in the context of being part of the environment which we humans have made and states that it includes our artifacts as well as laws, myths, and the special ways we view our environment. Others who attempt to capture the essence of culture consider it as the things that various people share in common such as religion, language, and economic status, to mention a few. Fairchild (1970) defines culture as all behavior patterns socially acquired and socially transmitted by means of symbols, including customs, techniques, beliefs, institutions, and material objects. In a somewhat different approach, Triandis (1972) does not attempt to define culture but indicates that it is in our heads. He further states that culture is absorbed by individuals in the process of socialization rather than actively taught and effortly acquired.

These various definitions of culture appropriately illustrate that there are numerous variables contributing to the cultural makeup of an individual or group of individuals. Therefore, the primary lesson to extract from this failed exercise in defining culture is to never generalize about culture. It is very tempting to neatly categorize specific cultural groups, such as African American culture, American Indian culture, Hispanic/Latino American culture, Asian American culture, and identify characteristics that appear to be shared by members within each group and proclaim to the world that this constitutes the cultural composition of the group. However, despite that there may be some shared characteristics in cultural groups such as skin color, hair texture, and speech patterns, there are also as many, if not more variations within these groups as there are shared traits.

As always, definitions vary according to the definer's point of view. Let us analyze several other definitions to determine if some common view points can be found. Some social scientists defined culture as the "way of life" of a people, including the sum of their learned behavioral patterns, attitudes and collection of material things. Lee (1989) and Axelson (1993) state that culture is the collective reality of a group of people and remind us that it is from this collective reality that attitudes, behaviors and values are formed and become reinforced among a group of people over time. As previously stated, Fairchild (1970) defines culture as behavior patterns which are socially acquired and socially transmitted including customs, techniques, beliefs, institutions, and material objects. And Triandis (1972) argues that culture is in our heads and is composed of the shared experience and knowledge of a self-perpetuating and continuous human group and is part and parcel of our personal reality. His belief is that culture is learned through socialization rather than learned through an active teaching process.

Though these definitions vary, there are, however, some common points one can observe and they are: (1) Culture is a group orientation. Stated another way, culture is common behavior, beliefs, attitudes, and values shared by a group of people; (2) Culture is learned behavior, attitudes, beliefs, and values, not inherited; (3) Culture is learned via socialization rather than through a formal teaching process. Therefore, at the risk of breaking my rule of not generalizing an operational definition that will be used in this book is as follows: Culture is commonly held characteristics such as attitudes, beliefs, values, customs and patterns of behavior possessed by a group of people, which have been learned and reinforced through a socialization process.

Additional Evaluation of Culture

As one gives casual thought to the topic of culture, we frequently associate culture with racial background. Decades of stereotyping have resulted in linking specific behavior to certain racial groups and this association has become so strong that in part the group as a whole is defined by these characteristics. The association of the behaviors to one's racial background is so interwoven that some regard the "cultural traits" as inherited. In other words, some people view culture and race as inseparable. Ashley Montagu (1997) contradicts this view by informing us that race and culture do not appear to be in any way connected. He further points out that culture is determined by one's experiences rather than anything innate; therefore, culture is the human-made part of the environment. Consequently, what we observe as a common characteristic of a group is a reflection of the similar experiences of its group members, and because these characteristics differ from our own we tend to categorize them as being unique unto that group.

As an example, one of the cultural traits often associated with African Americans is athletic ability. Because of the success that African Americans have experienced in professional athletics such as basketball, football, boxing, and baseball, some non-African Americans believe that African Americans are born with superior athletic abilities and/or they are better physically equipped to excel in athletic endeavors than other racial groups. The truth is instead of innate abilities, the prowess of African Americans in many athletic arenas can be attributed to their life experiences. Countless number of hours of athletic competition among friends and neighbors account for their athletic skills rather than a racial inheritance. Therefore, true to what Montagu postulated, it is one's experiences that determines culture.

Ironically, while Euro-Americans attribute numerous cultural traits to racial minority groups, it is the clustering (living in close proximity) of these racial groups which is stimulated by the dominant Euro-American society that causes similar beliefs, customs, ideas, and values of these minority groups. It is, therefore, quite understandable that a group of individuals who are experiencing similar things will develop similar beliefs, ideas, and other like ways of interacting with their environment. Thus culture must be evaluated with regard to the group's background. The following comments by Montagu (1997) adequately summarizes this point:

> Culture must be evaluated in relation to their own history, and carefully, not by the arbitrary standard of any single culture. Judged in relation to its own history, each culture is seen as the resultant of the responses to the challenges which that history may or may not record. If those challenges have been limited in nature, so will the culture reflecting their effects. If the challenges have been many and complex in character, then the culture will reflect that complexity.

Ashley Montagu's statements clearly indicate that the range and quality of experiences individuals encounter help determine the complexity of one's culture. While this is correct, however, the value which society places on this culture is often determined by the dominant culture. For example, if the dominant culture determines that aggressive behavior is desirable, but subordinate cultures are discouraged or not allowed to be aggressive, their cultural trait of meekness is devalued. If the dominant culture values productivity but places subordinate cultures in positions where their abilities to be productive is limited or the type of productive output of the subordinate cultures is devalued, again the subordinate cultures are placed in a disadvantaged situation. While it is true, that experiences determine the complexity of cultural development, another reality is that the dominant culture determines to a considerable degree the kinds of experiences one encounters. Further, the dominant culture determines the values to be placed upon these cultural traits. It is therefore the devaluing of their culture that minorities including persons with disabilities and other subordinate groups have experienced that causes negative human relations and human interaction.

Culture or Cultures

In previous discussion, reference has been made to inaccurate thoughts of race and culture as inseparable; similarly we tend to group individuals together and associate a particular culture to that group, i.e., Asian American culture, or African American culture. As we give deep and serious thought to the idea of culture, we begin to realize that there is no one culture that fits any group of people. Stated succinctly, there is no one African American culture, nor one American Indian culture. There are numerous cultures associated with any ethnic group. An African American reared in Harlem, New York, will have some experiences similar to an African American reared in rural Oklahoma; however, the two will have many different experiences which will mean their cultural backgrounds will be different. From a cultural standpoint, with the exception of some physical appearances such as skin pigmentation and hair texture, there may be more cultural similarities between the African American reared in rural Oklahoma and a Euro-American reared in rural Oklahoma than between the African American New York native and the African American Oklahoma Native. This is not intended to indicate that the two African Americans, although from different regions of America, will not experience similar acts of discrimination and oppression. This point emphasizes that as a helping professional, one cannot afford to fall into the trap of accepting the conventional view, that there are specific racial cultural characteristics that can be generalized to all members of that racial group.

Is There a Disability Culture?

As previously stated, when one thinks of cultural groups the thoughts are generally associated with racial and/or ethnic groups; however, upon examining my operational definition of culture, "Culture is commonly held characteristics such as attitudes, beliefs, values, customs, and patterns of behavior possessed by a group of people, which have been learned and reinforced through a socialization process," one should raise the question, "Is there a culture, or cultures, associated with being a member of the community of persons with disabilities?" Based upon this definition, one could argue that any group of people who share common characteristics which have been obtained and/or imposed upon them by a socialization process qualifies as a cultural group; therefore, one may conclude that persons with disabilities qualify as a cultural group. However, if one takes the anthropological view of culture, which primarily identifies culture from a racial and ethnic standpoint, then there is no disability culture. Certainly disabilities cannot be traced back in time to a common language such as Spanish for persons of Hispanic/Latino background, nor can disabilities be traced to a country or continent of origin such as Africa. Persons with disabilities are perhaps the most diverse group of people on Earth; the group consists of all human characteristics in existence, all racial and ethnic backgrounds, all social and economic levels, and both genders. Given this cornucopia of human conditions, reality dictates that disability is one variable among many that constitutes a person's being. Race, ethnicity, and gender are also variables and we attach cultural significance to persons who are considered members of these groups. With this in consideration, should we attach cultural significance to each human variable? The answer is no; one obviously could take the attaching cultural significance to an extreme. Another logical question is, "Why should we consider persons with disabilities as being part of a cultural group?" While it is true that persons with disabilities as a group do not have a mother language that distinguishes them from other groups and thousands of years into the future archeologists will not unearth artifacts that relate to a society of disabled persons; however, persons with disabilities have experienced not only within America, but throughout the world, treatment and attitudes that have caused them to be treated differently than the so-called "nondisabled." Both society-at-large and persons with disabilities have been socialized to think of persons with disabilities as being different from others. Persons with disabilities have a long and unique history as a group of people. The reality is that a person with a disability has more in common with his "nondisabled" neighbors than he does with another person with a disability; he nevertheless is perceived to have a common bond with other persons with disabilities and as a result has been classified and characterized as being part of a different and unique group of people. It is for these reasons this author has concluded that there is a disability culture.

There may be disagreement whether there is a disability culture, but there is virtually no disagreement that persons with disabilities are integral to the

diversity of American society. Tainter (1995) supports this view with the following:

> The term diversity is most often used when discussing issues regarding ethnic
> minority groups and women. Another group which deserves consideration
> consists of persons with disabilities. Americans with disabilities are an integral
> part of the fabric of diversity, sharing a common thread with African
> Americans and other groups in their demand for acceptance as individuals,
> respect for abilities and celebration of their differences.

The Nature of Culture

The United States Congress, with the enactment of the Rehabilitation Act
of 1973, the Americans With Disabilities Act of 1990, and the Rehabilitation
Amendments of 1992, recognized persons with disabilities as a class of people who have been discriminated against similar to some racial minorities.

As previously stated, there is no one culture for any group, i.e., American
Indian Culture, African American Culture, or Asian American culture. Likewise, there is no one culture of persons with disabilities. The fact is there are
numerous cultures for each group. In fact, each individual belongs to many
cultures, rural, southern culture, African American southern culture, African
American person with a disability culture, and African American female person with a disability culture and the list could continue. Each individual
moves in and out of various group cultures. When one physically moves
from one part of the United States to another, she probably moves into
another cultural group and may or may not maintain membership in previous cultural groups. The point of this brief discussion with regard to the
sometimes transient nature of culture is to explode the myth that there is a
universal culture for African Americans, Asian Americans, American Indians, Hispanic/Latino Americans, and yes, persons with disabilities. There
are African American cultures and Native American cultures, etc.

Despite the reality that there are multiple cultures for each group, the perception remains that there is a universal culture particularly with respect to
racial minority groups. Consequently, a set of characteristics are ascribed to
the group and all that belong to the group are generally considered to possess these characteristics. In some instances, these characteristics are positive,
but in most cases they represent a less than complimentary opinion of the
group. Regardless of whether they are positive or negative, applied universally, they are a gross misrepresentation of a group of people. Because these
characteristics often become the benchmark by which individuals within that
group are judged, they create obstacles of stereotypes and prejudice through
which the individual is unable to navigate and set himself free.

Tainter (1995) identifies what he considers cultural experiences of persons with disabilities which fit the universally-applied characteristics category. One cultural experience is the view of persons with disabilities as "damaged goods." Tainter points out that to overcome this image, the person feels he must strive to get rid of the differences. Perhaps this impact explains why some persons with disabilities deny their disability and engage in unwise behavior, attempting to be "normal." Another common cultural experience of persons with disabilities which is shared with racial minority groups is the belief that people within these groups who succeed are extraordinary. As Tainter reminds us, this is a patronizing concept which implies if persons with disabilities try hard enough they can succeed. Henderson and Bryan (1997) add to the list of universally-held common cultural experiences by identifying the following common perceptions of persons with disabilities: people with disabilities are inferior, are less intelligent, totally impaired, dependent and need charity, and prefer the company of others with disabilities.

Persons with disabilities who are members of a racial minority group also have the added cultural experience of their minority group. In universally-held cultural misperceptions, the person can be placed in a situation of double jeopardy in that he must navigate his way through the mazes of misconceptions of both cultural groups. Because of the misconceptions of cultural experiences of racial minority persons with disabilities and the peril at which they are often placed because of this inaccurate understanding, there is a tremendous need for more study and better understanding of the cultures of racial minorities and persons with disability and the impact of the intersection of the two cultures, especially by those who are helping professionals.

Understanding Cultural Diversity

In expressing his influential opinion with regard to how the newly formed government's education system should be developed, Thomas Jefferson emphasized the point that persons should be educated to manners, morals and habits that were congruent with those of the country. The manners, morals and habits to which President Jefferson referred were Euro-American cultural values which had been established as the dominant cultural views of the new nation. This point of view coupled with the melting pot theory, which promoted the blending of all cultures in the United States into one culture, a unique American culture, entrenched the idea that Euro-American lifestyles, morals, values, attitudes, and beliefs were the standards by which all Americans should both live and be judged. To restate a previous point, there always have been and probably always will be a "dominant" culture.

This is a reality of life; however, the extent to which other groups' cultures are subordinated and the negative or positive evaluations the group members experience as a result of being judged by the dominant culture's standards determines the impact the dominant culture has upon subordinate cultures.

For decades Euro-American culture has been the dominant culture in America and has had a major influence on virtually every aspect of life including how helping professionals interact with their clients. Recently, helping professionals have begun to question the appropriateness of using one standard to evaluate diverse groups of people who have many life experiences which are considerably different than the dominant cultural standards. Helping professional educators have begun to review their training standards and ask some probing questions about the validity of teaching and training counselors, social workers, rehabilitation counselors, psychologists, psychotherapists, and other helping professionals to evaluate all of their clients and patients with one measuring stick, especially the evaluation of racial minority and persons with disability group members. Both the helping professional educators and the helping professionals themselves have begun to review past as well as present experiences of not taking appropriate consideration of their client's/patient's own cultural background in the helping process. They have begun to question whether the fact that over 50 percent of racial minority persons do not return for counseling after the first session may be attributed in part to the helping professional demonstrating a lack of understanding of the person's cultural standards. Likewise, the low percentage of minority clients/patients following through with treatment plans is also added to the list of things to consider with regard to inadequate understanding of diverse cultures.

The "assumption of universality" is how Keisier (1966) refers to the belief that helping professional practices formulated on the basis of Euro-American cultural standards could be applied uniformly to all clients. Keisier and a growing number of authors (Bryan, 1996; Henderson and Bryan, 1997; Ridley, 1995; Sue, 1990; and Atkinson, Morton and Sue, 1993) have taken exception to this approach which has been widely used in the helping professions. These authors as well as others argue that most traditional theories and practices are biased in favor of white middle-class males. Concurrent with this opposition, numerous books, articles, monographs, and results of proceedings have been published with the expressed purpose of sensitizing helping professionals to the cultural diversity within their client/patient population. Additional discussion of these and other relevant points are put forth in the chapter "Minorities and Disabilities."

Multiculturalism

At first glance, the term "multiculturalism" appear to be a safe and nonoffensive word meaning many cultures. Proponents of multiculturalism view it as a concept of giving recognition to the viewpoints of all cultures which contribute to American society. They further think of multiculturalism as understanding, giving value to and accepting the contribution made by the various cultural groups in America. The concept of many cultures tends to be in conflict with the idea of the melting pot theory which promotes the idea of one culture made from many cultures. The multiculturalists' view the idea of promoting a one-culture or blending various cultures in one "American Culture" as being detrimental to the cultures being blended. In fact, the multicultural view is that it is not a blending but a forced acculturation into the dominant culture. In other words, it is not a melding of cultures into a unique culture which fairly and accurately represents all cultures (if this is possible) but an acceptance of the dominant culture's viewpoint, thus relegating other cultures to a position of lesser importance. The multiculturalists do not necessarily fault the dominant culture's values as being evil or wrong, but find fault that the views, attitudes, and ideas of the dominant culture have become the benchmark for American society and oppose the degree to which attempts are made to impose its will and standards upon the subordinate cultures. From the multiculturist's viewpoint, too often in an attempt to impose its will, the dominant culture degrades the subordinate cultures for not "attaining" the standards of the dominant culture. In the view of multiculturalists, many, if not most, of the dominant culture's standards are good but not the only way.

In America, Euro-Americans are the dominant culture and there are some specific characteristics and standards that are highly respected by this group which serve as the benchmark by which other groups tend to be judged. A brief review of four of these characteristics illustrates the absence of a multicultural approach:

1. *Individualism*–Many Euro-Americans value independence. From elementary schooling through high school, rugged individualism is emphasized. The pioneering efforts of early Euro-American settlers is romanticized in textbooks, television, movies, etc. This results in early identification with the idea that independence is valued and dependency is less valued. This sends the message that every individual should be as independent and self-reliant as possible. Individualism is more important than a group. If one is reared and educated to believe in this philosophy it is difficult to find any fault with this belief; however, from the viewpoint of those who subscribe to multiculturalism, the idea that the individual is more important than the group and independence is valued more than a collective effort does not provide suffi-

cient value to some Asian or Pacific American cultures which emphasize sublimating individual efforts for the good of the group. Perhaps not to the extent some Asian and Pacific Americans emphasize group efforts over individual ventures, some America Indian tribes view the tribal agenda as more important than individual achievement. There has been negative impact on persons with disabilities with regard to the emphasis placed upon independence and individualism, particularly those persons by virtue of their disability having a need for assistance. The multiculturalist would propose that the devaluing of dependency may cause some persons with disabilities to feel inadequate and be treated in a like manner.

2. *Achievement*–Within America's dominant culture, individual achievement is equated with success and in an economically-based society, success is equated with the accumulation of goods and property. The idea of achievement, from the multiculturalist standpoint, is not wrong. America would not be and could not continue to be a world leader if it did not value achievements. The multiculturalist may take issue with overwhelming emphasis on accumulation of material goods. This emphasis does not allow room for valuing those cultures which deemphasize the collection of individual wealth. The implication for persons with disabilities relates to the emphasis on individual achievement and more important is how success is determined. For many persons with disabilities, both individual achievement and accumulation of goods are difficult.

3. *Verbal Expression*–Euro-Americans place more value on verbal communication than interpreting nonverbal communication; therefore, those individuals who can eloquently express themselves verbally are perceived to be more intelligent than the shy quiet person. Multiculturalists would remind us that some Asian and Pacific American cultures and American Indian cultures place considerable value upon silence and/or nonverbal communication.

4. *Nuclear Family Structure*–The nuclear family is considered to be the father, mother, and unmarried children. The influence and contributions of relatives and close friends are minimized. Children within the nuclear family concept are considered equal to the parents, in that their ideas and expressions are to be given as much consideration as adults. As will be discussed in other chapters of this book, the extended family which encourages the input of other relatives such as grandparents, uncles, aunts, and cousins is an integral part of some minority cultures.

These are a few of the cultural values many Euro-Americans hold in high esteem and by which subordinate cultures are judged. Those who subscribe to multiculturalism would argue that all of these values are good as well as beneficial in some settings; however, they would remind us that their objections revolve around the idea that there are other viewpoints which exist and when appropriate, need to be given equal consideration instead of being sublimated to the dominant culture's points of view.

Opponents of multiculturalism view the concept as a part of Affirmative Action and they further view it as a way of condoning preferential treatment for minority groups. Those opposed to multiculturalism make reference to the areas of education and employment especially hiring priorities as examples of what they consider as its undesirable effects.

Opponents of multiculturalism appear not to have strong opposition to making the educational curriculum more culturally representative by including the accomplishments of various racial and ethnic groups in history texts. However, they have taken exception to making what they consider fundamental changes in curriculum such as was proposed in including Ebonics as a form of English. The strongest opposition in the area of education targets what they believe to be preferential admission of minority students. To be more specific, they contend that lesser academically qualified minority applicants are being admitted to colleges and universities than nonminority applicants. They further identify the practice of designating specific scholarships for racial minorities as further evidence of multiculturalism advocating preferential treatment. Therefore, from their perspective, multiculturalism is synonymous with discrimination.

Bradford Wilson, executive director of the National Association of Scholars (1998) articulates that group's opposition to Affirmative Action and multiculturalism with the following remarks:

> The focus on race-conscious affirmative action policies fit naturally into a discussion of multiculturalism because such policies substitute noninntellectual criteria–race and ethnicity–for intellectual criteria–standardized test scores, grades, and scholarships–in the way that multiculturalism uses group identify to justify curriculum upheaval and faculty hiring.

Part of what multiculturalism is concerned about is the focus on racial and ethnic identity as the defining characteristic of an individual. Racial preferences or race conscious affirmative action policies are rooted in the idea that a person's race or ethnicity is sufficient reason to take them seriously or not take them seriously.

Some opponents of multiculturalism make the point that the proponents of this concept support it on the basis that it helps minorities overcome the effects of past discrimination; however, in their opinions, multiculturalism actually does more harm than good in the educational arena in that persons who are poorly prepared academically are admitted, thus experiencing failure and lowering of their self-esteem.

Similar arguments are presented as opponents attack the concept of multiculturalism with regard to employment. Those that support the multicultural concept point out that access to quality education and technological training which would prepare racial minorities and persons with disabilities for career status jobs have traditionally not been available; therefore, to require them to compete for jobs with those who have had access to appropriate education and training is ridiculous. The opponents counter with the argument that employers should not be forced to hire less qualified individuals. They suggest that an answer is to develop the needed training and make the training available to everyone.

The unanswered question in this debate revolves around "prejudice." If those that have been excluded are trained and brought to the knowledge level of those who have not been excluded, will employers hire minorities and persons with disabilities at the same rate they hire others or will past prejudices and preconceived stereotypes enter into and hamper the hiring decision? For those who contend that prejudice will be a factor in hiring decisions, they contend outside intervention will be required. Multicultural opponents counter by saying that in this scenario, any time a minority or person with a disability is not hired, the employer will be accused of being prejudiced.

Cultural Accommodation

What does "understanding diverse cultures" mean? With regard to the helping professions, does this mean developing a theory and practice for each of the racial minority groups as well as persons with disabilities, women, and the elderly? Do culturally sensitive helping techniques imply the opposite of the assumption of universality to which Keisier referred? These are valid and important questions. These and other relevant questions will be addressed in subsequent chapters.

Acculturation

Within a given society, of all the cultural groups which exist, in most cases one will become the dominant culture and as previously stated, many of that society's activities, belief systems, values, and standards are determined by the dominant culture. In an attempt to be accepted by and be considered part of the society, subordinate cultures attempt to emulate the dominant culture. This is a form of acculturation. Some social scientists say that acculturation, within the context of American society, refers to the degree to which an individual identifies with the attitudes, lifestyles, and values of the predominant culture. In American society, there are numerous dominant cultural characteristics and the extent to which individuals and groups of individuals deviate from those characteristics and standards determines how much they are devalued. Likewise, the closer they mimic and/or incorporate them in their lifestyles, the more they are valued. Many of Euro-American cultural standards are so well woven into the fabric of American society that not only do members of the dominant culture accept them as the correct standards by which to live, but in many instances the subordinate culture also makes this same judgement. Unless carried to an extreme, there is, generally speaking, nothing wrong with Euro-American standards. The major problem in American society has been the extent to which the dominant culture has suppressed the subordinate cultures. The lack of consideration given to other points of view and ways of doing things as well as lifestyles is what has been questioned, not the right or wrong of Euro-American cultural standards. One might correctly observe and point out Chinese culture in China is dominant and serves as a benchmark by which societal standards are judged in that country. Also in some countries, societal standards are based upon a religious orientation and one religious sect dominates all other groups, religious and nonreligious oriented. Appropriate responses to these observations are: (1) The fact that one culture completely dominates another in any part of the world is no justification for such occurrences in other parts. This would be similar to justifying oppression by pointing to country X and saying that it has a high standard of living for the majority of its people despite a restrictive society. (2) America is composed of many different groups of people who have worked together to develop the country and society into a world leader; therefore, each cultural group should be valued. (3) The uniqueness and greatness of America has, to a large extent, been based upon the diversity of ideas. The freedom to think, dream, and work toward moving those dreams into realities has been a hallmark of American society. Therefore, one fact that has distinguished America from many other societies has been its diversity.

As diversity is considered in America, it is unfortunate but not surprising that persons with disabilities are often overlooked. Zawaiza (1995) feels that diverse, underserved and/or special populations are usually euphemisms for persons from minority groups. As a society, what we often fail to realize is that persons with disabilities are the most diverse group of people in America, both numerically and in composition. First, they are the largest minority group, and second, they are composed of every segment of American society, represented by all age groups, all racial groups, both genders, and all economic strata. Few groups in America can claim this level of diversity. Despite the diversity, persons with disabilities are too often viewed as one-dimensional. For example, in the helping relationship, the professional helper will too frequently consider only the person's disability or her racial background. When more than one factor is considered, it most often is gender and racial background rather than gender, race, and disability.

The following comments by Tainter, Compisi, and Richards (1995) provide insight into why persons with disabilities must be considered as an integral part of the diversity of America.

> Developing strategies to include people with disabilities in our communities, including the workplace, this is a view that considers disability as part of the fabric of diversity. It must embrace the diversity of all persons with disabilities and consider them as members of the disability community. This community in itself is a cultural group that has come to be identified as a civil rights minority group that requires the same strategies and remedies for inclusion as other minority groups. For persons with disabilities from ethnic minority backgrounds, we must acknowledge and respect all aspects of their diversity. Ignoring any one aspect of a person's background, be it ethnicity, gender, or disability does not benefit the person or the society as a whole. It is a view that asks for the presentation of persons with disabilities in a context of dignity and quality, not pity and patronization.

Davila (1995) recognizes that in the past, persons with disabilities have been viewed one-dimensionally and the result has been a disregard of the needs of this significant group of people. To avoid this deletion of needs in the future, Davila tells us that it is incumbent upon us to recognize persons with disabilities from all backgrounds to ensure that their concerns are placed on the national agenda, and that persons with disabilities receive their share of resources, moreover persons with disabilities must demand that they receive the skills and knowledge needed to succeed in life.

Many of the characteristics of the disability culture have negative connotation such as persons with disabilities are often considered inferior to the person without a disability. Persons with disabilities are often thought to be less intelligent. In some instances, persons with disabilities are considered docile and in other cases, they are considered aggressive. In the instances when they are thought of as aggressive, it is often associated with rebelling against one's condition or status in life, again a negative connotation to being a person with a disability. When these cultural characteristics and values are placed beside and compared to the following dominant culture's values of perfectionism, independence, aggressiveness, self-expressiveness, autonomy, self-determination, accumulation of goods, task-oriented, materialistic, achievement, control, and competitiveness, one not only obtains a view of the level to which persons with disabilities must become acculturated as well as the difficulty they may experience in attaining these levels.

Conclusion

Cultural diversity in America is inevitable; cultural diversity in America is good and desirable, and because of cultural diversity many aspects of

American society will experience change. Another fact about cultural diversity is that persons with disabilities, including persons with disabilities from ethnic/racial minority backgrounds, are part of this diversity; thus a relevant question is, "What are some of the changes that will have to occur to accommodate persons with disabilities and what will be some of the effects of more and more persons with disabilities becoming part of the American mainstream?" Books are written on changes that will take place in the twenty-first century as a result of America becoming more diverse; therefore, this conclusion cannot adequately address the many changes. However, two major changes must occur for persons with disabilities to feel as part of the mainstream of American society.

The major problem that most persons with disabilities encounter is the negative attitudes of others with regard to what the person with a disability can do. As a society, too often we think of disability as "can't" such as blind people can't see, deaf people can't hear, paraplegic people can't walk, mute people can't talk and the list could go on. While it is true there are things that a person with a disability cannot do, is this not true for all humans? We do not observe persons without disabilities and think of the things they cannot do, when in fact, if careful analysis were made, there are probably as many things they cannot do as there are things the person with a disability cannot do. It is true that one of the reasons we think of what the person with a disability cannot do is that his limitations are often visible, while so-called nondisabled person's limitations are hidden. Regardless, thinking of a person's inabilities is acquired through a socialization process and can be unlearned and not perpetuated by passing on to the next generation. Instead, our society must learn to acknowledge the limitation(s) of a person with a disability and concentrate upon the things he can do, encouraging and assisting him to strengthen his assets just as we would a person without a disability.

Closely associated with removal of negative attitudes toward persons with disabilities is removing the stigma associated with having a disability. Persons with disabilities learn to dislike themselves because society too often views them as inferior humans. Some of the words we use to describe disabilities and those that possess them give some clue to the intensity of the stigma attached—words such as "cripple," "crazy," "dumb," and "gimp" can be devastating. The exclusion, the denial of opportunities, and benign neglect that many persons with disabilities experience have the effect of deepening the feeling of inferiority.

To eliminate stigma attached to disabilities, our society must teach our children that there is nothing shameful about having a disability. We must impress upon these future adults that there is nothing wrong with having friends who are different and there is nothing bad about socializing, dating, and marrying persons with disabilities. Most of all, we must emphasize that persons with disabilities are as good and useful as persons without a disability. Once children learn to accept persons with disabilities and their limitations, they will experience few, if any, difficulties working, socializing, and living with persons who have disabilities.

Because of technical advances, the world of work is changing and opportunities for persons with disabilities are increasing and will continue to do so. For persons with disabilities, to take advantage of these employment opportunities equal opportunity to quality education must be made available. New methods of assessing intelligence and abilities are being acquired and concurrent with this is the need for new attitudes and perceptions of persons with disabilities' intellectual capabilities so that they can have fair and reasonable opportunities to be educated and trained for present and future jobs. Finally, as persons with disabilities are able to successfully compete for career-type jobs, they will have the resources to enjoy the many fine recreational resources of America.

In summary, America must view diversity as impacting all areas of society.

Review Questions

1. Why is it difficult to define what culture is?
2. Do you believe there is a disability culture? Defend your position.
3. Explain what the "assumption of universality" means.
4. What does multiculturism mean to you?
5. What does acculturation mean?
6. How would a person with a disability attempt to become acculturated?

Suggested Activities

1. Interview someone from a cultural background different from your own to learn about their customs, beliefs, rituals, etc.
2. Interview a person with a disability with the goal of determining how he/she feels with regard to being a person with a disability.
3. Research the concept of multiculturalism and identify both the pros and cons of the concept.
4. Contact your state's Vocational Rehabilitation Office to determine how many persons with disabilities reside in your state, and of them, how many are from racial/ethnic minority groups and how many are male and female.

References

Atkinson, D. R., Morten, G., & Sue, D. W. (Eds.). (1993). *Counseling American minorities: Crosscultural perspective* (4th ed.). Madison, WI: William C. Brown.

Axelson, J. A. (1993). *Counseling and development in a multicultural society* (2nd ed.). Pacific Grove, CA: Brooks/Cole.

Bryan, W. V. (1996). *In search of freedom.* Springfield, IL: Charles C Thomas.

Davila, R. R. (1995). Leadership for a new era. *Disability and diversity: New leadership for a new era.* President's Committee on Employment of People With Disabilities, Jan:24–27.

Fairchild, H. P. (Ed.). (1970). *Dictionary of sociology and related sciences.* Totowa, NJ: Rowan and Attanheid.

Henderson, G., & Bryan, W. V. (1984). *Psychosocial aspects of disability.* Springfield, IL: Charles C Thomas.

Keisier, D. (1966). Some myths of psychotherapy research and the search for a paradigm. *Psychological Bulletin, 65.*

Lee, C. C. (1989). Multicultural counseling: New directions for counseling professionals. *Virginia Counselors Journal, 17*:3–8.

Montagu, A. (1997). *Man's most dangerous myth: The fallacy of race.* Walnut Creek, CA: Alta Mira.

Ridley, C. R. (1995). *Overcoming unintentional racism in counseling and therapy: A practitioner's guide to intentional intervention.* Thousand Oaks, CA: Sage.

Sue, D. W., & Sue, D. (1990). *Counseling the culturally different: Theory and practice* (2nd ed.). New York: John Wiley and Sons.

Tainter, B., Compisi, G., & Richards, C. (1995). Embracing cultural diversity in the rehabilitation system. *Disability and diversity: New leadership for a new era.* President's Committee on Employment of People With Disabilities, Jan. 28–32.

Triandis, H. C. (1972). *The analysis of subjective culture.* New York: John Wiley.

United States Bureau of the Census. (1990). Washington, D.C.

Walker, S., Orange, C., & Rackley, R. (1993). A formidable challenge: The preparation of minority personnel. *Journal of Vocational Rehabilitation, 2*(1):46–53.

Wilson, B. (1998). Seeing no evil. *Black Issues in Higher Education, 14*(23):18–20, January.

Suggested Readings

Betancourt, H., & López, S. R. (1993). The study of culture, ethnicity and race in American psychology. *American Psychologist,* June:629–636.

Carkhuff, R. R. (1986). *The art of helping.* Amhurst, MA: Human Resource Development Press.

Carney, C. B., & Kahn, K. B. (1984). Building competencies for effective cross-cultural counseling: A developmental view. *The Counseling Psychologist, 12*:111–119.

Davenport, D. S., & Yurich, J. M. (1991). Multicultural gender issues. *Journal of Counseling and Development, 70*:64–71, September-October.

Jahoda, G. (1984). Do we need a concept of culture. *Journal of Cross Cultural Psychology, 15*:139–151.

Thurer, S., & Rogers, E. S. (1984). The mental needs of physically disabled persons: Their perspectives. *Rehabilitation Psychology, 29*:239–249.

Chapter 2

DIVERSITY AND DISABILITY

Chapter Outline
• Introduction
• Melting Pot
• American Culture
• Diversity
• Diversity and Disability
• Diversity in the Workplace
• Conclusion

Chapter Objectives
• Identify why the "melting pot" theory has not succeeded in America
• Articulate the importance of diversity in America
• Identify why America is becoming a culturally diverse nation
• Articulate why persons with disabilities must be included in America's
  Diversity
• Understand why persons with disabilities are considered as a cultural group

Introduction

The Declaration of Independence represented a utopian dream of its architects who, at the time of its construction, knew that its words did not accurately represent the status of some of its inhabitants. Nor would it, for many years to come, be a reality for some groups of people. Despite the exalted language, the reality was that many persons of African descent were being subjected to slavery and the indigenous people now called American Indians were being denied both human and civil rights while being treated as unwanted strangers in their own land.

Perhaps these two racial minority groups were the most visible of the ones being unjustly denied their rights, but another group was also being separated from the mainstream of American society and being denied the rights guaranteed by the Constitution and that group included both males and females from the African American and American Indian groups as well as members from the dominant culture. The group was then and remains today the largest minority group in American, that group being persons with disabilities.

Melting Pot

The myth of freedom and equality for all was further perpetuated by the "melting pot" theory which was espoused as immigrants from various ethnic, cultural, and philosophical backgrounds migrated to America. The idea was that all of these various attributes which constitute a person's existence would blend together with their fellow immigrants to form a new and unique American. As these early immigrants came to America, social scientists and others proposed the idea that the various cultures brought by these immigrants would be blended and a new and unique culture would emerge– "the American culture." As appealing as this idea sounded, something went wrong and as some have stated, there were some cultures which were not included into this cultural melting pot. Perhaps only the uninformed would disagree and choose to believe that the blending of all cultures into "the American culture" has been successful. Given the reality that there are some cultures which did not fuse into the American culture, a couple of relevant questions must be posed: (1) Were these cultural groups not allowed to do so; or (2) Did these cultural groups tenaciously hold on to their motherland cultures and refuse to blend, believing that to do so would deprive them of their heritage. The answer to these questions may be the third option–a combination of one and two. Bea Wehrly (1995) offers her explanation:

> For a time, it was thought that the United States would become a melting pot of all the cultures brought by the immigrants and an idealized blended national culture would emerge. As more and more immigrants came to the United States in the late 19th and early 20th centuries, the white European men in power became concerned about the different values and behaviors brought by immigrants, and so the norm was changed from the melting pot to that of assimilation. Cultural assimilation, as practiced in the United States, is the expectation by the people in power that all immigrants and all people outside the dominant group will give up their ethnic and cultural values and will adopt the values and norms of the dominant society–the white, male Euro-Americans.

In reviewing the history of human relationships in America, it is obvious that some groups were more readily accepted into the mainstream of

American life. Primarily the immigrant groups most quickly accepted were those coming from European countries, although this is not accurate in all cases because there were instances when, for a variety of reasons, others such as Italians and Jews found it to their respective advantage to isolate themselves. Even though the first generation of these groups initially found some resistance to their total inclusion, succeeding generations were included and have become integral parts of the American culture.

To a major degree, early generations of persons of African, Asian Pacific, and Hispanic/Latino descent, as well as American Indians also experienced this exclusion and from a basis of self-survival, determined that it was to their advantage to isolate themselves. In the case of these groups, the isolation was more imposed than voluntary. A major difference between the accepted groups and the excluded groups was that in most cases, succeeding generations of those excluded often experienced the same difficulties in being included as their ancestors. One result of this exclusion was the maintaining by these groups of their motherland culture. An interesting side note of the maintaining of the motherland culture relates to African Americans; at one time it was believed that because of slavery African Americans had lost their African culture. Recent studies of some African and African-American behavior, values, and beliefs reveal that African Americans have maintained some of the belief systems, values, and rituals of the mother country, although because most of their ancestry was not allowed to record their African heritage over successive generations, the origin of the attributes have been lost.

American Culture

With regard to the establishment of a dominant "American Culture," the reality is that the Europeans who left their homelands, often to escape persecution and prosecution, established in the new land a government that subjected some minority groups to similar restrictive and dehumanizing laws, as the ones from which they (Europeans) had been subjected in their homelands. In the process, they established cultural values and standards that were familiar and beneficial to their survival. It is difficult to argue against the idea of self-preservation except when the standard of living established is based in part at the expense of other humans and their existence.

Reality dictates that in any society one group will become dominant; therefore, that group's standards, values, belief system, and morals will often become the dominant culture. This fact is neither good nor bad, simply a fact of life. However, it is the extent to which the dominant culture extends itself to include or exclude other belief systems, values, and standards as a significant part of the overall society that causes the dominant group's motives and actions to be considered oppressive or inclusive.

Euro-American culture has been the dominant culture in America for several hundred years and its domination has been so encompassing that virtually all other cultures have either been suppressed, assimilated, or eliminated. Critics of the domination of Euro-American standards would argue that other cultures have had to conform to the Euro-American culture's standards or risk being significantly diminished. Euro-American culture has been the benchmark by which most everything in America is judged. This is not intended to imply that Euro-American cultural standards are inherently bad, but that the total domination has allowed little room for consideration of other group differences.

How does one culture maintain dominance over other cultures? One method is to deny other groups the same rights and privileges that the dominant group enjoys. By inhibiting rights such as to vote, to own property, to be educated, to have gainful employment, to socialize with whom one wishes, and to live where one can afford and want to live places subordinate groups in an inferior position—a position which not only blocks that generation from advancing in society but also dooms further generations of offspring to similar inferior positions. Conversely, a way that subordinate groups can overcome their inferior positions is to demand their rights and once received, use them to create a more open and inclusive society for all cultures.

Although it has taken far too long and is not complete, Americans are to be credited for recognizing wrong and attempting to correct the mistakes. Many discriminatory laws have been ruled unconstitutional and have been replaced by humane and empowering laws such as the 1964 Civil Rights Act and the 1990 Americans With Disabilities Act. Some observers of America's political and civil rights scene would argue that as a result of these laws and the increased numbers of minority and persons with disabilities demanding their rights, the dominant culture has had little choice but to consider the cultural differences these persons represent.

Diversity

During the decade of the 1990s persons who have professional as well as personal concerns with regard to the fields of education, employment, counseling, and other helping professions, such as rehabilitation, human relations, and human resource development, just to mention a few, began to pay close attention to the issues of cultural diversity. They became keenly aware of the demographic expectation that during the first half of the twenty-first century the aggregate population of African Americans, American Indians, Asian Americans, and Hispanic/Latino's will become the majority population in America. The displacing of Euro-Americans as the numeric majority can and will have a profound impact upon how daily living and many activities are conducted in America. For example, bilingual education in public schools will become more common in areas where there is a large Spanish-speaking population, also within all levels of education–kindergarten through graduate school–issues and case studies which have relevance to ethnic minorities will become more common as part of the daily curriculum. The area of employment will see increased numbers of faces which are black and brown and shades in between, seeking employment. Moreover, some of these will have physical and/or mental disabilities; therefore, management must become better prepared to manage, work alongside, and assist persons of color who have disabilities and come from different backgrounds than many Euro-Americans. Finally, with regard to the impact cultural diversity will have upon the way commerce is conducted within America, as businesses are preparing their marketing strategies, they cannot afford to ignore either the Euro-American or non-Euro-American who has a disability and his or her purchasing power.

As one considers the following information, both the potential economic and political impact of persons with disabilities becomes apparent. Approximately one-fifth (1/5) of the American population has some type of disability. To add emphasis to the economic and political impact persons with disabilities can have–for every person with a disability there is an average of one person who has a significant, if not personal, interest in the person with a disability. Therefore, it is clear that a large group such as this can have major economic and political impact on American society.

The purpose of these issues is to emphasize that diversity is a fact of life which brings many changes, adjustments, and modifications with regard to the way we think, act, and react to daily life in America. Diversity in America is good and desirable. The most obvious benefit for recognizing and embracing diversity first comes from the moral and human rights point of view. By virtue of being a human, one has the God-given right to fair, equal, and humane treatment. Second, aside from the altruistic viewpoint, diversity is beneficial to America from an economic position. To be more specific, by embracing diversity and ensuring that all citizens have equal rights and fair opportunities to develop one's maximum potential means that America has a better educated, better trained, and better informed population which will help insure America's place as a world leader.

Diversity and Disability

Helping professionals can rejoice that just as they have recognized the increase in cultural diversity in America, many other Americans have become cognizant of the need for being more aware of differences, particularly cultural; however, the rejoicing perhaps could be tempered if the largest minority group in America, persons with disabilities, are not included within the groups which are being given long overdue consideration of their cultural differences. The following comments by Bryan (1996) provide clues as to why persons with disabilities have in the past been excluded from being considered as part of the cultural diversity of America.

> Until recently, persons with disabilities were not widely considered a minority group. In fact, it was not until the Rehabilitation Act of 1973 that they were considered a "class" of people. Persons with disabilities are members of other groups of people, they are male or female, and they have an ethnic identity; their rights and privileges are associated with whatever cultural and/or gender group they belong.

Persons with disabilities who are members of a racial minority group must be considered from two perspectives when considering cultural diversity. The first is as a class of people–persons with disabilities; and second, as a minority within a minority. Stated another way, they must be viewed as persons who have a disability who are a member of a racial minority group (i.e,. African American person with a disability, Asian American persons with a disability or a American Indian with a disability). It is vitally important that racial minorities with disabilities be considered when plans are being made to restructure curriculum, sensitize counselors, social workers, psychotherapists, and other helping professionals to be more responsive and sensitive to the needs of these groups. Because not to do so means one cultural aspect, race vs. disability, is considered while the other is ignored. Frankly, the difference can mean success or failure. The following comments of the National Council on Disability (1992) provides some insight into why we should consider the needs of persons with disabilities.

> The combination of disability and ethnicity, race and/or cultural background often results in a double form of discrimination. Individuals with disabilities who are members of ethnic, racial and or ethnic cultural groups frequently experience discrimination disproportionately in comparison to their White or European counterparts.

Emphasis is added to the need to become sensitive to minority persons with disabilities when one considers that juxtaposition with the increase in population of racial minorities will be an increase in the population of persons from those minority groups who obtain a disability. Offered as proof of the previously mentioned statement, according to a 2002 U. S. Census Bureau report on racial minorities with severe disabilities, 7.2 percent of Asians or Pacific Islanders has a severe disability and 14 percent of African Americans have a severe disability. Zawaiza (1995) reminds us that American Indians are substantially worse off than the dominant culture and as bad or worse off than other minorities. Compared to the dominant culture, over twice as many American Indians are unemployed or live in poverty. A disproportinate number of American Indian students drop out of high school before the twelfth grade. Additionally, the prevalence of diabetes among American Indians exceeds 20 percent in many tribes and reaches 50 percent among some tribes. Henderson and Bryan (1997) characterize the American Indian as being at the bottom of the economical ladder in the United States. Likewise, Autaubo (1995) takes the position that when compared to other minority groups in the United States, Native Americans are among the poorest of the poor.

As one considers the danger involved in the types of jobs that are available to many minorities, the lack of appropriate and adequate health care, and the void of preventive measures to decrease the chances of illness as well as the minimal economic standards by which many minorities live, it becomes easy to state with a considerable degree of accuracy that the numbers of minorities with disabilities will continue to grow. Leung and Wright (1992) underscores this point by emphasizing that persons with disabilities will increasingly come from minority populations. They further stated that persons with minority status will no longer be the exception and concluded their comments by making the observation that the needs and future work force of America will most likely be met not only by its diverse racial and ethnic populations, but also by persons within those populations who have disabilities.

As previously stated, America has become and will continue to be a culturally diverse nation and persons with disabilities are an integral part of that diversity. When considering cultural diversity, it would be a mistake of considerable magnitude to disregard this group as part of that diversity; likewise, when considering racial minority groups and their needs, it would be a major error to fail to consider persons with disabilities within those groups. Perhaps stated more succinctly, when working with a person who has a disability one has to have an awareness and sensitivity of both the person's racial background and her disability. To further this understanding of culture and cultural diversity, culture will be defined, additionally the need for developing an understanding of various racial cultures will be discussed, as well as the impact of culture on the helping process and various aspects of acculturation.

An underlying theme of all these discussions, although not always directly stated, is the inclusion of disabilities as a factor within a cultural group.

Diversity in the Workplace

As we have become a more inclusive society, American employers have, in many cases, attempted to structure their workforce so that it is somewhat representative of its local population. In this noble effort, ethnic/racial minorities and women have benefited by securing jobs in greater numbers than in previous years. Despite these increased employment opportunities, there remain inequities in the rate of employment of these minority groups verses the employment rate of Caucasians. Additionally, there are tremendous inequities in the salaries earned by these groups in comparison with their Caucasian counterparts and in the case of women, of all ethnic/racial backgrounds, with men.

Although increased employment opportunities have accrued for ethnic/racial minorities and women, unfortunately the same cannot be said for persons with disabilities. Thus, true diversity in the workplace has not occurred in the United States.

The most conservatives estimates of the number of persons in the United States indicates at least one-fifth of the population have some type of disability, yet the unemployment rate of persons with disabilities over the past two decades consistently has remained in the thirty plus percent range. When one looks closer at the unemployment rate, by examining the rate for ethnic/racial minorities and women, the percentage increases beyond the 30 percent range. Additionally, because of the lack of employment the majority of persons with disabilities live on incomes below 25,000 dollars annually. Again, when income is examined by ethnicity, race and women the average income is much lower than 25,000 dollars.

Despite Title 1 of the Americans with Disabilities Act, which prohibits discrimination because a person has a disability, the unemployment rate for persons with disabilities has not significantly improved. Given this fact, one is prompted to ask the question—why is this true? Is the lack of employment diversity with regard to persons with disabilities a result of prejudice, discrimination, ignorance, or combinations of all of the previously mentioned?

The answer appears to be a combination of the previously mentioned reasons. Title 1 of the Americans with Disabilities Act requires an employer to provide **reasonable accommodations** for persons with disabilities in the interview and employment stages, unless the accommodations create an **undue burden**. An undue burden is determined on a case by case basis, but is generally considered to mean that the accommodation will be too expensive and/or will change the nature of the business. In some cases, employers claim an undue burden because they mistakenly think that making accommodations will be too expensive. The reality is that most businesses that have made accommodations report that most changes cost less than 1,000 dollars. It would appear that making reasonable accommodations for employees with disabilities would be considered good business practices, since employers routinely make accommodations for employees to improve their work performance under the name of ergonomics. Therefore isn't ergonomics a form of reasonable accommodation?

The numerous myths that have hampered employment of persons with disabilities have been proven to be untrue and inaccurate. Myths exist, such as a company's insurance rate will increase if persons with disabilities are hired, other employees will not accept working with a person with a disability, persons with disabilities are unsafe workers and are accident prone, and employees with disabilities are unproductive and will have very high absenteeism rates. Despite the debunking of these myths, the unemployment rate of persons with disabilities, as previously mentioned, remains a disgrace to a nation with the resources that exist in the United States.

Given the dismal record of lack of adequate employment in the United States for persons with disabilities, the question of what can be done to correct this situation must be addressed. Some solutions may be found by looking back a few decades to the late 1970s and the decades of the 1980s and 1990s when the United States was addressing the issue of lack of ethnic/racial diversity in the work place. One of the problems identified was a lack of appropriate education and training for certain jobs, specifically jobs in the fields of medicine, dentistry, nursing, allied health areas, engineering, teaching (mathematics and science areas), and law, to mention several professions where ethnic/racial minorities were underrepresented. To remedy these deficiencies, federal and state agencies awarded grants (on a competitive basis) to colleges, universities, and in some cases public and private schools to identify and educate ethnic/minority and other disadvantaged students in basic courses and skills to increase their chances of being successful with regard to entering and completing the proscribed course of study. In most cases, these programs met with success; certainly they helped increase the number of ethnic/racial minority and disadvantaged persons entering into the previously mentioned occupations. In this author's opinion, similar programs should be developed for persons with disabilities. To make the programs stronger and increase chances of success, these programs should be instituted as early as elementary school and also be focused toward vocational training as well as college-level education. To be more specific, at the earliest point when a student has been identified as having a disability, counselors trained to work with persons who have disabilities should be assigned to work with the student and his/her parents and/or significant others to help monitor the student's progress. The Individual Education Plan (IUP) that is used for students with developmental disabilities perhaps is a plan that could be used with some modifications. These counselors/advocates would work with the students and families throughout the persons public or private school education. Aptitude and vocational testing as well as appropriate counseling should be available at any point in the student's progression thorough the educational system. This type of program works best if decisions with regard to the direction (career choice or future educational choice-vocational school or college) the student will go is made early, preferable in the first year of high school. In this author's opinion, every student, regardless of whether he or she has a disability, if he or she plans to attend college, should also learn a vocational skill. It is understood that there are issues that would have to be addressed in implementing this or a similar program, issues such as funding, concerns regarding special treatment, and how to identify participants for the programs.

The previously mentioned program can help increase the pool of qualified trained persons with disabilities; however, there remains another key ingredient, that being employers willing to hire persons with disabilities. In this author's opinion, most employers are interested and willing to be fair in their employment practices; however, a major concern must be the ability of their businesses to survive. With this thought in mind, programs of incentives and education will work. There have been and probably will continue, for some time, to be tax incentives for hiring persons with disabilities. Associated with these incentives should be a requirement that an employer receive education regarding persons with disabilities, and must require employees to also receive similar education. The education for the employer and supervisory personnel could be designed to dispel myths regarding persons with disabilities as well as relevant information with regard to possible needs of persons with disabilities. The training for nonsupervisory personnel would be designed to impress upon them that persons with disabilities make good coworkers and do not need sympathy, nor are they some mysterious persons.

Review Questions

1. Why did some racial minority groups such as African Americans, American Indians, and Hispanic/Latinos not fully blend into the American melting pot?
2. What are some experts predicting about the shift in America's population in the first half of the twenty-first century.

3. Why is it important to consider one's race/ethnicity as well as disability when developing rehabilitation plans for racial/ethnic minorities with disabilities?
4. What are some things that can be done to prepare persons with disabilities for gainful employment?

Suggested Activities

1. Contact your state's employment agency and determine the state's unemployment rate; also determine what percentage of that total are persons with disabilities.
2. Determine job training opportunities for persons with disabilities in your city and/or state.
3. Determine the unemployment rate of minority persons with disabilities in your city and/or state.
4. Determine the percentage of persons with disabilities enrolled in colleges and universities in your state.
5. Determine the number and/or percentage of minority persons with disabilities enrolled in colleges and universities in your state.

References

Autaubo, D. (1995). *American indians: Multidimentional factors of disability.* Oklahoma City, OK: Unpublished paper, University of Oklahoma Health Sciences Center.

Bryan, W. V. (1996). *In search of freedom.* Springfield, IL: Charles C Thomas.

Henderson, G. & Bryan, W. V. (1984). *Psychosocial aspects of disability.* Springfield, IL: Charles C Thomas.

Leung, P., & Wright, T. J. (1992). Minorities with disabilities: An introduction. *The unique needs of minorities with disabilities: Setting an agenda for the future.* Jackson, MS: National Council on Disabilities and Jackson State University, pp. 1–2.

Wehrly, B. (1995). *Pathway to multicultural counseling competence.* Pacific Grove, CA: Brooks/Cole.

Suggested Readings

Banks, W. (1997). Group consciousness and the helping professions. *Personnel and Guidance Journal, 55*:319–330.

Massey, D. S., & Eggers, M. L. (1990). The ecology of inequality: Minorities and the concentration of poverty, 1970–1980. *American Journal of Sociology, 95*(5):1153–1188, March.

Pape, D. A., Walker, G. R., & Quinn, F. H. (1983). Ethnicity and disability: Two minority statuses. *Journal of Applied Rehabilitation Counseling, 14*(4):18–23.

Chapter 3

RELIGION AND DIVERSITY

Chapter Outline
• Introduction
• Christianity
• Judaism
• Islam
• Buddhism
• Hinduism
• Implications for Rehabilitation and Other Helping Professionals
• Conclusion

Chapter Objectives
• Provide a brief discussion of Christianity
• Provide a brief discussion of Judaism
• Provide a brief discussion of Islam
• Provide a brief discussion of Buddhism
• Provide a brief discussion of Hinduism
• Provide information about the importance of religion as a variable in the helping process

INTRODUCTION

Perhaps as long as human kind has existed on earth, we have in some way paid homage to a supreme power or powers. The deities to which we have expressed humbleness sometime were called God or gods and in some instance they were called spirits. In antiquity, humans attempted to explain frightful events by assigning a supreme power or powers as the controlling being responsible for the action. Thunder and lighting, floods, fires, destructive winds, plagues, and famine are but a few of the extraordinary events that early humans attempted to explain and justify by indicating that the gods or spirits were angry. Not only were they attempting to explain the cause of supernatural events, they were also acknowledging that there was a power or powers greater than they as individuals and collectively as a group. They also were acknowledging that this power or powers had the potential to significantly influence their lives and they needed to, in some ways, humble themselves to them, or perhaps suffer disastrous consequences.

In the areas of cultural diversity and multiculturalism, when attempting to understand variables impacting the life of an individual, we ascribe considerable importance to one's ethnicity, race, and or gender as though they are the most important variables to consider. However, for those who believe in a supreme being, their **faith** is as important as ethnicity, race, and gender, and perhaps influences their actions and beliefs more than these previously mentioned variables. In America, we attempt to separate church and state and perhaps this is the reason, when we discuss cultural impact, faith or religion is secondary to ethnicity, race, and gender, when in reality, for many people, faith/religion is **dominant**.

It has been said that the question is not whether we worship God, but the real question is which god. There is considerable truth in this statement; because everyone worships some god. For some, it is a spiritual being; for others, including atheists, it may be the worship of a material god—money, clothes, automobile, etc.

Religion or the expression of faith goes beyond attending religious services. The expression of faith includes adhering to some, if not all, of the basic principles and beliefs that serve as the foundation of the faith. Additionally, the expression of faith also includes recognition and at least occasional celebration of important historical events of the faith. Similar to ethnic/racial groups who celebrate or recognize significant events related to that part of their culture, individuals of a religious persuasion also place great importance in significant events related to their faith. Therefore, for some people, their religious faith transcends all the other variables of their cultural composition.

The need for rehabilitation and other helping professionals to understand the impact faith may have in the helping process is very important. For those persons who believe in a supreme being, if they practice their faith, they will in all probability rely on the same in stressful situations or times of crisis, and for those who believe in a supreme being but may not be actively practicing their faith, in stressful situations, many will seek help from a higher power than mortal humans.

This chapter will provide a brief overview of the following major faiths/religions: **Christianity, Judaism, Islam, Hinduism, and Buddhism**.

This author is very much aware that scores of books have been written about each of the faith/religions mentioned in this chapter, which indicates that there is a tremendous amount of information on each subject; therefore, no attempt is being made to give detailed coverage of any of the previously mentioned faith/religions. It is hoped that the reader will be inspired to do additional research to increase his/her knowledge.

Christianity

Brief History of Christianity

Christianity was established in Palestine by followers of Jesus of Nazareth. Rome and the Roman Empire's army during the time of Jesus Christ's physical appearance on earth were the military and political rulers of the region in which Christianity developed. Christianity and its influence spread throughout the Roman Empire and later throughout the rest of Europe; as we know today, Christianity has also spread thoughtout the rest of the world. Christianity, which is one of the most influential of the major world religions, is also one of the youngest religions.

Currently there are three major divisions within the Christian faith: Roman Catholic, Eastern Orthodox, and Protestant. Within the Protestant group are numerous denominations such as Baptist, Methodist, and Church of Christ, to mention only three. Within the various branches of these denominations are further divisions such as the Southern Baptist and Free Will Baptist to mention only two. Further division can also be seen along ethnic/racial lines. While most Protestant denominations have become open to persons of all ethnic/racial groups, most, however, remain segregated, perhaps not by edict, but by tradition. This is especially true in the case of African Americans. During the period of slavery and reconstruction, primarily in southern American states, although not exclusively in those areas, African Americans were not welcome in churches where the congregations were predominately Caucasians. Denied access to their home countries' religions, many African Americans adopted and developed branches of the Caucasian-dominated churches, to help serve their religious inclinations. Thus the separation of religious congregations along racial lines in America continues today. Regardless of the division or denomination of the church, the Holy Bible is the scared text of all groups.

As previously stated there are three major divisions of the Christian religion. The Eastern Orthodox formed the second division when it broke away from what some consider the original Christian church, the Roman Catholic Church in 1054 A.D.; the division occurred as a result of disagreement over doctrine and ecclesiastical authority. Even thought most Eastern Orthodox churches have common beliefs, principles, and doctrines, each tends to be oriented toward the nation in which it resides, Russian Orthodoxy, Romanian Orthodox, and Bulgarian Orthodox to name only three as examples.

Protestant, being the third division, emerged as a result of the Protestant Reformation which was lead by Martin Luther. Martin Luther was a university professor at Wittenberg, Germany; he believed that salvation came as a free gift of God through the forgiveness of sin. In essence, Martin Luther was denouncing the authority of the Pope and the Bishops of the Roman Catholic Church. His belief gave every person direct access to God and His forgiveness.

Some Basic Beliefs of Christians

Although there are three divisions and numerous denominations within the Christian religion, there are some beliefs that are held in common by all. Some of them are:
- All Christians believe in one God, who is the Father and Creator of all human kind.
- All Christians belied in the Trinity: the Father, the Son and the Holy Spirit.
- All Christians believe that Jesus of Nazareth is the Christ and is the Son of God, born of a Virgin and was sent to Earth to live a sinless life, thus setting an example for earthly faithful to follow.
- All Christians believe in the Virgin birth.
- All Christians believe that Jesus was crucified for human kinds sins and was buried and resurrected in three days and ascended to Heaven.
- All Christians believe the Bible is the Holy Scripture provided as encouragement and guidance by which they are to live.

Significant Events

There are numerous events and significant dates that are important to Christians; however, not all Christians observe each of them. Despite this, the two most important events in Christianity and, generally speaking, observed by all Christians are Christmas Day, which represents Jesus Christ's birthday, and Easter, which represents the resurrection of Jesus Christ.

Judaism

Brief History of Judaism

It is impossible to understand the history of Judaism without discussing the history of the Jewish people. Much of the early history of Judaism is told in the first five chapters of the Old Testament of the Bible (Torah). Abraham is considered the founder of the faith, which is called Judaism. When one traces the lineage of Abraham, it is recognized that some of the best known persons of the **Torah** are of the seed of Abraham. Isaac, and Jacob, also known as Israel, whose decedents were called Israelites, all are of the lineage of Abraham. According to Scripture, descendants of Jacob migrated to Egypt where they were enslaved and Moses received the Law from God and lead them from bondage.

The history of the Jews is replete with conflicts, victories, and defeats as they struggled to attain and retain the "promise land." Today, the Nation of Israel, which was established in 1948, is recognized by Jews as their homeland. The word homeland is somewhat misleading in that not all Jews originate from the current State of Israel. To better understand what a Jew is, one needs to understand that from a cultural standpoint, the term Jewish is not a designation of a race of people. Anyone through the process of conversion can become a Jew; therefore, a Jew can be of any race or ethnicity. Additionally, one does not have to be born in Israel to be a Jew. Also one does not have to be born a Jew, as previously stated, he/she can become a Jew by going through the process of converting to Judaism. Given this information, to a large extent, being a Jew is a way of life and perhaps a state of mind. Furthermore one does not have to be religious to be a Jew.

To further understand Judaism, one must understand that currently there are three major sects or versions of Judaism: **Orthodox, Reform,** and **Conservative**. Orthodox Judaism believes in the teachings of the concepts in the Torah and further believes that they are unchanging and should be followed unaltered as outlined in the Scripture. Reform Judaism does not strictly adhere to all Jewish traditions as do the Orthodox Jews. Conservative Judaism believes in the scholarly study and interpretation of the Torah. Stated another way, followers of the Conservative philosophy believe that the beliefs of Judaism should be open to evaluation and interpretation and be changeable based upon contemporary scholarly findings, study, and interpretation.

One can see that defining Judaism is both complex and a multifaceted endeavor and as previously stated, it is almost impossible to define Judaism without defining what a Jew is. For Orthodox and Conservative Jews, a Jew is defined as any person whose mother was or is a Jew or any person who has completed the process of conversion to Judaism; whereas, for the Reform Jews, children whose mother or father was or is a Jew is Jewish as long as they were reared as a Jew.

Some Basic Beliefs of Judaism

In listing some of the beliefs of Judaism, only some of the beliefs held by the three major sects of Judaism have been listed. There are other beliefs held by Orthodox Jews that Conservative and/or Reform Jews may view in different ways.

The basic theological premise of the Jewish faith is namely that God exists, that He created the world by His will, and that He revealed His will to Israel and mankind at Sinai (Donin, 1972). Jews believe in one God. As previously stated, the Torah, or the first five books of the Hebrew Bible (Old Testament), is the foundation of doctrine, customs, and observances. The Oral Torah served to provide clarification for many of the commandments; this served as the cornerstone for what was to become the Talmud.

The bond between the Jewish people and the land of Israel began during the time of Abraham. When the children of Israel fled oppression and slavery in Egypt, they sought the land that had been promised them in Deuteronomy 34:4 (Trepp, 1980).

In summary some of the basic beliefs of Judaism are:

• God exists.
• God is the Creator of all that exist.
• God is incorporeal (without a body)
• God has communicated through prophets.
• The Torah was revealed by God to Moses.

Significant Events and Traditions

Halackhah: The system of Jewish law is Halackhah; its major emphasis is on deeds as it asks for a commitment in behavior. The law also deals with ethical obligations and religious duties.

Sabbath: Day of rest, starting at sundown on Friday evening and lasting through sundown Saturday.

Kosher: Kashrut, more commonly known as keeping kosher, sets forth what Jews may eat, the acceptable method of slaughter of animals, and the cooking utensils and cleaning methods that may be used. With regard to acceptable foods to eat, generally speaking, the rule is that Jews may eat any land mammal that has cloven hooves and chews its cud; this includes sheep, cattle, goats, and deer. From the water, they may eat anything that has fins and scales. Shellfish such as lobsters, oysters, shrimp, clams, and crabs are excluded. With regard to fowl, birds of prey may not be eaten; however, fowl such as chicken, geese, ducks, and turkeys are permitted. Rodents, reptiles, amphibians, and insects are forbidden (Rich, 2005).

There are restrictions with regard to combining foods. One may not eat meat and dairy together; however, eating fish and dairy, or dairy and eggs is acceptable. These are a few of the rules and/or restriction; for more information, one should consult a Jewish dietician or Rabbi. Also one must be aware that not all Jews adhere to all of these practices.

Jewish Festivals: Some of the festivals observed by Jewish people are **Rosh Hashanah, Yom Kippur, Sukkoth, Hanukkah, Passover** and **Shavuot.**

Rosh Hashanah is the Jewish New Year, which occurs in the fall.

Yom Kippur, the Day of Atonement, is the climax of the High Holy Day season. It is considered a day of spiritual reckoning where Jews spend the entire day in the synagogue in prayer, meditation, and fasting.

Sukkoths is a thanksgiving festival. This is a time of rejoicing, engaging in hearty meals which symbolize a bountiful harvest.

Hanukkah is perhaps the second most observed Jewish holiday. This holiday is based on a historical story of a miracle. The story relates that the Greeks had entered the temple and desecrated all of the holy oil except for one flask. Based upon volume, this oil should have lasted only one day, instead it lasted eight day. Thus the tradition of lighting candles for eight days.

Passover is the most observed holiday for the Jewish people (Rich 2005). Passover celebrates the Jewish peoples' exodus from Egypt and their bondage in that area. On the eve of the exodus, the Jews marked their doorpost with lambs' blood, and the angel of death which killed all Egyptian first-born children passed over the houses marked with the blood. As a result of this event, it is written that Pharaoh released the slaves and allowed them to leave Egypt.

Shavuot celebrates the giving of the Torah to the Jewish people (Rich, 2005).

Islam

Brief History of Islam

Islam is the youngest of the major religions of Christianity, Judaism, Hinduism, and Buddhism The faith that we know as Islam began in Mecca during the Seventh Century A. D. The Islamic **Prophet Muhammad**, who was born around 570 A. D. in Mecca Arabia is said to have had a revelation from the Archangel Gabriel which lead to the establishment of the religion Islam. The revelation among other things revealed to Muhammad that there was only one God, **Allah**, and He is the Creator of the world. It should be noted that during that period of time in the Arabic region of the world, as well as other part of the world, belief in and worship of more than one god was common.

After this revelation, the Prophet Muhammad was able to convert some of his relatives, including some in-laws and his wife Khadija, to Islam. The Arabic word Islam means the submission or surrender of one's will to the only true God worthy of worshiping, Allah, and anyone who worships Allah is called a **Muslim**. Additionally, the word Islam means peace, which is a natural consequence of total submission to the will of Allah.

According to the Islamic religion, Adam was the first prophet sent by Allah. It is noted that Muhammad is a prophet, not a god nor considered the Son of God. Additionally, the Islamic religion considers Jesus and Abraham prophets.

After the death of Muhammad in 632 A. D., there was an ideological split in the Muslim world; the division produced two major groups: the Sunni and the Shi'a. The division appears to have been primarily over earthly leadership of the Muslim faith. Today there are a number of Muslim sects around the world. In the United States, within the past century there has been a development among African Americans groups, commonly referred to as **Black Muslims or Nation of Islam**. Regardless of the sect, all follow many of the teachings of the Prophet Muhammad and acknowledge Allah as the one and only God.

Basic Beliefs and Traditions

The **Quran** is the holy scripture of Islam which was revealed to the Prophet Muhammad by Allah. To Muslims, the Quran is the word of God and these words express to them His will. The relevance of the Quran to Muslims can be compared to the relevance of the Torah to Jews and the Holy Bible to Christians. The Quran is divided into 114 chapters and the chapters are divided into verses.

According to John Sabini (1994), there are **Five Pillars of Islam**; these pillars are actions that all Muslims must perform, if possible, to remain on the correct path. These pillars are giving testimony to: **faith, prayer, alms-giving, fasting,** and **pilgrimage**. The following explanation of the five pillars is based upon the writings of John Sabini.

Testimony: This is the profession of faith. "There is no god but God; and Muhammad is the messenger of God."

Prayer: Every adult Muslim, male or female, of sound mind and body, is required to pray five times a day-at sunset (beginning of the Muslim day), in the evening, at dawn, at noon, and in mid-afternoon. The Quran promises that those who pray and perform good deeds will enter Paradise, and tradition also states that each prayer absolves one of minor sins. An important fact that helping professions should know is that a Muslim at prayer should not be interrupted, stared at, or photographed, and a person should not walk in front of the praying person (Sabini, 1994).

Almsgiving: Benevolence and giving to the less fortunate is highly valued. Not only is it valued, it is mandated by the Quran.

Fasting: According to Sabini, fasting is meant to test the self-denial and submission of the faithful Muslims and permit those that have abundant resources to experience the deprivations of the poor. Both men and women and all but the youngest children are required to fast. Once a year for a period of one month, Muslims are required to abstain from food, drink, smoking, and sexual relation during the hours of daylight. This occurs during **Ramadan**, the ninth month of the Islamic calendar. It is noted that the Islamic calendar is based on the Lunar months which have twelve months in a year; however, the Lunar year is shorter than the solar year by about ten days.

Pilgrimage: The major pilgrimage is called the **Hajj**. The Quran requires that every adult Muslim of either gender and in sound body and mind make a pilgrimage to Mecca at least once in a lifetime, if possible. The destination is the Holy Mosque in Mecca.

Significant Events

There are a number of celebrations and events associated with Islam, and as is the situation with the other major religions, not all Muslims fully participate. Also, some events are celebrated more fully within one Muslim country and not so in another. Most of the major events have been outlined in the belief section.

Buddhism

Brief History of Buddhism

The founder of Buddhism, or as he referred to himself, **way-shower**, was **Siddhartha Gautama**. He was born in approximately 560 B. C. in the area that is present-day Nepal, India. Gautama's father was a local ruler who practiced Hinduism; therefore Siddhartha Gautama was reared in the ancient

Hinduism religion. Much of the narrative of Gautama's life is weaved with legends in that most of his history was written long after his death. By way of legend, it is said that a white elephant touched the side of Gautama's mother and by this action, she knew she was with child. The white elephant was considered a divine animal, and its action of touching the side of his mother became evidence of the divine destiny of the coming child. Legend also records that his mother gave birth to him in a standing position while holding on to a branch that had miraculously lowered itself to assist her. With regard to his birth, it is also reported that he did not emerge through the womb, but emerged painlessly from the side of his mother, thus saving him the trauma of a vaginal birth. This method of birth is important in that it is believed that a vaginal birth wipes out the memory of past lives and is further believed by Buddhists that Siddhartha Gautama retained memory of all of his previous lives. It should be further explained that Buddhists believe that one is born, dies, and reborn until he/she attains **Nirvana**. Nirvana is considered to be a state of existence where suffering no longer exists.

As previously stated, Siddhartha Gautama was born into royalty, privilege, and affluence, but at approximately age twenty-nine, he had a life changing experience that provided direction to the rest of his life. While out riding, he encountered four sights that would change his life and began his quest for enlightenment, or Buddha (the term Buddha means enlightenment). The sights he saw were: an old man, a sick man, a dead man, and a holy man (Ganeri, p. 10). Because he had led a sheltered life, he had not experienced many of the realities of life, infirmity, death, and illness. These sights gave him cause to contemplate the many aspects of life. Because of this contemplation, Gautama decided to leave the comfortable life he had known in search of answers to the question of how to find the positive counterparts of the suffering states of birth, aging, illness, death, sorrow, and corruption (Armstrong, p. 5). He then began to devote his life to extreme asceticism, which he later abandon because he was not finding the answers to the perplexing questions and devoted his life to meditation.

While meditating under a tree, Siddhartha Gautama found the answer. This discovery became know as **the middle way**. The middle way is the principle that between extreme asceticism or depravity and indulgence is a rationed life in which the body is given what it needs to function optimally, but no more (Novak & Smith, p. 8). A result of his meditation, and what contemporaries call revelations, there have developed within the Buddhist tradition **Four Nobel Truths** and an **Eight-Fold Path**, which will be explained in the next section basic beliefs.

Some Basic Beliefs

As have previously been mentioned, Siddhartha Gautama was reared in the Hindu religion, but he did not think that some of the precepts of the religion answered some of the basic questions of life, such as why do humans suffer? Although he did not find the answer to this and other questions of life through Hinduism, he retained one of the basic Hindu beliefs, that being reincarnation after death. Gautama believed, and this became a major part of Buddhist belief, that one is born, dies, and is reborn again and again until one attains the state of Nirvana. As previously mentioned, Nirvana is considered to be a state of existence where suffering no longer exists and the causes of suffering have been removed.

Also as previously mentioned, Buddhists believe there are Four Nobel Truths and these truths explain suffering. They are (1) life is suffering. This basic truth is saying that suffering is part of living and being human. (2) Cravings cause suffering. (3) To end suffering, one must end cravings. (4) The means to end cravings can be found by following the Eight-Fold Path. If one follows the Eight-Fold Path, it will lead him/her to **Enlightenment** (Buddha). The steps along this path are (1) Right Views, (2) Right Intentions, (3) Right Speech, (4) Right Action, (5) Right Livelihood (occupation), (6) Right Effort, (7) Right Contemplation, and (8) Right Meditation. As one can extract from these steps to Enlightenment, they deal with morality. If one has the correct morality and intentions, he/she is on the correct path to Enlightenment.

There are a number of versions or sects of Buddhism and some appear to have elevated Gautama to the status of deity; however, he did not proclaim himself a deity. He said he was a way-shower.

Significant Events

As is the case with the other major religions, there are a number of celebrations; however the two most important festivals for most Buddhists are **Wesak** and **Dharma Day**. **Wesak** is the celebration of the Buddha's enlightenment, and is considered the most important celebration in the Buddhist year. Buddhists plan most things around a lunar calendar; therefore, this festival is held on the full moon of May/June. **Dharma Day** celebrates the day in which the Buddha arose from his session of enlightenment.

Hinduism

Brief History of Hinduism

Identifying the history of Hinduism is more difficult than identifying the history for the other major religions, because there is no one central individual or figure to which one can associate its development. Some Hindu individuals say the religion has existed forever. Hinduism is **henotheistic** with regard to its identification of deities. Stated another way, Hindus believe in a central deity, called **Brahman**, which is a pervading spirit or oneness of the universe, present in all things considered sacred and honored. In addition to Brahman, some may also worship what is considered minor deities.

The few historical things that are known about Hinduism indicate that the basis of the religion is a mixture of an ancient civilization of people, and their religious beliefs, who lived over 5000 years ago in the Indus Valley region of the Indian continent and the religious beliefs of Aryan people who invaded the Indus Valley region approximately 3000 years ago. Although the history of Hinduism is difficult to identify, what is known is Hinduism is the oldest religion of the major religions, Christianity, Judaism, Islam, and Buddhism, and perhaps the oldest religion in the world. Hinduism is the dominate religion of India.

Some Basic Beliefs

Perhaps the best understanding of the Hindu religion does not come from its history, but from its basic beliefs and goals. A major goal of people who are Hindu is to attain **moksa**, or **enlightened liberation** of the **Atman** or **self** from the wheel of rebirth or the cycles of birth and death. **Reincarnation**, or **samsara**, is the belief that one is reborn after death. The physical form of rebirth is determined by the level of spiritual purity that the person has achieved by the time of his or her death.

The belief in **Karma** is a major aspect of the Hindu religion. Karma is the law of action and reaction. For every action taken, we face a reaction in the future. Therefore, chance and luck, from the Hindu perspective, do not exist. Consequently, everything happens according to the positive or negative energy stored from our actions in the Karma. In coordination with Karma, the **Dharma** is used to assure spiritual growth toward moksa. Dharma is a set of moral codes and correct behaviors that are taught in ancient texts and rituals. Hinduism promotes the belief in meditation and rejection of the material world as the final step to **Nirvana** where the Atman (self) and Brahman (absolute spirit) are reunited resulting in the individual attaining moksa (enlighten liberation).

As previously stated, the Hindu religion is a henotheistic religion which believes in the oneness of spirit (Brahman) but may worship that spirit by way of a multitude of gods who are seen as coming from a divine source. The sacred texts of the Hindu religion are the **Vedas** (wisdom). The Vedas are four collections of religious writings, believed by Hindu followers to be inspired, composed approximately 3000 years ago. Vedas are considered the oldest and most profound source of Hindu wisdom available to study. Vedic chants are used in modern worship ceremonies. The **Brahmans** and **Upanishads** are texts that seek to explain the Veda and are often used as reference material and are the basis of specialized branches of Hinduism. The religion does not have explicit doctrine or institutional forms of worship; therefore, the practices have become regional in expression. Stated in other terms, in different areas and regions of the world where the Hindu religion is practiced, each has developed its own expression of the faith.

Considering the fact that expression of the Hindu faith is regionalized, one source of identity is which creator god they choose to follow. The three major figures of the modern creation gods are **Brahma** (the creator), **Vishnu** (the preserver), and **Shiva** (the destroyer). These three represent a **Trimurti** (trinity) of perspectives about the universe. Vishnu is the generative and positive force. Shiva is a destructive force which is necessary in the creative process. Brahma balances these two opposing forces. The three are not separate beings but different aspects of the one universal spirit.

Significant Events

Because Hindu religion is regionalized, it is virtually impossible to list all of the significant events and festivals.

Implications for Rehabilitation and Other Helping Professionals

What does religion have to do with the helping process? What does religion have to do with cultural diversity? As helping professionals, when we delve into religious background or lack of same, aren't we getting into a sensitive area? As helping professionals, don't we have enough to consider when analyzing clients without involving ourselves in perhaps a controversial area such as religion? These are perhaps similar questions that were either asked or crossed the minds of professional helpers when the issue of considering race and ethnicity as variables in the helping process emerged.

As a helping professional, involving one's self into a client's religious beliefs can be risky. However, what is being proposed is not trying to change a client's religious beliefs but understanding those beliefs and their impact upon the client's behavior. This understanding is necessary when attempting to develop a reasonable rehabilitation helping plan. This understanding is similar to considering one's race and/or ethnicity and the experiences associated with these variables as well as some of the beliefs and values to which the person's cultures expose him/her. Likewise, beliefs and values learned from religious association provide powerful influences on a person's belief systems.

This author contends that if a client/patient believes in a power or powers greater than oneself, this devotion and the beliefs and rules associated with this devotion are a stronger force upon one's behaviors than racial and ethnic influences. For persons who have some devotion to religious beliefs, these beliefs have an impact upon their health belief system. Some clients/patients, if they are influenced by religious beliefs, may feel that their illness and/or disability is the will of God; therefore, their recovery and/or rehabilitation is determined by His will. Similarly, where the person's religious doctrine promotes cause and effect, the person may believe that past behavior is the reason for his current situation. Do these predestination beliefs mean there can be no helpful intervention? The answer to this question is, intervention is possible. One goal should be to help them understand that intervention is not meant to change their beliefs, but the fact that there are numerous dimensions to human life should be pointed out to them and that spirituality is a very important dimension that can be used to aid in the healing, recovery, and rehabilitation process. The approach a helper should take will be determined by the type of help that is being offered.

If the helper does not feel comfortable involving himself in the client/patient's religious life, he should seek the assistance, with the permission of the client/patient, of a helper who is trained in this area.

An important fact the helper should remember is that he does not have to become an expert on religion and religious beliefs. However, as it is important to understand some things with regard to a client's racial and ethnic cultural background, it is equally beneficial to have basic information about religious background and/or orientation. If one does not know, ask.

Conclusion

Unless one is involved in some type of religious counseling, religion as a cultural variable is often overlooked. The truth of this statement is greater perhaps in the United States than it is in some other countries, which do not promote separation of church and government. Despite the separation of religion and governmental affairs, in the United States, for many people, religious doctrines provide considerable guidance and comfort. The influence of one's religious faith often is demonstrated at times of crisis and conflict. Despite the impact that religious faith can and does have on some persons' decisions and actions, especially in times of discomfort, helping professionals often overlook this important variable. Through the process of failing to recognize the influence and impact of this variable, the helping professional may be overlooking a component which can have significant influence on the outcome of the helping plan.

The purpose of this chapter was not to recommend a process by which the helping professional could incorporate religion in the helping plan, nor was it intended to recommend ways to minimize the impact religion may have in the helping process. The purpose of this chapter has been to make the helper aware of the possible importance of religious faith with regard to working with some clients. Additionally, the purpose was to increase the awareness of helping professionals with regard to the major religions in the world and their meanings and importance to those persons who live by their precepts.

Review Questions

1. What are the three (3) major religious divisions within the Christian faith?
2. What are the three (3) major beliefs of the Christian faith?
3. What are the three (3) major sects or versions of Judaism?
4. What is the name of the first five (5) books of the Hebrew Bible?
5. Within Judasim, what does Kosher mean?
6. What is the meaning of Yom Kippur?
7. Within the Islam faith, who is the Prophet Muhammad?
8. What are the Five Pillars of Islam?
9. What does the term "the middle way" mean in the faith of Buddhism?
10. What are the Four Nobel Truths in the faith of Buddhism?
11. Within the Hindu faith what does the term "Dharma" mean?
12. Within the Hindu faith what does the term "Karma" mean?

Suggested Activities

1. Discuss with someone of the Christian religion some of the basic beliefs of his/her religious faith.
2. Discuss with someone of the Jewish faith some of the basic beliefs of his/her religion.
3. Discuss with someone of the Islamic religion some of the basic beliefs of his/her faith.

4. Discuss with someone of the Buddhist faith some of the basic beliefs of his/her religion.
5. Discuss with someone of the Hindu religion some of the basic beliefs of his/her faith.

References

Armstrong, K. (2001). *Buddha.* New York: Penguin Groups.

Donin, H. (1972). *To be a Jew: A guide to Jewish observance in contemporary life.* New York: Basic Books.

Ganeri, A. (2001). *Buddhism.* Srl, Florence, Italy: McRae Books.

Novak, P., & Smith, H. (2003). *Buddhism: A concise introduction.* New York: Harper-Collins.

Rich, T. (2005). Judaism 101. Kashrut: Jewish dietary laws. Retrieved June 20, 2005. http://www.jewfag.org/kkashrut.htm.

Sabini, J. (1990). *Islam: A primer.* Washington, DC: Middle East Editorial Associates.

Trepp, L. (1980). *The complete book of Jewish observances: A practical manual for the modern Jew.* New York: Simon & Schuster.

Part Two

DISABILITY

Chapter 4

DISABILITY AND REHABILITATION

Chapter Outline
- Introduction
- Definition of a Disability
- Who Are Persons with Disabilities?
- Affects of Labeling
- Rehabilitation
- Conclusion

Chapter Objectives
- Present a definition of disability
- Provide an analysis of the disability definition
- Provide information with regard to the number of persons with a disability in America
- Identify disabilities among racial minorities
- Identify key pieces of legislation that have contributed to the rehabilitation of persons with disabilities

Introduction

What is a disability? How many people in America have a disability? At what point does a limitation become a disability? Who should be considered a person with a disability? And what is the appropriate terminology to use when referring to someone who is considered to have a disability? These are but a few of many questions the world of rehabilitation encounters frequently and society in general is attempting to answer.

As the medical and psychological professions have become better at diagnosing physical, mental, and emotional conditions, likewise, educational specialists have developed and learned more accurate ways of assessing learning styles and potential. Moreover, sociologists and social workers are contributing their knowledge toward the understanding of the impact social environmental factors have toward creating disabling conditions.

In the arena of education, increasing numbers of students are seeking assistance from counselors on the basis of having a learning disability. Stress-induced disabilities are being identified as a major problem by persons who work or have worked in jobs which are filled with high pressure activities such as the military, financial investors, and air traffic controllers to mention a few. Office workers, especially those who spend a considerable amount of time manipulating a computer terminal, are reporting various problems ranging from visual impairment to various forms of muscle strains. Given these problems, some new and others a variation of old physical, mental, or emotional issues, a relevant question is "What is the definition of a disability?"

Definition of a Disability

The definition of a disability appears to be dynamic; it has evolved over the past several decades as science and technology have revealed different methods of detecting and successfully treating many life situations which create limitations to one's abilities to successfully carry on with life activities. In retrospect, we find that what was considered a disability depended upon the society in which the person(s) with the limitation lived. In some ancient societies such as Rome, just the fact that a person "significantly" deviated from the "norm" appeared to be grounds for declaring the person as disabled, thus warranting abandonment and exclusion from society. In other societies such as the period of time when America was primarily an agrarian society, the classification of persons as being disabled, to a large degree, was predicated upon their abilities to be physically productive. If they were able to work the land and extract a living from the soil, they were accepted, perhaps viewed as being "different" but not disabled. Therefore, early definitions of disability emphasized a person who had a physical or mental condition which limited his/her ability to be gainfully employed. Later, emotional conditions were added as part of the evolving definition of disability.

In referring to Beatrice Wright's early works on defining the difference between a disability and handicap, Charlene P. DeLoach and Associates (1983) provide the following as further evidence of how our thinking has evolved with regard to what constitutes a disability:

> First, a disability has an "objective aspect," in contrast to a handicap, which is relative in nature. The second important point is that a disability is a "condition" resulting from illness, injury or congenital causes. Often people equate disability with illness. Disability should be understood as an ongoing condition that is a result of an injury, illness or congenital cause. And finally, a disability

limits or impairs physical or mental functioning. A person with a disability will have functional limitations and these limitations are used as a means of describing the effects of the disability upon the person.

Though lengthy, this explanation of a disability remains fairly accurate but has one major limitation, that being the foundation for a disability is a medical condition or more precisely, one that can be defined through medical interrogation. This was also the limitations of a definition given by Henderson and Bryan (1984). They defined a disability as a condition of impairment, physical or mental, having an objective aspect that can be usually described by a physician. This limitation of describing a disability solely on the basis of medical observations is a vivid indication of the evolution of the description of a disability as we view the currently acceptable definition which was issued as part of the Americans With Disabilities Act (ADA).

The Americans With Disabilities Act provides what is considered a "three-prong" definition. The following is an identification of each prong and a brief analysis.

First Prong

Definition–A person with a physical or mental impairment that substantially limits one or more major life activities such as walking, seeing, hearing, speaking, breathing, learning, working, or caring for one's self.

Analysis–the key words are "substantially limits." As an example, a broken leg is usually temporary, therefore, not considered a disability because it does not substantially impair walking on a permanent basis. However, if the break is severe enough to require permanent or long-term use of a mobility aid, it may be considered a disability.

As one reviews the major life activities, it will be noticed that the inability to perform is often determined by medical review; however, one life activity–learning–is often determined by educational specialists. It is true that the causes of some forms of learning problems such as mental retardation and brain damage are medically and/or psychologically determined, but several others such as Attention Deficit Disorder are often determined by nonmedical personnel. The point made is that the inclusion of learning as a disability, or more precisely, the lack thereof is an evolution in the thinking of what constitutes a disability.

Second Prong

Definition–a person is considered to have a disability if he/she has a record of such a physical or mental impairment.

Analysis—This definition deals in part with the stigma attached to having a disability. It speaks to "one who has a record of such a physical or mental impairment." This means that even though the person's condition may be controlled by medication or through rehabilitation, he/she can still be considered as having a disability because society's perception and reaction probably will continue to be one of viewing the person as having a disability. An illustration of this is a person who controls his epileptic seizures with medication is considered to have a disability because there is a record of seizures even though they are medically controlled; employers and others may think of him as having a disability. This will probably be the case despite his education and the fact that training has prepared him for employment in areas which, if he were to have a seizure, would be at minimum risk to himself and others. Another example is this book's author had polio many years ago which resulted in a weak right leg and a limp. Although he has a doctorate, has been a college professor and administrator for over thirty years, and the effects of polio have not impaired his ability to carry out any major life activities, he is considered as having a disability because, in this case, there is both a record of having a disability and there is visual evidence of same. Therefore, society does perceive him to be a person with a disability.

Third Prong

Definition—A person is considered as having a disability if he/she is regarded as having such an impairment.

Analysis—Similar to the second prong, this also deals with perception and to some extent, stigma; however, it differs in that it is referring to persons who may not have a disability but have conditions that are perceived as being disabling. For example, a person who has a large visible birthmark on his face which does not limit any of his major life activities may be perceived or stigmatized by employers and others as a person with a disability; therefore, he can be classified as having a disability.

As an overall analysis of the latest definition (ADA), we find that it differs from the older definitions in that they were based upon the limitations being clinically proven and the older definition did not take into consideration the impact of stigma and perception; whereas the ADA definition is more inclusive allowing more conditions to be considered.

Is "Handicap" an Offensive Word?

Some persons within the disability rights movement believe that applying the word "handicap" to a person with a disability should never be done. The major reason behind the rejection of the label is the negative images projected by the word. The word "handicap" is derived from an old English term which means cap-in-hand or stated more succinctly–beggar. Many years ago in England, one of the few groups which were allowed to beg in the streets were persons with disabilities; therefore, to a large extent the terms "handicap" and "beggar" have become synonymous.

Bryan (1996) convincingly argues that both terms "handicap" and "disability" for the uninformed illuminate negative images of persons with disabilities. He concludes his comments with the following:

> Many people believe the words "handicap" and "disability" mean the same: two words used to describe the same human condition. Too often the words "handicap" and "disability" create images of a person who cannot work and cannot take care of daily life functions. This image may be altered somewhat when they encounter a person with a disability; however, the image of a person unable to function at the same level as someone who does not have a disability is often the replacement. These ideas about handicap and disability are what most nondisabled persons use to judge persons with disabilities.

Perhaps Wright (1960) has the correct approach to handicap when she referred to the term meaning the obstacle that one faces in pursuing one's life goals. This view does not place handicap either as an extremely negative term or in the exclusive domain of persons with disabilities. In reality, every human faces many handicaps in his or her lifetime.

Undoubtedly scholars, rehabilitation professionals and others will continue the debate with regard to the usefulness or lack thereof of the terms handicap and disability. Until a definitive answer emerges, the most appropriate and least offensive approach is to place the person first and the limitation as secondary, thus "a person with a disability or a person with a handicap" is preferred.

When Is a Person Rehabilitated?

If a person is considered to have a disability if he/she has a physical or mental impairment that substantially limits one or more major life activity, then is he rehabilitated when there is no longer a limitation to a major life activity? Is the person rehabilitated when he is gainfully employed, thus able to provide for his basic needs? Is a person to be considered rehabilitated when, through the use of assistive devices or personal assistance, he is able to carry through with his major life activities?

These are only a few of the valid questions rehabilitation and other helping professionals encounter as they develop rehabilitation plans. In any academic course such as planning or evaluation and measurement, students are told that to determine success or failure one must establish his or her objectives in measurable terms; therefore, we return to the question, "How does one determine when a client is rehabilitated?" Some rehabilitation professionals define rehabilitation as the restoration of the person to the fullest physical, mental, social, vocational, and economic usefulness of which he or she is capable. This appears to be a comprehensive and reasonable definition in that it does not limit rehabilitation to any one life function. In the past, many vocational rehabilitation agencies considered a client to be rehabilitated when the client had been employed on a job for a specific period of time. The employment generally occurred after the client had been trained in an area commensurate with her abilities and/or had been provided physical restoration services that allowed her to become employable. The limitations of this approach to defining rehabilitation is obvious in that for those because of the severity of their disability employment is not realistic, it is virtually impossible for them to be considered rehabilitated.

Who Are Persons with Disabilities?

Membership in the world of disability is open and has no boundaries. Anyone, regardless of race, gender, ethnicity, social or economic status, faith and age is subject to become a member at anytime in his/her life. It is true, as will be discussed later, that some groups have a greater chance of becoming a member than others and from a parity standpoint, is overrepresented; equity of inclusion notwithstanding, people with disabilities are the largest open-class minority group in the world.

Class of People

In passing the 1990 Americans With Disabilities Act, the United States Congress recognized persons with disabilities as a class who have been discriminated against, similar to the way ethnic minorities have experienced discrimination. To support this pronouncement, Congress acknowledged the following realities:

1. Society has isolated and segregated individuals with disabilities;
2. Persons with disabilities have been victims of serious discrimination;
3. Discrimination against persons with disabilities continues to be a pervasive social problem;
4. The result of discrimination against persons with disabilities continues to be problematic in the critical areas of employment, housing, public accommodation, education, transportation, communication, institutionalization, health services, voting, and access to public services;

5. There has been no legal recourse for persons with disabilities who have been victims of discrimination;

6. Some of the acts of discrimination encountered by persons with disabilities are blatant and intentionally exclusionary;

7. Persons with disabilities occupy an inferior status in the American society; and

8. Persons with disabilities are a minority group which has been relegated to a position lacking political power in the American society.

In passing the Rehabilitation Act Amendment of 1992, the American Congress reemphasized its belief that persons with disabilities are treated as an underclass of people by stating:

1. Individuals with disabilities constitute one of the most disadvantaged groups in society; and

2. Individuals with disabilities continually encounter various forms of discrimination.

With the statements from the Americans With Disabilities Act and the Rehabilitation Act Amendments of 1992, Congress appears to be describing persons with disabilities as a class of people who have been continually and consistently denied their civil rights.

Number of Persons with Disabilities

It is difficult at best to provide an accurate count of the number of persons with disabilities in America. The methods of identifying persons with disabililties is the major obstacle to receiving a complete and accurate count. As one reviews the methods used to collect statistics with regard to persons with disabililties a myriad of data-collecting techniques come into view. Some statistics are based on "self-identification," others may be work related, while others exclude persons who are institutionalized. Still others are based upon a certain age range, generally age 14–64, while some researchers consider a person as being disabled if he/she was injured or sick and unable to work for a given period of time. Finally, none of these methods are able to include the person who has an "invisible" disability, such as heart condition, diabetes, various forms of seizures, and some mental and emotional problems unless the person is willing to disclose the disability.

An excellent example of discrepancies in the estimate of the population of persons with disabilities occurs when one views the 1990 statistics. The Americans With Disabilities Act estimated the number of persons with disabilities to be 43 million, while in the same year, the National Health Interview Survey (NHIS) estimated the population to be 33.8 million.

Despite the various methods and their shortcomings, with regard to determining the number of persons with disabilities in America, the most widely accepted estimate is that approximately one-fifth of the American population has a disability. An obvious observation of the percentage of persons with disabilities is that the community of persons with disabilities represents a significant portion of the American population. This causes one to consider the impact a population of this size can have toward improving their life conditions when they unite to pursue common causes. The sphere of influence increases dramatically as one considers the number of persons with disabilities plus for every person with a disability there is at least one significant other who has concerns with regard to that person's well being and one can also conservatively estimate that there are a significant number of people in America that make all or a part of their income from working with persons with disabilities. As one contemplates these facts it is abundantly clear that the community of persons with disabilities and those that care for and have an interest in their well being comprise a considerable portion of the American population. Therefore, all of these forces working together can cause significant change to occur in American society.

Tracing Disability Rate Increases

As the population of America has increased over the past quarter century, likewise the rate of disabilities have also increased. The increases can be attributed to several factors:

1. Demographic shifts associated with the aging of the American population. This trend will continue as life expectancy continues to increase.

2. Advanced medical technology is causing more lives to be saved today as compared to twenty-five years ago; this is particularly true of the very young and the elderly.

3. More individuals are disclosing their disability. While there still remains a stigma attached to having a disability, the severity of societal condemnation has decreased. Additionally, there are more laws to protect persons with disabilities and more services are available to persons with disabilities.

4. Conditions heretofore not appropriately diagnosed, such as learning disorders, are considered a disability.

Disability Among Racial and Ethnic Groups and Women

The results of most surveys of the percentage of disabilities in America reveal a picture of a higher rate of disabilities among racial minorities and women than Caucasian males.

When viewed from the standpoint of ranking the prevalence of disabilities among racial minority groups, Native Americans have the highest rate followed by African Americans with Caucasians being third; persons of

Hispanic origin ranked fourth and Asian or Pacific Islanders fifth. This same rank order occurs as one compares women and their racial background. When women are viewed as an aggregate without respect for racial background survey results confirms that women have a higher rate of disabilities than men.

As one views the living and working conditions of some minorities and women, plausible reasons for the high rate of disabilities are revealed: with respect to American Indians, alcohol and alcohol-related accidents and violence account for a significant number of disabilities, also the fact that many American Indians appear to be susceptible to diabetes contributes to the increased rate. A significant number of disabilities among African Americans and Hispanic/Latino Americans can be contributed to the fact that many persons of these groups work in jobs where the accident rates are abnormally high. Also, many Hispanic/Latino are agricultural workers and agricultural accidents are among the highest among all occupations. Working conditions and the stress of being mother, spouse, and employee contribute heavily to the high disability for women. Detailed discussion will be provided in the chapters that discuss disability and ethnicity.

Effects of Labeling

As a society of categorizers, attaching labels to help describe events, ideas, theories, individuals, and groups is important to establishing and maintaining an orderly society. This, in theory, is correct and would remain so if all of our labels could be "neutral" bestowing neither good nor bad significance to the individual or object being labeled. Of course, we recognize that this is not the case and in reality is not practical in many instances. Significance of good or bad, right or wrong, as well as degrees in-between in some cases is very useful. For instance, labeling or identifying an action such as smoking as being bad for one's health is useful; also labeling certain behaviors in public as inappropriate is useful in socializing children toward that society's acceptable behaviors. Therefore, labeling, in most instances, is a useful process.

The use of labeling similar to the use of medicine, while developed to be helpful, if used incorrectly it can have the opposite effect and do more harm than good. Perhaps the most obvious negative impact of attaching a label to describe humans can be seen in the various meanings society has associated with the terms used to describe and identify persons with disabilities. First, the contemporary terms used are disabled and handicapped. These terms, along with many others such as crippled, impaired, lunatic, deformed, stupid, and crazy all leave the impression of an inferior person. Robert Funk

(1987) described the influence of persistent negative labeling such as persons with disabilities as being deviants, incompetent, unhealthy objects of fear who are dependent upon the welfare and charity of others as sufficient societal justification for exclusionary action, such as segregation of persons with disabililties and denial of equal opportunities.

Most of the negative labeling terms used to describe persons with disabilities are not original creations of the current generations of our population; these terms have been associated with persons with disabilities for decades. If one reviews old hospital records of mental institutions the use of terms such as lunatic, deranged and imbecile were considered to be acceptable medical terms of the time. Similarly, the word "crippled" was liberally used in most hospitals; in fact, less than fifty years ago many pediatric orthopedic hospitals were named "crippled children's" hospital. As previously stated, all of these terms imply inferiority. Myron Eisenberg and associates (1982) believe we construct an ideology to explain the perceived inferiority of persons with disabilities by using stigmatic terms such as cripple, moron, and gimp in our daily language. The noted author Beatrice A. Wright (1988) believes this type labeling develops a negative bias and this bias steers perception, thoughts, and feelings along negative lines to such a degree that positive qualities remain hidden. She continues by stating that the negative bias becomes a powerful source of prejudice that ill serves those who are already disadvantaged.

Perhaps the ultimate tragedy of negative labeling is what Eisenberg and associates (1982) describe as "buying into the stigmatization process" and they describe the process as the stigmatized individual holding the same beliefs and self-identity as does the rest of society. As we review the following comments of Joseph Stubins (1988), one gains the impression he agrees with Eisenberg's point:

> The toughest item on the agenda of disabling is that modern America has no need for most disabled persons. In the rehabilitation community this conclusion is unthinkable, although such a conclusion is both plausible and real. Even those disabled citizens who lead conventional lives tend to repress their status and patronizing attitudes of the able-bodied and internalize the value of the straight world.

It is the internalization of the values of the nondisabled that is of concern to rehabilitation professionals and rehabilitation advocates. By accepting nondisabled persons descriptions, views, and attitudes toward them, persons with disabilities are in effect allowing the nondisabled population to exert unwarranted control over their lives. The following comments by Joseph Stubins (1988) succinctly places in perspective the hazards of persons with disabilities buying into the nondisabled labeling:

Disability can be viewed as a particular kind of relationship between a person with an impairment and the social and physical environment. What kind of relationship is this? (1) It is a superordinate subordinate one; able-bodied persons have power over those with impairments. (2) This power relationship is manifested by the able-bodied population's defining critical words from their perspective, e.g., in saying that disability is in the person rather than the relationship, and having control of the environment. (3) The relationship is characterized by the able-bodied person's asserting the right to determine what kind of rehabilitation services disabled people need.

These three points appear to have been key elements in the rise of the disability rights movement. While the attitudes expressed within these points do not represent a mean-spirited approach of the nondisabled, in interacting with persons who have disabilities, it nevertheless represents oppression; and this and other forms of oppression was considered by the disability rights movement leadership as stumbling blocks which had to be removed before rehabilitation services could be considered effective and meeting the needs of the population it was intended to serve.

The remainder of this chapter will deal with various efforts put forth, both past and present, to insure that the rehabilitation needs of persons with disabilities are being met.

Rehabilitation

The American federal government can be credited with laying the foundation for the beginning of state and federal government's participation in the rehabilitation of persons with disabilities when in 1917 Congress passed the Smith-Hughes Act which established the Board of Vocational Education. This landmark act is considered an education act rather than a rehabilitation act; however, it indirectly provided services to persons with disabilities as a result of providing for vocational education. The initial venture into the area of the federal government authorizing and funding services to persons with disabilities was begun with the enactment of the Smith-Sears Veterans' Rehabilitation Act of 1918 and its main purpose was to provide "vocational" rehabilitation services and return to employment persons with disabilities who had been discharged from military service. It should be noted that to this point all of the federal rehabilitation efforts were established to provide service to veterans; therefore, persons with disabilities who had no connection to the military, if they could afford services, had their rehabilitation services provided by charitable organizations or private rehabilitation facilities.

Public rehabilitation programs came into existence in 1920 with the enactment of the Smith-Fess Act. As Bryan (1996) points out, the Act provided only for vocational guidance, training, occupational adjustment, prostheses, and placement services, thus establishing the guidelines that federal funding for rehabilitation services for persons with physical disabilities would be oriented toward preparing the person for employment. This meant that physical restoration, except providing prostheses which was provided to make the person more employable, and sociopsychological services were excluded. This philosophy continued for twenty-three years until the Barden-LaFollette Act of 1943 was enacted. This Act provided more funds and allowed additional program options such as providing physical restoration as well as funding research programs for in-depth study of more effective and efficient ways of rehabilitation and delivering rehabilitation services and finally it provided training funds for rehabilitation specialists such as physicians, nurses, rehabilitation counselors, physical therapists, occupational therapists, social workers, and psychologists.

The philosophy of directing vocational rehabilitation programs toward preparing persons for employment to the exclusion of other forms of rehabilitation was so deeply imbedded within the rehabilitation policy-makers and the United States Congress' mind that when the Mental Retardation Facilities and Community Health Centers Construction Act was passed in 1963, it was not placed within the vocational rehabilitation program partly because of its lack of emphasis on vocational goals. While maintaining its passion for strong emphasis on vocational goals as being a central theme of the vocational rehabilitation program, Congress continued to strengthen the program with the Vocational Rehabilitation Amendments Act of 1965. In this piece of legislation, Congress used three approaches to improve services: (1) Congress provided monies to states for innovative projects that developed new methods of providing services; (2) Congress created a broader base of services to people with disabilities, including individuals with socially handicapping conditions; and (3) Congress eliminated economic need as a requirement for rehabilitation services. It is noteworthy that prior to this amendment act, persons had to demonstrate that they could not pay for certain services; also social conditions were not considered a disability.

During the early and mid 1960s, persons with disabilities and various disability advocate groups began to give increased attention to the almost exclusive emphasis Congress was placing on vocational goals in most rehabilitation programs. The concerned community of persons with disabilities as well as many of their family members did not oppose "a" goal of employability, but believed that employment as "the" goal was rendering persons with severe disabilities who did not have much promise for sustained employment, to a life of dependency, institutionalization, and handouts. Additionally, these disability rights groups were equally concerned about other issues such as the lack of input persons with disabilities and their families had with the development of rehabilitation plans, deinstitutionalization, demedication and self care to mention a few. An outgrowth of these concerns was the uniting of various groups of persons with disabilities for the purpose of demonstrating their concerns with a show of unity. Previously, one of the major weaknesses of efforts to promote the needs of persons with disabilities was the inability of the various groups to come together in a common cause. Two major obstacles existed–one was that advocacy was based along the lines of disability category such as polio association, multiple dystrophy, multiple sclerosis, etc.; and two, most of these organizations were headed by persons who did not have a disability.

Gartner and Joe (1987) believe that one of the most notable features of the disability activism years was the central role played by persons with disabilities and the coalitions of people with different disabilities. They further inform us that perhaps for the first time persons with disabilities were the leaders of the movement. This was important because Congress and other rehabilitation policy makers were seeing persons with disabilities in new roles: as leaders and as their own advocates rather than in the passive subservient roles to which they had grown accustomed. The community of persons with disabilities had observed the success that African Americans and other racial minorities experienced through their marches and sit-ins which culminated in the passage of the Civil Rights Act of 1964.

As the community of persons with disabilities gained experience at coalition building and lobbying, their message began to be heard and heeded by rehabilitation policy makers. In 1975 the Education for All Handicapped Children Act (name later changed to Individuals With Disabilities Education Act–IDEA) was passed. The Act provided each child who had a disability a free, appropriate education in the least restrictive environment. Another important provision gave parents of children with disabilities the right to be involved in the process of determining the type and nature of their child's education.

During the early 1970s the community of persons with disabilities were not only concerned with education issues, they were also keenly aware that total rehabilitation meant independent living for those that were able to live independently. To this community, independent living was not restricted to those who were ambulatory or considered mentally competent, as was normally the restriction for independent housing. They strongly believed that persons with severe disabilities such as those with spinal cord injuries, mental retardation, as well as severe visual limitations should have the same opportunity as others, both with and without disabilities to be independent and exert control over their own lives. Stimulated by what they considered the failure of the traditional rehabilitation programs, they formed the American Coalition of Citizens with Disabilities (ACCD). One of the several acts that spurred the creation of the American Coalition of Citizens with Disabilities was the veto by President Nixon of the Vocational Rehabilitation Act of 1972 on the grounds the legislation "strayed too far from the essential vocational objective of the program." Of considerable importance to the community of persons with disabilities was that within the Act were provisions of federal financial support for independent living centers. Through the efforts of ACCD and others within the community of persons with disabilities as well as families, friends, and other advocates, independent living centers were funded through the Rehabilitation Comprehensive Services and Developmental Disabilities Act of 1978 (Rehabilitation Amendment of 1978).

Prior to the enactment of the Rehabilitation Amendment of 1978, there were nongovernment supported independent living centers which had been developed as a result of persons with severe disabilities moving into communities and contracting for services that they could not provide for themselves. Through this method of independence, persons with severe disabilities were able to exert considerable control over their lives. An obvious limitation to the nongovernment-supported programs was financial support. Therefore, to expand opportunities to a larger population, funding provided by state and the federal government was needed. This was achieved by the enactment of the Rehabilitation Amendment of 1978.

The independent living center concept has evolved into an important addition to the nation's rehabilitation program as well as a tremendous benefit to persons with disabilities. Currently there are over 300 centers representing every state in the country. This concept is also used throughout Europe.

From a rehabilitation viewpoint, a relevant questions is, "What are independent living centers?" According to Bryan (1996), services vary in an effort to accommodate the needs of the population served; moreover, most centers reflect a common goal which Townsend and Ryan (1991) describe as advocating for "independence" in decisions about one's life which may not necessarily mean physically performing daily living tasks. With respect to the roles of independent living centers, they categorize them into four areas: (1) control and direct personal and community services including planning and organizing transportation, finances, paid work, cooking, laundry, housekeeping, and general assistance; (2) encourage regular participation in leisure and recreational activities including social skills, emotional stability, motivation, attitudes, and interaction support to participants at home or outside the home; (3) assist with the development and use of individual potential and talents, i.e., individual's vision of the possibilities for overcoming barriers which limit fulfillment of aspirations; and (4) contribute to the well-being and betterment of society, including the ability to give as well as take to combat a sense of dependency on others. Moreover, the major emphasis is on the consumer, in this case person with a disability, making choices about how he/she wants to live, choosing who or what will provide the services as well as how they will be provided.

The disability rights movement and the push for independent living centers developed simultaneously with the effort to pass the Rehabilitation Act of 1973 which would provide the greatest strength of the rehabilitation program that heretofore had existed. Title V, with its Sections 501-504 was the heart of the Act:

Section 501: This section established the Interagency Committee on Handicapped Employees. This committee is charged with overseeing federal hiring, placement and job advancement of persons with disabilities within the federal government system.

Section 502: The Architectural and Transportation Barriers Compliance Board was established by this section to monitor the construction of new federal buildings and remodeling existing structures to ensure they are accessible to persons with disabilities.

Section 503: This section requires every employer who enters into a contract for more than $2500 with the federal government comply with affirmative action in hiring persons with disabilities.

Section 504: As a result of this section, every American institution receiving federal assistance must take steps to ensure that persons with disabilities are not discriminated against in employment.

There is little question that the Rehabilitation Act of 1973 was the strongest piece of legislation for protecting persons with disabilities from discrimination in the area of employment to that date; however, there was one major weakness–the Act affected only those private employers who did business under contract with the federal government for more than $2500. Granted, this was sufficient to cover the Fortune 500 companies as well as most other large companies, but the majority of American businesses are small, many of whom do not necessarily contract with the federal government. Therefore, many neighborhood or local "mom and pop" businesses were not affected.

In 1990, this flaw was corrected with the enactment of the most comprehensive piece of legislation for persons with disabilities in the form of the Americans With Disabilities Act (ADA). This is a Civil Rights piece of legislation that prohibits discrimination against persons with disabilities and protects their civil rights by requiring all persons and all businesses to adhere to the provisions. The core of the Act is contained within five titles: Employment, Public Service, Public Accommodation and Services Operated by Private Entities, Telecommunication Relay Services, and Miscellaneous Provisions. A brief description of each title is provided below.

Title I: Employment was phased in with two steps. Phase one was effective July 26, 1992, and covered all employers who had twenty-five or more employees. Phase two included employers who had fifteen or more employees and it went into effect July 26, 1994. Companies with fewer than fifteen employees are exempt and may be covered by the public accommodation provisions.

The employment provision prohibits discrimination in the hiring process of persons with disabilities because of the person's disability. The law requires that the employer provide "reasonable accommodations" whenever needed unless proof of undue hardship is provided.

Title II: Public Services prohibits discrimination of persons with disabilities in all services, programs, and activities provided by or made available by state and local governments.

Title III: Public Accommodations and Services operated by Private Entitles prohibits discrimination of persons with disabilities with regard to their access and use of public accommodation.

Title IV: Telecommunications Relay Services' primary goal is the provision and expansion of telecommunication services for persons with hearing impairment.

Title V: The Miscellaneous Provisions section is a "catch all" provision to emphasize that ADA's goal is to strengthen existing laws, both state and federal, as they relate to providing equal access for persons with disabilities. It further points out that if a state or federal law provides more protection to a persons with a disability than the ADA, that law supercedes the ADA; conversely, if the ADA provides better protection to the person with a disability, the ADA supercedes the weaker law.

Conclusion

Work or employment play such a central role in most American's lives to the point that we are defined, in part, by our occupation. Work provides us with not only income allowing us to take care of basic needs and hopefully enjoy some of the nonbasics, but also has an impact upon our self-esteem. According to Childs (1971), work is more than a means through which goods and services are purchased; it is a means by which an individual purchases his/her dignity. Given the lofty position that work occupies in our lives, there is no surprise that rehabilitation of persons with disabilities is synonymous with employment. To be more specific, in some instances, persons with disabilities are not considered to be rehabilitated until they have become employed. However, Ondusko (1991), and Satcher and Dooley-Dickey (1992) remind us that through the years individual and group prejudices which are based on unfounded myths have caused workers with disabilities to be relegated to dead-end jobs, if any at all. It is these negative attitudes which too often serve as the greatest hurdle that people with disabilities have to overcome in their quest for gainful employment. As long as the Puritan work ethic is attached to mores and behaviors concerning the worth of individuals, it will be through work that persons with disabilities are considered as economically productive citizens.

Although work will continue to be a central factor in American lives, the fact exists that some persons, because of the nature of their disability, will not be employable or at best be able to maintain minimal employment. Therefore, these persons should not be devalued or considered as nonrehabilitated. Our society must begin to look at the whole person, not one aspect, particularly the aspect of limitations. In other words, rehabilitation means more than work; it also means being able to make decisions about one's life situation and being able to "assist" in taking care of oneself, and in some cases "assist" means giving instructions and informing others of one's needs.

Review Questions

1. How does the Americans With Disabilities Act define a disability?
2. How does the Americans With Disabilities Act's definition of disability differ from previous definitions?
3. What are some of the difficulties encountered in attempting to obtain an accurate count with regard to the number of persons with disabilities in America?
4. Percentage-wise, which racial group in America has the fewest persons with disabilities?
5. What are some of the reasons for high disability rates among some American minority groups?
6. The first federal legislation with regard to rehabilitation of persons with disabilities was established for which group?
7. What are independent living centers?
8. What was the major weakness of the Rehabilitation Act of 1973?
9. What are the five (5) titles that constitute the 1990 Americans With Disabilities Act?

Suggested Activities

1. Conduct an informal survey by interviewing at least ten (10) persons, asking them to give you their definition of a disability; also ask them to identify ten (10) disabilities.
2. In the previously mentioned survey, ask the participants at what point would they consider a persons to be rehabilitated.

3. Research information on the Americans With Disabilities Act and identify relevant facts with regard to each title then list how each title impacts persons with disabilities.
4. Visit a rehabilitation center and learn about the latest techniques used to rehabilitate persons with disabilities.
5. Visit at least two (2) independent living centers and observe the types of services provided to its occupants.
6. Interview a rehabilitation counselor with regard to the types of services provided to persons with disabilities by his/her agency to persons with disabilities.

References

Bryan, W. V. (1996). *In search of freedom.* Springfield, IL: Charles C Thomas.

Childs, G. B. (1971). Is the work ethic realistic in an age of automation? In H. Peters, & J. C. Hansen (Eds.), *Vocational guidance and career development.* New York: Macmillan.

DeLoach, C., Wilkins, R. D., & Walker, G. W. (1983). *Independent living, philosophy, process and services.* Baltimore: University Park Press.

Eisenberg, M. D., Giggins, C., & Duval, R. J. (Eds.). (1982). *Disabled people as second-class citizens.* New York: Springer.

Funk, R. (1987). From caste to class in the context of civil rights. In A. Gartner & T. Joe (Eds.), *Images of the disabled.* New York: Praeger.

Gartner, A., & Joe, T., (Eds.). (1987). *Images of the disabled.* New York, Praeger.

Henderson, G., & Bryan, W. V. (1984). *Psychosocial aspects of disability.* Springfield, IL: Charles C Thomas.

Ondusko, D. (1991). Comparison of employees with disabilities and able-bodied workers in janitorial maintenance. *Journal of Applied Rehabilitation Counseling, 22*:19–24.

Satcher, J., & Dooley-Dickey, K. (1992). Attitudes of human resource management students toward persons with disabilities. *Rehabilitation Counseling Bulletin, 35*:248–252.

Stullins, J. (1988). The politics of disability, In Yuker, H. E. (Ed.), *Attitudes towards persons with disabilities.* New York, Springer.

Townsend, E., & Ryan, B. (1991). Assessing independence in community living. *Canadian Journal of Public Health, 82*:52–57.

Wright, B. (1960). *Physical disability: A psychological approach.* New York: Harper and Row.

Wright, B. A. (1988). Attitudes and the fundamental negative bias: Conditions and corrections. In H. E. Yuker (Ed.), *Attitudes toward persons with disabilities.* New York: Springer.

Suggested Readings

Barton, L. (1993). The struggle for citizenship: The case of disabled people. *Disability, Handicap and Society, 8:*235-248.

Brown, I. (1994). Promoting quality within service delivery systems. *Journal on Developmental Disabilities, 3*(2):i–iv, 1994.

Bryan, W. V. (1996). *In search of freedom.* Springfield, IL: Charles C Thomas.

Flynn, M. (1989). *Independent living for adults with a mental handicap: A place of my own.* London: Cassel.

Henderson, G., & Bryan, W. V. (1997). *Psychosocial aspects of disability* (2nd ed.). Springfield, IL: Charles C Thomas.

Jongbloed, L., & Crichton, A. (1990). A new definition of disability: Implications for rehabilitation practice and social policy. *Canadian Journal of Occupational Therapy, 57:*32–38.

Livneh, H. (1988). Rehabilitation goals: Their hierarchical and multifaceted nature. *Journal of Applied Rehabilitation Counseling, 19*(3):12–18.

McPherson, G. (1990). Are you ready for the revolution? *Canadian Journal of Rehabilitation, 3:*1–5.

Meyer, L. H., Peck, C. A. & Brown, L. (Eds.). (1990). *Critical issues in the lives of people with severe disabilities.* Baltimore: Brookes.

Mondros, J., & Wilson S. (1994). *Organizing for power and empowerment.* New York: Columbia University Press.

Oliver, M. (1990). *The politics of disablement.* London: Macmillan.

Renwick, R., Brown, I. & Nagler, M. (Eds.). (1996). *Quality of life in health promotion and rehabilitation: Conceptual approaches, issues and applications.* Thousand Oaks, CA: Sage.

Chapter 5

DISCRIMINATION AND DISABILITY

Chapter Outline
- Introduction
- Brief History of Discrimination
- What Is Discrimination?
- Legacy of Discrimination
- Prejudice
- Blaming the Victim
- Fear of the Powerless
- Attitude Formation
- Understanding Stereotypes
- Destroying Stereotypes
- Conclusion–The Ism's

Chapter Objectives
- Better understanding about why we are prejudiced
- Identifying the five phases of prejudice
- Better understanding of the impact discrimination has had on persons with disabilities
- Better understanding of how attitudes are formed
- Better understanding of how stereotypes are formed and ways of eliminating them

Introduction

A holistic approach to treating and interacting with a client/patient in a helping relationship whether the helping relates to the field of rehabilitation, medicine, counseling, social work, or psychotherapy requires the helper to go beyond understanding the injury, the pathology of the disease, and/or the symptoms of the ailment and seek an understanding of the "whole" person. Most persons who consider themselves as professional helpers will quickly acknowledge that an understanding and awareness of

74

many factors influencing a person's life (educational, social, and family to mention only a few) provide the helper with a better basis for assisting the person being helped. In the quest for a complete understanding, one has to be equally vigilant of both positive and negative factors influencing the person's life. One of the most insidious negative impacts is discrimination.

Without evidence to the contrary, one is forced to assume that discrimination is not of recent origin. In fact, there is overwhelming evidence to comfortably support the theory that discrimination is as old as humankind. Discrimination in some form has existed for many, many centuries. Not offered as a defense, but as a fact, humans have been at various times and often concurrently discriminated against because of strength, or more precisely lack thereof, religious beliefs, gender, age, language, and physical stature to list only a few. Despite the fact that in America, as is true in most countries, there are a number of forms of discrimination; however, currently we too frequently hear about and concentrate on racial and gender discrimination. As discussed in Chapter 1, the changing demographic trends are prompting many aspects of American life to reevaluate and develop plans to reconstruct the ways in which we interact with persons here-to-fore ignored.

Persons with disabilities have been one of those groups that has been adversely affected by discrimination. Although modern-day discrimination of persons with disabilities does not have the malicious intent of elimination that early day "survival of the fittest," had. The fact remains that persons with disabilities have been discriminated against in various ways that have had a negative impact upon their lives. Persons with disabilities who are from a minority group too frequently experience "dual discrimination," as a member of a racial/ethnic minority group and as a person with a disability. As helping professionals, we may overlook the duality of their life situation and concentrate upon the impact of the person's disability to the exclusion of the contributing factors of race and/or gender or the reverse may occur of focusing all attention on the person's race and/or gender overlooking the impact the disability has on the person's life. Clearly to maximize the potential of successfully rehabilitating clients, the rehabilitation/helping professional must take a holistic approach and examine various aspects of the client's life situation.

All persons with disabilities who are minorities have experienced discrimination both from being a person with a disability and being a member of a racial minority group. Attitudes toward persons with disabilities, societal reactions to persons with disabilities, and perceptions of worth of individuals with disabilities over the past half century have received considerable attention by researchers and educators; however, relatively little attention has been given to the impact of an individual experiencing discrimination both as a person from a minority culture and a disability culture. In-depth discussion of the impact of dual discrimination will be provided in the chapters on disability and ethnicity. At this point the author would like to provide a foundation for future discussion by exploring the following topics: "A Brief History of Discrimination," "What Is Discrimination" and "Why Are We Prejudice?"

Brief History of Discrimination

Survival Techniques

Undoubtedly prejudice and discrimination have existed in some form as long as there have been groups of people. As previously stated, it is not uncommon for people to elect to associate with others who share similar interests, beliefs, and values. This form of natural selection is normal. During the earliest history of human existence, individuals grouped together for survival; they assisted each other with their safety and sustenance needs. Undoubtedly, selection into these ancient groups was not only based upon one's ability to contribute to the group's well-being but was also based upon attributes that were familiar and nonthreatening to the group. Persons who looked different, acted different, communicated different, walked different, and perhaps smelled different than what the group was accustomed were rejected for inclusion into the group. This was perhaps one of the first forms of human discrimination. Those who were rejected as members of one group probably banded together with others who had similar characteristics, thus forming another group which perhaps rejected others who did not look, act, communicate, walk, or smell as they. This natural selection continued and many groups came into existence. Each one of these groups not only rejected "abnormal" would-be members, but in the process became suspicious of the person and the groups the "rejects" eventually formed. Because these people were "different," contact with them was deliberately avoided. Due to the lack of contact, suspicions developed in their curious minds which led to preconceived ideas about the group and its behavior. Active minds sometimes invented behavior for the group and these preconceived ideas and prejudgments were told around campfires with the young listening at a distance, absorbing many of the interesting details and these stories were repeated around their campfires when they became adults with their young attentively listening. Each group was equally guilty of creating fictional stories about the other groups. As groups engaged in battle against each other, their distrust, dislike, and discrimination became more ingrained into their interaction patterns.

Tool of Power

Over the centuries, discrimination has evolved from a survival technique into a "tool of power." The "in"-group characterizes the "out"-group(s) as inferior and bestows many negative connotations to the attributes of the out-group and its members. By lowering the status of the out-group the in-group's status is increased and a feeling of superiority is embedded in the members' minds. For "keeping the out-group members in their places," in-group members are rewarded with privileges such as better paying jobs, higher quality of education, etc. In summary, the in-group obtains a position of power over the out-group and consistently uses this to keep the out-group in subordinate positions.

The purpose of this brief historical time travel along the road of discrimination is to illustrate that discrimination probably began as a survival technique and discrimination of one group against another has been passed down for several hundred generations with each generation believing it has both the right and the reason to behave in the manner they do. As times have changed and humanity has progressed, likewise discrimination has made changes. No longer is our survival dependent upon discrimination, if in fact it ever was, but we persist in finding ways to exclude, avoid, and attack others and, yes, occasionally even exterminate people we consider different and inferior to ourselves. The additional point to be made is currently that there is not justification nor valid reason for discriminating against each other. Natural group selection is normal and is likely to continue as long as humans exist; however, the viciousness of discrimination is not normal and does not have to be perpetuated generation after generation.

What Is Discrimination?

According to Ritzer, Kammeyer, and Yetman (1982), discrimination is the behavioral expression of prejudice. Gordon Allport (1979), in his seminal work on prejudice, presented a model of acting out prejudice which consists of five phases: antilocution, avoidance, exclusion, physical attack, and extermination. His model ranges from a mild form of discrimination to the ultimate act of discrimination. Understanding these forms of discrimination provides us with a prospective on prejudice and how one form of prejudice without being controlled may progress to more severe forms of discrimination. The model also provides us with knowledge of how prejudice impacts the victim. The interpretation of the stages draws considerably upon the writing of Ponterotto and Pedersen (1993).

Antilocution is perhaps the least aggressive form of prejudice and is represented by prejudicial conversation conducted by individuals sharing similar opinions. Most individuals engaged in this type of behavior will vehemently deny their behavior is prejudicial in any way. Rather, they indicate this is simply a matter of expressing their opinions. Although this form of prejudice is nonaggressive, it can be very dangerous in that it can have both a multiplying and inciting affect. An opinion may multiply when an opinion is shared with another person, he then shares it with someone else and so on until a much larger group is expressing this viewpoint. Additionally, in the process of multiplying the opinion, individuals may become incited to take aggressive action.

An example of this level of prejudice is two or more persons expressing their opinions that an independent living center for persons with severe mental disabilities proposed for their neighborhood is going to create a safety risk for their families. At this level of prejudice, the discrimination is only talk and in most instances the information discussed is based upon hearsay, rumors, and stereotype rather than fact. However, as previously implied, without facts that contradict misinformation, the next level of discrimination (avoidance) occurs.

Avoidance goes beyond talk and places into action efforts to avoid individuals and/ or groups declared unwanted. The persons engaged in conducting the avoidance generally are willing to accept some inconveniences to eliminate interaction with those being avoided. As an example, a family moving their children from public neighborhood schools and sending them several miles away to an expensive private school to avoid having their children interact with children of different cultures and/or racial backgrounds.

During the integration period, mid-1950s and the decades of the 1960s and 1970s, the avoidance behavior was common as racial minority students were given their rights to an equal education and began to attend formerly nonminority schools. At considerable expense, some parents either moved to areas where there were no minorities or placed their children in expensive, private schools. This was repeated when neighborhood covenants were declared illegal. This was the practice where homeowners would either sign an agreement or it was placed on their title to their property that they would not sell their property to persons of certain races. Again, when this was declared to be illegal, some owners, rather than live next to or in the neighborhood with those they had attempted to exclude, often would sell their homes, sometimes taking a loss. Today we continue to hear of similar behavior. In some cases, families have elected to move when the decision is made to locate a facility for persons who have a mental disability or a halfway house for former substance abusers in or near their neighborhood.

Exclusion is the third level of discrimination which may take the form of getting a petition signed to exclude an individual or group, for example, from membership in a social club or organization. An appropriate example is when homeowners in a neighborhood may circulate a petition to block the development of an independent living center in their area. Additionally, the neighborhood covenants discussed in avoidance is also an excellent example of exclusion.

Physical Attack is the fourth level of discrimination which becomes much more serious than those already mentioned. This stage requires heated and often irrational emotional reactions which lead to physical violence. Physically abusing the occupants of the mythical independent living center or breaking the windows in the center are examples of a physical attack. Numerous examples from the American Civil Rights Movement could be cited; however, the author believes that the reader recognizes the point.

Extermination is the final stage of discrimination which is the ultimate act of discrimination represented by taking the life of a person from another culture or racial background. This was illustrated in the bombing of African American churches in the southern United States during the Civil Rights era of the 1960s. Also, the elimination of thousands of Jewish people by the Nazi forces is a constant reminder of the extremity of extermination.

The last two stages, physical attack and extermination, indicates that prejudice has reached the stage of hatred and the victim of the discriminatory act is thought to represent some type of threat to the perpetrator.

Discrimination and Disability

Throughout the centuries, persons with disabilities have been subjected to each of the five levels of discrimination, although most discrimination today rarely exceeds the avoidance level. Most nondisabled persons have a sympathetic approach to dealing with persons with disabilities; therefore, they may avoid reacting aggressively toward them even though they may harbor feelings and emotions to which they feel ashamed to admit. Rather than deal with these feelings, too often nondisabled persons avoid contact with persons who have disabilities.

Except for rare incidents in today's society do persons with disabilities face physical attack and almost never extermination, although not many years ago some persons who were mentally retarded were sterilized and this is a form of extermination. However, throughout history, persons with disabilities have been subjected to both physical attack and extermination. In some ancient societies, it was acceptable to destroy babies who had a disability; similarly, persons who were considered to be "different" were physically attacked and driven from the community. For a more in-depth review of historical treatment of persons with disabilities read *In Search of Freedom* (Bryan 2005) and *Psychosocial Aspects of Disabilities*, (Henderson & Bryan 2004).

In summary, the human relationship of dealing with persons who have disabilities has consisted of a mixture of discriminations ranging from being threatened with extermination to actual extermination.

Legacy of Discrimination

One of the physical laws of nature is that for every action there is a reaction. With regard to discrimination and disabilities there have been numerous reactions such as low self-esteem and a dependency on others for resolution of some of their problems, just to mention two. Perhaps the major impact or legacy of discrimination can best be seen in the areas of education, employment, economics, housing, communication, and transportation. The impact of discrimination of persons with disabilities in an economically-driven society is that poor educational attainment serves to limit one's employment potential which in turn impacts one's earning ability. The lack of adequate financial resources severely limits one's ability to purchase necessary goods and services, not to speak of items that go beyond the necessities of life which makes for a more comfortable existence and can improve one's position on life's status totem pole. Too frequently, the result of this chain of events set into motion by discrimination is a dependency upon local, state, and/or federal public assistance, thus continuing some of the negative feelings about persons with disabilities. At this point the legacy of discrimination will be viewed as it relates to education, employment, and the economical condition of persons with disabilities.

Education–A dissertation does not have to be written to explain the educational status of a large segment of the population of persons with disabilities. The following statement taken from the National Organization on Disability/Louis Harris Survey of Americans With Disabilities (1994), while dated provides a convincing summary. Based upon a comparison of the survey of a national cross-section of adults eighteen years of age and older who did not have disabilities, the conclusion is "it is clear that adults with disabilities are less educated than those without disabililties." The results from a similar survey conducted by the same organizations in 1998 indicate that this statement remains true. A closer analysis of this survey reveals: adults with disabilities are twice as likely as adults without disabilities to have less than a high school education (22% vs. 9%).

Without question, the previously stated facts demonstrate that discrimination has placed some persons with disabilities in a disadvantaged position with respect to educational attainment; despite this information, a comparison of this survey (1998) with a similar survey conducted in 1986 provides hope in that there has been some improvement of the educational level of persons with disabilities. The comparison provided the following results: (1) in 1986, forty percent (40%) of adults with disabilities had not completed high school, whereas in the 1998 survey, the percentage had decreased to 22 percent. (2) Approximately three in four adults with disabilities have at least a high school education, whereas in 1986, three in five had a high school education. Perhaps the trend toward improved educational status of persons with disabilities, especially those requiring special education, can be attributed in part to legislative action such as the Individuals With Disabilities Education Act (IDEA) which, according to Zawaiza (1995), is the primary source of federal aid to state and local school systems for instructional support services to children with disabilities. Through the passage of this act, Congress attempts to insure that all children with disabilities are provided a free, appropriate education in the least restrictive environment. The Act also gives the parents of children with disabilities the right to be involved in the process of determining the type and nature of their child's education through an individualized plan (Bryan, 1996).

Economics–In 1994, a Harris survey compared the economic situation of persons with disabilities in that year with persons with disabilities in 1986 and the survey results indicated that Americans with disabilities may have been better educated than their counterparts of 1986; however, their income or earnings had not kept pace with their educational attainments. The 2002 U. S. Census Bureau report shows that in the first decade of the twenty-first century, people with disabilities economically lag behind nondisabled persons. Of persons age 25 to 64 with no disability, 39.3 percent had personal income of less than 20,000 dollars and 12.3 percent lived in households with total household income below 20,000 dollars. In comparison, among persons with nonsevere disabilities, 47.6 percent had personal income less than 20,000 dollars and 18.3 percent lived in households with total household income below 20,000 dollars. Among persons with a severe disability, the gap widens considerably in that 76.6 percent had personal income below 20,000 dollars, and 37.8 percent lived in households with total household income below 20,000 dollars.

Employment –Perhaps no one feature defines an American more than the type of work he/she performs. We frequently identify persons by their job. Pete, the janitor; Fred, the plumber; Mary, the attorney; and Sarah, the dentist; the job attached to their names tells us a great deal about them. One, we are able to judge their level of education; two, we get some idea of their economic status; and three, we are able to judge a little about their working environment. In short, a person's line of work defines a large number of things about the person. Likewise, to be unemployed and/or not able to work defines things about the person also. Unfortunately, much of how we think of an unemployed person (unless they are retired) is negative. True, persons who are unemployed by virtue of a disability are often not painted with the same negative brush stroke as a person who does not have a disability and is unemployed; never-the-less, there is a specter of devaluation. While a major reason for employment difficulties of persons with disabilities is attitudinal barriers of employers and other nondisabled persons, the author is not implying that every person with a disability who is unemployed is so because of discrimination.

The discrimination that persons with disabilities encounter is one of the most difficult forms of discrimination to eradicate. First, the discriminator is often unaware that his behavior toward persons with disabilities constitutes discrimination. From a point of view of ignorance, we act in a patronizing manner; we may speak for, think for, and act in behalf of persons with disabilities, thinking that we are sparing them the trouble or embarrassment of failing. Second, persons without disabilities will strongly deny their prejudices. As previously indicated, it generally is not socially acceptable to express negative feelings with regard to persons with disabilities. Despite our denial of prejudice, our actions often reveal our inner feelings. Third, the discriminator, through various acts of charity and avoidance of personal contact, cleanses his conscious from feelings of guilt. Today most discriminatory acts are not blatant and are nonviolent and often issued without malicious intent; therefore, convincing oneself that no discrimination has occurred becomes much easier. Without recognizing that a problem exists, extermination of the problems becomes extremely difficult.

Prejudice

A simplified explanation of prejudice is "prejudging" or making decisions about someone or a situation before obtaining sufficient facts necessary to make an informed decision. Given this definition, prejudice can be either positive or negative; however, in most instances when we speak of or think about prejudicial action or statements, it is usually within a negative connotation. Likewise, when we consider the meaning of prejudice, it is often associated negatively with a racial situation. Persons with disabilities in the past as well as presently have been prejudged. First, we will look at why we are prejudiced then view prejudices with regard to disability and next we will look at prejudice associated with race and finally we will intersect the two factors of disability and race.

Why Are We Prejudiced?

According to Allport (1979) and Ponterotto and Pedersen (1993), three factors contribute significantly to the development of prejudicial views: (1) ethnocentricism, (2) lack of significant intergroup contact, and (3) preference for categorization.

Ethnocentricism–The American Heritage Dictionary defines ethnocentricism as the belief in the superiority of one's own ethnic group. Without doubt, everyone should have pride in their cultural background; therefore, there is nothing wrong with being proud of one's heritage. Group identity is strengthened when one has reasons to speak proudly of his group's standards and accomplishments. Being proud is not the problem, but the feeling of superiority and the extent to which group members will express this superior feeling create the problem and set the wheels of discrimination in motion. Ethnocentricism can lead to racism in that as group members began to "buy into" the belief that their ethnic group is superior to all other ethnic groups, they often will confer benefits to its members to the exclusion, and in some cases at the expense, of other groups. These benefits may take the form of political, social, economic, and educational advantages to mention a few. Except for the most blatant racist, the awarding and receiving of favorite individual or group status is often unintentional or covert prejudice rather than openly overt prejudice. For some ethnic groups, ethnocentricism is so deeply ingrained in their daily lives that most members of the group do not give much thought to the favorite or superior status which they enjoy. Perhaps the following illustration will provide an example: When one has been awarded a job for which she competed against a person from another ethnic and/or cultural group who had comparable skills and credentials, it is ego satisfying and psychologically safer to think that the job was awarded based upon one's superior skills and credentials rather than preference being given because of one's group membership. Another example of not being aware of receiving benefits based upon one's group membership is one ethnic and/or cultural group receiving lower bank loan interest rates because of a perceived better credit risk status of the ethnic group over other groups. Perhaps Lee (1989) summarizes the issue of ethnocentricism with his comments that the manner in which group members view themselves in relation to others can shape attitudes, behaviors, and values.

Lack of Significant InterGroup Contacts–Ponterotto and Pedersen (1993) provide the essence of this problem with their comments that separation between human groups is common–people often prefer the company of their own kind as a matter of convenience. However, despite the fact this behavior is accepted as natural, this preference to associate primarily with like-minded individuals leads to a form of cultural ignorance. The lack of contact with persons from different racial and cultural backgrounds from one's own is often a major reason for the development of stereotypes, prejudice as well as other misperceptions. This certainly is the situation with regard to racial minority groups and persons with disabilities. With regard to racial minorities, many erroneous ideas, attitudes, and beliefs were developed about them as being inferior mentally and morally bankrupt to justify the treatment to which they were subjected. As a result, many racial minority groups have been shunned and the result is a poor and inaccurate understanding by the dominant culture.

Spicer (1989) offers the following remarks which add emphasis to the negative impact of the lack of intergroup contact:

> Throughout the world, many people tend to value their way of life and reject other lifestyles. Our sense of belonging and social harmony can be disrupted when we encounter other cultures and we often seek to maintain our equilibrium by viewing these other people as inferior and even dangerous. Because our prejudices are largely unconscious these negative stereotypes can persist and, without our knowing it, have an impact on our interaction with other people.

Ironically, minority groups have a better understanding of the dominant culture than the reverse. The major reason for this is the subordinate cultures have to understand and correctly interpret the actions of the dominant culture to survive in the society dominated by them. For most people dealing with the "unknown" is difficult, resulting in our tendency to avoid same. As a society, we have experienced considerable difficulty in understanding disabilities because we have had a tendency to limit our contact with those who possess them. Although considerable medical advances have occurred over the past fifty years which have provided us with much information with regard to the causes of disabilities, the fact remains that we continue to struggle with our lack of understanding of why two persons may have similar medical conditions and one makes a complete recovery while the other experiences a disability. Throughout the ages, the collective wisdom of humans pondering this and other situations associated with disabilities have often ended in frustration realizing that there are probably some things associated with human existence we will never completely understand.

Preference for Categorization—We are a society of categorizers. We classify people by race, gender, economic status, physical condition, height, weight, hair color, religious preference, and so on. We categorize because it is convenient to do so and in reality in some instances, it is helpful to do so. Classifying these attributes provides us with a quick and convenient way of identification. During the process of classifying individuals and/or groups, we attach labels to them and unfortunately sometimes those labels are less than complimentary and the description of those labeled are too often based upon false information and equally false perceptions. Regardless of the inaccuracy, once applied, these labels stick and generation after generation of group members suffer the consequences. After generations of these prejudiced labels have been perpetuated, they become accepted as truth. Forgotten is the fact that these labels were based upon our need to categorize people and the assigning of attributes without having sufficient intergroup contact.

Prejudice and Disability

Today, few people, if any, desire to be considered prejudiced against persons with disabilities; therefore, we are most likely to hear complimentary comments with respect to the courage and determination with which persons live with their disabilities. In addition to that type of remark, we tend to avoid contact with persons with disabilities primarily because we feel uncomfortable being around them, especially if the person has a visible and severe disability. In fact, the lack of contact with persons who have a disability often leads to the complimentary comments. While on the surface one may think that if one is inclined to make comments without sufficient facts (prejudice), it is best to be prejudiced in a positive manner. The reality is that positive comments not based upon facts have also served as stumbling blocks for persons with disabilities. The comment that persons with disabilities are courageous too often leaves the impression that all persons with disabilities have an inner reservoir of strength from which they draw to deal with daily obstacles encountered as a result of being a person with a disability; thus, when a person with a disability is observed struggling to deal with his disability, the thoughts of persons without disabilities is that this person is maladjusted.

Persons with disabilities have lived a curious existence throughout humankind's existence on earth. Perhaps their perceived value to a particular society determined the role they played in the society and consequently the judgment of their human worth was determined accordingly. The prejudgment of them has ranged from gods to demons, from valuable wise persons to village idiots, and from communal assets to community leeches. In some societies, it was appropriate to display negative reactions to persons with disabilities; conversely, in others it was thought that bad luck would befall anyone who harmed or acted negatively toward a person with a disability. Throughout human history, persons with disabilities have had to react to an ambiguous world. Perhaps as much as any group of people, they have experienced prejudice, albeit not all negative.

Prejudice and Race

Without question, one of the most visible stains on the fabric of American society is prejudice based upon one's racial background. The extent to which segments of American society have been willing to display their prejudice has at times shaken the foundation of American democracy. America did not invent prejudice, nor was it the first nation to discriminate against a major portion of its population; however, in the twentieth century, with the possible exception of South Africa, no country exhibited the degree of prejudice against people because of their racial group affiliation as America did.

What is the underlying reason for race-based prejudice? As will be discussed in the section on understanding racial minorities, the foundation for prejudice and discrimination based upon one's racial background is economy and fear.

American Indian's land was taken and they were assigned to what often was considered unproductive land so that the Euro-American culture could "develop" the confiscated lands. Africans were brought to America and forced to develop the land generally without compensation. Asians were brought to America also to work and develop the new country at often below subsistence wages. The same appears to be true for Hispanic/Latino people. The result was a supply of very cheap labor that provided the captains of commerce higher levels of profit than they would have received had they been required to pay fair salaries and/or did the work themselves.

To keep the racial minority groups subservient, the dominant culture had to project an image of these people as being inferior. To instill inferiority in the minds of the subservient racial group many aspects of their lives were degraded. In the case of Americans of African descent, their homeland, Africa, was attacked as being a place where subhumans lived; also the African Americans' skin color was debased. The color black and the word dark were synonymous with evil and bad. Today these words still carry the same connotations - think of what "dark" clouds imply, "black" lie vs. "white" lie, "black" hat vs. "white" hat.

Blaming the Victim

Although in the southern United States, Americans of African descent were responsible for performing the majority of the work, they were considered lazy and unintelligent, thus a group of people the dominant culture had to closely supervise. While none of this was true, these images and perceptions were passed down from generation to generation until the idea was accepted as fact by many Euro-Americans and unfortunately by some

African Americans. While there have been definite elements of discrimination reaching Allport's elimination stage, the majority of the discrimination could be considered phase four–physical attack.

In the case of the American Indians, they were depicted as savages, and uncivilized, when in reality, they themselves were often the victims of savage treatment. As they attempted to defend themselves from unjust treatment, this was used as evidence to reinforce the attitude that they were savages. The prejudice and subsequent discriminatory action leveled at American Indians reached phase five–extermination – of Allport's model of discrimination. Prejudice against persons of Asian descent was often based on their different lifestyles, the types of food they ate, their clothing, and their speech, all of which were foreign to Americans of European descent. Prejudice against and treatment of people of Spanish descent was based in part on their different cultural values and also that they were descendants of countries that had engaged in and lost wars with America.

Fear of the Powerless . . . Why?

Much of the fear associated with race-based discrimination is difficult to understand. In America, racial minorities' lifestyles, values, beliefs, and behaviors are often devalued resulting in a perception of inferiority. In many respects, racial minorities, and to some extent, women of all colors, are powerless. With this in mind, a logical question is, "Why should the dominant culture fear the powerless?" The following are three reasonable responses to that question:

1. *Fear of the unknown*–As previously stated, an initial step along the path of discrimination is avoidance by the dominant culture of the subordinate culture. This avoidance means that the dominant culture becomes ignorant of what makes the subordinate culture tick, what motivates subordinate cultural members, what their true values are, how they really feel about issues, etc. When dominant culture members stop and give concentrated thought about subordinate culture, it becomes apparent that they have only a superficial understanding. Conversely, the subordinate culture generally has an excellent knowledge and understanding of the dominant culture because their survival depends upon this understanding.

2. *Fear that the oppressed will rise in power*–This fear by the dominant culture continually fuels the fires of discrimination. This second point is indicative of the oppressed versus the oppressor syndrome. Since antiquity some groups have oppressed other groups; in some cases, it has been one religious sect against another, in others it is one nationality against another or one philosophical view vs. and opposing view. In all of these cases the oppressed have

attempted to overthrow their oppressor, sometimes with success and other times their attempts ended with disastrous results; regardless of the result there appears to be something embedded within the human spirit that will not allow us to remain in bondage whether that bondage is spiritual, mental, physical, and/or emotional.

3. *Fear of contamination*–The dominant culture has been so successful in creating the perception that the subordinate culture is immoral, savage, and unintelligent that often these attributes are accepted as fact. Because these ideas have been passed from generation to generation and accepted as fact, there is a fear that to associate with "those people" will result in being contaminated with their inferior qualities. This impact explains the reluctance by some to socialize, date, and marry persons from cultures different from and considered inferior to their own.

Attitude Formation

Attitudes, feelings, and values often make objective thinking difficult and as human beings we have attitudes. But as Henderson and Bryan (1997) convincingly argue, it is behavior not attitudes which create major problems in human interaction. What people think about others is important and can have an impact upon them; however, the most devastating impact is how people act out their prejudices. Past decades have produced considerable racial struggles in America where racial minorities have spoken and demonstrated against prejudicial attitudes and discrimination. Consequently, much media attention has been focused on these confrontational conflicts, thus informing Americans of the impact prejudicial attitudes and associated behavior have on their victims. Because of the attention given to racial conflicts, as one observes the popular mass media, it is easy to gain the impression that racial minorities are the only group of people discriminated against in America, but prejudice is not limited to skin pigmentation. Women of all colors as well as persons with disabilities from all racial groups routinely experience discrimination in America. For persons with disabilities who experience the dual or triple (in the case of women) discrimination of having a disability and being a person of color, prejudice and discrimination can become an insurmountable stumbling block.

Being social animals, we learn from, and to a major extent, survive by interacting with others of our kind. A result of this socialization process is the development of attitudes about things that affect our lives as well as other humans we encounter. The formation of an attitude begins as we receive information with regard to a subject, individual, and/or group of individuals and we store much of this information in our memory bank. Every day we receive hundreds, if not thousands, of pieces of information, most of which are information bits; however, some information bits are reinforced by the person observing things that in his/her mind confirms the bits of information and/or is told by group members (family, friends and other influential people) that the bits are true. It is through the constant reinforcement that these bits of information become attitudes. Once these bits of information are accepted as facts and in the process of internalizing the information the fact begins to take on an emotional status with the individual, the result is an attitude. The attitude can be either positive or negative. Attitudes lead to behavior and the behavior may range from the process of talking and passing on the attitude to others, to acting out the emotional aspects of the attitude and/or inciting others to act in a manner consistent with these emotional feelings with regard to the attitude.

Attitudes are based upon either objective judgments or prejudgments. Objective judgment means the person has carefully weighed the pros and cons of a situation and has made an informed decision with a minimal amount of emotions affecting the decision. This does not mean that the person does not have emotions attached to the attitude; however, he does not allow emotions to overrule facts. Conversely, prejudgment is a "rush to judgment"; decisions are significantly influenced by emotions. Prejudgment also means the individual reacts more to concepts than proven facts and often has a closed mind. As the saying goes, "Don't confuse me with the facts; my mind is made-up."

All humans have attitudes and most give little thought to how they were developed. Given the universality of attitudes, the following is some of what we know about their formation:

1. Attitudes are learned; we are not born with an innate trust, distrust, like or dislike of anyone. This is learned through a socialization process. The most insidious prejudices are negative attitudes directed toward groups of people. They take the form of assumptions or generalizations about all or most members of a particular group. Once negative attitudes are learned and accepted as group standards, the individuals of which the group is composed tend to reinforce the attitude by selectively observing behavior and/or slant the interpretations of the behavior of the "out group" or group to which the negative attitude is directed.

2. Attitudes are learned mainly from other people. Most attitudes are learned through our association with other people. As we are socialized by the various groups of which we are members, we both consciously and subconsciously attain the attitudes to which the groups ascribe. Most humans prefer to think of themselves as independent thinkers, "making up" their minds independent of what others think; however, the reality is that most of

us are better followers than we are leaders. Even as leaders, our opinions and attitudes are influenced by the thinking and action of others.

The pattern of formulating certain attitudes begins when we are young. Some authors and researchers have concluded that very young children are aware of various dimensions along which to describe and characterize themselves and other people and come to hold adult preferences and stereotypes. Other writers and researchers such as Jones and Sisk (1967 & 1970); Weinberg (1978); Periman and Routh (1980); and Richardson (1970) confirm the fact that attitudes toward persons with disabilities are learned early in life. According to Gellman (1959), Roeher (1961), and Weinberg (1979), antidisabled attitudes have been detected in children as young as three years old. It should be noted that young children use hate words and display negative attitudes before they fully understand the implications; thus, attitudes are developed as early as three years of age; however, quite often they do not become firm until between eight to ten years of age (Henderson & Bryan, 1997). If children learn attitudes early in life, from whom do they acquire these attitudes? The answer appears to be that attitudes are passed down by parents and other influential persons in children's lives. Psychologists and sociologists have studied cultural attitudes toward sickness and disabilities and several frameworks have been developed which may contribute to a better understanding of the attitude toward persons with disabilities. Sociocultural conditioning, by way of norms standards and expectations passed on from parent to child, often lead to negative attitudes. According to Killingsworth (1994), aesthetic aversion has been found to play a role in formation of judgments about the individual's mental abilities and is known to play a role in maternal child bonding. Additionally, many other influences of attitudes occur during childhood and are initiated by parenting. These occur in all stages of development and are associated with fears of loss or mutilation, parental emphasis on the importance of health and the use of threats as discipline.

In American society, there is a strong emphasis on health, the perfect body, personal productiveness, achievement, and the ability to be socially and economically competitive. Negative attitudes with regard to unemployment, poverty and public assistance held by society are too often associated with having a disability. Again, these are attitudes learned, but not from just anyone; primarily attitudes are learned from "significant others."

3. Attitudes are learned from those who have high or low prestige. As previously stated, significant others perhaps have the greatest influence on an attitude formation with an individual; however, there is a "flip side" to this, that being people tend to adopt attitudes opposite to those groups with low prestige. Such attitudes are likely to be held for one of two reasons: (1) Certain groups may have low prestige for people because they have rejected

those people who adopt attitudes opposite to their's as a means of rejecting them in turn; or (2) certain groups are poor role models for people; thus, the people elect not to imitate them (Henderson and Bryan, 1997).

4. Once attitudes have been learned, they are reinforced. Once formed, an attitude may serve various other motives. Most people learn negative attitudes toward racial minorities, women, and persons with disabilities from family and friends and quite often the action (discrimination) taken resulting from the attitude(s) is both socially- and economically-based. Socially, minorities, women, and persons with disabilities are categorized and restricted to certain roles which, in most instances, are inferior positions to Euro-American, nondisabled males. The social motive appears to revolve around "power." By placing minorities, women, and persons with disabilities in subordinate or inferior positions, the dominant individuals can control many aspects of their lives. Their levels of educational attainment as well as their employment opportunities are, to a large extent, dependent upon the benevolence of the dominant group. This leads to the second motive that reinforces attitudes—economics. As Henderson and Bryan (1997) argue, it is economically advantageous for one group to keep another group out of certain kinds of work, to deny them adequate legal protection in bargaining for their labors, to keep their aspirations low or even on occasion to exterminate them. Because minorities', women's, and persons with disabilities' social, economical, and educational development are often suppressed, their lower-level of achievement serves as a reinforcement of the attitude of inferiority. Finally, as humans, it is often difficult for us to admit we are wrong; therefore, we use "selective observations" to reinforce our attitudes rather than change them. Additionally, we tend to associate with people who maintain similar views as our own, thus adding additional reinforcement of our attitudes.

Understanding Stereotypes

According to Tallchief (1996) stereotypes are oversimplified attitudes or judgments. She makes the analogy of stereotypes to cartoons; they may be based on something real; however, they are not an accurate view of any group of people and are usually exaggerated. Stereotypes are often used to reinforce the attitude that certain groups are inferior to the dominant group. Stereotypes can be applied to any group of people and unfortunately, many are negative. Stated as examples, black people are lazy, blondes are silly, Asians are sneaky, Jews are stingy, and persons with disabilities are unhappy and depressed. These and other stereotypes have been repeated and reinforced many times; consequently, we accept them as fact without questioning their validity. Spicer (1989) is convinced that because our prejudices are largely unconscious, these negative stereotypes can persist without our knowing their existence, thus having an impact on our interaction with other people.

Stereotypes are often developed as we attempt to categorize people. Because certain characteristics stand out, such as skin color, speech patterns, language, and physical attributes, they are used to classify people. It is not the use of these attributes which are at fault, rather the stereotypes that we associate with them. As Spicer (1989) has pointed out, the stereotypes that surround race and skin color are some of the most persistent and inaccurate images. With respect to disabilities, some of the stereotypes associated with persons with disabilities are extremely devastating. Hays (1994) lets us know that stereotypes worsen when misinformation such as those surrounding skin color and physical appearance are applied across the board to every member of a particular group and then judgements are formed.

In the following comments, Spicer (1989) clearly identifies some of the pitfalls in the across-the-board application of stereotypes.

> Skin color is one of the most mutable human physical characteristic; for example when used as a method for classification, it combines a four-foot six-inch African Pygmy and a six-foot Haitian immigrant living in Florida into one race. The error is compounded when we attempt to predict behavior by assuming that these "Blacks" have the same values, speak a similar language, and share the same view of the world. But because skin color is a visible sign of differentness it has become the simple means of classifying people used by the prejudiced who inevitably view people of their pigmentation as superior.

Although Spicer speaks of skin color, one can easily envision all persons with disabilities as being stereotyped in a similar manner.

Destroying Stereotypes

Inaccurate perceptions are often based on years and sometimes decades of misinformation. Stereotypes occur as a result of inadequate contact with the individuals being stereotyped. Lack of contact hampers the opportunity to learn factual information, thus leading to the development of attitudes and opinions based upon perceptions, second-hand and prejudicial information. Not only does inadequate contact lead to lack of understanding but also leads to unwarranted fears; therefore, many individuals tend to stereotype members of a particular group if they feel threatened by them as they do not understand or know them. Because of the lack of understanding, we may consider those that appear to be different from us as uncivilized, dangerous, lazy, and unintelligent. They may be either ignored or punished by removing some of their privileges, or in some cases such as persons with disabilities, society attempts to protect and control them either "for their own good" or the good of society.

Without doubt, stereotypes, particularly negative stereotypes, do nothing to improve the quality of life of those being stereotyped and diminish the moral stature of the persons responsible for the stereotyping. Given the insidious nature of stereotyping, helping professionals in particular should work toward not developing stereotypes and breaking those that they have. Hays (1994) offers the following tips for eliminating stereotypes:

1. Expose oneself to a broad range of experiences,
2. Build friendships with persons of other races,
3. Take an interest in a culture different from your own, and
4. Get to know people on a one-to-one basis.

Conclusion–The Ism's

We have established that discrimination is the behavioral or acting-out of one's prejudice; therefore, racism, sexism, and handicapism or disablism are forms of discrimination. Charles V. Willie (1984) correctly argues that racism and sexism are forms of institutional oppression. This author would add to the list–handicapism. United States Supreme Court Justice Thurgood Marshall described racism as demeaning to individuals and the nadir of social responsibility and further stated that it condones oppression and tramples on fundamental rights. Pierce (1969) relates racism to a disease that consists of an attitude, ideation, and behavior based upon the assumption of the superiority of the dominant culture's skin color. Pettigrew (1973), in describing racism, viewed it as the acting out of intergroup prejudice against a race other than one's own in a way that limits the opportunity and choices open to the victimized group. Ridley (1989) described racism as "any behavior or pattern of behavior that tends to systematically deny access to opportunities or privileges to members of one racial group while perpetuating access to opportunities and privileges to members of another racial group."

Although the preceding discussion and descriptions relate mainly to discrimination based upon one's race, sexism and handicapism are similar except in sexism the group that is victimized is either male or female, but in the situation of handicapism, the victims are both male and female and the discriminating factor is the person's physical, mental, and/or emotional condition.

The acts of discrimination which most often receive publicity are related to one's race. An individual or group of individuals being insulted by the issuance of racial epithet often followed by violence against one's person because of his/her skin color and/or racial group affiliation is an example of what is often associated with racism. While these acts actually happen and one is too many, the reality is that this form of racism occurs the least in number within America. A minority person is far more likely to be passed over for promotion on her job, or be ignored in a work conference conversation, or simply be excluded from meetings that involve the making of policy than she is to be physically and/or visibly abused. Likewise, discrimination based upon one's sex or physical, mental, and/or emotional condition is more likely to be in the form of exclusion, ignoring, and patronizing than elimination by physical means. The overt forms of discrimination of physical and/or verbal abuse have receded and given rise to what many human and civil rights specialists feel is as destructive, if not more so, especially to the human spirit, that being covert discrimination which is represented by exclusion, ignoring, and other subtle forms of denial of rights. Overt discrimination, which often is illegal, generally can be dealt with better because the action and its perpetrators's intentions are obvious. One does not have to expend time and energy attempting to convince the perpetrator and others that a problem exists. Even though the creator of the act may believe he is justified in his actions and beliefs, the inappropriateness of same is readily observable to most objective-minded persons. Therefore, actions to correct the problem can begin. Conversely, covert discrimination is subtle and difficult to detect and more difficult to prove. The persons involved in covert discrimination will vehemently deny that they are prejudiced and offer strong objections to the suggestion that they discriminate. When confronted with the reality that he has failed to hire an African American female who has a disability, supervisor "A" denies that his decision was based on either her race, gender, or disability. When provided with additional facts that the person he failed to hire had more experience and generally was better qualified than the person hired, his answer probably will continue to be one of denial. Several reasons will be offered, such as "I did not think she could physically handle the job," or "I hire the best qualified person regardless of race, sex, or disability and it was my opinion that the person I hired was the best qualified." A difficulty with covert discrimination is the denial. Until the persons are convinced that their actions represent a stumbling block to others, corrective action is difficult. The person who is guilty of covert discrimination not only denies discrimination but often truly believes his actions are nondiscriminatory. This is a good indicator that he subconsciously has accepted many of the stereotypes and prejudgments that surround minorities, women and persons with disabilities and have accepted them as fact and are acting upon these misconceptions. If one thinks of the many stereotypes and misconceptions associated with a minority group, then women, and next, persons with disabilities, and finally combine all within one person (an African American female with a mental disability), one can easily imagine a very difficult set of circumstances that individual has to overcome.

The result of racism, sexism, and handicapism is the disenfranchisement of a group of people. They are often denied through discrimination their rights promised to them by the laws of America, and to add insult to injury, they are frequently blocked in their attempts to better their conditions.

There will be additional discussion of racism, sexism, and handicapism and its impact upon the helping relation in future chapters. Additional tips on how the helping professional can overcome these effects and keep this type of discrimination out of the helping relationship will also be discussed in future chapters.

Review Questions

1. List the five (5) phases of prejudices and give an example of each which relate to persons with disabilities.
2. What have been some of the impacts of discrimination against persons with disabilities?
3. What are the three factors listed in this chapter that contribute to the development of prejudicial views?
4. What is the foundation of race-based prejudice in America?
5. What are some ways attitudes are formed?
6. What are some of the ways one can eliminate stereotypical thoughts and ideas with regard to persons of different cultures?
7. How can discrimination be used as a "tool of power?"
8. What is meant by discrimination as a "survival technique?"

Suggested Activities

1. List ten (10) stereotypes you have with regard to persons with disabilities. How many are negative?
2. Interview a person with a disability who is also a member of a racial minority group; ask the person if he/she has experienced discrimination as both a racial minority and as a person with a disability. If he/she indicates having experienced discrimination, ask which was the most difficult to handle–racial discrimination or discrimination on the basis of his/her physical, mental, and/or emotional status.
3. Think about the origin of your beliefs and attitudes about both racial minorities and persons with disabilities.

4. Imagine that a transitional house for persons with a mental and/or emotional disability is being planned for your community and you are hired by the city government to work with the community in an effort to get the community to accept the facility and its occupants. Develop your strategy to combat stereotypical attitudes and avoid possible discrimination of the future occupants of the proposed transition house.

5. Research your state's governmental structure to determine which agency(ies) handles discrimination complaints and how they are handled. Also, determine if the agency has had complaints of discrimination based upon disability.

References

Allport, G. (1958). *The nature of prejudice.* New York: Doubleday, Anchor Books.

American heritage dictionary (3rd ed.). (1992). Boston: Houghton Mifflin.

Bryan, W. V. (1996). *In Search of Freedom.* Springfield, IL: Charles C Thomas.

Gellman, W. (1959). Roots of prejudice against the handicapped. *Journal of Rehabilitation, 40:*4–6.

Hays, S. R. (1994). *Life issues: Racism.* United Kingdom: Marshall Cavendish Corporation.

Henderson, G., & Bryan, W. V. (1997). *Psychosocial aspects of disability* (2nd ed.). Springfield, IL: Charles C Thomas.

Jones, R. L., & Sisk, D. A. (1970). Early perceptions of orthopedic disability: A development study. *Rehabilitation Literature, 31:*34–38, 1970.

Killingsworth, N. (1994). *Attitudes toward the disabled.* Oklahoma City, OK: unpublished paper. University of Oklahoma Health Sciences Center.

Lee, C. C. (1989). Multicultural counseling: New directions for counseling professionals. *Virginia Counselors Journal, 17:*3–8.

Marshall, T. (1994). Quoted in Racism's Impact on Mental Health, Carter, J. H. *Journal of the National Medical Association. 86*(7):543–547.

N.O.D. (1998). *Harris Survey of Americans With Disabilities.* New York: Louis Harris and Associates.

N.O.D. (1994). *Harris Survey of Americans With Disabilities.* New York: Louis Harris and Associates.

Perlman, J. L., & Routh, D. K. (1980). Stigmatizing effects of a child's wheelchair in successive and simultaneous interactions. *Journal of Pediatric Psychology, 5:*43–55.

Pettigrew, T. F. (1984). Racism and mental health of white Americans. Quoted in *Racism, sexism and elitsm,* Willie, C. V. Institute for Responsible Education, Boston.

Pierce, C. M. (1994). Is bigotry the basis of the medical problems of the ghetto? Quoted in Carter, J. H., *Journal of the National Medical Association, 86*(7):543–547.

Ponterotto, J. G. & Pedersen, P. B. (1993). *Preventing prejudice: A guide for counselors and educators.* Newbury Park, CA: Sage.

Richardson, S. A. (1970). Age and sex differences in values toward physical handicaps. *Journal of Health and Social Behavior, 11*:207–214.

Ridley, C. R. (1995). *Overcoming Unintentional Racism in Counseling and Therapy,* Thousand Oaks, CA: Sage.

Roeher, G. A. (1966). Significance of public attitudes on the rehabilitation of the disabled. *Rehabilitation Literature, 22*:66–72.

Spicer, J. (1989). *Counsling ethnic minorities.* Minnesota: Hazeiden.

Sue, D. W., & Sue, D. (1990). *Counseling the culturally different: Theory and practice* (2nd ed.). New York: John Wiley and Sons.

Tallchief, P. (1996). *Respecting cultures in institutions of higher education.* Oklahoma City, OK: unpublished paper. Southern Nazarene University.

Weinberg, N. (1978). Preschool children's perceptions of orthopedic disability. *Rehabilitation Counseling Bulletin, 21*:327–331.

Willie, C. V. (1984). *Racism, sexism and elitism equity and choice: Institute for responsible education.* Boston.

Zawaiza, T. W. (1995). Stand and deliver: Multiculturalism and special education reform in the early twenty-first century. In *Disability and diversity: New leadership for a new era.* Washington, D.C.: President's Committee on Employment of People With Disabilities and Howard University.

Suggested Readings

Abramowitz, S. S., & Murray, J. (1991). Race effects in psychology. In R. M. Crystal, & R. J. Alston, Ethnicity and culture in rehabilitation counseling: The perspective of three prominent counselor educators. *Rehabilitation Education, 5*(3):209–214.

Bradsher, J. E. (1997). Disability among racial and ethnic groups. Disabilities Statistics Abstracts #10, Disability Statistics Center, University of California, San Francisco.

Brodwin, M. G.; Hong, G. K, & Sorian, M. (1992). Discrimination, disability and cultural considerations; Implications for counselors. *California Association of Counseling and Development Journal, 12*:9–14.

Eisenberg, M. G., Giggins, C., & Duval, R. J. (Eds.). (1982). *Disabled people as second-class citizens.* New York: Springer.

Fine, M., & Asch, A. (1988). Disabilities beyond stigma: Social interaction, discrimination and activism. *Journal of Social Issues, 44*:3–21.

Funk, R (1987). From caste to class in the context of civil rights. In A. Gartner & T. Joe (Eds.), *Images of the disabled.* New York: Praeger.

Graham, S. (Ed.). (1992). Most of the subjects were white and middle-class. *American Psychologist, 47*:629–639.

Hahn, H. The politics of physical differences: Disability and discrimination. *Journal of Social Issues, 44*:39–47.

Kundu, M. M. (1992). Reaction to the vocational rehabilitation of minorities. In T. J. Wright, and P. Leung (Eds.), *Proceedings of The unique needs of minorities with disabilities: Setting an agenda for the future.* Washington, D.C.: National Council on Disability, pp. 98–107.

N.O.D. (1998). *Harris Survey of Americans With Disabilities.* New York: Louis Harris and Associates.

Stubbins, J. (1988). The politics of disability. In H. E. Yuker (Ed.), *Attitudes toward persons with disabilities.* New York: Springer.

Vash, C. (1987). Quality of life issues affecting people with disabilities. In Emener, W. (Ed.), *Public policy issues impacting the future of rehabilitation in America,* proceedings of the Second Annual Education Forum, Stillwater, Oklahoma: National Clearinghouse of Rehabilitation training Materials, pp. 2–35.

Walker, S., & Turner, K. A. et al. (Eds.). (1995). *Disability and diversity: New leadership for a new era.* Washington, D.C.: President's Committee on Employment of People With Disabilities and Howard University.

Walker, S., Belgrave, F. Z., Nichols, R. W., & Turner, K. A. (1991). Future frontiers in the employment of minority persons with disabilities. *Proceedings of the National Conference, President's Committee on Employment of People with Disabilities,* Howard University.

Wright, B. A. (1988). Attitudes and the fundamental negative bias: Conditions and corrections. In H. E. Yuker (Ed.), *Attitudes toward persons with disabilities.* New York: Springer.

Wright, T. J., & Leung, P. (Eds.). (1992). *The unique needs of minorities with disabilities: Setting an agenda for the future.* National Council on Disability and Jackson State University.

Part Three

DISABILITIES AND MULTICULTURALISM

Chapter 6

MINORITIES AND DISABILITIES

Chapter Outline
• Introduction
• Civil Rights Movement's Impact on Mental Health Process
• Characteristics of Counseling which Cause Conflict for Some Minorities
• Racism in the Mental Health System
• Multicultural Counseling
• Questions, Issues, and Answers
• Things a Helping Professional Must Do to Become Culturally Sensitive
• Additional Steps to Take
• Things a Culturally Sensitive Helping Professional Must Do in Assessing
  Culturally Different Clients
• Conclusion

Chapter Objectives
• Identify reasons some minorities distrust the American mental health process
• Identify ways traditional counseling may create conflict for some minorities
  and persons with disabilities
• Identify how racism affects the helping process
• Identify what multicultural counseling is
• Identify the benefits of multicultural counseling
• Identify what a helping professional has to do to become culturally sensitive
  and the implications for the rehabilitation process
• Identify ways a helping professional can assess culturally different clients and
  the implications for the rehabilitation process

Introduction

Perhaps it was a beautiful sunny day or it could have been a dreary, gloomy day; history does not acknowledge the climatic conditions of the day in 1619 when the ship from Africa docked at Jamestown, Virginia, and deposited its human cargo of twenty Africans. The climatic conditions are not important; however, the event itself is certainly more than noteworthy in that it began an era of oppression, suppression and discrimination against people of African descent, the result of which is felt today by the descendants of those first passengers and subsequent passengers of similar ships.

The act of controlling other humans' lives was not new to a group of people whose ancestors only a few generations earlier had relocated to America to escape similar treatment that had been imposed upon them in Europe. Upon arriving in America, the European immigrants were welcomed by the indigenous people of America, today called American Indians or Native Americans. Despite the helping hands that were extended by the Native Americans, not many years later the indigenous people found themselves in a struggle with their uninvited guests for their land and survival of their lives and ways of living. As a result of wars with the European strangers and the introduction of European diseases for which the first Americans had no immunity, a major portion of the Native population was destroyed.

As has been the case with African Americans, the results of actions, policies, and beliefs exhibited by Euro-Americans continue to have an impact upon the lives of the current generation of American Indians. The impact will be discussed in more detail in Chapter 10.

A review of American history reveals that at one time Spanish-speaking people owned considerable portions of southwest United States and some parts of southeast America. Hostile engagements such as the battle of the Alamo branded Mexicans as enemies of America and through the process of generalization, other Spanish-speaking persons such as those from South and Latin America were painted with the same paint brush of opinion. Consequently, current Americans whose ancestors originated from Spanish-speaking areas are impacted by the dominant society which has branded their way of life as abnormal and inferior. Finally, Asian and Pacific Americans, similar to the other American racial ethnic minorities, African Americans, American Indians, and Hispanic/Latino Americans, experience a lower position on American life's social totem pole because of events associated with their ancestors. Sue and Sue (1990) provide a chronicle of events (discussed in Chapter 8) that have contributed to Asian or Pacific Americans' current position in American society's "pecking order." As the authors inform us, the Chinese were the first Asian group to arrive in America in significant numbers and most settled on the west coast of the United States to secure jobs on the railroad and in other local industries. When the economy of that area began to falter, they became an economic threat to Euro-Americans. The fact that many of their customs, speech, and dress were considerably different than Euro-Americans added to the desires by the dominant culture to exclude them from the mainstream of American society. The desire to exclude and limit Asian or Pacifics' participation in American society resulted in the passage of immigration laws which blocked the immigration of Chinese to America. The next largest group of Asian or Pacific immigrants to come to America was the Japanese and they did not fare any better than the Chinese. Moreover, attempts were also made to limit the number of Japanese immigrating to America; however, without doubt, the most atrocious act was the internment of over 100,000 Japanese Americans in concentration camps because the empirical Japanese government bombed Pearl Harbor.

As Sue and Sue point out, other Asian or Pacific groups such as Filipinos and Koreans have experienced considerable discrimination while attempting to become part of mainstream America. These facts tend to illustrate that one of the major obstacles minorities in America have in the past and currently have had to face is prejudice and discrimination.

These accounts of minority experiences in America are not being offered as a history lesson with regard to discrimination in America, nor is the primary goal of this book to illustrate the history of minority groups within America. These accounts are, however, being presented to: (1) establish that ethnic minorities have a long history of being discriminated against in America; (2) establish that there are historical factors influencing the customs, behavior, and other cultural attributes of minorities of which the helping professional must be aware to be successful in the helping process; (3) increase the awareness of helping professionals with regard to reasons some minority groups have a distrust of the mental health process; and (4) emphasize the importance of helping professionals understanding and considering the backgrounds and experiences of minorities with disabilities as they work with them in the rehabilitation process.

With regard to understanding the history of minorities in America and how past actions impact present behavior, authors such as Draguns (1996), Lee (1989), Giordano and Giordano (1976), Axelson (1985), Ridley (1995), Ridley and Lingle (1996), and Locke (1992) have stressed the importance of helping professionals and educators be cognizant of the history of minorities, especially the history of oppression. Ridley and Lingle (1996) emphasize that a counselor must be sensitive to minorities and their "cultural data." Lee (1989), believes that a knowledge of cultural realities has become a professional imperative. Giordano and Giordano (1976) argue that it is useful to know about the history of minorities existence in America because to understand their traumatic memories as well as their current preoccupations, anxieties, and insecurities provides a clear and more concise understanding of behavior. Although referring to one specific helping profession (education), perhaps Locke (1992) summarizes the essence of all the previously mentioned writers with the following remarks:

Educators cannot explore only those factors relating to individuals' experience in the present. They must understand and have empathy for those events from the past or future that have an impact on the present. Likewise, while there is much evidence that the history of culturally diverse groups in the United States often is unpleasant, educators must be willing to explore this unpleasant materials so that culturally diverse individuals can better deal with events in the present. For some culturally diverse persons it is a recollection of the past or even the reading of history that contributes to this willingness or unwillingness to interact with the dominant culture. Teachers and counselors must explore what this actual or vicarious oppression has done to the psychological adjustment of culturally diverse students or clients.

As helping professionals increase their efforts to work more effectively with minority clients and patients, an understanding of factors which have played significant roles in shaping a person and/or group's culture is essential. An awareness of factors which have had an impact upon a person's culture will bring to the forefront of the helping professional mind that there is not a single culture for any minority group. In other words, there is no African American culture, American Indian culture, Hispanic/Latino American culture, or Asian/Pacific American culture. However, there are African American cultures, etc. If the helping professional learns very little about minorities other than this point, he will have made significant progress in his quest to become a more effective helper of people, because being aware of individual and within group differences will help him eliminate from his mind stereotypes and prejudices. Most certainly, the aim of this book is to aid the understanding of the helping professional far beyond the recognition of intragroup and individual differences.

To promote these and other factors' relevance to minorities, the following chapters will present information with regard to African Americans, Native American Indians, Asian and Pacific Americans, and Hispanic/Latino Americans regarding: (1) a historical prospective of their lives and times in America, (2) factors which contribute to the high rate of disabilities among minorities, (3) current social issues impacting their lives, (4) economic issues impacting their lives, (5) employment facts contributing to their existence, (6) educational status, (7) family dynamics to include family structure, (8) the impact of being part of an ethnic minority group as well as being a person with a disability, and (9) intervention strategies.

Civil Rights Movement's Impact on Mental Health Process

The civil rights movement of the 1950s and 1960s did more than make racial minorities aware that they had civil rights which had been abridged; it also had the effect of confirming to oppressed minorities that many of the negative things credited to them were not totally their fault. The many evils of discrimination were placed before the nation so that all Americans could see its terrible impacts. Below standard educational achievement, substandard living conditions, inadequate health care, and high rates of unemployment as well as underemployment were shown not to be the result of low morals, lack of ambition, and inferior intelligence of a group of people, but the result of racist laws, insensitivity on the part of those making policy, and a complacent population that erroneously believed that separation of the races was best for the nation.

The same civil rights movement which stimulated millions of minorities to demand their rights also caused helping professionals to do a self study of mental health services to determine if as Helms (1985) questioned, "Had cultural issues that had been ignored in society in general also been ignored in the counseling process?" The answer to this questions was yes, and as supporting evidence, helping professionals such as Sue, Allen and Conway (1975); and Sue, McKinney, Allen and Hall (1974) pointed to the American minorities' (African Americans, Asian and Pacific Americans, Hispanic/ Latino Americans, and American Indians) underutilization of the traditional mental health services.

Characteristics of Counseling Which Causes Conflict for Minorities

While the rate for Euro-Americans terminating counseling after one contact is high (30%), it is higher (over 50%) for American racial/ethnic minorities such as African Americans, Asian and Pacific Americans, Hispanic/ Latino Americans, and American Indians (Sue & Sue, 1990). The high rate of termination of counseling after only one contact indicates that racial minorities have serious concerns with the current mental health system of America. Derland W. Sue and David Sue (1990) have identified several items which they consider major characteristics of counseling that may act as a source of conflict for racial minority groups.

1. Most theories of counseling emphasize verbal, emotional and behavioral expressiveness and the obtaining of insight. As will be discussed in detail in the chapters on racial minorities, specifically for some Asian and Pacific Americans and American Indians, and outward displays of emotion may be considered inappropriate.

2. Counseling, being traditionally a one-to-one activity, encourages clients to discuss intimate details of their lives. For some minorities it is highly inappropriate to discuss sensitive family matters especially without the consent of family elders. Again, this and other characteristics will be analyzed in detail in the chapters on racial minorities.

3. The counseling setting is often an ambiguous situation with the counselor listening and the client talking. This approach fails to recognized that some minorities view talk therapy as ineffective because they are action-oriented, and many of their problems need immediate attention.

4. Typical counseling sessions are monolingual. Clients for whom English is not their primary language or those that do not express themselves well with conventional English may find counseling ineffective.

5. Some counseling theories emphasize long-range goals. For some minorities their problems may demand immediate results; therefore, they function in the-here-and-now rather than being future-oriented.

6. Traditional counseling makes a distinction between physical and mental well being. Some Asian and Pacific American cultures do not make such a distinction.

The point being made is that traditional counseling practices have been based upon Euro-American values, specifically those values expressed by middle-class, Euro-American males and some of these values are not congruent with values by which some minorities have been reared. Other mental health professionals such as Hoare (1991), Ivey (1993), Atkinson et al. (1989), and Katz (1985) support Sue and Sue's contention that dominant Euro-American values have had the major influence on mental health therapy in America. Most mental health helping professionals would not argue that these Euro-American values are bad, but will point out that the problems revolve around using these characteristics and values as the yardstick by which all clients are measured. By using these values as the benchmark, clients with other values are forced to acculturate into the Euro-American standards or risk being misdiagnosed by mental health and other helping professionals who are not sensitive to other cultures.

Racism in the Mental Health System

Charles Ridley (1995) takes a strong stand in support of the need for culturally sensitive counselors by indicating that the lack of cultural sensitivity allows racism to enter into the mental health system. He contends that minority clients experience within the American mental health system, abuse, neglect, and mistreatment at the hands of counselors. The following listings by Ridley explain how, in his opinion, minority clients, in comparison to Euro-American Clients, receive unfavorable experiences:

• Diagnosis–Minority clients tend to receive a misdiagnosis, usually involving more severe psychopathology.

• Staff assignment–Minority clients tend to be assigned to junior professionals, paraprofessional or non-professionals for counseling rather than senior and more highly trained professionals.

• Treatment modality–Minority clients tend to receive low-cost, less preferred treatment consisting of minimal contact, medication only or custodial care rather than intensive psychotherapy.

• Utilization–Minority clients tend to be represented disproportionately in medical health facilities, specifically minority clients are underrepresented in private treatment facilities and overrepresented in public treatment facilities.

• Treatment duration–Minority clients show a much higher rate of premature termination and dropout from therapy or they are confined to much longer inpatient care.

• Attitudes–Minority clients report more dissatisfaction and unfavorable impressions regarding treatment.

While Ridley's declaration of racism in counseling is a strong statement, he accurately points out that counselors may not think or feel that they are racist, but it is their actions that constitute racism. To illustrate his point he identifies five factors which he considers predisposes counselors to racist practices.

1. Ridley states that most counselors have good intentions and it is the counselor's beliefs that these good intentions automatically make them helpful. Because they are ignorant of their inappropriate procedures and practices they continue to repeat their mistakes without being aware of the damage being done.

2. The second factor identified by Ridley is that traditional counselor training perpetuates the idea that existing counseling theories and techniques are appropriate for all people, regardless of their race, ethnicity, or culture. Therefore, being trained in this philosophy, some counselors may not see the necessity of altering their practices. Derland Sue and David Sue (1990) support Ridley's view with the following statement:

> With respect to training, counselor education programs need to do several things. First and most important is the recognition that no one style of counseling will be appropriate for all populations and situations A program that is primarily psychoanalytically oriented, cognitively oriented, existentially oriented, person-centered oriented or behaviorally oriented may be doing a great disservice to their trainees. The goals and processes espoused by the theories may not be those held by culturally different groups.

Sue and Sue (1990) address a possible solution to this problem by indicating that Euro-American counselors must rid themselves of their "white racism" and "white ethnocentric views." They feel that "attempts to teach effective cross-cultural counseling will be doomed to failure unless trainees address their own white racism."

3. Many counselors have limited their understanding of cultures to their own culture, thus leading to Ridley's third factor–"cultural tunnel vision."

Because of this limited understanding, these counselors attempt to program their clients into viewing life situations as they—the counselors—interpret events. Broadening one's cultural field of vision is imperative to eliminating cultural tunnel vision. Numerous authors, counselor educators, and researchers including Pedersen (1997); Sue and Sue (1990); Paniagua (1994); Corey, Corey, and Callanan (1993); and Wehrly (1995) warn against the narrow view of culture, and Paul Pedersen (1997) perhaps summarizes their views with the following comments:

> This tendency to depend on one authority, one theory and one truth has been demonstrated to be extremely dangerous in the sociopolitical setting. It is no less dangerous in a counseling context. The encapsulated counselor is trapped in one way of thinking that resists adaptation and rejects alternatives. By contrast, a broader definition leads counselors toward a more comprehensive understanding of alternatives and a more complex perspective of one's own beliefs.

4. Blaming the victim, according to Ridley, may take the form of the helping professional justifying his inability to successfully interact with the minority client by labeling him as uncooperative. In the helping relationship the balance of power resides with the professional helper and he must be aware that with the stroke of his pen he can negatively label a client and this negative evaluation will probably follow the client throughout the mental health process and affect the type of future treatment. In short, the helpee should not become the victim of the helper's inadequacies.

5. The final factor outlined by Ridley is called "either/or" thinking. This type of thinking places emphasis on the belief that "there is only one way," "there is only one view," and "there is only one correct way." This approach may force clients to react in ways that are not only foreign to them but also against their group's value system, thus causing stress and anxiety.

After reviewing these five factors as well as the major characteristics identified by Derland and David Sue, that in their opinions acts as a source of conflict for racial minorities, one develops a clearer view of why there is a high nonreturn rate for minorities after their first encounter with the mental health system.

Multicultural Counseling

To overcome what has often been unintentional discrimination of minorities by some helping professionals, cross-cultural or multicultural approaches to helping have been and continue to be promoted. Multiculturalism within the helping professions engenders both proponents and opponents. Some of the issues with regard to multiculturalism in the helping professions will be addressed in this discussion of multiculturalism as a factor in the helping process.

Over the past three decades there has been increased discussion with regard to the role multiculturalism plays in the helping profession. The concern with regard to the need to have counseling that is sensitive to ethnic minorities' different world views has led Paul Pedersen (1990, 1991) to declare multicultural counseling as the "fourth force" in counseling, coequal in its importance to the three traditional forces – psychoanalytic, behavior modification, and humanistic counseling. Clearly, Pedersen and a host of other leading helping professionals, including Clement Vontress (1971), C. Gilbert Wrenn (1962), Derland W. Sue (1978) and Allen Ivey (1977) believe multicultural sensitivity to be an essential factor in being an effective helper.

Before further discussion of multicultural counseling can be carried forward, multicultural counseling needs to be defined. Most researchers, educators, and helping professionals identify multicultural counseling with an operational definition which states that multicultural counseling is infusing within one's counseling/helping technique sensitivity to the client's culture and considering its impact upon how he/she views and interacts with the world. It is generally felt that multicultural counseling should take place when the helper is of one cultural background and the helpee is from another. Multicultural counseling is often considered along racial lines, in other words, the helper being from one racial group and the helpee from another; however, the helper and helpee can be from the same racial background, but have different cultural orientations. This can be illustrated by the helper and helpee being from the same racial group; however, the helper may be nondisabled and middle class while the helpee has a disability and considered from a lower socioeconomic background.

With regard to minority group and the dominant group interaction in the helping relationship, most people would agree that some minority groups have different cultural experiences than their Euro-American counterparts and that these cultural differences may in fact cause them to have a different view of world events. Derland and David Sue (1990) argue that "the world view of the culturally different is ultimately linked to the historical and current experiences of racism and oppression in the United States." They continue with the following insightful comment, "The world view of the culturally different client who comes to counseling boils down to one important question: what makes you, a counselor/therapist, any different from all the others out there who have oppressed and discriminated against me?"

While we think of multicultural counseling as a recent concept, in reality, the idea of the influence culture has on a person's world view has been discussed for many years. Bea Wehrly (1995), in her book *Pathways to Multicultural Counseling Competence,* and Joseph G. Ponterotto and associates (1990), in their edited book *Handbook of Multicultural Counseling,* provide excellent historical perspectives of multicultural counseling. Morris Jackson (1995) points out that during the 1940s and 1950s when the American Personnel and Guidance Association (former name of American Counseling Association) was being established, African Americans and other minorities were not involved in the building of this association and consequently the counseling profession. In his opinion, this explains why the cultural prospective of these groups were not considered as the foundation of the counseling profession was being laid.

Bea Wehrly (1995) credits the work of Abraham Maslow (1954), George Kelly (1955), Theodora Abel (1956), C. H. Patterson (1958), and C. Gilbert Wrenn (1962) with early identification of the necessity of understanding and considering the impact that culture has on personality as well as the therapeutic process. More recent authors, D. W. Sue and D. Sue (1990), S. Sue and N. Zane (1987), J. G. Ponterotto and P. B. Pedersen (1993), F. A. Paniagua (1994), C. R. Ridley (1995), J. M. Casas (1995), D. R. Atkinson, G. Morten and D. W. Sue (1993), J. A. Axelson (1993), and A. E. Ivey (1993), have strongly promoted the concept of multicultural counseling.

The following comments by Michael D'Andrea and Judy Daniels (1995) more than adequately sum up the philosophical views of those who promote the concept of multicultural counseling:

> Every generation inherits a unique set of challenges. Today, the counseling profession faces a major challenge regarding how it will respond to the cultural/racial/ethnic diversification of our contemporary society. This diversification is forging a new sociopolitical reality in which counselors will be called upon to work with very different types of client populations. These clients will present mental health professionals with unique developmental perspectives and personal concerns that are different from those presented by the individuals that most practitioners have typically been accustomed to serving in the past.

Questions, Issues and Answers

Today, most responsible counselors and other types of helping professionals acknowledge the need for cultural sensitivity in the helping process. This acknowledgment does not mean that there are not serious questions asked and issues raised about multicultural counseling. Relevant questions raised are: Should separate counseling and other helping techniques be developed for each ethnic minority group? How far does one carry the concept of multicultural counseling? As an example, Euro-Americans can be divided into several groups based upon their country of origin; therefore, how much consideration should be given to the differences that exist among these groups? "Does multiculturalism with regard to the helping professions include socioeconomic status?" Stated in other words, economically poor people may in fact have a different world view than more affluent individuals resulting in part from experiencing discrimination similar (but not the same) to what ethnic minorities experience. Should demographic variables such as gender, particularly women, be considered? Are persons with disabilities to be considered separate from their racial and/or their gender background?

Are Separate Helping Techniques Needed?

With regard to the question of whether separate helping techniques should be developed for each ethnic minority group, Pedersen et al. (1996) addressed this issue with the following comments:

> Moreover, culture in some ways is not unlike the fourth "time" dimension of modern physics of space. As such, cross cultural counseling does not abrogate, or even compete with these three established theoretical orientations. Instead, it extends each of these three frameworks and makes them optimally more applicable and realistic in contemporary multicultural contexts.

Ponterotto (1995) supports Pedersen's argument by stating that in the multicultural settings, cultural differences in all counseling relationships should be the rule rather than the exception.

What Pedersen and Ponterotto are saying is consideration of the impact of culture will fit within any of the currently accepted helping professional theories. The wise helper will use cultural orientation as a tool to help him/her interpret the helpee's perception of his life situation. For example, the helper interviewing his client is surprised to learn that the client allows her children to spend considerable periods of time with a series of cousins and family friends. On the surface, it appears to the helper that the client provides inadequate parental care of her children. However, by looking into this person's background, the helper discovers that these cousins were reared with the client and are thought of as sisters and brothers and the friends are long-time friends who are also the client's church brothers and sisters. In other words, these persons are the client's extended family. A cultural understanding of the role of the extended family enables the helper to develop a more accurate picture of this client's life situation.

How Far Must We Go?

With regard to the question of how far should one proceed with identification of culture as a factor within the helping process, the answer is if the helper's cultural orientation (i.e., values, belief system and patterns of behavior) are different from the helper, it would without doubt benefit the helper to understand the helpee's cultural orientation. This is not to imply that the helpee's orientation will be correct or that the helper must modify his cultural orientation to conform to the helpee, but that an understanding of "what, why, and how", the helpee thinks and acts will aid the helper in his efforts to be more effective. Relatedly, this indicates that cultural differences go much deeper than racial lines, thus the helper must consider the helpee's culture in every client regardless of whether the helper and the helpee are members of the same racial group. The helper can make a mistake of significant proportion if he assumes that because he and the helpee are from the same racial group there is no need to consider cultural factors in assessing the helpee, or the reverse assuming that because he and the helpee are from different racial groups, this automatically makes their cultural orientations completely different. Freddy Paniagua (1994) refers to this issue as "cultural match" and "cultural mismatch." Cultural mismatch can be two persons sharing the same racial background (African American helper and African American helpee) but with different cultural orientations (beliefs, values, attitudes). Similarly, a cultural match can be two persons from different racial backgrounds (Caucasian helper and Hispanic/Latino helpee) but sharing a similar cultural orientation. From this it is clear that two persons sharing the same racial background can be either a cultural match or cultural mismatch. The point is that the helper cannot make the mistake of assumption.

Does Helper and Helpee Have to Be From Same Background?

To a large extent, the previous discussion answers the questions whether the helper and helpee have to be from the same racial background to have an effective helping relationship. Adding support to the contention that racial match does not guarantee an effective helping relationship, Sue, Fujino, Hu, Takeuchi, and Zane (1991) found that except in the case of Mexican Americans, racial match failed to be a significant predictor of treatment outcome. As Paniagua (1994) points out, the factors which appear to have the most impact upon treatment outcome are counselor/helper sincerity and sensitivity. If the helper is sensitive to other views and sincere in his efforts to be fair and as unbiased as possible, his race should have little impact upon treatment outcome. Significantly, racial match is less important than cultural match and there is a difference between the two.

Socioeconomic Status as a Variable

One's socioeconomic status certainly can have an impact upon one's views of world events and his/her particular environment. Socioeconomic status is a very important cultural variable to consider in the helping relationship, especially if there is a significant difference between the socioeconomic status of the helper and the helpee. In most cases, the helper's socioeconomic status will be middle class whereas the helpee may be from a lower socioeconomic background. One only has to think of the stereotypes and negative comments often made about persons who receive public or welfare assistance to understand the need for the helper to be vigilant with regard to his need to understand how a helpee from this type of background may interpret the helper's attempts to be helpful. This is not to imply that all or the majority of clients/helpees are from low socioeconomic backgrounds. The need to understand socioeconomic impact equally applies to persons from high socioeconomic backgrounds. Offered as an example, is a vocational rehabilitation counselor working with a person who is an attorney and has recently had a stroke which has affected his memory and speech. Prior to the stroke, the attorney was earning a yearly salary in excess of $200,000. In this scenario, the vocational rehabilitation counselor must be concerned about change in social interactions and changes in perception of one's self-esteem to only mention a few. Having an understanding of the helpee's socioeconomic status will aid the counselor in being sensitive to the helpee and his significant others to adjust to his new life situation.

Gender as a Variable

Women in America, as well as worldwide, have been subjected to discrimination and oppression as much as any group. America gained its independence over 200 years ago, but women have only enjoyed some aspects of independence, particularly the right to vote, for less than 100 years. Today, women are engaged in struggles for equality, attempting to remove the barriers imposed by "men only" type institutions such as the military, military academies, social clubs, and until recently, some higher education institutions. Although these and other barriers to women's full participation in American society is slowly being eliminated, still today one may view with amazement at the opposition which is sometimes raised when there is discussion of integration of women into what formerly was an all-male institution.

From a cultural perspective, clearly women represent considerable diversity which offers a challenge of some significance to a professional helper. In some cases, the helper may be faced with single cultural discrimination

(Caucasian female), in other instances double discrimination (American Indian female) and in some instances, triple discrimination (African American female with a disability). The answer to the question, should women be considered in the concept of multicultural counseling, the answer is obviously yes.

Persons with Disabilities

As an aggregate, persons with disabilities are among the most diverse group of people on Earth. For a variety of reasons, persons with disabilities have been oppressed and discriminated against and the result of same has had numerous effects upon these individuals. As has been stated before, persons with disabilities have more in common with their nondisabled counterparts; however, society perceives them as a group of people that has numerous and significant things in common. Despite this perceived commonality, until recently, the concept of disability culture did not exist. Also, as previously discussed, one may seriously debate whether a disability culture actually exists, the fact remains that as long as persons with disabilities are discriminated against and treated as second-class citizens, there is a need for counselor/helper sensitivity to the life situation of persons with disabilities.

Finally, with regard to the umbrella question of whether there should be separate counseling/helping techniques for each minority and/or cultural group, the answer is no. Giving the diversity within groups the idea of separate techniques for each racial group is not feasible nor warranted. This is not to imply that the current theories and techniques do not need to be altered to take into consideration the uniqueness of different groups. The remainder of this chapter is devoted to identifying things a culturally sensitive, helping professional must consider when encountering persons from various racial and cultural backgrounds who have a disability in a professional helping relationship.

Things a Culturally Sensitive Helper Must Do

Self Analysis–Perhaps one of the first things any person should do as one considers becoming a helping professional is to take an introspective look at oneself. This is especially true when one is aware that he/she will be engaged in multicultural interactions. Don Locke (1986, 1992) contends that awareness of self is the first step to understanding others. He suggests that as a start toward self-awareness one might address the following questions.

1. What is my cultural heritage? With what cultural group do I identify?
2. What is the cultural relevance of my name?

3. What values, beliefs, opinions, and attitudes do I hold that are consistent with the dominant culture? Which are inconsistent? How did I learn them?

4. How did I decide to become a teacher or counselor? What cultural standards were involved in the process?

5. What unique abilities, aspirations, expectations, and limitations do I have that might influence my relations with culturally diverse individuals?

The author would like to add an additional question:

6. What are my attitudes, beliefs and perceptions of a person with a disability?

As one answers these questions, he/she will consider the issues of stereotypes. There are stereotypes about almost everything and helping professionals are not immune from being influenced by them. In fact, most stereotypes are learned at an early age, generally from our parents and other significant others. As stated in Chapter 3, stereotypes can be either positive or negative, but regardless of the direction these stereotypes take, if they are untrue, they are a misrepresentation of a group of people that someone professing to be a helper can ill afford to have. If one possesses inaccurate stereotypes, they will influence the helper's perceptions of the individual(s).

A culturally-skilled helping professional is one who recognizes that he has prejudices with regard to persons who are different from himself and under the best of circumstances has dealt with and eliminated them or at least has put them aside and is willing to be objective in his interaction with the helpee. Everyone has prejudices and a helper should not be ashamed to admit that he has prejudices and acknowledge that if they are not checked, they will be counterproductive within the helping relationship. The key is to recognize the prejudices, be willing to admit their existence, and eliminate them.

Perhaps Derland Sue and David Sue (1990), with the following five points, provide a clear summary of what a culturally-sensitive counselor/helper is. In making their case, they refer to counseling psychologist; however, the points, in the opinion of this author, apply to any type helping professional:

1. The culturally skilled counseling psychologist is one who has moved from being culturally unaware to being aware and sensitive to his/her own cultural heritage and to valuing and respecting differences.

2. The culturally skilled counselor is aware of his/her own values and biases and how they may affect minority clients.

3. Culturally skilled counselors are comfortable with differences that exist between themselves and their clients in terms of race and beliefs.

4. The culturally skilled counselor is sensitive to circumstances (personal biases, stage of ethnic identify, sociopolitical influences, etc.), that may dictate referral of the minority client to a member of his/her own race/culture or to another counselor in general.

5. The culturally skilled counselor acknowledges and is aware of his/her own racist attitudes, beliefs and feelings.

The helper, attempting to become more culturally sensitive, will assess his/her comfort level with regard to being around and interacting with persons who appear to be different from himself, such as racial/ethnic minority and persons with disabilities. If one does this in a manner which does not involve attempting to deny deeply entrenched feelings, one comes fact-to-face with biases and prejudices that one has learned to effectively hide. Certainly, sublimating these feelings is one way of handling the situation; however, if one fails to recognize that such emotions exist, there is little chance of determining how one acquired them and a greater chance of these emotions subconsciously surfacing within the helping process, thus increasing the chances of failure.

In analyzing one's comfort level with regard to the culturally different and biases and prejudices held toward same, the helper should, as previously stated, explore the origins of these feelings asking such questions as: were these feelings held and emotions displayed by my parents, grandparents, and significant others? Are these feelings based upon any concrete incident or were they acquired and reinforced by my social group(s)? What attempts have I made to modify and/or address these feelings? Finally, why do I still possess them?

Becoming a culturally sensitive helper is not an optional skill that the helper acquires; culturally sensitive skills are required skills in order for the helper to be considered professionally competent. Success or failure of the helping relationship with culturally different persons to a major extent will depend upon this competency.

Determine how much he/she adheres to the dominant culture standards–As stated in an earlier chapter, the "rightness" or "wrongness" of America's dominant culture's standards is not being questioned; however, what is questioned is the domination of these standards over other cultural standards and points of view. Considering this line of thought, the helper must determine to what extent he/she is vested in the dominant culture's viewpoints. The helper should not feel guilty for having many of these cultural beliefs (as long as they are not bigoted points of view); however, he must examine these views and his embracement of them, asking "Am I accepting of other points of view?" The answer to that question will give the helper clues to his sensitivity of other cultures. As an example the American dominant culture values expressiveness, thus the more articulate one is the more she is valued. As a vocational rehabilitation counselor who has been reared and/or trained to accept this point of view, what will be his evaluation of a Chinese American client who will only answer questions and offers no additional elaboration?

Determine his/her views of the helping process**–**One of the major points of contention which has helped promote the concept of multicultural counseling is the belief that a major reason racial minorities do not trust the mental health system is that they distrust the process; additionally, some of the values of the helping process is contrary to their cultural belief system.

Again, I refer to Sue and Sue's (1990) excellent book, *Counseling the Culturally Different,* to identify some of the helping professional's processes and values. They list four characteristics of Euro-American-dominated helping professions:

1. Counselors often expect their counseled to exhibit some degree of openness, psychological-mindedness or sophistication. They place a high premium on verbal, emotional and behavioral expressiveness and obtaining of insight.
2. Counseling is traditionally a one-to-one activity that encourages clients to talk about or discuss the most intimate aspects of their lives. Individuals who fail to or resist self-disclosure may be seen as resistant, defensive or superficial.
3. The counseling or therapy situation is often an ambiguous one. The client is encouraged to discuss problems while the counselor listens and responds. Relatively speaking, the counseling situation is unstructured and forces the client to be the primary active participant. Patterns of communication are generally from client to counselor.
4. Other factors identified as characteristics of counseling are (a) monolingual orientation, (b) emphasis on long-range goals, (c) distinction between physical and mental well-being, and (d) emphasis on cause and effect.

Too much emphasis cannot be placed upon the need for the helper understanding the previously mentioned helping process characteristics as well as others and their impact upon his/her culturally different helpees. The helper must realize that he is the primary enforcer of these "unspoken" helping profession's rules when he adopts them. If he implements them without consideration to possible cultural conflict, he is adding fuel to the flames with regard to the elimination of the culturally different from the helping process.

The previously mentioned counseling/helping professional characteristics as well as others will be given further attention in each of the chapters which discuss racial minorities. At this point a foundation is being laid so that we can have an indepth discussion of the impact these characteristics have upon the racial or ethnic minority groups of African American, Asian and Pacific American, American Indians, and Hispanic/Latino American persons with disabilities.

Inventory one's strengths and weaknesses**–**Every helping professional should periodically sit down and list at least five strengths that she has that contribute to her being an effective helping professional and list five weaknesses that need to be strengthened for her to become a more effective helper. As one is attempting to become more culturally sensitive and/or test one's sensitivity toward other cultures, she may want to add some strengths and weaknesses specific to culture.

Dedicate oneself to learning about other cultures–One of the many negative legacies of legal segregation in America has been the lack of contact between persons from different racial and cultural backgrounds. With regard to persons with disabilities, although there was no legal segregation, separation nevertheless occurred, primarily separation by choice of the nondisabled. Regardless of the reason for separation of cultures, the fact is and continues to be a lack of understanding primarily by the dominant culture, of other cultures with regard to their beliefs, traditions, and attitudes toward the dominant culture to mention only a few. Given this gap in knowledge between cultural groups, it is incumbent upon the helper (particularly if he is from the dominant culture and/or represents the dominant culture's views) to learn about other cultures.

As the helper approaches this task, several questions probably will enter his mind. Some of the questions which will be raised are as follows: "How many different cultures must I learn?" "How much should I learn with regard to these cultures?" "How do I learn about these cultures?"

The idea of learning about cultures different from one's own can cause some stress within the helper. As one surveys the racial groups of African American, Asian and Pacific American, Hispanic/Latino American, and American Indians and considering the differences within each of these groups, the helper quickly realizes that it is impossible to learn all there is to know about these cultures. The ideal solution would be that the helper would learn about all cultures; however, as previously stated, this is impractical, if not impossible. Given this reality, what should the helper do? First, the individual should assess the variety of cultures represented within his/her caseload or population that he/she serves. Considering the current housing patterns which are often typified by racial/ethnic groups living in close proximity of each other (concentration of African Americans living in a specific part of town), in all probability the helper will have a limited number of different racial groups within the population he/she serves. If this is the case, he/she should concentrate on those groups. This is an ideal situation from the standpoint of being able to devote one's attention to a limited group of people. In reality, while the concentration of racial/ethnic groups is often true, the fact remains that in many sections of town in America there are a variety of cultures represented, although there may be a concentration of one specific group. Even though there may be only a few from other cultural groups, understanding their points of view is also important; therefore, the helper must learn about all of the cultural groups represented within the population he/she serves. A good starting point is to explore the history of these groups. Authors such as Sue and Sue (1990), Paniagua (1994), Locke (1992), and Ho (1987) support this position. It is felt that by understanding the history of various minority groups one obtains an understanding of many aspects of the group's culture, the things they value, the reasons they react to certain things, as well as their beliefs and attitudes. For example, an understanding of African American history will provide an understanding of why religion and the church play such a significant role in the lives of many. An overview of the history of African Americans, Asian and Pacific Americans, Hispanic/ Latino Americans, and American Indians as well as other important facts with regard to these groups will be discussed in Chapters 7-10.

Additional Steps to Take

Additional ways of learning about other cultures, particularly racial/ethnic groups, is to determine some of the group's social outlets such as social organizations, clubs, and athletic organizations and visit with some of the leaders and members of these groups ascertaining their origin, purpose, goals, and objectives. A word of caution is appropriate at this point, in that the helper must be careful not to pick one or two social clubs, etc. and generalize that these organizations define the status of the entire group. The helper will find beneficial information about the community through visiting with the religious leaders of the community. In most racial/ethnic minority groups, the religious leaders/elders perhaps have the best view of the conditions that prevail in their communities. In his search for knowledge, the helper should avoid making the mistake that many outside observers make in assessing a community, that being to assume that the most knowledgeable persons with regard to community affairs are the ones that are most vocal, in other words, those individuals who tend to appear on television, radio, and in the print media. In many cases this is not true. Their visibility does not represent leadership but is more indicative of their abilities to attract the spotlight.

Additional concerns with regard to the most visible being considered the most knowledgeable is that in some cases the dominant power structure of a city will identify persons with whom they feel comfortable and designate them as the community leaders by giving them the previously mentioned visibility. On the other side is the community activist who may be militant and gains attention through his/her persistent action. In either case neither group may represent the mainstream beliefs, attitudes and desires of the community; therefore, it is imperative that the helper does a careful analysis of the community.

Because of the complexity of humans and their cultures, it is impossible for anyone to know about all aspects of any particular group's culture; therefore, the helper must be willing to acknowledge information difficulties to his clients and ask them to explain a matter of which he has no or limited knowledge. This acknowledgment can be therapeutic in that it demonstrates the concern and caring of the helper.

Things a Culturally Sensitive Helping Professional Must Do in Assessing Culturally Different Clients

Determine level of acculturation–In an earlier chapter, the "melting pot" theory was discussed, indicating that the melting pot concept did not become a reality for most racial/ethnic minorities in America because they did not assimilate into one unique culture–the American culture. Instead, Euro-American, middle class, male values became the dominant cultural standard for America. Now, rather than assimilating into one unique culture, subordinate cultures such as racial/ethnic minorities must become acculturated to be considered as part of mainstream America. Acculturation for many racial/ethnic minorities means giving up part of their culture and accepting Euro-American cultural standards. Thus far I have used two terms–assimilating and acculturation–which are often used interchangeably; however, in the mind of this author there is a difference, albeit subtle. Donald Atkinson, George Morten, and Derland Sue (1993) argue that "acculturation refers to cultural assimilation or the acquisition of the cultural patterns of the core or dominant society." However, they point out that assimilation refers to more than acquisition of cultural patterns but implies an equalness with the dominant culture. Stated in other terms, assimilation implies a contribution to the dominant culture and that contribution being incorporated and treated as equal value to other aspects of the dominant culture. Keefe (1980), as quoted in Atkinson et al. (1993), admits that acculturation is a term that is frequently used, especially by social scientists, but few can agree upon its meaning. Keefe continues by acknowledging that "most contemporary social scientists describe acculturation in the United States as a unilateral process in which immigrant groups are expected to adopt the dominant culture but contribute little or nothing to it." This implies an unequalness. The subordinate culture is expected to assume the dominant culture's views and contribute little or nothing from their culture to the dominant culture. It is easy to conclude that this view of acculturation requires the subordinate culture to relinquish some or all of its culture to become part of the American mainstream. Reviewing the subtle difference between the terms assimilation and acculturation, assimilation refers to being included or contributing to the dominant culture's makeup, whereas acculturation implies little or no contribution to the dominant culture and, in fact, giving up some of one's culture in the process of accepting the dominant culture.

Returning to the notion that the helper must assess the client's level of acculturation, Don C. Locke (1992) offers four levels of acculturation which a culturally sensitive helper may consider in assessing a client's acculturation:

1. bicultural, able to function as effectively in the dominant culture as in their own, while holding on to the manifestations of their own culture;
2. traditional, holding on to a majority of cultural traits from the culture of origin while rejecting many of the traits of the dominant culture;
3. marginal, having little real contact with traits of either culture; and
4. acculturated, having given up most of the cultural traits of the culture of origin and assumed the traits of the dominant culture.

Locke continues his advice to culturally sensitive helpers by pointing out that "looking at the degree of acculturation one must also seek to determine at what level(s) individuals belonging to culturally diverse groups have acculturated in terms of marital, attitudinal, behavioral, civic, structural and identification factors."

In addition to assessing the client's level of acculturation, one must also determine the degree of acculturation of the client's family. This assessment is very important if there are generational age differences existing within the same household. To be more specific, for some minority families, such as Mexican Americans and some Asian and Pacific Americans, it is not uncommon for three generations to be living within the same house, and each of those generations may be at a different level of adjustment to the dominant American culture. To use the Mexican American family as an example, the first generation immigrated to America from Mexico and located in an area where there were other Mexican immigrants, thus maintaining much of their Mexican culture including the language. Their daughter, being twelve years of age when they moved to the United States, attended American schools for six years, adapting somewhat to the dominant American culture, learning to speak English, however, retaining most of her Mexican culture; thus she developed a dual cultural orientation. The daughter's son, born after she completed high school, has spent all of his life in America and is heavily influenced by the dominant American culture, preferring the American lifestyle over the Mexican culture of his grandparents and the Mexican and American cultural mixture of his parents. In this scenario there are three levels of acculturation living within one household; if the helper is working with any member of this extended family, she must take into account this fact.

To this point, a strong case has been made for the helper to determine level(s) of acculturation. Now, let us discuss how to determine level(s) of acculturation. This is where interviewing skills become of paramount importance. Through the interviewing process and by skillfully wording questions, one can glean considerable information with regard to one's cultural beliefs regarding traditional versus folk medicine, religious orientation, child-rearing practices, work ethics, and education, to mention a few. Having a knowledge of the history of the person's racial group, coupled with skillful interviewing, one will be able to determine many of the things both tangible and intangible that the person values, as well as some of his sociopolitical viewpoints. Through skillful interviewing, the helper should be able to determine any conflicts that may exist with regard to the client's degree of comfort with his level of acculturation. Stated another way, is he comfortable with his level of acculturation or is there interconflict with feelings that he is accepting too much or not enough of the dominant culture's values.

Throughout this discussion, an emphasis has been placed on "skilled" interviewing; perhaps the following simplified scenario will highlight a difference between skilled and unskilled interviewing:

Scenario: *Helper.* "In our discussion, you have mentioned that you and your family have had some health problems. How have you handled them?" *Client/helpee.* "We use home remedies and we ask the elders at our church to pray for us." At this point the unskilled interviewer believes that he can safely assume that the family is holding onto their traditional culture and rejecting the prevailing dominant culture's approach to health care. The skilled interviewer would not assume; he would ask additional questions:

Scenario: *Helper.* "Do you prefer home remedies to physician care? *Client/helpee.* "No." *Helper.* "Why do you use home remedies rather than going to a physician?" *Client/helpee.* "We do not have medical insurance and cannot afford a physician's charges." At this point, one can see that with a few more questions, a different view of the client emerges. Therefore, careful and skillful interviewing will aid the helper assess acculturation level(s) of racial/ethnic minority individuals.

***Implication for the rehabilitation process*–**The next issue to address is the person with a disability who is from a racial minority background. Assessing this individual's level of acculturation with regard to his/her racial/ethnic group affiliation is the same as previously discussed; however, disability becomes an extra dimension that must be considered in assessing acculturation level(s). This extra dimension of disability makes the assessment of a racial minority client with a disability a challenge for the helper; thus, it is easily understood why many helping professionals have concentrated on one dimension (race or disability) to the exclusion of the other. The assessment of an individual and/or his family's level(s) of disability acculturation will primarily revolve around attitudes. Attitudinal barriers tend to be the major stumbling block for most persons with a disability. Additionally, in far too many cases, the attitudes toward disabilities are negative and the general feeling is that to be accepted into the mainstream of America, a person with a disability must somehow overcome society's negative attitudes toward disabilities.

The process of assessing the disability culture of a person with a disability should be as follows:

1. The helper must have a sound knowledge of societal attitudes toward disabilities and those who possess disabilities.

2. The helper must have an awareness of the subtle and sometimes not-so-subtle ways society expresses attitudes toward persons with disabilities.

3. The helper must be knowledgeable of the client's "environment attitudes," toward disabilities, and the ways in which these attitudes are manifested. Environmental attitudes refers to the client's local surrounding such as neighborhood, city, state, etc. The environmental attitudes may differ considerably from societal attitudes in that the client's local environment may or may not have taken more aggressive steps toward eliminating negative attitudes toward its citizens with disabilities than the overall American society.

4. The helper must determine the client's attitudes toward himself and his disability.

5. The helper must determine the attitudes of the client's family with regard to disabilities in general and specifically his life situation.

Determine family structure–Perhaps the oldest human institution is the family. Regardless of whether the family consists of all blood relations or a combination of relatives connected by blood or by friendship or social ties, the family generally serves as the most influential force in most persons' lives. Child abuse, spousal abuse, and parental abuse speak to the more hideous side of family relationships; however, these acts are unfortunately a reality and also have an impact upon each of the family members. Fortunately, most families are nurturing, caring, and loving, thus aiding in the healthy development of each of its members. In most instances, one cannot determine by mere observation whether a family is functional or dysfunctional; therefore, the importance of assessing family structure cannot be overemphasized.

Bryan (1996) sets forth a convincing argument that the presence of viable family structure has been credited with helping individuals survive incredible conditions. The family structure of some ethnic minorities, such as low income African Americans and Hispanic/Latino Americans quite often receive considerable criticism of their position on the "social totem pole," especially from those who are positioned above them. They are chided because many live barely surviving on local, state, and/or federal assistance; however, the survival of these people has been greatly enhanced by the fact that an extremely strong family structure exists. Even the very thing for which they are criticized, large families, ironically serves as the primary means of survival. It is not uncommon to have two and three generations living within the same household and the circle of influence extending to uncles, aunts, and cousins. Therefore, the presence or absence of a constructive family structure will contribute to the family's ability to cope with various life situations including the presence of a person with a disability.

The culturally sensitive helper must determine whether the family structure is nuclear or extended family. Nuclear family structure generally is considered parent or parents, and unmarried children living at home, whereas extended family is considered to consist of parent or parents, children, and close significant others such as grandparents, uncles, aunts, cousins and close family friends. The structure of the family will provide clues as to the authority structure in the family, child-rearing practices, and other family dynamics such as how decisions are made within the family and how family resources are allocated and used. With regard to minority families, it is helpful to determine the role played by each family member within the family drama. A helper who is oriented toward middle-class, American family roles may be somewhat surprised to find that in some minority families, children, especially the older children, play a more significant role within the family than is normal within most Euro-American, middle-class families.

***Implications for the rehabilitation process*–**Knowledge of the family structure with regard to the authority figures, who makes decisions, how decisions are made, child-rearing practices, and the role of each family member are of vital importance when working with a person with a disability.

A person with a disability within a family unit, regardless of whether the onset of the disability was sudden, gradual, or congenital, does not necessarily mean that a family will be rendered ineffective and thrust into a state of crisis. Desiring to be helpful, rehabilitation counselors as well as other helping professionals may assume that the family will have difficulties adjusting to the family member with a disability, and that the expected change within the family social system will be so great that a crisis is unavoidable. It is true that in many cases the family will experience difficulties with respect to adjustment; however, difficulties do not always equate to crisis. Conversely, the helping professional should not assume that crisis does not exist or will not occur simply because members of the family do not speak of any problems or show any outward signs of potential problems. In summary, the helping professional assessing a family with a member who has a disability must not assume that a crisis is imminent because a family member has a disability; nor should he assume that a state of crisis does not exist simply because of family members' denial of any problems. The point being made is the helping professional must carefully assess the family in the following manner:

1. Assess the family as a unit and attempt to determine how stable the family has been historically,
2. Assess how the family was prepared for this situation, and
3. Assess the family's current resources for handling the situation.

By closely observing the family, one will get an opportunity to examine each family member's reaction to the situation which will often reveal strengths and weaknesses within the family unit, particularly as they relate to problem solving. Knowing a family's strengths and weaknesses will be of tremendous benefit to the helper as he works with the family.

Determine support systems–Throughout most life situations, both good and bad, the family serves as the major supporting force for most individuals; however, the best functional families cannot be an island unto themselves and supply all the needs of their members. Therefore, the culturally sensitive helper's identification of other support systems or lack thereof will be revealing. The identification of support groups will provide valuable information with regard to the influences within the client's life. To a significant degree many of our attitudes and beliefs take shape by discourse and observation of those with whom we frequently interact. Institutions such as churches, social clubs and intellectual clubs often provide a safe haven for individuals to address issues surrounding both happy and sad occasions.

In many minority communities, the church provides many services in addition to the spiritual service. The church may serve as a social club, civic club, and meeting house. Many minority individuals do not have either the time nor the money to join and participate in social or civic clubs and their activities; therefore, the church often fulfills those needs.

While it certainly is true that many minority individuals, for a variety of reasons, do not join formal social and civic clubs, many do, however, belong to informal social groups such as domino and card groups as well as getting together on weekends to share laughter and libation. Thus, in assessing support systems for minority individuals, the helper must be cognizant of both formal and informal groups.

Implication for the rehabilitation process–The culturally sensitive helping professional should be aware that for persons with disabilities and their families, effective support services are essential. Petr and Barney (1993) report the results of a study which outlines what parents and families of persons with disabilities state as their most urgent needs: (1) the need for a greater variety of services; (2) the need for advocacy; (3) the need for the system of care to better reflect certain attitudes and values; (4) the need for emotional support; (5) the need for social support, and (6) the need for financial support. Additionally, families frequently report that a major support service need is for respite care and access to other families that are experiencing or have experienced similar situations.

Checking the client's support system needs using the previously mentioned needs as a template could prove to be an excellent start for the helping professional.

Determine the client's world view–According to Derland W. Sue (1977, 1978) world view refers to how a person perceives his/her relationship to the world. Ivey, Ivey and Simek-Downing (1987), as quoted in Sue and Sue (1990), add their thoughts as to what world view means by indicating it is how one thinks the world works. It is clear from these definitions that world view is based upon one's perceptions of events and these perceptions are formed through interacting with others. Consequently, everyone has world views, thus the helping professional needs to understand both his and his client's view of the world. Conflict and/or misdiagnosis may occur if the helping professional expects his clients' views of the world to conform to his and attempts to reconstruct the clients' views to conform to his views. As Sue and Sue (1990) remind us, for many minorities in America, a strong determinant of world views is based upon their experiences of racism and the subordinate position they occupy in society.

Implication for the rehabilitation process–As all other humans, persons with disabilities, regardless of whether they are from a racial minority group, will have world views based upon their interactions with others, accuracy of views notwithstanding. These views of their place in the world are often based upon whether they view themselves as being accepted or rejected by society. Similar to racial minorities, many persons with disabilities view themselves as occupying subordinate positions in society. Additionally, they view themselves as societal objects of pity, persons who are dependent upon the charitable nature of their fellow beings.

The helping professional working with a racial minority person who has a disability, attempting to assess the world views of this person, must take into consideration the views engendered by virtue of being a minority person as well as the view developed from viewing the world through the eyes of a person who has a disability. No doubt this can become a formidable challenge; however, to be successful, the helping professional must rise to the occasion. The helper must keep in mind that he cannot afford to concentrate upon one factor (race or disability) to the exclusion of the other.

Never generalize–Human beings have found the process of categorizing to be convenient. The distribution of goods and services is often based on our ability to identify reasonable categories. Despite the good that often occurs as a result of our various classification systems, there is at least one negative aspect, that being categorization can lead to overgeneralization. Two areas in which this occurs too frequently are race and disability. While most anthropologists and social scientists agree, there is no such thing as race, nevertheless, as a society we find the convenience of classifying according to some arbitrary standards as sufficient grounds for ignoring facts, thus creating racial groups. Once these artificial group classifications have been made, we continue the avoidance of fact by ignoring within group differences by implying that all persons placed within the group are all alike, sharing similar beliefs, attitudes, likes, and dislikes. Also based upon these classifications, we ascribe certain characteristics to all the individuals placed within the group.

Implication for the rehabilitation process–An almost identical scenario as previously described occurs for persons with disabilities. As has been stated before, persons with disabilities have more in common with nondisabled persons; however, as a society, we tend to classify most persons with a disability as having considerable commonalities.

Conclusion

Rehabilitation, whether that takes the form of employment, independent living, physical and/or improving the quality of life through removal of various barriers, is the ultimate goal of all rehabilitation programs. The rehabilitation counseling/helping professional, in his/her attempt to assist the client reach the rehabilitation goal, must not only be extremely knowledgeable with regard to his/her area of expertise, but must also be knowledgeable with respect to human nature. In far too many cases as the rehabilitation helping professional has worked with his minority clients, the client has had to adjust to the therapy or helping technique. In other words, little consideration has been given to the uniqueness of the individual and how that uniqueness translates into perhaps a different view of the world than what is often considered as the standard view (Euro-American middle-class male). Given the continued diversification of American society, considerably more attention is being given to other views of the world, particularly those views held by some minority individuals.

Counselors, social workers, and other helping professionals have become more concerned with regard to understanding racial minority individuals and how their life experiences affect their views of the world, thus affecting the helping relationship. Counselors and other helping professionals who work with persons with disabilities have a formidable challenge before them as they work with racial minority persons who have a disability. They must learn to assess at least two cultures; the culture associated with being a member of a racial minority group and the culture of disability. No longer can the helping professional afford to concentrate on one variable (race or disability) to the exclusion of the other. Successful rehabilitation outcome depends upon the helping professional becoming an expert at assessing both and sometimes three variables within one individual.

Review Questions

1. What are some of the experiences African Americans, Asian and Pacific Americans, Hispanic/Latino Americans and American Indians have in common?
2. Identify some of the counseling characteristics which cause conflict for some minorities and indicate the implications for persons with disabilities.
3. What is multicultural counseling and how does this type counseling impact the rehabilitation process?
4. Are separate helping techniques needed when working with persons with disabilities who are from a minority group? Defend your answer.
5. Identify some steps a helper can take to become more sensitive to his/her culturally different clients including persons with disabilities.
6. Is there a difference between assimilation and acculturation? Defend your position.
7. What is meant by "client's world view?
8. What are some of the support systems parents of persons with disabilities have indicated they need?
9. Why is it important to determine family structure in working with persons with disabilities who are from a minority group?

Suggested Activities

1. Interview a rehabilitation counselor or social worker and attempt to determine how he/she works with clients who are from a different racial and/or cultural background than his/her background.
2. Interview a person from one of the racial/ethnic minority groups and determine the level of acculturation of the persons.
3. Interview two families, one that represents the nuclear family concept and the other that represents an extended family concept. Compare the differences with regard to decision making, child rearing, authority structure, etc.
4. Interview several helping professionals to obtain their opinions with regard to multicultural counseling.
5. Interview several families of persons with disabilities to determine the type of support systems they need and the availability of same.

References

Abel, T. M. (1956). Cultural patterns as they affect psychotherapeutic procedures. *American Journal of Psychotherapy, 10*:728–740.

Asbury, C. A., Walker, S., Maholmes, V., Rackley, R., & White, S. (1991). *Disability prevalence and demographic association among race/ethnic minority population in the United States. Implications for the 21st Century.* Washington D.C.: Howard University Research and Training Center.

Atkinson, D. R., Morten, G., & Sue, D. W. (1989). *Counseling American minorities: A cross-cultural perspective.* Dubuque, IA: W. C. Brown.

Atkinson, D. R., Morten, G., & Sue, D. W. (1993). *Counseling American minorities: A cross-cultural perspective* (4th ed.). Madison, WI: Brown and Benchmark.

Axelson, J. A. (1993). *Counseling and development in a multicultural Society* (2nd ed.). Pacific Grove, CA: Brooks/Cole.

Bryan, W. V. (1996). *In search of freedom.* Springfield, IL: Charles C Thomas.

Corey, G., Corey, M. S., & Callanan, P. (1993). *Issues and ethics in the helping professional* (4th ed.). Pacific Grove, CA: Brooks/Cole.

D'Andrea, M., & Daniels, J. (1995). In J. G. Ponterotto et al. (Eds.), *Handbook of multicultural counseling.* Thousand Oaks, CA: Sage.

Draguns, J. G. (1996). Humanly universal and culturally distinctive: charting the course of cultural counseling. In Pedersen, P. D. et al. (Eds.), *Counseling Across Cultures.* Thousand Oaks, CA: Sage.

Helms, J. E. (1985). *Cultural identity in the treatment process.* In P. Pedersen (Ed.), *Handbook of cross-cultural counseling and therapy.* Westport, CT: Greenwood Press.

Ho, M. K. (1987). *Family therapy with ethnic minorities.* Newbury Park, CA: Sage.

Hoare, C. H. (1991). Psychosocial identify development and cultural others. *Journal of Counseling and Development, 70*:45–53.

Ivey, A. E. (1977). Cultural expertise: Toward systematic outcome criteria in counseling and psychological education. *Personnel and Guidance Journal, 55*:296–302.

Ivey, A. E. (1993). Reaction, on the need for reconstruction of our present practice of counseling and psychotherapy. *The counseling psychotherapist, 21*:225–228.

Ivey, A. E., Ivey, M. B., & Simek-Downing, L. (1987). *Counseling and psychotherapy: Skills theories and practices.* Englewood Cliffs, NJ: Prentice-Hall.

Jackson, M. L. (1995). *Multicultural counseling: Historical perspectives.* In J. E. Ponterotto et al., *Handbook of multicultural counseling.* Thousand Oaks, CA: Sage.

Katz, J. (1985). The sociopolitical nature of counseling. *The Counseling Psychologist, 13*:615–624.

Keefe, S. E. (1980). *Acculturation and the extended family among urban Mexican Americans.* In A. M. Padilla (Ed.), *Acculturation: Theory, models and some new findings.* Boulder, CO: Westview Press.

Kelley, G. A. (1955). *The psychology of personal constructs* (Vols. 1-2). New York: Norton.

Lee, C. C. (1989). Multicultural counseling: New directions for counseling professionals. *Virginia Counselor Journal, 17*:3–8.

Locke, D. C. (1992). *Increasing multicultural understanding.* Newbury Park, CA: Sage.

Maslow, A. H. (1954). *Motivation and personality.* New York: Harper.

Paniagua, F. A. (1994). *Assessing and treating culturally diverse clients.* Thousand Oaks, CA: Sage.

Patterson, C. H. (1958). The place of values in counseling and psychotherapy. *Journal of Counseling Psychology, 5*:216–223.

Petr, C. G., & Barney, D. D. (1993). Reasonable efforts for children with disabilities: The parents' perspective. *Social Work, 38*(3):247–254.

Ponterotto, J. G., & Pedersen, P. B. (1993). *Preventing prejudice: A guide for counselors and educators.* Newbury Park, CA: Sage.

Ridley, C. R. (1995). *Overcoming unintentional racism in counseling and therapy.* Thousand Oaks, CA: Sage.

Sue, D. W., & Sue, D. (1990). *Counseling the culturally different* (2nd ed.). New York: John Wiley & Sons.

Sue, D. W. (1977). Counseling the culturally different: A conceptual analysis. *Personnel and Guidance Journal, 55*:422–424.

Sue, D. W. (1978). Eliminating cultural oppression in counseling: Toward a general theory. *Journal of Counseling Psychology, 25*:419–428.

Sue, S., Allen, D., & Conaway, L. (1975). The responsiveness and equality of mental health care to Chicanos and Native Americans. *American Journal of Community Psychology, 45*:111–118.

Sue, S., Fujino, D. C., Hu, L., Takeuchi, D. T., & Zane, N. (1991). Community mental health services for ethnic minority groups: A test of the cultural responsiveness hypothesis. *Journal of Consulting and Clinical Psychology, 59*:433–440.

Sue, S., McKinney, H., Allen, D., & Hall, J. (1974). Delivery of community health services to black and white clients. *Journal of Consulting Psychology, 42*:794–801.

Sue, S., & Zane, N. (1987). The role of culture and cultural techniques in psychotherapy: A critique and reformulation. *American Psychologist, 42*(1):37–45, 1987.

Vontress, C. E. (1971). Racial differences: Impediments to rapport. *Journal of Counseling Psychology, 18*:7–13.

Wehrly, B. (1995). *Pathways to multicultural counseling competence.* Pacific Grove, CA: Brooks/Cole.

Wrenn, C. G. (1962). The culturally encapsulated counselor. *Harvard Educational Review, 32*:444–449.

Suggested Readings

Atkinson, D. R., Furlong, M. J., & Poston, W. C. (1986). Afro-american preferences for counselor characteristics. *Journal of Counseling Psychology, 33*:326–330.

Casas, J. M., & Casas, A. (1994). The acculturation process and implications for education and services. In Matiella, A. C. (Ed.), *The multicultural challenge in health education.* Santa Cruz, CA: ETR Associates, pp. 23–49.

Folensbee, R., Draguns, J. G., & Danish, S. Counselor interventions in three cultural groups. *Journal of Counseling Psychology, 33*:446–453.

Hacker, A. (1992). *Two nations: Black and white, separate, hostile, unequal.* New York: Scribner.

Locke, D. C. (1992). *Increasing multicultural understanding.* Newbury Park, CA: Sage.

Lowery, L. (1983). Bridging a culture in counseling. *Journal of Applied Rehabilitation Counseling, 14*:69–73.

Pearson, J. C. (1985). *Gender and communication.* Dubuque, IA: W. C. Brown.

Ponterotto, J. G., & Benesch, K. F. (1988). An organizational framework for understanding the role of culture in counseling. *Journal of Counseling and Development,* *66*:237–245.

Ponterotto, J. G., Casas, J. M., Suzuki, L. A. & Alexander, C. M. (Eds.). (1995). *Handbook of multicultural counseling.* Thousand Oaks: Sage.

Ponterotto, J., & Casas, M. (1991). *Handbook of racial/ethnic minority counseling research.* Springfield, IL: Charles C Thomas.

Richardson, B. L. (1991). Utilizing the resources of the African American church: Strategies for counseling professionals. In C. C. Lee & B. L. Richardson (Eds.), *Multicultural issues in counseling: New approaches to diversity.* Alexandria, VA: American Counseling Association, pp. 65–75.

Ridley, C. R. (1995). *Overcoming unintentional racism in counseling and therapy.* Thousand Oaks, CA: Sage.

Ruiz, A. S. (1990). Ethnic identity: Crisis and resolution. *Journal of Multicultural Counseling and Development, 18*:29–40.

Sue, D. W. A conceptual model for cultural diversity training. *Journal of Counseling and Development. 70*:99–105

Sue, D. W. (1990). Culture specific strategies in counseling: A conceptual framework. *Professional Psychology, 24*:424–433.

Sue, D. W., Arredondo, P., & McDavis, R. J. Multicultural counseling competencies and standards: A call to the profession. *Journal of Counseling and Development, 70*:477–486.

Sue, D. W., & Sue, D. (1990). *Counseling the culturally different: Theory and practice* (2nd ed.). New York: John Wiley & Sons.

Wrenn, C. G. (1962). The culturally encapsulated counselor. *Harvard Educational Review, 32*:444–449.

Chapter 7

DISABILITY AND AFRICAN AMERICANS

Chapter Outline
- Historical Perspective
- Social Issues Impacting African Americans
- Educational Issues
- Employment and Economic Issues
- African Americans and Disability
   Major Health Issues
- Family Dynamics
- Attitudes
- Intervention Strategies
- Assessment
- The Revised Cross Model
- Conclusion

Chapter Objectives
- Identify significant historical events which have impacted the lives of African Americans
- Identify the prevalence of disabilities among the African American population in the United States
- Identify, social, educational, and economical issues which impact the lives of African Americans
- Identify how social, educational and economical issues affect the lives of African Americans with disabilities
- Identify the leading causes of disabilities among African Americans
- Identify critical cultural issues of which rehabilitation helping professionals must be aware with regard to African Americans
- Identify the impact families have on African American persons with disabilities, and
- Provide suggestions with regard to ways of effectively working with African American persons with disabilities.

Historical Perspective

The author of this book has chosen to segment the existence of African Americans in America into five periods; some periods are overlapping: (1) Slavery 1619-1865, (2) Reconstruction 1865-1877, (3) Segregation 1877-1964, (4) Black Nationalism 1930-1964, and (5) Integration 1964 to present. Certainly these are arbitrary segments of periods of time and events, others may choose to use different classifications. Offered as an example, the integration period of 1964 to present includes the significant period of Affirmative Action, some may wish to add a unique time period for this era.

Slavery (1619–1865)

The cruelty of indentured servitude and slavery has been part of the human experience for thousands of years. There is ample evidence that the first appearance of Africans and persons of African descent in America was not as slaves but as explorers and ship navigators sailing to North America among other areas in the territory to become known as the United States of America. This noble entrance of black people in America notwithstanding, the beginning of the permanent existence of persons of African descent began in August 1619 when the colonial government at Jamestown, Virginia, purchased twenty blacks from a Dutch frigate. Some historians indicate that the first Africans were indentured servants. This event opened the period of slavery which linked America to the long list of nations, empires, countries, and territories which had engaged in the inhumane practice of human bondage.

The purpose of slavery in America is clear, that being to provide an inexpensive and steady, controlled labor force to work the fields, shops, and homes of the owners. Meager as the efforts were, questions can be raised as to the cheapness of feeding, clothing, housing, and the occasional medical care of the slaves; however, certainly slavery to their owners had one major advantage that made the institution more desirable than employing persons for wages—the ability to control the work force. Slavery did not allow for demands of higher wages and work stoppage if the demands were not met. Slavery was never intended to be an on-the-job training program; therefore, the impact was as emotionally and psychologically devastating as the practice was cruel. The emotional and psychological cost to the slaves were so severe that the impact has been felt by generations of their offspring. Additionally, the impact has affected the entire nation of American citizens in various ways. Some of the major impacts upon the slaves and their generations to follow are: (1) labeled as inferior, (2) branded as immoral, (3) stereotyped as unable to be educated, and (4) deprived of normal family relationships.

To make the institution of slavery work effectively, the slave owners had to cause their human subjects to feel inferior thus allowing themselves to be dominated by "superior beings" who would determine what was best for their lives and provide accordingly. One may incorrectly think that physical intimidation was the only means the slave owners used to force their wills upon slaves; however, physical intimidation was only one of several methods. The process of destroying the slaves' self-worth began on the slave ship where persons from the same tribe and/or spoke the same language were separated so that communication would be difficult. This form of separation was continued once they were placed under the control of the purchaser. The unfamiliar surroundings, inability to communicate effectively, and punishment for behaving in ways which were natural to them was more than enough to confuse and intimidate the slaves. Add to this years of humiliating living conditions as well as consistently being referred to as subhuman and stupid, one can easily sketch a picture where feelings of inferiority serve as the primary background of life for the slaves.

Other actions taken during the slavery period which had profound effects upon future generations of African Americans were: (1) the practice of separating families, particularly not allowing most males to establish normal family ties, thus bonding with their children; (2) forcing many of the males and females to serve as producers of future laborers by forcing the males to mate with numerous females and then selling the offspring. The act of using some males as breeders is a classic example of the concept of "blaming the victim" in that despite being forced to live in this manner they were branded as immoral for their actions; (3) degrading the institution of marriage by not allowing couples to participate in the religious ceremony associated with marriage, instead having them jump over a broom handle or some other meaningless act; (4) not allowing slaves to be educated; and (5) treating the slaves as livestock to be bought and sold with their last name changing to the name of their current owner.

These, as well as other actions had the effect of causing the person who was forced to be a slave to feel inferior to the person who proclaimed to own him. Additionally, it sowed the seeds for a matriarchal dominated family and the process of African Americans being deficient in the educational arena was begun. As one might expect, as years have passed, many of these negatives have been continued and in some instances such as poor educational attainment have been magnified while other groups have made steady progress.

Undoubtedly slavery has had many negative affects on the persons who were enslaved as well as their progeny; however, there is a growing voice within America which is expressing the belief that over 100 years of "freedom" should have erased many of the deficits. This is perhaps a reasonable assumption to make, but inaccurate none-the-less. One could argue that it is unreasonable to think that 100 plus years could erase almost 250 years of deprivation. A more effective argument is that because of the discrimination to which African Americans have been subjected they have not experienced 100 years of freedom.

Slavery was certainly a cruel and inhumane form of discrimination, and the period of reconstruction was no less discriminatory for the African American.

Reconstruction (1865–1877)

With the end of slavery in 1865, persons who had been enslaved were legally free. While freedom had long been the dream of African Americans who were not free, it was unfortunate that most were not prepared to live as free individuals. They knew how to farm but most were not knowledgeable of the ways of managing a farm, additionally if they had possessed the management tools they would have had difficulty implementing them, because as a result of the Civil War, much of the infrastructure of the Southern states had been destroyed. In short, if they were able to raise crops, how would they market them? These were some of the conditions that the period of reconstruction began for persons who had been considered slaves. It is true that promises of land and livestock had been made, but very few saw those promises become reality. Instead of being a period of time when the Southern states were rebuilt and persons who had previously been enslaved were being prepared to live lives free from discrimination and intimidation, selfish intentions and greedy-minded persons chose to use the situation for their benefits.

History correctly records that some progress was made with regard to African Americans, such as being elected to Congress and to important local positions in several southern state legislatures. Ironically it was this trend toward moving from being powerless to having some voice in the building of their lives that cut short this phase of reconstruction. Former slave owners and their descendants had hopes of the "South" returning to its former position of southern grandeur and the slight elevation of their former human property was a definite threat to those dreams. To place an end to what they considered "foolish efforts," they began to devise ways to place fear within the hearts and minds of the ex-slaves, the results of which were the establishment of the Ku Klux Klan (KKK) and other white supremacy groups. The Klan had as its major goal putting "blacks" in their place, which was being subservient to white people and they attempted to do this through beating, burning of blacks' homes and churches, as well as lynching. Unfortunately, these activities were condoned by many of the southern local and state authorities. Their activities to a large extent brought to an end the experiment of reconstruction of the South, particularly any positive involvement by African Americans. Instead, began the new era of segregation or separation of the races, particularly the black and white races. No doubt, one of the legacies of the reconstruction period with regard to African Americans was the deepening realization that either as slave or ex-slave they had very little control of their lives and that they were at best second-class citizens who had very little recourse to seek grievance for wrongful acts committed against their person. In other terms, the seeds of distrust of the dominant society had begun to grow.

Segregation (1877–1964)

As the southern politics and other day-to-day activities returned to the control of the former land owners, two things high on their agenda were to insure that the ex-slaves were powerless and that there was complete separation of the black and white races as much as possible. The impact of these decisions was to last for many years and to a considerable extent continues to play a role in the daily lives of many African Americans today. Some of the measures taken were: (1) denial of the right of African Americans to vote in the former Confederate states; (2) segregated public school systems with the black schools inadequately funded; (3) segregated public and private facilities such as denying African Americans the right to dine in facilities where whites dined and separate restroom facilities to mention a couple; (4) the denial of African Americans the right to purchase homes wherever they could afford; (5) the denial of the right to worship wherever one desired; (6) the basic denial of free speech; and (7) relegation to menial tasks and receiving lower salaries than their white counterparts.

In fairness to the southern states, it must be noted that African Americans were to some degree denied these same rights in virtually every state of the Union. It was the southern states that most vigorously and aggressively promoted and practiced these discriminations. They were the ones who held on to these practices long after other parts of the country had begun to experiment with different ways of interaction between the two races. It is interesting to note that these same states which held the hardest line with regard to race relations today appear to be making better adjustment in this area than some of the states which did not practice segregation with the same fervor as the former Confederate states.

The impact of the denial of these rights have had and continue to have an impact upon the lives of African Americans in the areas of education, economics, employment, and the social realm. These impacts will be explored later in this chapter. At this point, we are establishing a historical basis for why the lives of many African Americans have been affected in the ways they are.

Black Nationalism (1930–1964)

Considering the many restrictions and denial of rights, the ex-slaves and their descendants must have been asking the question, "What is freedom for black people?" As generations of African Americans continued to experience the effects of segregation, several trains of thought began to develop with regard to the question of what is freedom for black people—one was Black Nationalism. Black Nationalism had different meanings to the various groups seriously debating the plight of the African American. Representing the two extremes, one group led by a fiery black man from the West Indies, Marcus Garvey, it meant returning to Africa, other groups proposed that several southern states be given to African Americans to be turned into "all-black" states. Neither the "back to Africa" movement nor the "all-black states" efforts succeeded. Mr. Garvey was deported from the United States and perhaps the all-black state idea was doomed from conception. Since neither effort met with much success is not the point; the idea worth keeping in one's mind is that African Americans' dream of exerting control over their lives was kept alive. Later movements such as the Nation of Islam (Black Muslim) promoted similar ideals.

The period of black nationalism overlaps the segregation period and, as previously stated, the exclusion of African Americans from the mainstream of American society gave rise to the black nationalism movement. A significant impact of the black nationalism movement was the questioning by African Americans of whether American society would ever accept them and allow them to truly be free. Further, the thought of many African Americans was that if they were not going to be accepted into American society as first-class citizens, they should separate themselves from mainstream America. In short, the roots of distrust of the dominant society was beginning to deepen.

Integration (1964 to Present)

Perhaps not as loudly heard during the peak period of the black national movement, but certainly a persistent voice for moderation, living within and changing from within the system were voices such as the National Association for the Advancement of Colored People (NAACP) and the Urban

League to mention only two. These voices became louder and would later be joined by other forceful organizations such as the Southern Christian Leadership Conference of which Dr. Martin Luther King, Jr. emerged as a leader.

The NAACP legal defense fund led by Thurgood Marshall was successful in winning the Brown vs. Topeka Board of Education decision which was the beginning of the end of segregated school system. Through marches, sit-ins, demonstrations, work stoppages, and refusing to shop at the segregated facilities and ride city busses, segregated facilities were integrated. The brevity of this account tends to make the efforts and results appear easy, which is not the case, as many lives were lost and/or destroyed in the struggle. Most certainly, America went through a social transformation it had not experienced since the Civil War.

Social Issues Impacting African Americans

During the twentieth century, and continuing into the twenty-first century a major social issue faced by Americans of African decent has been and continue to be "inclusion." Inclusion into a society which at best viewed them as second-class citizens. As discussed previously, many years after legalized slavery was abolished, the posture of the nation was segregating black people into what was farcically called "separate but equal" facilities. This separation has created a societal imbalance which, in most cases, favors Euro-Americans. Certainly much has been accomplished toward reducing the inequality that exists between African Americans and Euro-Americans. Laws and attitudinal changes have accounted for much of the progress. However, despite this progress, as the twenty-first century has become a reality, inclusion and equality remains a major "social issue of the day."

Equality struggles have been a hallmark of African American existence in America. While the efforts have met with some degree of success, such as access to educational opportunities, advancements in employment and personal security, the difficulties of the struggles, coupled with the slow pace of progression, has been attributed for some of the social issues that will be continued for quite sometime. The failure of integration to produce a color-blind society as well as the regression in civil rights during the decades of the 1980s and 1990s has produced considerable frustration on the part of many African Americans. For some, this frustration has led to their abandonment of the age-old principle of delayed gratification practiced by many African Americans. Particularly, some younger African Americans appear to have taken the attitude that if their paths to the American dream is going to be blocked, they will create their own roads to success. Too frequently and unfortunately those roads have led to negative encounters with law enforcement and too often have resulted in disastrous results.

According to Massey and Egger (1989), among young African American males, the leading cause of death is homicide and "legal intervention," which generally means death resulting from intervention of law enforcement. Astonishment is frequently the reaction as one reviews the death rate of African American males resulting from homicide, especially when observing the rapid increase from 1960 to 1987. The African American male homicide rate per 100,000 male population in 1960 was 36.7, by 1980 this rate had risen to 66.6. By way of comparison in 1987, homicide and legal intervention accounted for the deaths of 85.6 per 100,000 African American males ages 15-26; 98.9 per 100,000 between 25-34 and 78.4 per 100,000 between 35-44. The 1987 statistics of 98.9 for age group 25-34 is in stark comparison to 13.2 deaths per 100,000 for Euro-American males of the same age range.

These figures, shocking as they are, reveal only part of the story. The other parts that more directly impact rehabilitation and other helping professionals are the thousands who survive violence and become a person with a disability.

While the overwhelming majority of young and older African Americans are law abiding, concern has been voiced by African Americans with regard to the number of African Americans who are being lost to violence, crime, substance abuse, and overreactive law enforcement. Statistics indicate that violence involving America's youth is increasing. Gordon, Gordon, and Nembhard (1994) documented that African American males have a disproportionate involvement in violence and violent behavior.

In 1996, slightly more than 30 percent of all arrests in America were that of African Americans. Even as alarming as that statistic is 27 percent of all arrests under the age of 18 were black. Also in 1996, 41 percent of all jail inmates were black. While these figures represent both African American males and females, well over 50 percent are African American males. Such a large number of African American males, particularly between 18-34 years of age, has caused many African Americans to consider this as a form of genocide.

One may ask, "If this is a form of genocide, isn't it self-imposed and why are African American males disproportionately involved in violence and violent behavior?" In an attempt to address these and other relevant questions, Earl Washington (1996) conducted a survey of the literature and gleaned the following sociologic theories and concepts: (1) poverty-social disorganization theory, (2) racial oppression-displaced aggression theory, (3) subculture of violence theory, and (4) compulsive masculinity theory. It should be noted that these concepts and theories are by no means the extent of speculation of why African American males are disproportionately involved in violence and violent behaviors. These will provide the reader with some of the current thought with regard to this subject.

Poverty-Social Disorganization Theory

According to Voss and Hepburn (1968), this theory indicates that there is a correlation between the high rate of criminal involvement among African American men and the high rate of poverty within African American communities. Those that place credence in this theory postulate that poverty contributes to social conditions, which are conducive to criminal violence such as chronic unemployment, teen pregnancy, female-headed families, academic failure, welfare dependency, inadequate socialization, and substance abuse.

Racial Oppression Displaced Aggression Theory

This theory posits that anger and frustration built up within African American men and youth as legitimate means to success, such as academic achievement, upward mobility, financial success and gainful employment are blocked by society. As a result, the inability to attain goals creates anger; however, fear of retaliation by Euro-Americans forces African Americans to internalize the anger; consequently the frustration is displaced in the form of violence against other African Americans and African American communities.

Subculture of Violence Theory

This theory maintains that the majority of African Americans are law abiding and maintain values that promote conforming to the prevailing laws; however, there are subculture values and norms which condone violence as an acceptable means of resolving interpersonal conflicts. The theory also emphasizes that during late adolescence to middle-age, African Americans develop attitudes which view trouble, toughness, sexual conquests, manipulation, autonomy, and excitement as ways of confirming one's manhood.

Compulsive Masculinity Theory

First proposed by Parson in 1947 and intended to explain male behavior in general, not specifically any ethnic groups, this theory put forth the proposition that all males at some point in their lives attempt to repudiate identification with their mothers and identify with what is considered masculine;

thus his behavior becomes the antithesis of what he perceives as feminine. If one subscribes to this theory, an important factor will be to identify the male influences in the young man's life, in that his perception of masculinity will be greatly influenced by those contacts.

The Broken Promise Concept

This author proposes his own concept which postulates that the overinvolvement of young African American males in violence and violent behavior is not based upon low morals or lack of self-control but upon anger and frustration relating to society's broken promises. As African Americans emerged from the cruel bonds of slavery and began the struggle to build lives within whatever framework the American society allowed, a guiding principle that sustained black people in America has been the societal promise that if one obeys the laws, becomes employable and works hard, there would be no limitations to obtaining the key to the door marked "success." Many African American youth heard stories of their grandparents' struggles and they observed their parents' struggles only to realize that each generation basically begins the struggle in the same position or at a less-advantageous position than the previous generation. As they contemplate their futures they see a similar situation awaiting them. Unwilling to accept the same fate, they take charge (in their belief) of their lives. For too many, taking charge translates into violent and illegal behavior. Unfortunately, this behavior will continue until society "makes good on its promises."

Teenage Pregnancy

Regardless of race, teenage pregnancy occupies the nation's concerns. According to the American March of Dimes Birth Defect Foundation, almost one million teenagers become pregnant annually and more than half give birth. Also, in 1995, over 13 percent of all births in the United States were to teenagers. Teenagers of African American descent have a high rate of pregnancy. The March of Dimes provides the following information with regard to health risks to teenage mothers, health risks to the baby, and consequences of a teenage pregnancy. All issues deal with why there is considerable concern within the African American community.

Health risks to a teenage mother and her baby:

- Teenage mothers are more at risk of pregnancy complications such as premature labor, anemia, high blood pressure, as well as placental problems.
- Because of immaturity, teens are at risk for sexually transmitted diseases such as chlamydia, syphilis, and AIDS.

- Of all maternal age groups, pregnant teens are least likely to get early and regular prenatal care.
- Because of poor dietary habits, pregnant teens increase the risk of their babies being born with health problems.
- Of all maternal age groups, pregnant teens are less likely to gain an adequate amount of weight which increases the risk of delivering a baby with low birth weight. March of Dimes states that in 1995, 9.3 percent of mothers ages 15-19 had low birth weight babies, 13.5 percent of mothers under the age of 15 had low birth weight babies. This is in comparison to 7.3 percent for mothers of all other ages. Low birth weight babies, defined as weighing less than 5.5 pounds, are often at-risk babies in that their organs may not be fully developed leading to respiratory problems. Also, they are 40 times more likely to die in their first month of life than normal-weight babies.

Consequences of Teenage Pregnancy. The results of teenager pregnancy frequently impact rehabilitation counselors and other helping professionals in that teen mothers are more likely to drop out of high school. The absence of a high school diploma generally leads to other problems such as inability to secure employment that will adequately support a family, causing the family to rely in part on some type of public assistance. Also, interrupted high school education can result in securing what is considered unskilled jobs which too often have elements of danger possibly leading to disabilities. Because of immaturity, teens often have not had the time or experience to develop good parenting skills. Sadly, a by-product of the inability to deal with the stress of rearing a child is child abuse.

Changing Influence of the Family

Another social issue which certainly is not unique to African Americans or any other ethnic minority group is the changing influence of the family. As America has become more mobile and information about distant shores more accessible, the closeness that families enjoyed particularly during our agrarian period has diminished considerably. This same scenario has impacted African Americans, but perhaps the greatest threat to family stability among African Americans are the things that have previously been discussed, the youth being influenced by gangs and teen pregnancies robbing young girls of their formative years.

Educational Issues

Few, if any, would disagree that education is one of the keys to the survival of any society. Whether the education is a primitive group passing along knowledge of hunting and shelter preparation or an industrialized nation brainstorming with regard to ways of improving access and participation to its kindergarten through college educational programs, education occurs. Therefore, there is no question that education occurs, rather the questions are to what extent, how accessible, quality thereof, and level of participation. The answers determine how far a society advances.

The United States of America, one of the most technologically advanced countries in the world, has reached this enviable status by having an advanced national education system. Many would argue that the United States is not as advanced as it should be given its resources and educational system. Questions have been raised with respect to the quality of education as well as whether the educational system is demanding enough regarding demonstrations of educational competency. These are valid and legitimate questions and concerns. Another concern is the rate of participation of the minority/ethnic groups, particularly, African Americans, Asian and Pacific Americans, Hispanic/Latino Americans, and American Indians.

With regard to African Americans, as previously stated, during legalized slavery, it was illegal for slaves to be formally educated. After its abolishment, African Americans were educated in separate facilities from Euro-Americans and without question, their education was not equal to their Euro-American counterparts. Legal education segregation continued until the landmark Brown vs. Topeka Board of Education ruling in 1954.

While morally wrong, prior to the 1960s, America could afford to have an unequally educated population in that jobs requiring unskilled laborers were plentiful. Unfortunately, America accepted ethnic minority groups as being less educated, thus filling the roles of unskilled workers. With current technological advances, countries wishing to compete in the global market cannot afford to undereducate any segment of their population.

African Americans in Higher Education

Distinguished Scholar Reginald Wilson identifies two major events which have had a significant impact upon African Americans attending college. The first was the passage of the G.I. Bill for educational benefits in 1945. This bill was not specifically designed to increase minority attendance in colleges; it was established to avoid millions of veterans from saturating the job market after the Korean War. Regardless of the intent, it has had the effect of making higher education affordable for many African Americans as well as other ethnic minorities. The second event was the 1964 Civil Rights Act which placed emphasis on equality for all American citizens. Following the passage of this landmark Civil Rights Act, acknowledgment was given that ethnic minorities in general, and specifically African Americans, had not been afforded equal opportunities to attain formal education. With this acknowledgment also came the realization that special services would be helpful to many African American college students to help remand the effects of past discrimination; therefore, programs such as Upward Bound, Talent Search, and Affirmative Action came into existence.

Today, considerable discourse is conducted with regard to the need for and fairness of having such programs for specific groups of people. Despite these discussions, these programs, as well as other efforts, appear to have produced positive results. The positive results were proclaimed in a 1997 issue of *Black Issues in Higher Education* as the article announced that African American baccalaureates surged by 30 percent from 1991 to 1995.

Reginald Wilson informs us that African American females are the primary cause of this phenomenal growth in African American baccalaureate recipients. The following comments by Professor Wilson provide additional analysis of the growth and what it means:

> For African American men there has been an incremental increase of 2,000 new baccalaureates a year, but African American women have gained by 4,000 a year.
>
> During the same period of time, the number of whites receiving baccalaureate degrees declined slightly, meaning that African Americans represented a larger percentage of the college-going population.

The impressive growth of African American baccalaureate recipients has to a large extent been made possible through the efforts of Historically Black Colleges and Universities (HBCU). Although increased enrollment of African Americans in community and junior colleges as well as increased enrollment at predominantly white institutions (PWI) have decreased the historically black colleges and universities share of African American student enrollment, they continue to produce the majority of African American baccalaureates as well as awarding a significant number of graduate degrees.

Historically Black Colleges and Universities–A Quaker group in Philadelphia established the first public black college in 1837, Cheyney State College (Payne 1994). Later in that century, in 1862, the Morrill Land grant Act was passed which established grants of land to each state (30,000 acres for each member of congress). The proceeds were to be used to establish what is known as Agricultural and Mechanical Colleges (A&M). In the 1862 Act, only one black college (Alcorn State) was established. The other colleges established were white institutions of higher education. In 1890, another Morrill Land grant Act was passed which created 16 black colleges (Wilson 1994).

During the period of legal segregation, historically black colleges and universities were the primary means of obtaining higher education for African

Americans. Additionally, these institutions served as the principle employers of black intellectuals. With regard to educating African Americans, Reginald Wilson reminds us that during their over 100-year history, historically black colleges and universities not only were the primary access to higher education for African Americans, but with its open door policy, they accepted both the best prepared students and many that were not as well prepared which would not have been admissible to other colleges and universities.

With the end of legal segregation access to traditionally white institutions became somewhat easier resulting in a decline in the position of African Americans who attended historically black institutions. Despite the decline, most historically black colleges and universities remain viable institutions.

Education is of considerable importance to most every American and of particular value to African Americans in that for many years, education has been promoted as their ticket out of poverty and a weapon to be used in the war against oppression and discrimination. In most instances, increased education is associated with increased opportunities, specifically employment opportunities.

Employment and Economic Issues

In an economic-based society such as exists in the United States, gainful employment is essential. Work, to a large degree, defines who we are, how we feel about ourselves, and how others perceive us, as well as our ability to purchase goods and services. In identifying how work helps satisfy the basic needs, Ann Roe (1956) outlined Abraham Maslow's hierarchy of needs:

> In our society there is no single situation which is potentially so capable of giving some satisfaction at all levels of basic needs as is the occupation. With respect to the physiological needs, it is clear that in our culture the usual means for allaying hunger and thirst, and to some extent, sexual needs and other is through the job, which provides the money that can be exchanged for food and drink. The same is true for safety needs. The need to be a member of a group and to give and receive love is also one which can be satisfied in part by the occupation. To work with a congenial group, to be an extrinsic part of the function to the group, to be needed and welcomed by the group are important aspects of the satisfactory job.
>
> Perhaps satisfaction of the need for esteem from self and others is most easily seen as a big part of the occupation. In the first place, entering upon an occupation is generally seen in our culture as a symbol of adulthood and an indication that a young man or woman has reached a stage of some independence and freedom. Having a job in itself carries a measure of esteem. What importance it has is seen most clearly in the devastating effects upon the individual of being out of work. Occupation as a source of need satisfaction is of

extreme importance in our culture. It may be that occupations have become so important in our culture just because so many needs are so well satisfied by them.

Given the important role employment plays in our lives, African Americans tend to be at risk for experiencing difficulties in fulfilling some of life's basic needs in that they experience high rates of unemployment and underemployment.

Unemployment

The high rate of unemployment of African Americans, particularly African American males, has such a long standing history that the figures tend to have lost their shock value. Because of the changing nature of employment, the quoting of current employment or unemployment statistics becomes of little value; however, what is of vital importance are the trends. At any point in time, one comparing Euro-American and African American employment/unemployment rates will see that the unemployment rate for African Americans is twice that of Euro-Americans. To paint an even more distressing picture, the unemployment rate for African American teenagers is consistently in the 20 plus percent range.

Gang activity and violent behavior, as well as other illegal actions committed by African American youth have been a byproduct of unemployment. While no excuse justifies disregarding just laws, as a society, we must look at the impact of a segment of our population being denied equal opportunities. Teenage unemployment generally is considerably higher than adult unemployment, but for African American youth the rate is triple that of their Euro-American counterparts.

African Americans and Disability

According to a 2002 U. S. Census Bureau report, among the ethnic and racial groups of Asian or Pacific Americans, Caucasians, and Hispanic/ Latino, African Americans have the greatest prevalence of disabilities. The same is true when severe disabilities are considered.

A review of data indicates that too many African Americans continue to experience the same or similar problems that have plagued them for decades. These problems answer the question of why there is a high rate of disabilities among African Americans. The following provides clues that also answer the question of why:

1. Since over 50 percent of the working African American population work as unskilled laborers, they are more susceptible to disabling injuries.

Except for farm labor, African Americans work under some of the most dangerous conditions, most with a high probability of producing employee injuries.

2. Approximately 50 percent of the African American population's income places them in what is considered the low-socioeconomic class. This generally means their living environment is consistent with their income level, relegating them to live in areas where there may be exposure to lead and other chemical hazards as well as being at greater risk of physical violence. These hazards, added to poor lighting, heating, and ventilation provide an environment conducive to acquiring a disability.

3. Lack of access to adequate health care has historically been a major problem for African Americans. Additionally inability to afford health insurance causes those in need of health care to delay attending to health needs until the problems are critical. This has happened with frequency causing some social reformers to call for a national program guaranteeing reasonable access to all Americans without regard to wealth or lack thereof.

4. Poor dietary habits such as excessive consumption of fatty foods, salt, and/or high sodium content is a major contributor to development of health conditions leading to disabilities.

5. Unhealthy lifestyles such as smoking and excessive use of alcohol.

Major Health Issues

Some of the leading health problems are hypertension, heart conditions, diabetes and strokes. There are a number of factors which contribute to the onset of these problems, and some have already been discussed; however, one factor—stress—has not been mentioned. Stress appears to be a common link to most of these problems, particularly heart condition, stroke, and hypertension. It is theorized that the various coping and defense mechanisms African Americans use to deal with the many forms of prejudice and discrimination cause stress to build within their bodies, resulting in heart attacks, strokes, and elevated blood pressure.

Heart Disease: To emphasize the magnitude of the heart disease problem for African Americans, one should look at heart disease mortality. According to the U. S. Health Chartbook (1993), in 1991, heart disease mortality was almost 40 percent greater for African American men than for Euro-American men and 64 percent greater for African American women than for Euro-American women. Also, the heart disease mortality was more than 60 percent greater for African American men than African American women. While dated, these statistics have not significantly changed.

As previously stated, I am using mortality rates which do not speak to the numbers that survive and have some type of limitation. However, mortality rates are used to indicate the extent of the problem.

Strokes: The death rate for stroke is almost twice as great for African American men as the rate for Euro-American men and significantly higher for African American women than the rate for Euro-American women.

Family Dynamics

Historical Perspective of African American Families

The African American family, its effectiveness, its roles, and values have been greatly maligned in the American society. Considerable amount of mis-perceptions and injurious information concerning African American families began with slavery where, in most cases, marriage among slaves was treated lightly. To formalize a union between two slaves, jumping over a broomstick was considered sufficient and this action in no way guaranteed that the union and their offspring would not be separated through selling one partner and/or some or all the children. According to Blassingame (1972), although some slave owners did not view slave marriages in the same light as their own, they had a tendency to keep slave families together in that from the slave owner's viewpoint, a married slave who was concerned about his or her family was less likely to revolt. Because the slave family had little, if any, con-trol over their destinies, it has been theorized by some behavioral scientists that slave families were unstable and set into motion destructive psychologi-cal and sociological tendencies which impact some African Americans today–factors such as absentee fathers, single parent families, and female-dominated families. John Blassingame (1972) argues that despite these theo-ries of the destruction of the family system under slavery, the African American slave family was a most important survival mechanisms for slaves. Abzug (1971), in his earlier work, laid the foundation for Blassingame's point of view with the following comments:

> It was in the family that the slave received affection, companionship, love and empathy with his suffering under this peculiar institution. Through the family he learned how to avoid punishment, cooperate with his fellow slaves, and retain some semblance of his self-esteem. The socialization of the slave child was another important function for the slave parents. They could cushion the shock of bondage for him, inculcate in him values different than those the mas-ter attempted to teach him, and represent another frame of reference for his self-esteem besides the master.

The primary nurturing role in the slave family was the responsibility of the mother and that role has not appreciably changed in today's society. However, some feel that the role of today's African American mothers has expanded considerably beyond being the emotional glue that bonds the family together.

Role of Mother

A major flaw in analyzing African American families, particularly segmenting individual roles, is that the family and its members' roles are compared to Euro-American, middle-class families and family members' roles. Because of unequal access to education, employment, and housing as well as income, in this author's opinion, this makes a comparison harmful. Harmful because conclusions are reached which often place African American families and the members' roles in negative positions. Perhaps a good example is to view the African American mother as domineering. This concept has been fostered in that a large percentage of African American married women are employed and in some cases are more gainfully employed (in terms of income) than their husbands. In comparison, it has been within the last several decades that a significant number of Euro-American females worked. Because African American females have been in the paid labor force since the abolishment of slavery, their status has been elevated by social scientists. The African American male's status has been devalued, thus the unfair labeling of African American females as being bossy and dominant within the family.

While it is an untrue characterization of African American females as being aggressive, domineering, and demanding, it is true that in many instances it is easier for an African American female to secure employment than African American males. Therefore, African American females may be visible to those who are not familiar with some of the oppressive struggles African American females face as being the primary economic provider for the family again perpetuating the myth that the female within an African American family is the dominant force. Robert Staples (1988) effectively debunks the myth of the dominating black female with the following:

> From the time of slavery onward, she has resisted the destructive forces that she has encountered in American society. During the period of slavery, she fought and survived the attack on her dignity by the slave system, relinquished the passive role ascribed to members of her gender to insure the survival of her people, and tolerated the culturally endured irresponsibility of her man in recognition of this country's relentless attempts to castrate him. Too often, the only result of her sacrifices and suffering have been the invidious and inaccu-

rate labeling of her as a matriarch, a figure deserving respect but not love. The objective reality of the black women in America is that she occupies the lowest rung of the socioeconomic ladder of all sex-race groups and has the least prestige. The double burden of gender and race has put her in the category of a super-oppressed entity.

Also adding to the myth of the dominating female is that approximately one-third of the African American households are headed by a female (no male present). At this junction, several points should be made with regard to female-headed households:

• When we think of female-headed households, we logically think of absence of a male, and visions of "deadbeat dads" quickly enter the picture. There is no question that a high percentage of the households are void of a male (husband and father) because of no marriage, divorce, and/or abandonment; however, there is a considerable number who are widowed. The African American female is expected to live almost nine years longer than the African American male; therefore, there is a good chance that a considerable number of female-headed households are results of death of the male.

• Niara Sudarkasa (1993) contends the increase in female-headed households is of recent origin and is a result of the welfare policy and public housing policies. The point is that in past generations (pre 1960s), unwed teenagers would live with other adults, parents, grandparents, or other relatives; however, today public assistance programs along with housing authority policy encourages unwed mothers to live apart from relatives, thus being counted as heads of households.

• Female-headed households can and most often are stable households. Generations of advice and experience are passed down from parent to daughter with regard to surviving within the American society. Moreover, considerable resources such as kinfolk, church members, and friends are available to assist with household-related matters.

• Female-headed household does not mean absence of male influence. Brothers, uncles, and grandfathers as well as male friends and other male relatives are available to assist with the guidance of children.

• As Sudarkosa points out, female-headed households are not totally the result of teen pregnancy, but in part females reacting to the demographic, economic, political and social plight of black life in America.

Considering the several myths surrounding the role of African American women, it is not surprising that there is misunderstanding of their roles within the family setting. Succinctly stated, African American women are coproviders sharing equal roles and status with their male partners in the handling of family matters.

Role of Father

Similar to the African American female's role, the African American male's role is shrouded in misperceptions, some of which have their roots in the treatment of African American males during slavery. In slavery, to maintain control over the black male, he was generally degraded. He was helpless in defending himself from being whipped like a child, he was unable to protect his family from any action the slave master decided to perform, and he was labeled as lazy, ignorant, and not worthy of trust. Some of these labels are applied to the current generation of African American males. The following comments by Robert Staples (1988) clearly identifies some of the perceptions held with regard to African American males.

> Along with the economic conditions that impinge on their role performance, black men are saddled with a number of stereotypes that label them as irresponsible, criminalistic, hypersexual, and lacking in masculine traits. Some of these stereotypes become self-fulfilling prophecies because the dominant society is structured in a way that prevents many black men from achieving the goals of manhood. At the same time, the notion of the castrated black male is largely a myth. Although mainstream culture has deprived many black men of the economic wherewithal for normal, masculine functions, most function in a way that gains the respect of their mates, children and community.

The lack of economic prowess to which Professor Staples refers is a major obstacle faced by African American men's quest to provide a better standard of living for their families. Factors such as high unemployment and low salaries for those who are employed create situations that decreases the African American males' chances of fulfilling the role of primary economic provider for his family.

Staples (1988), while using the works of Lewis (1975) Scanzoni (1971), Cazanave (1979) and Daneal (1975), makes two important points. First, recent literature has refuted the long-held view that African American males are ineffective and indifferent to their children. Instead, current literature produced by Lewis and Scanzoni indicates that black fathers are warm, nurturing, and play a vital role in the rearing of their offspring. Second, the works of Cazanave and Daneal found better parenting patterns among middle class, African American fathers. Thus, indicating that when African American fathers have the economic resources to provide for the family, they are able to be more effective parents.

African American Family Characteristics and Child-Rearing Practices

It is well documented that the family serves as a major force in the psychological, social, and emotional development of children; therefore, the manner in which the parents react to events, the belief system they promote, the attitudes they project, the behaviors they display, and the values they embrace influence the maturation of the children. Robert Hill (1972) identifies strong kinship bonds, strong achievement orientation, adaptability of family roles, strong religious orientation, and strong work orientation as strengths of African American families. Janice Hale-Benson (1988) contends that the following are common characteristics of many African Americans: People-oriented, authoritarian in their child-rearing practices, positive attitudes toward child bearing (meaning little, if any, stigma is attached to bearing a child outside of wedlock), strong attention to nonverbal communication and style orientation (importance is not only placed on what one does but how one does it).

Kinship Bonds

Parental type influence upon African American children generally extends beyond the immediate family members. A long-standing practice of many African American parents has been to seek and accept advice and emotional and sometimes financial support from their parents, grandparents, uncles, aunts, highly respected cousins as well as non-relatives such as close friends and select church members. It is not uncommon for close friends, especially church member acquaintances, to be referred to as uncle, aunt, or in some cases as the person's "play mother." This informal adoption of non-relatives into the family circle is a means of showing respect and acknowledgment of the level of the family's regard of their friendship. Children grow up hearing of these persons being referred to as relatives and treat them with the same respect and regard they have for blood relatives.

Achievement Oriented

Education has always played a prominent role in the lives of African Americans. As stated before, most African Americans view education as the key to unlock the doors of success. Most African American parents stress to their children they want them to have a better life than their lives and emphasize that being educated will help ensure that they are able to secure jobs that will afford them the better things in life.

Work Oriented

Despite the stereotype of African Americans, particularly African American males, as lazy persons, African Americans have a very strong work ethic. The high unemployment rate of African Americans is most often a result of discrimination, lack of education, and lack of skills necessary to successfully compete for certain jobs than it is of lack of ambition and drive. Most families emphasize work as much as education, in that work is viewed as the reward for being educated.

Adaptability of Family Roles

Versatility has been one of the keys to the survival of the African American family. This is evident as African American females have stepped forward to provide economic support in times when the male is either unemployed or underemployed. Similarly the male may assume many of the housekeeping duties as the female is keep busy with work outside of the home. African American children learn early to be adaptable in that the older children are quite often called upon to take care of the younger children, serving as substitute parents–providing services ranging from basic babysitting to determining appropriate discipline.

People Oriented

Janice Hale-Benson (1988) contends that black children are taught to be aware of people's moods, emotions, and body language as much, if not more, than actual words. Therefore, African American children learn to be excellent readers of nonverbal communication. Sometimes African Americans who are quiet are viewed by the uninformed as being inattentive and nonaggressive, when they do not ask many questions, in actuality they do not feel the need to ask questions when they have obtained the answers through observance of nonverbal communication.

Authoritarianism

Many African American parents are very direct in their child-rearing practices. In disciplinary situations, "talking back" is often not tolerated. Stated in other terms, when the parent is disciplining a child, he/she does not allow nor does the child expect to give a lengthy discussion on how unfair he/she believes the punishment to be. The parent will tolerate some discussion, but when the decision on punishment has been made, the parent expects (and generally receives) compliance without much input from the child. Physical discipline is not uncommon in African American families. In most cases, the physical part of the punishment does not reach the stage of being a beating;

however, in an age where corporal punishment may be considered child abuse, more than one black parent has been shocked to learn that what they consider firm direct punishment is considered by others to be abusive.

Attitudes Toward Childbearing

Although childbearing outside of wedlock is not encouraged by African Americans, when it does occur, the child is not considered illegitimate. The child is generally accepted and loved as any child would be. Most often unwed females are not encouraged to have an abortion or place the child for adoption. This is not to imply that there are only a few abortions or adoptions, but to emphasize that the abortions and adoptions are often not driven by shame but more because the person or family determines that they do not have the resources to adequately care for the child.

Style

From a very early age, black children learn that what one does is important and the style with which one does things is equally important. Style is a way the black child puts his personal signature to whatever he/she is doing. This emphasis is carried over into adult life. A very good example is the personal touch black basketball players put into dunking a ball or the way in which a professional football player reacts when he has made a spectacular play.

Intervention Strategies

Persons in the helping professions, such as rehabilitation counselors, social workers, psychologists, and educational counselors to mention a few, would love to have a "menu" type book that would identify a group, list the characteristics of that group, and based upon those characteristics the helper would be provided with a how-to-do list of techniques that will be applicable in the situation at hand. Because we are dealing with humans and currently no two are exactly alike, therefore this approach is not practical. Despite this common-sense knowledge, too frequently books, journals, and articles list common characteristics of African Americans, Asian and Pacific Americans, etc. as though all persons in those groups have had the same experiences, have the same backgrounds, and came from the same social and economic background. Most helping professionals probably have read that Asians are polite, quiet, and reserved and African Americans are loud and concrete thinkers. The truth is that some Asians are quiet and some African

Americans are loud; likewise, some Asian Pacific Americans are loud while some African Americans are very good at abstract thinking. The point is that there is no one set of characteristics which adequately describe all members of any group. There is a variety of factors to consider when attempting to assess a client to determine the appropriate helping approach.

Assessment

In assessing a client one must get to know the person, his background, and his experiences so that he does not rely on identifying the client through stereotypical ideas of the person and the group to which he is associated. The concept of giving consideration to one's cultural background when engaged in the rehabilitation helping process is of tremendous value; it frees the professional helper from the tunnel vision of observing everything from one perspective, primarily the dominant culture's viewpoint. As liberating as this concept is, it can also be equally destructive if the helper takes a monolithic view of minority group attitudes and behaviors as stated by Donald Atkinson and his associates (1989). By this they mean disregarding within group differences and viewing all members of a particular minority group as having the same experiences, beliefs, attitudes, and value systems. One can easily see that this point of view is as unproductive as judging everyone by the dominant culture's standards.

To avoid making either of the previously mentioned mistakes, the professional help would be wise to assess the client from a variety of diagnostic viewpoints: pride and identification with one's culture and heritage, level of acculturation, communication styles, expectations of the helping process, value orientation, and situational control (influence of family, religious influence, and social influence). This will be the format for discussing intervention with African Americans; likewise, a similar format will be used with the other racial/ethnic minority groups of Asian and Pacific Americans, Hispanic/Latino Americans, and American Indians.

Pride In and Identification With One's Culture and Heritage

Because of the reasons why African Americans became permanent residents of America, pride in who they are and from where they originated was degraded by the majority of Euro-Americans. In essence, African Americans were taught to hate themselves and loathe their black identity. In too many cases, this effort was very successful, resulting in African Americans attempting to emulate Euro-Americans. As discussed in the historical background section, considerable effort has been made to restore pride in being black people. Consequently, African Americans are at various stages of pride, identification, and acceptance or rejection of their culture and heritage.

Several distinguished scholars, including Thomas (1971), and Cross (1971) have contributed to the literature with regard to African Americans moving from a Euro-American orientation to a black identity orientation and this concept has been referred to as the Black Identity Model. Social scientists such as Janet Helms (1985) believes that the racial identity model has potential diagnostic value. Additionally, Derald Sue and David Sue (1990) indicate that research now suggests that a minority individual's reaction to counseling, the counseling process, and the counselor is influenced by his/her cultural/racial identity and not simply linked to minority-group membership. They further point out the high failure-to-return rate of many culturally different clients seems intimately linked to the mental health professional's inability to accurately assess the cultural identity of the client.

Perhaps William Cross (1971), in his original work and in his revisions (1991) which he calls Nigrescense, has done as much as anyone to promote this model as a technique by which professional helpers may trace the developmental stages blacks encounter in moving from a form of self-hating to a self-healing and culturally affirming self-concept. One can certainly question the model and Cross acknowledges that not all African Americans engage in a self-hatred process. Some persons will correctly point out that many African Americans do not indulge in self-hatred and that their self-concept is firmly rooted in pride in being a black person.

The author is suggesting that rehabilitation and other helping professionals can use this model as a tool in evaluating the stage of black racial identity of their African American clients. It should also be recognized that the author believes a value of this model is not that each African American goes through all of the stages, but that each African American client when being seen by the helper is at some stage of black identity and development and this model serves as a valuable tool in understanding the stage.

The Revised Cross Model

Stage 1: Pre-Encounter: Cross describes persons in this stage as holding attitudes toward being black as ranging from race neutral to antiblack. He further indicates that because there is this range of attitudes, some persons at this stage believe their happiness and well-being are not the product of their race but have more to do with other factors of life such as religion, lifestyle, and professional status. The antiblackness group loathes other blacks and feels alienated from other blacks as well as the black community.

Implications for the Rehabilitation Helping Professional Process: When working with an African American client who has a disability and/or his significant other, it is helpful in an interview (whether initial or later depending on circumstances) to ask a series of questions related to the person's attitude toward being black. Questions would include the following:

• Has being black helped or hindered you in your life?

• How do you feel that being a black person is going to affect your current situation?

• What type of discrimination, if any, have you encountered in your life?

• What type of discrimination, if any, do you expect to encounter as a black person with a disability?

If the client for mental and/or emotional reasons is unable to respond to these questions with slight modifications, these same questions can be asked of the clients' guardians/significant others. This is important in that their views and their stage of black identity is important to the rehabilitation process. The answers to these and other well considered questions should provide the helper with an idea if the person fits into the pre-encounter stage.

Stage 2: Encounter: In this stage the person experiences an event or events which cause her to rethink her position on "blackness." The event may be negative, such as a racist remark made by a Euro-American person for whom she has high regard, or it may involve a position which she has desired and for which she has worked hard being given to a Euro-American male who has less experience and qualifications than she. It may be positive in that she has seen a documentary of an African American freedom fighter and she decides to read more about the person resulting in a change in attitude toward being black. In most cases, once the person has had the encounter(s) he/she will begin to develop a different view of Euro-American people and Euro-American values.

Implications for the Rehabilitation Helping Professional Process: Clients and/or their significant others at this stage may insist on having a helping professional of the same racial background as their own. Additionally, they may question the Euro-American helper's motives—his abilities to understand their needs and express an inability to work with the helper.

State 3: Immersion–Emersion: This stage is represented by transition, transition from what he was to what he wants to become. It is the latter that is unclear. The Immersion part is an attempt to absorb everything that represents positive blackness. Cross describes the emersion phase as:

> The second part of the stage is emergence from the emotionality and dead end, either/or racist and oversimplified ideological aspects of the immersion experience. The person begins to "level off" and feel in control of his or her emotions and intellect. In fact, the person cannot continue to handle the intense

emotional phases and concentrated effect levels associated with conversion and is predisposed to find ways to level off.

Thus, as one is engulfed within the emersion phase she begins to recognize that her entire life does not have to be absorbed with "blackness" and that Euro-Americans are not the devils she believed them to be during the immersion phase.

Implication for the Rehabilitation Helping Professional Process: While the client and/or his significant others are in the immersion phase, the reaction will be much as in the encounter stage. However, if the Euro-American helper can withstand this stage and/or become involved with them when they are in the emersion phase, productive rehabilitation efforts can be made. That is, the client will have less resentment and bitterness toward the nonblack helper. This does not, however, mean that the client has complete faith and trust in the helper. It is at this point that the helper must demonstrate multicultural skills and awareness if she hopes to execute a successful rehabilitation plan.

Stage 4: Internalization: As the name implies, the person begins to internalize his concept of blackness and its value to his life. Cross identifies three dynamic impacts internalization has on an individual:

- It helps him defend and protect himself from psychological insults that stem from living in a racist society;
- It provides a sense of belonging and social footage; and
- It provides a foundation for interacting with people of other cultures that may have a different world view.

Implication for the Rehabilitation Helping Professional Process: Perhaps Cross' statement that "the successful resolution of one's racial identity conflicts makes it possible for the person to shift attention to other identity concerns" relatedly the African American person with a disability, once he has internalized his blackness, can move on to accepting his disability. This may be best described by comparing this with Abraham Maslow's hierarchy of needs; one cannot actualize until he has met some of the basic needs. In this case it may be difficult for the African American with a disability to accept his disability if he is having difficulty accepting who he is as an individual.

Stage 5: Internalization–Commitment: There is not a great difference in this stage from the previous stage with the exception the individual works at maintaining his positive view of himself as a black person.

Implications for the Rehabilitation Helping Professional Process: Rehabilitation is easier to accomplish if the person knows who he is and can use his self-pride to withstand undesirable life events.

Level of Acculturation: Since acculturation is the subordinate culture accepting the values and characteristics of the dominant culture, Cross' Black

Identity Model, to a large extent, helps determine level of acculturation of African Americans. Two additional points with regard to African Americans and acculturation must be understood. (1) It is impossible to live in America and not adopt some of the dominant culture's values; therefore, regardless of which stage of black identity in which an African American is, he will exhibit some Euro-American values. (2) Because most African Americans have for many years been disconnected from their African heritage, most of the values they hold are based in Euro-American culture.

Implication for the Rehabilitation Professional Helping Process: This is not to say that African Americans and Euro-Americans are exactly alike; however, it is this author's contention that because of historical circumstances, the two racial groups are culturally more alike than they are different. The extent to which African American values differ from Euro-American values relates to the extent Euro-Americans prohibit African Americans from implementing these values.

Expectations: There are two aspects to expectation: (1) the helper's expectations and the client's expectations; and (2) the client's knowledge of the rehabilitation helping process.

Helper's Expectations and Client's Expectation

The rehabilitation process goes smoother and is more likely to be successful if both the helper and client have the same expectations. Early in the contact with the client, the rehabilitation helper determines what outcome she expects as a result of this relationship. Failure is the most conceivable outcome if the helper is working toward rehabilitation to prepare the client for a job when the client's expectations are to be certified as being disabled to qualify for disability income. Therefore, it is incumbent upon the helper to determine if there is a congruence between her plans and the client's plans.

Client's Knowledge of the Rehabilitation Process

The rehabilitation professional must ensure that the client understands the rehabilitation process. Particularly why certain things are required such as income information, matters concerning the family such as number of children, spouse's occupation, etc. This is particularly relevant to African Americans. Because of a history of discrimination, many African Americans distrust "government" agencies, especially when they ask a number of questions. In the past, they may have been accustomed to answers to these types of questions being used to disqualify them for some services they were seeking.

Implications for the Rehabilitation Helping Professional Process: The helping professional should not be surprised nor angered by resistance to providing information needed for the rehabilitation process. By being honest, understanding, and nonthreatening in his approach as well as being careful to explain the why's and what for's, the professional helper increases his chances of success.

Value Orientation

Derald Sue and David Sue (1990) discuss values with regard to how some minority groups view time and its use differently than many Euro-Americans. There used to be a statement among African Americans with regard to life, that they function on "black people's time", which meant if one wanted an activity that involved African Americans, to begin at 11:00, it should be set at 10:30 because of the casual manner in which some African Americans relate to time. Helping professionals oriented to Euro-American standards of punctuality may have difficulty accepting any client who does not adhere to schedules. In fact, they should insist on punctuality in that a casual adherence to scheduled meeting time disrupts other appointments and that is unfair to the helper and his other clients. The professional helper should discuss appointments and the importance of being on time, if he detects a tendency to be late.

The important point made with regard to African Americans and time is that the rehabilitation professional should not tolerate unjustifiable lateness. However, he should not view the client's initial casual approach to timeliness as a sign of lack of concern and interest in the rehabilitation process.

With regard to other values that many African Americans hold, having a knowledge of the person's ethnic cultural heritage including important events and customs will aid the professional helper in understanding the values of some African Americans. At this point the helping professional may be thinking that expecting her to learn about this history, customs and traditions is too much to ask. The response to this is African Americans have always had to learn Euro-American history, customs, and traditions.

Situational Control

Situational control refers to how much control the African American client believes she has over situations and events that affect her life. The assessment in this area should relate to whether the client believes others or outside forces control what happens to her or whether she is in control of her life and the decisions and actions she takes will make a difference between accomplishing her goals or nonaccomplishment of the goals. These are extremely important distinctions to make when one considers that for a large portion of the existence of African Americans in the United States, their lives have been influenced by laws and unwritten codes designed to control their lives. Thus, some African Americans in the rehabilitation process may feel that regardless of what they want, someone else is going to decide what they will receive and be allowed to do. For those clients who believe their fate is predetermined, it is imperative that the rehabilitation helping professional work toward empowering the client.

Other situational control influence assessments should relate to how much influence the family has on the client. The client's ability, or lack thereof, to participate in the rehabilitation process will determine to a large extent how much involvement and influence the family has with the client. The helper must be aware that for some African Americans, the family will need to be part of the rehabilitation plan in that family members will play a prominent role in the rehabilitation process–roles ranging from being a care giver to babysitter. Additionally, the helper may need to view the family beyond the immediate members and include extended family members such as friends, cousins, and grandparents. Another situational influences may be religion. Some religious doctrines teach that situations such as illness and disabilities are acts of God and beyond the control of humans. Thus, prayer is the answer. Knowing whether the client has beliefs of this nature will certainly affect the rehabilitation process. In cases such as this, the helper should respect the person's religious beliefs and incorporate religion as much as possible. Incorporating religion may mean meeting with the client's religious leader (with the client's permission) to discuss how they may assist the client in meeting his goal of becoming rehabilitated.

Conclusion

Many African Americans' world views have been influenced by the manner in which they have been treated by the dominant culture. For example, older African Americans who experienced the period of segregation has his/her views influenced by strict separation of the African American and Euro-American races. In many instances, these experiences affect the level of trust the African American client will have in a Euro-American rehabilitation helping professional.

Discrimination associated with segregation resulted in unequal educational opportunities, high unemployment and underemployment of African Americans, particularly African American males. A combination of unequal educational opportunities and discrimination has resulted in many African

Americans being employed in jobs which are physically and/or environmentally hazardous; therefore, placing them in situations where injuries and disabilities frequently occur. The low income associated with these jobs, as well as public assistance at or below the substance level, often force African Americans to live in environments which put them at risk for acquiring disabilities. Additionally, the daily stress of attempting to support a family and educate children while underemployed and underpaid eventually leads to physical and/or emotional conditions that may warrant the assistance of a helping professional.

Many African American communities are attempting to address critical issues such as gangs, gang-related activities, and teen pregnancy. Gang violence and young girls cutting their formative years short through having babies are problems of monumental proportion that require the expertise of helping professionals. Rehabilitation helping professionals' expertise is needed when these situations go beyond being problems and become debilitating.

Because of these reasons, as well as many others, rehabilitation helping professionals will probably see increased numbers of African American clients. The rehabilitation specialist must assess the African American client from the prospective of being an African American with a disability instead of a client with a disability. This implies that some of the views and many of the experiences of African Americans will be different from those of Euro-Americans. Therefore, making judgements based upon Euro-American standards in many instances will decrease the chances of a successful rehabilitation plan. Likewise, understanding the world view of an African American client will increase the chances of a successful rehabilitation plan.

Review Questions

1. What, if any, are the benefits of a counselor/rehabilitation helping professional understanding the historical background of African Americans?
2. What impact is violence having on African American youth and what is the relevance of violence among African American youth to the area of rehabilitation?
3. To what do the following theories and concept relate: Poverty-Social Disorganization theory, Compulsive Masculinity theory, and Broken Promise concept?
4. What are some of the reasons African Americans have a high rate of disabilities?
5. Among African Americans, which has the highest rate of disabilities, males or females?

6. What are some of the negative stereotypes of African Americans and how can they impact the rehabilitation process?
7. Name the five stages of the Revised Cross Model of Black Identity and some of the implications for the rehabilitation process.
8. What does situational control mean and how does this affect the rehabilitation process?
9. How can the rehabilitation helping professional insure that the client's expectations of the rehabilitation process and his expectations are congruent?

Suggested Activities

1. Determine the number and/or percentage of African Americans living in your state.
2. Determine the percentage of your state's African American population that has disabilities.
3. Determine the five leading causes of disabilities of African Americans in your state.
4. Make a list of at least five agencies and/or organizations in your state that specialize in assisting African Americans. These organizations do not have to be connected to disabilities. Also, identify the type of services these organizations provide. This can be the beginning of a community service file that you can use as a rehabilitation helping professional.

References

Abzug, R. H. (1988). The black family during Reconstruction. Quoted in C. H. Mindel et al. (Eds.), *Ethnic families in America* (3rd ed.). Englewood Cliffs, NJ: Prentice-Hall.

Blassingame, J. (1972). *The slave community.* New York: Oxford University Press.

Carter, D. J., & Wilson, R. (1990). *Minorities in higher education—Ninth annual statistics report.* Washington, D.C.: American Council on Education.

Cazanave, N. (1979). Middle-income black fathers: An analysis of the provider role, the family coordinator, 28 (November) In C. H. Mindel et al. (Eds.), *Ethnic families in America.* (3rd ed.). Englewood Cliffs, NJ: Prentice-Hall.

Chenoweth, K. (1997). Phenomenal growth. *Black Issues in Higher Education, 14*(10):34–36, July 10.

Congressional Task Force on the Future of African Americans. (1989). *The future of African Americans to the year 2000.* Washington, D.C., p. 149.

Cross, Jr., W. E. (1971). The Negro-to-black conversion experience. *Black World, 20*:13–27.

Cross, Jr., W. E. (1995). The psychology of negriscence. In J. G. Ponterotto et al. (Eds.), *Handbook of multicultural counseling.* Thousand Oaks, CA: Sage.

Daneal, J. E. (1975). A definition of fatherhood as expressed by black fathers. Ph.D. Dissertation, University of Pittsburg. In C. H. Mindel et al. (Eds.), *Ethnic families in America* (3rd ed.). Engelwood Cliffs, NJ: Prentice-Hall.

Hale-Benson, J. E. (1988). *Black children: Their roots, culture and learning styles* (rev. ed.). Baltimore: Johns Hopkins University Press.

Helms, J. E. (1990). *Black and white racial identity.* Westport, CT: Greenwood Press.

Hill, R. (1972). *The strength of black families.* New York: Emerson Hall.

Hornor, L. L. (Ed.). (1998). *Black Americans: A statistical sourcebook* (1988 ed.). Palo Alto, CA: Information Publication.

Justiz, M. J., Wilson, R., & Bjork, L. G. (Eds.). (1994). *Minorities in higher education.* Phoenix, AZ: American Council on Education.

Lewis, D. R. (1975). The black family: Socialization and sex roles, Phylon 36 (Fall):221–237. In C. H. Mindel et al. (Eds.), *Ethnic families in America.* (3rd ed.). (1988), Englewood Cliffs, NJ: Prentice-Hall.

March of Dimes Teenage Pregnancy Fact Sheet. (1997). Http://www.noah.cuny. edu/pregnancy/marchofdimes/pre_preg.plan/teenfact.html.

Massey, D. S., & Eggers, M. L. (1990). The ecology of inequality: Minorities and the concentration of poverty, 1970-1980. *American Journal of Sociology, 95*(5):1153–1188, March.

1988 Commission on the Cities. *The Kerna Report updated, Race and Poverty in the United States Today.* Report of a National Conference, pp. 2–3, March 1, 1988.

Nystrom, J. (1996). Socioeconomic and environmental factors affecting the lives of African Americans. Unpublished paper. University of Oklahoma Health Sciences Center.

Parsons, T. (1947). Certain primary sources of aggression in the social structure of the western world. *Psychiatry, 10*:167–181.

Payne, N. J. (1994). Maintaining the competitive tradition: In M. J. Justiz et al. (Eds.), *Minorities in higher education.* Phoenix, AZ: Oryx Press.

Roe, A. (1956). *The psychology of occupations.* New York: John Wiley and Sons.

Scanzoni, J. (1971). The black family in modern society. In C. H. Mindel et al. (Eds.), *Ethnic families in America* (3rd ed.). Englewood Cliffs, NJ: Prentice-Hall.

Staples, R. (1988). The black American family. In C. H. Mindel et al. (Eds.), *Ethnic families in America* (3rd ed.). Englewood Cliffs, NJ: Prentice-Hall.

Sudarkasa, N. (1993). Female-headed African American households. In H. P. McAdoo (Ed.), *Family ethnicity.* Newbury Park, CA: Sage.

Sue, D. W., & Sue, D. (1990). *Counseling the culturally different* (2nd ed.). New York: John Wiley and Sons.

Thomas, C. W. (1971). *Boys no more.* Beverly Hills, CA: Glencoe.

U. S. Department of Commerce, Bureau of the Census. (1991). *America's black population, 1970 to 1990: A statistical review.* p. 129.

U. S. Department of Education: National center for educational statistics. High school completion rates: http://nces.ed.gov/pubs/dp95/97473-0.html.

U. S. Department of Health and Human Services. *Health, United States, 1989 and Prevention Profile,* p. 128.

U. S. Department of Health and Human Services. (1985). *Report of the secretary's task force on black and minority health. Volume 1: Executive Summary.* August, p. 101.

U. S. Department of Health and Human Services. (1985). *Report of the secretary's task on black and minority health, 1: Executive Summary,* August, p. 63.

Voss, H., & Hepburn, J. R. (1968). Patterns of criminal homicide in Chicago. *Journal of Criminal Law, Criminology, and Police Science, 59*:499–508.

Washington, E. M. (1996). A survey of the literature on theories and prevention of black male youth involvement in violence. *The Journal of Negro Education, 65*(4), Fall.

Wilson, R (1997). Quoted in Phenomenal growth. *Black Issues in Higher Education, 14*(10):34–36, July 10.

Wilson, R. (1994). The participation of African Americans in American higher education. In J. M. Justiz et al. (Eds.), *Minorities in higher education.* Phoenix, AZ: Oryx Press.

Suggested Readings

Cross, Jr., W. E. (1991). *Shades of black.* Philadelphia: Temple University Press.

Gutman, H. (1976). *The black family in slavery and freedom 1750–1925.* New York: Pantheon.

Helms, J. E. (1990). *Black and white racial identity.* Westport, CT: Greenwood Press.

Phinney, J. Stages of ethnic identity development in minority group adolescence. *Journal of Early Adolescence, 9*:34–49.

Ponterotto, J. G., & Pedersen, P. B. (1993). *Preventing prejudice: A guide for counselors and educators,* Newbury Park, CA: Sage.

Staples, R. The black American family. In C. H. Mindel et al. (Eds.), *Ethnic families in America: Patterns and variations* (3rd ed.). Englewood Cliffs, NJ: Prentice-Hall, pp. 303–324.

Sudarkasa, N. Female-headed African American households: Some neglected dimensions. In H. P. McAdoo (Ed.), *Family ethnicity: Strength in diversity.* Newbury Park, CA: Sage, pp. 81–89.

Chapter 8

DISABILITY AND ASIAN AND PACIFIC AMERICANS

Chapter Outline
• Historical Background
• Social Issues Impacting Asian and Pacific Americans
• Asian and Pacific Americans and Disability
• Economic and Employment Issues
• Educational Issues
• Family Dynamics
• Intervention
• Communication Style
• Expectation
• Value Orientation
• Conclusion

Chapter Objectives
• Identify specific historical events which have impacted the lives of Chinese, Japanese, Korean and Filipino Americans
• Identify the diversity of Asian and Pacific Americans
• Identify social, educational and economical issues which impact the lives of Asian Pacific Americans
• Identify how social, educational and economical issues impact the lives of Asian Pacific Americans with disabilities
• Identify the impact families have on the lives of Chinese, Japanese, Korean, and Filipino Americans with disabilities
• Identify critical cultural information of which rehabilitation helping professionals must be aware
• Provide suggestions with regard to ways of effectively working with Asian and Pacific Americans with disabilities

Historical Background

While Asian and Pacific Americans constitute slightly less than three (3) percent of the United States population, there has been a phenomenal growth of approximately 800 percent increase in the population over the past 35 years. Similar to the Hispanic/Latino ethnic group, Asian or Pacific Americans are not a homogeneous group. In fact, Asian or Pacific Americans are a much more diverse group than most Americans realize. The group consists of those whom we normally consider as Asian or Pacific Island countries such as China, Japan, Korea, and the Philippines. In addition there are a number of other countries included as Asian Pacific and they include India, Brunei, Burma, Indonesia, Malaysia, Bangladesh, Pakistan, Sri Lanka, Vietnam, Cambodia, Laos, Thailand, and there are others that could be named; however, the author's intent is to make the point of Asian and Pacific Americans as being a very diverse group of people. Once again, the author wishes to caution the reader not to overgeneralize by assuming that there is a single Asian and Pacific American culture. Unfortunately, space does not permit a discussion of each of the various subgroups that comprise the Asian and Pacific American ethnic group. Because of the aforementioned limitation, most of the discussion will relate to the subgroups of Chinese Americans, Filipino Americans, Japanese Americans, and Korean Americans. Books and journal articles will be listed in the suggested reading section of this chapter which will provide the reader with information regarding some of those subgroups not extensively covered.

Similar to the debate as to exactly when and under what conditions Africans first tread water and walked on American soil, it is unclear as to the date and circumstances surrounding Asian Pacific Islanders' entry into America. Cordova (1983) contends that in the 1760s a few natives of the Philippines removed themselves from a Spanish merchant ship in Louisiana and found their way to what is now New Orleans. Similarly, Jensen (1988) contends that during this same period a few, Asian Indians were delivered as indentured servants to the East Coast of America. While these accounts are probably based upon documented facts, the official beginning of Asian and Pacific immigration to the United States began in the 1840s and Rowena Fong (1992) lets us know that there was a variety of reasons for the immigration: political freedom, economic advancement, personal aspirations, and/or family pressure.

Chinese Americans Historical Background

The Chinese were the first of the Asian Pacific subgroups to immigrate to the United States in significant numbers. The discovery of gold in the

Sacramento Valley attracted the attention of many groups, both domestic and international. In addition to seeking their fortunes in the gold fields of California, many Chinese helped build the transcontinental railroad.

There has been some debate with regard to the intent of many of the Chinese immigrants; some say most of the early immigrants came as sojourners, meaning they intended to return to China, and those proponents point out that the majority of these immigrants were males who, if they were married, had left their families behind. On the other hand, some researchers indicate that the immigrants' intentions were to send for their families after they had secured enough money to establish a home in America. Whatever the intent, it is clear that they came to take advantage of the employment opportunities that were available in America. In the early days of immigration, while they were not exactly welcomed by the frontiersmen, they were accepted because they were a source of cheap labor particularly to mine and railroad owners. In the last 1860s, circumstances began to change and Sue and Sue (1990) inform us that a series of business recessions, coupled with the completion of the Union-Central Pacific Railroad, began to create competition for jobs. Morrison Wong (1995) adds to our understanding of the attitudes being displayed at that time by Euro-Americans regarding Chinese immigrants by pointing out that xenophobic and racist attitudes begin to be common among the general population which caused considerable anti-Asian feelings. Rowena Fong (1992) succinctly places the Euro-Americans' self-serving views in perspective as she states, "The main complaint was that Chinese immigrants worked too hard for wages that were too low and thereby undercut the wages of Euro-American workers."

A result of this anti-Chinese sentiment was physical violence against Chinese people such as the riot in Los Angeles's, Chinatown that Sandermeyer (1973) described, or the physical attack upon Chinese immigrants in Rock Spring, Wyoming that was outlined by Kitano (1969). Additionally, laws that were detrimental to Chinese people were being passed throughout the United States such as the 1853 California Foreign Miner's Tax which imposed a tax on noncitizen miners. In 1870, San Francisco implemented a Cubic Air Ordinance which was designed to eliminate large numbers of Chinese sleeping in a single room together. In 1852, California levied a $50 per head tax on each Chinese arriving ship passenger. In 1882, the United States Congress passed the Chinese Exclusion Act which Morrison Wong (1995) describes as "the first and only immigration act to specifically designate an ethnic, racial or nationality group for exclusion." Wong provides further information with regard to the Act in these comments, "The act prohibited all Chinese laborers, whether skilled or unskilled from entering the United States for ten years. All other Chinese entering the United States had to have identification certificates issued by the Chinese government. The Chinese Exclusion Act was extended by the U. S. Congress for another ten years with the 1892 Geary Act, and in 1902, Congress passed legislation that made permanent the exclusion of immigration of Chinese persons. Not until the 1943 Magnuson Act was passed by the United States Congress was the Chinese Exclusion Act of 1882 effectively repealed."

Because of the early discrimination Chinese immigrants faced, coupled with the lack of protection from harm received from local, state, and/or federal authorities, Chinese individuals and families banned together for self-protection and survival. This resulted in the development of what we now call Chinatowns. In addition, other Chinese organizations such as Chinese Consolidated Benevolent Association were formed to maintain Chinese culture and serve as a voice for the Chinese people to the Euro-American authority structure (Fong 1992). There has been several other legislative acts since the 1943 repeal of the Chinese Exclusion Act which have impacted Chinese immigration to the United States. Perhaps the greatest impact has occurred as a result of the 1965 Immigration Act which lifted many of the immigration quotas and according to Morrison Wong (1995), "By abolishing the national origins system, this act became the first immigration policy that practiced the principles of racial equality." The Immigration Act of 1965 was amended in 1981 which also had the effect of increasing Chinese immigration.

According to the U. S. Census Bureau 2004 report, the Chinese population in America exceeds 4,000,000. An important fact for helping professionals to remember about the Chinese population is that a significant number of this population is first and second generation immigrants. This is an important fact, especially from the standpoint of acculturation, values, education, socialization, and customs. More discussion of these and other factors will be presented later in this chapter.

Japanese Americans Historical Background

Following the immigration efforts of the Chinese were the Japanese; however, as Rowena Fong (1992) reminds us, the Japanese government attempted to avoid some of the pitfalls that the Chinese immigrants encountered by screening the Japanese men who were to immigrate to the United States. Once in the states the Japanese government would consult with the U. S. government on behalf of Japanese immigrants. The first large immigration of Japanese occurred in the 1880s as Malays were recruited and contracted to work in the Hawaiian sugar cane fields. As a result, the Japanese eventually became the largest ethnic minority on the Hawaiian Islands. In the 1890s, Japanese began to arrive on the U. S. mainland, primarily in California, to work the farm fields and the gold mines.

Similar to what had happened to the Chinese, the Japanese began to experience prejudice and discrimination, especially from Euro-American workers. Some Euro-American workers began to advocate violent actions to exclude Japanese from working. In part to avoid confrontation beginning in 1900, President Theodore Roosevelt and the Japanese government developed what was called a "Gentleman's Agreement" which in simple terms restricted the immigration of Japanese for the purpose of being a laborer. This agreement was renewed in 1905 and in 1908.

Setsuko Nishi (1995) reminds us that in 1924, the Oriental Exclusion Act was passed which had the effect of virtually stopping Japanese immigration for the next thirty years. In 1952, immigration of Japanese began again with the passage of the McCarren-Walter Immigration Act. The next major immigration of Japanese came as a result of the passage of the 1965 Immigration Act.

Without a doubt, the most devastating insult to Japanese Americans was the collecting and virtually imprisoning of over one hundred thousand persons after the government of Japanese attacked Pearl Harbor in 1941. These Japanese American citizens were taken from their homes, supposedly out of fear they would aid the Japanese government, although they were American citizens and had no loyalty to the Japanese government. This act has had a tremendous psychological impact upon Japanese Americans which is felt even today. This is a fact to which rehabilitation and other helping professionals should be aware. More discussion will occur later in the chapter.

Filipino Americans Historical Background

The second largest population of Asian or Pacific American subgroup is Filipino Americans. Currently their population count exceeds two million. As mentioned at the beginning of the chapter, persons from the Philippine Islands may have been the first Asian Pacific persons to come to the United States. Pauline Agbayani-Siewert and Linda Revilla, (1995) using Cordova (1983) and Espina (1982) work as documentation, propose that "the first Filipino settlements in the United States began in the late eighteenth century," when Filipinos escaped from Spanish ships and found their way to Louisiana.

There is a significant Spanish influence in most Filipino heritage as a result of Spain's colonization of the Philippines for over 300 years. Thus, the majority of Filipinos are of the Catholic faith. Spain's rule of the Philippine Islands ended as they were defeated by America in the Spanish-American war. At the end of this war, the Philippine government declared itself as an independent nation, which lead to the Philippine-American War, or as the American government preferred to label it, the Philippine Insurrection.

The Philippine Islands became an American colony after losing the insurrection/war, thus making Filipino persons U.S. nationals with the right to open entry into the United States. The period of America's colonization of the Philippines continued until 1946 when the country was granted its independence.

Agbayani-Siewert and Revilla (1995) separate the Filipino immigration to the United States into two waves–the first came as a result of the U.S. Congress passing the 1903 Pensionado Act which, according to those authors, "Provided support to send young Filipinos to the United States for education on American life." They further pointed out that many of this group returned to the Philippines after they had completed their education. The second wave consisted primarily of Filipinos immigrating to the U.S. to work. They were often recruited as cheap labor in Hawaii, Alaska, and in the western United States.

Rowena Fong (1992) provides an idea of where Filipino individuals worked in the United States with the following comments:

> As Japanese and Korean labor immigration ended about 1905, Hawaiian plantation owners began to look elsewhere for cheap workers. Like the Chinese and Japanese laborers, the Filipinos were persuaded by sugar plantation owners to go to Hawaii and work under contract. In 1907, 150 Filipinos were sent to Hawaii. Others soon arrived on the mainland and the Filipinos became successors to Chinese and Japanese in western farms and canneries. They numbered about 100,000 from the 1930s through the 1950s, with about equal numbers on the mainland and in Hawaii. Besides working on farms and in canneries, Filipinos also worked as cooks and did domestic labor.

Although Filipinos were United States nationals, they also experienced discrimination. Sue and Sue (1990) reports Filipino immigrants experienced discrimination from labor unions led by the American Federation of Labor who espoused the idea that Filipinos were cheap labor lowering the standard of living for Euro-American workers. In addition, Fong (1992) points out that there was physical violence such as a mob attack on a California Filipino club, including beatings and one murder.

Despite the hardships imposed by violence and discriminatory behavior, Filipinos continued to immigrate to the United States. Besides economic opportunities, there are primarily two reasons Filipinos immigrated to the United States and continue to do so–one, because of the Unites States' early colonial involvement, most Filipinos have a good understanding and feel comfortable with many U.S. customs and values; and two, because of the U.S. military presence in the area, Filipinos marry service personnel and become United States citizens.

Korean Americans Historical Background

The noted Asian Pacific American scholar Pyong Gap Min (1995) divides Korean immigration to the United States into three distinct periods: Old immigration (pioneer period), intermediate period, and new immigration. The dissection of Korean's migration to the U.S. into these three periods provides an excellent overview of the reasons behind their immigration to the United States:

Old Immigration (1903–1905): Similar to many Chinese and Japanese immigrants, the first Koreans appear to have immigrated to Hawaii to work on the sugar plantations. During the early 1900s to 1905, professor Min informs us that a modest number of Koreans were recruited by the sugar plantation owners to replace Japanese workers who had moved to California or were engaged in strikes or work stoppages. This period of immigration ended partly because the Korean government halted immigration from Korea upon suspicion that Koreans in America were being mistreated and partly because of pressure applied by the Japanese government. Upon winning the Russo-Japanese War, Korea became a colony of Japan in a sense, which afforded the Japanese government considerable control over Korea's affairs.

Intermediate Period (1950–1965): There appears to have been two major groups of immigrants during this period. First group were brides of U.S. servicemen who were stationed in South Korea during the Korean War and the second group were orphans of the Korean War. Soldiers adopted children who had lost both parents as a result of the war. According to Min (1995) later non-military U.S. Citizens began to adopt Korean orphans.

New Immigration (1965–Present): As was the case in increases in Chinese and Japanese immigration, the 1965 Immigration and Naturalization Act has had the greatest impact upon increasing Korean immigration.

Social Issues Impacting Asian and Pacific Americans

Collectively, Asian and Pacific Americans have been characterized by the mass media as the "model minority." With this title those that subscribe to this belief are saying that Asian and Pacific Americans have either reached or succeeded the national median of indicators which are often used as measures of success in America such as income and education to mention only two. The overall concept is that Asian and Pacific Americans have been discriminated against similar to other ethnic and racial minorities in America and have overcome this hideous stumbling block and achieved the "American dream."

The distinguished authors Derald Sue and David Sue (1990) take exception to this characterization of Asian and Pacific Americans but point out that at first glance this concept of the successful minority appears to have validity. They allude to the fact that the Chinese, Japanese and Filipinos have either equaled or exceeded the national median income and with regard to education, collectively the Asian and Pacific American subgroups complete a higher median number of grades than all other groups in America. Additionally, Asian or Pacific Americans appear to be better accepted by Euro-Americans than the other ethnic, racial minority groups in that interracial marriage between Asian or Pacific Americans and Euro-Americans appears to be more acceptable than any other ethnic racial group. Stated more succinctly, the "social distance" (prejudice and discrimination) seem to be less than for the other groups. Finally, Sue and Sue tell us that a variety of studies show that Asian and Pacific Americans demonstrate very few problems in areas such as juvenile delinquency and psychiatric disorders which serve as indicators of good mental health. All of these things taken together seem to indicate a minority group which has made a successful adjustment to life in America despite having to deal with prejudice and discrimination.

As previously stated, Derald and David Sue do not subscribe to the concept of model minority. Other authors and scholars Min (1995), Tsukada (1988), Wong (1982), Cabezas et al. (1987), and Toji and Johnson (1992) also take exception to the media-made concept of model minority. As one analyzes some of the areas previously mention as proof of the successful or model minority concept, one obtains a better perspective as to Asian and Pacific American life in America.

As previously stated, those who subscribe to the idea that Asian and Pacific Americans are a model minority point to the fact that their median family income exceeds that of Euro-Americans. However, upon close observation, the primary reason for this is in many cases that there are more wage earners in the Asian or Pacific American family than in the Euro-American family. Additionally, authors such as Wong (1982), Cabezas et al. (1987), and Tsukada (1988) convincingly argue that despite the educational attainment and/or training, Asian and Pacific Americans' labor positions and salary received is less than Euro-Americans with comparable education and training. In other words, Asian and Pacific Americans experience similar, glass ceilings and prejudicial career path blocks as other ethnic, racial minorities.

Sue and Sue (1990) continue to debunk the model minority myth by eluding to the fact that from an educational standpoint, many Asian and Pacific Americans continue to experience difficulty with English. They refer to a finding of Watanabe (1976) which indicates that some Asians who have lived in the United States for several generations continue to have difficulty mastering the English language.

While some may point to the ethnic gatherings that have produced Chinatowns, Japantowns, etc. as economic success, they too frequently forget that these areas came into existence as effort to avoid prejudice, discrimination, and violence. Additionally, as Sue and Sue (1998) remind us, some of these areas represent ghetto areas with prevalent unemployment, poverty, health problems, and juvenile delinquency.

In addition to misrepresenting the life situation of many Asian and Pacific Americans, other potentially damaging effects are (1) Possible resentment by other ethnic and racial minority groups toward Asian and Pacific Americans. By stating that Asian Pacific Americans have overcome all obstacles placed in their paths, this is implying that other minority groups could do the same if they had the motivation and determination to do so. (2) Denial of services to Asian Pacific Americans. Because of the positive stereotype, public officials and other policy makers may tend to exclude Asian and Pacific Americans from things such as Health and Human Service assistance programs and federal student financial aid for needy and/or underrepresented students to mention only two. (3) Hurh and Kim (1982) argue that as Asian and Pacific Americans begin to believe the concept of being a model minority, they began to develop "false consciousness," thinking they have attained middle-class status, failing to recognize that they are underemployed and over-worked.

Asian and Pacific Americans and Disabilities

Although the Asian and Pacific American population trails African Americans and Hispanic/Latino, they are one of the fastest growing ethnic minority groups in America. To illustrate, the 2000 U. S. Census Bureau count indicated that Asians were 3.6 percent of the U. S. population, four years later in 2004 the population had increased to 4.2 percent. The population growth of Asian and Pacific Americans is expected to continue to grow well into the twenty-first century.

With regard to disabilities, Asian and Pacific Americans have the lowest rate of disabilities among the racial/ethnic minorities of African Americans, Hispanic/Latino, and American Indians. Also they have the lowest rate of severe disabilities .

Economic and Employment Issues

As previously stated, the Asian and Pacific American median income is greater than the national average which gives the appearance of a highly economically successful group. A growing number of researchers and knowledgeable authorities with regard to Asian Pacific affairs indicate the economic success is an illusion in that the income figures are quite often generated by more family members than what generates the family income of Euro-Americans. Because economists and others have viewed the family income of Asian Pacific Americans as being above average, very little research exists to identify the standard of living these families experience.

Beth Hess and her associates (1995) discuss the economic position of Asian and Pacific Americans from the standpoint of their preparation for an entry into business, particularly businesses which they own. The authors point out that among Chinese Americans, the clustering together to form the Chinatowns has had a mixed blessing. On one hand, it has provided employment and a basis for bank and mortgage loans for new businesses and homes; however, on the other hand, they argue, for many of those who do not remove themselves from the Chinatown environment, especially new immigrants, they tend to live in poverty and are exploited at work. They continue by emphasizing that local merchants quite often become targets for groups of young Asians involved in the protection racket as well as drugs, gambling, and prostitution. With regard to the Japanese Americans, it appears they have become more diversified as they have become more socially mobile, moving into mid-level management jobs, particularly in the electronics and engineering areas.

With respect to the other Asian Pacific subgroups, Hess and her colleagues (1995) have this to say:

> In contrast, Asians from the Indian subcontinent entered the United States with educational credentials and technical skills and have found their economic foothold in the pharmaceutical industry and health-care facilities. Although they, too, have experienced discrimination, their economic success allows greater choice of where to live. Recent arrivals, from the Philippine Islands are also relatively well educated, with professional degrees in medicine, law and engineering, even though most have had to settle for less prestigious jobs. Immigrants from Korea lack the educational background of the Asian Indians and Filipinos, but compensate with a powerful commitment to self-employment for the entire family. Koreans have been successful in operating small grocery stores in urban neighborhoods, although this often brings them into conflict with other minority groups resentful of the Korean's presence.

This summary supports the idea that many Asian and Pacific Americans either come to the United States well prepared or prepare themselves for prestigious jobs but often discover that because of bias and discrimination, they are both underemployed and underpaid. Therefore, despite the myth of the model minority, Asian and Pacific Americans continue to experience discrimination in the workplace which has an impact upon their ability to earn so that their standard of living will be equal to their personal efforts.

Education Issues

The concept of model minority appears to permeate all aspects of Asian Pacific Americans' lives and education certainly is no exception. Bob Suzuki (1994) discusses the impact with the following comments:

> Due to the model minority stereotype, to even suggest that serious problems exist for Asians in higher education may seem to border on the absurd to many people, especially educators. Asian Pacific Americans, both students and faculty, are viewed as "overrepresented" in higher education in comparison with their proportion in the general population.

To be objective, let's look at both sides of the issue, why Asian and Pacific Americans appear to be successful and what are their strengths and what are their problems within the education area.

Strengths

• Asian and Pacific Americans' parents place considerable emphasis on education; therefore, many Asian and Pacific students are well prepared academically.

• A large percentage of Asian and Pacific Americans take college preparatory courses in the public schools.

• Because of the type of courses many Asian Pacific students take in elementary, middle, and high school, they are well prepared in analytical thinking which is the basis for many standardized tests.

• A larger proportion of Asian Pacific students take the Scholastic Aptitude Test (SAT) than students in general (HSIA 1988).

Weaknesses

• As Suzuki (1994) points out, the statistics on Asian and Pacific Americans with regard to enrollment into college would suggest that Asian Pacific students have no problem with gaining entry into U.S. colleges and universities, he indicates that this is true for some of the subgroups such as Chinese and Japanese, but for others as the southeast Asians and Filipinos, they in fact may be underrepresented.

• The return (salary) on the educational investment does not equal their Euro-American counterparts.

Family Dynamics

Because of their diversity, it would be a significant mistake to attempt a summarization of all Asian Pacific families by generalizing specific principles and values that this or any other author feels the various subgroups have in common. Therefore, I shall discuss each of the Asian Pacific American subgroups of Chinese American, Japanese American, Korean American, and Filipino American separately.

Chinese American Families

Since most of the current Chinese Americans are desendents of those first Chinese people to immigrate to America in the mid-1800s, a glimpse of the traditional Chinese family provides a foundation for understanding current behaviors. In particular, according to Morrison Wong (1988), we should look at customs that continue to influence Chinese Americans' lives as well as the degree to which the current generation has deviated from them by accepting Western values. Some of the traditional Chinese family dynamics are as follows:

- Extended kinship groups;
- Patriarchal—father and eldest son had the dominant roles in the family;
- Patrilocal, the married couple lived with the husband's parents;
- Filal Piety (respect) considered of paramount importance—The family came first; therefore, family obligations were more important than individual accomplishments;
- Arranged marriages.

As previously stated these were the roots which anchored the traditional Chinese family. Next, let's look at the modern Chinese American family dynamics. Wong (1988) separates the modern Chinese American family into two groups. The first is characterized by Lucy Huang (1981) and Evelyn Glenn (1983) as "dual worker family." The second is the middle class, white collar or professional Chinese American family.

The dual working family is generally represented by the Chinese who came to the United States and settled in Chinatowns. Some of the characteristics of the dual working family, according to Huang (1981) and Glenn (1983), are as follows:

- Both husband and wife are employed as craftsmen, laborers or service workers;
- Both husband and wife are coequals as wage earners;

- Because both parents work, they and the children are frequently separated; in fact, the parents may work different shifts, thus having little time together.

The middle class or professional Chinese American family may be characterized as follows:

1. Having earned enough money to move away from Chinatown and live in suburbs;
2. View themselves as more American than Chinese, according to Lucy Huang (1981), Harry Kitano (1985), and Melford Weiss (1970);
3. Highly educated;
4. Semi extended family structure (family members such as parents and grandparents) do not live with them but live close.

Father's Role: Similar to the traditional Chinese family, the father is the primary authority figure. He may maintain respect and authority over the family in a manner that appears to be emotionally distant to persons who are acculturated to Western standards.

Mother's Role: As in most American families, the mother is responsible for the children. While according to Wong (1988) she decides what is best for the children, gives them commands, and the children are expected to obey.

Child-Rearing Practices:

1. Public displays of affection is considered poor taste;
2. Independence and maturity are stressed early in the child's life;
3. Aggressive behavior is not condoned among siblings and young children, according to Richard Sollenberger (1968);
4. Older children are responsible for assisting young children in social activities and learning appropriate social behavior, according to Lucy Huang (1981);
5. Education is highly valued;
6. Control of children is often handled by the "sense of shame," as it is dishonorable to bring shame upon the family.

Japanese American Family

The various generations of Japanese Americans have been classified as Issei (first generation), Nisei (second generation), Sansei (third generation), and Yonsei (fourth generation).

Issei (First Generation): Issei constitute the first group of Japanese to immigrate to America. As stated earlier, most of this group were laborers contracted to work in the Hawaiian sugar cane fields and later migrated to the west coast of the contiguous United States to work on the railroads, canneries, and as farm laborers. Since the Issei represents the first group of Japanese immigrants, those who are alive are elderly. The purpose in mentioning them, other than to recognize them as the Japanese pioneers in America, is to establish that they represent the beginning of the Japanese American family.

The majority of the first generation of Japanese Americans came as bachelors with the intent of making their fortune and returning to Japan to establish a family. Some did; however, many stayed in America. Because there were laws against Japanese marrying Euro-American women, many who remained in America selected their Japanese wives from pictures who became known as "picture brides."

Sylvia Yanagisako (1985) contributes to our understanding of the early Japanese family as she informs us that as a result of the way the Issei selected brides, the families of the bride and groom were closely associated with all stages of the marriage. Therefore, the traditional Japanese kinship bond reached into America.

The early research of Frank Miyamoto (1939) identified what he considered four aspects of the Japanese family system which, to a large extent, characterized Japanese life that has been passed down from the first generation (Issei) to succeeding generations:

1. The concept of the Japanese community as one large family in which family norms are reinforced by the community;

2. Patriarchal family organizational structure which emphasizes male dominance;

3. Primogeniture and adoption family system, which means the family property and other valuables as well as family power and control flows to the eldest son;

4. Family customs such as marriage, anniversaries, and holidays are celebrated, thus playing a significant role in the social and cultural life of the Japanese.

Another important fact to remember about the first generation is that they and their children were the group placed in the internment campus during World War II. Without doubt, this had an impact upon the emotional and psychological development of both generations and subsequent generations as the memories of the event is passed along to them.

Nisei (Second Generation): There is a wide age range among the Nisei group, some are elderly and others are in their middle-age years. Because of the age range, some Nisei spent time in the internment campus while others were born after the war ended. According to Leonard Broom and John Kitsuse (1956), one can easily recognize the difference between those who spent time in the campus versus those who had spent their adolescent years in a much freer environment.

One begins to see the beginning of the effects of acculturation on Japanese Americans in the second generation, which according to Kitano and his associates (1984) conflicts between the first and second generations were common. The Issei was of the opinion that the Nisei were too quickly becoming Americanized, thus turning their backs on Japanese traditions.

Nisei families represent a variety of cultural models. The wide age range and degree of the Issei's influence determined whether the second generation continued with the conservative Japanese family tradition or whether they gravitated toward the American family norms.

Sansei (Third Generation) and Yonsei (Fourth Generation): These generations have had more exposure to American life than the previous generations; therefore, it is understandable that each subsequent generation has become more acculturated. Harry Kitano (1988) provides the following excellent summarization of current Japanese American family characteristics. He concludes:

1. There is a continuity from the first to the second and to succeeding generations.
2. Certain cultural styles have been retained including enryo (preference for ethnic peers), close family ties, ethnic celebrations, and high educational expectations. The retention of and changes in various cultural elements vary by family in terms of size, socialization, area of residence, influence of the ethnic community, and contact with the dominant community.
3. The most dramatic change in Japanese American families is that of out-of-group marriage. Sansei out-of-group marriage rates of over 60 percent may mean the eventual demise of a monolithic ethnic community.
4. Most Sansei families are similar to American models. However, there are some three-generation households, ensuring that the old ways are not completely forgotten.

Filipino American

Filipino Americans are excellent examples of why we should not aggregate Asian and Pacific Americans and generalize their cultures into one Asian Pacific culture. For example, traditional Filipino cultural values and beliefs not only encourage but expect women to work outside the home which is contrary to some other Asian Pacific subgroups. Also, the Filipino traditional marital relationship is rooted in egalitarian principles. Pido (1986) reminds us that Filipino women share most aspects of family responsibilities more equally with males than do most other Asian Pacific groups. Finally, the Filipino family is structured differently than some of the other Asian Pacific subgroups in that the power and authority flows differently. In many other Asian Pacific subgroups, the elders maintain considerable control over younger family members; whereas within Filipino tradition, the elderly are respected, but they do not continue to exert control.

Pauline Agbayani-Siewert and Linda Revilla (1995) increase our understanding of Filipino family characteristics with the following:

1. Open displays of anger or aggression are discouraged; whereas, displays of passive cooperative behavior are encouraged.
2. Family structure is more egalitarian than patriarchal.
3. Regardless of whether the relationship is by blood or fictive, kinship is highly regarded.
4. Fictive relations are incorporated into the family through the compadre (co-parent) system. Once accepted as a family member the individual is treated as blood kin.
5. Kinship takes precedence over persons outside the group. When a kinship member is threatened, the family will rally around the individual to provide protection and support.

Korean Family

Noted scholars of Asian Pacific American cultures such as Min (1995), Hurh and Kim (1984), Reitz (1980), and Yinger (1980) contend that Korean Americans have a higher level of ethnic attachment than most other Asian Pacific American groups. In essence, this implies that Korean Americans maintain and practice a considerable portion of their traditional culture. Pyong Gap Min (1995) provides three reasons for this strong ethnic attachment:

1. South Korea is a small culturally homogeneous country which has only one racial group that speaks the same language. This homogeneity means cultural rituals are virtually practiced by everyone and is reinforced from generation to generation.
2. Most Koreans are affiliated with Korean ethnic churches. Therefore, religious beliefs and practices are transferred generationally. Additionally, the church serves as a center for social activities. Thus, more than religious principles are conveyed.
3. The propensity to own and operate small businesses creates the ability to hire persons from their cultural group and in a sense maintain a mini-community of persons with similar cultural beliefs and backgrounds.

Considering the very strong ethnic ties to the traditional Korean culture one may conclude that the Korean families are very conservative and tradition-bound. This is evident by the low divorce rate, low percentage of female-headed families, and in general a more stable family structure than Euro-American families as well as some of the other ethnic minority groups. Additionally, Korean families tend to be traditional in their approach to children showing respect to their elders. However, as Korean Americans become more acculturated, we begin to view some acceptance of American culture. More specifically, according to Min (1995), in Korea, the wife is expected to remain in the home and be a full-time homemaker; however, in America, more Korean females work outside the home. Again, referencing the work of Min, three factors contribute to this:

1. The economic reality of living in America often dictates that the family needs the income of both husband and wife.

2. The salaries in America are seven to eight times greater than in Korea, which makes the American work force very attractive to Korean women. It is obvious that both the husband and wife see an opportunity to "get ahead" financially with two incomes.

3. Living in America has caused a change in Korean's attitudes with regard to gender roles.

Child-Rearing Practices:

1. Older Korean parents tend to be more authoritarian than Korean parents born and reared in America.

2. Korean parents place a high premium on education.

3. Punishment of children may appear to be more harsh than Euro-American standards.

4. Respect for others, especially elderly, is strongly emphasized.

Intervention

Level of Acculturation

It cannot be overstated that because of the diversity of Asian and Pacific Americans (at least 32 distinct ethnic or cultural groups) one should not generalize Asian Pacific cultures into one culture. In analyzing these cultures, the rehabilitation helping professional must take into consideration whether the client was foreign-born or born in the United States. Additionally, he must be aware of the generation the client represents because, as was discussed earlier in this chapter, the acculturation level probably will be different depending upon how long the person has been in America and the cultural generation he represents. Moreover, if the client is third or fourth generation that was reared in America, the helper must be cognizant of the environment in which the person was reared. As an example, a fourth generation Korean American who was reared in a Korean ethnic community probably will be less acculturated to the dominant culture standards than fourth generation Korean reared in suburban America. Frederick Leong (1986) contends that the more Asian Pacific Americans are acculturated to Western standards, the better they respond to counseling.

When working with some Asian and Pacific Americans, it is helpful to also determine the level of acculturation of the parents, if applicable. Because some groups, particularly Chinese, Japanese, and Korean, continue to respect the father's authority as the head of the family (regardless of whether the children are adults and married), therefore his level of acculturation will affect the client's actions.

Communication Style

Acculturation level also impacts communication style. The more an Asian or Pacific American identifies with Western culture, the greater the chance he will exhibit communication patterns that are similar to the dominant culture. Relatedly, the fact that Asian and Pacific Americans are such a diverse group and considering there can be tremendous variations within the group, the rehabilitation professional helper must put forth extra efforts to determine what, if any, influence cultural generation has on communication. As an example, a second generation Chinese American, as Fong Chan et al. (1988) point out, may have been taught by his parents to show respect to authority figures by not speaking until being spoken to; therefore, he may appear to be quiet and shy. The reality is that it is not a matter of being non-communicative but a matter of how he has been reared.

In addition to communication style from the standpoint of being verbal or non-verbal, the rehabilitation helper working with Asian and Pacific Americans has to be aware of language barriers, particularly if English is a second language for the client.

Expectation

Knowledgeable scholars of Asian Pacific American cultures, Chan et al. (1988), Sue and Sue (1990), Leung and Sakata (1988), and Ho (1987), inform us that with regard to mental health settings such as counseling, some Asian and Pacific Americans have quite a different expectation of the therapy process than many Euro-American clients. To be more specific, first they may be very reluctant to see a counselor because in their minds emotional issues are symptoms of physical problems, thus they may have difficulty in understanding and accepting the idea that "talk therapy" will provide a solution to their problems. Second, when they are seen by a counselor, they view him as "the authority," thus they may expect the professional helper to provide answers rather than pose questions. Given these concerns the rehabilitation professional helper would be wise to determine the client's perception of what is to occur between the two of them. An accurate understanding will allow the professional helper to explain what is to happen and also adjust his technique(s) to be more relevant to the client's understanding and expectations. This is not to say that the rehabilitation counselor has to completely change his approach, but it may very well be necessary to make some adjustments.

Value Orientation

Gargi Sodowsky et al. (1995) identify what they consider as core values of U.S. Asian groups. These values emphasize personality traits such as silence, nonconfrontation, moderation in behavior, self-control, patience, humility, modesty, and simplicity. Douglas Chung (1992) also adds to our understanding of Asian Pacific value orientation by identifying differences in Western culture which is pragmatic and individualistic in contrast to Eastern culture which is considered to be more idealistic and collective. Basically, this implies that some people influenced by Eastern cultures view group goals or the good of the group more important than individual accomplishments; therefore, working together is highly valued. These are important facts rehabilitation professional helpers would be well advised to remember when developing plans of action for some Asian Pacific Americans. As an example, a rehabilitation counselor working with a Chinese American client on vocational plans after his physical rehabilitation will probably be more successful if he includes the client's significant others and couch the vocational goals in terms of how his new occupation will be of benefit to both him and his family.

Social harmony, social control, and self-control appear to be the essence of Eastern cultures and they are anchored in family relationships. These points take us to the next area of assessment, situational control.

Sodowsky et al. (1995) provide us with information with respect to how social harmony, social control, and self-control are such an integral part of many Asian and Pacific American's lives.

Social harmony is achieved through structured family relationships that have clearly defined codes of behavior, including language usage and hierarchical roles. Some of these formal relationships are those of father and son, husband and wife, older brother/sister and younger brother/sister, grandparent and grandchild, and uncle/aunt and nephew/niece.

Filial piety, especially that of the eldest son, is the cornerstone of morality. Family identity is characterized by the interdependence of individual members, by individual members seeking the honor and good name of the family and protecting it from shame and by reciprocal duties and obligations that take precedence over individual desires.

Social control is obtained through demands for obedience and fulfillment of obligations. If these behaviors are not observed, the principal techniques of punishment employed by the family are arousing moral guilt and making the morally reprehensible person lose face through social/public shame.

Considering these facts, the family serves as a major influence within the lives of many Asian or Pacific Americans. Rehabilitation helping professionals cannot ignore this fact and after assessing the person for controlling factors within her life, he determines that indeed the family influence is significant he as the professional helper must bring the family into the rehabilitation plan. In fact, the helping professional may have to exercise control on his part as the client takes time to discuss and perhaps receive the approval of the appropriate family members with regard to aspects of the plan. In counseling situations where issues of mental and/or emotional problems are at the heart of the therapy, the professional helper must keep in mind the issue of not bringing shame to the family. To discuss issues of mental or emotional problems outside of the family and especially without the permission of the appropriate family members may be difficult if not impossible for some clients to do. In situations such as this, the professional helper must encourage the client to discuss his feelings about disclosing sensitive information and ask him what would make him feel comfortable enough to engage in conversation. Offers to consult with the client's family (with his permission) may resolve the impass. If the client refuses the offer and does not offer any solution, the professional helper has two choices: offer to refer the client, perhaps to someone with a similar cultural background, or explain to the client, given the circumstance, it appears no further progress can be made and the therapeutic relationship must be terminated. If this is to be done, the professional helper should provide the client with information on how to resume the therapy with him. Additionally, the client should be given the name of other helping professionals he can contact if he desires to again engage himself in therapy.

Conclusion

Most helping professionals know that Asian and Pacific Americans are a diverse group of people but often are treated as a homogeneous group. The fact that too often we think of Korean Americans as having the same cultural values as Filipino Americans causes helping professionals to react to them in a professional helping relationship similarly. This approach, coupled with the judgment made by using a Euro-American cultural yardstick, has caused a lack of return to the helping relationship after the first visit. As a result, the high rate of "no shows" clearly establishes that something is wrong with the helping professional system's approach to working with Asian or Pacific Americans.

An additional problem in working with Asian and Pacific Americans is created by the perception of them as the "model minority." While this title may be intended to be complimentary, it creates a false impression of Asian and Pacific Americans as a group of people who have no problems. They are considered to be above the United States averages for educational achievement and economic standards. Additionally, they are viewed as having a social network which takes care of its own, thus solving any problems that may confront them. These perceptions too frequently cause responsible agencies and organizations to overlook mental and emotional problems created by discrimination, poverty, and an unequal return on their educational investments.

The rehabilitation helping professional must become aware of the cultural background of the Asian and Pacific American subgroup with which he is working. Knowledge of level of acculturation as well as the significant influences on the person's life will provide valuable guidance with regard to strategies of assisting the client in the rehabilitation process.

Review Questions

1. Why have Asian and Pacific Americans been described as a "model minority?"
2. Identify some of the flaws in the concept of Asian and Pacific Americans as the model minority.
3. What do Issei, Nisei, Sansei and Yonsi mean?
4. Is the rate of disabilities among Asian and Pacific Americans high or low?
5. What are some Chinese cultural variables that may affect the rehabilitation process? How should the rehabilitation helping professional react to them?
6. What are some Japanese cultural variables that may affect the rehabilitation process? How should the rehabilitation helping professional react to them?
7. What are some Korean cultural variables that may affect the rehabilitation process? How should the rehabilitation helping professional react to them?
8. What are some Filipino cultural variables that may affect the rehabilitation process? How should the rehabilitation helping professional react to them?

9. Which of the Asian and Pacific American subgroups have the largest population in the United States?

Suggested Activities

1. Determine the number and/or percentage of Asian and Pacific Americans that live in your state.
2. Determine the percentage of your state's Asian and Pacific American population which has disabilities. Separate the population into the appropriate subgroups, such as Chinese American, Japanese American, etc.
3. Determine the five leading causes of disabilities among the various Asian and Pacific Americans subgroups in your state.
4. If there are any Asian and Pacific American ethnic communities such as Chinatown in your area, visit at least one and observe the range of acculturation within the community.
5. Make a list of at least five agencies and/or organizations in your state that specialize in assisting Asian and Pacific Americans. These organizations do not have to be connected to disabilities. Also, summarize the services provided.

References

Agbayani-Siewert, P. & Revilla, L. (1995). Filipino Americans. In P. G. Min (Ed.), *Asian Americans: Contemporary trends and issues.* Thousand Oaks, CA: Sage.

Broom, L. & Kitsuse, J. (1988). The managed casualty. In C. H. Mindel et al. (Eds.), *Ethnic families in America* (3rd ed.). Englewood Cliffs: Prentice-Hall.

Cabezas, A., Shinagawa, L., & Kawaguchi, G. (1987). New inquiries into the socioeconomic status of Filipino Americans in California. *Amerasia Journal, 13*:1–22.

Chan, F., Lam, C. S., Wong, D., Leung, P., & Xue-Shen, F. (1988). Counseling Chinese Americans with disabilities. *Journal of Applied Rehabilitation Counseling, 19*(4):21–25.

Chung, D. K. (1992). The Confucian model of social transformation. In S. M. Furuto et al. (Eds.), *Social work practice with Asian Americans.* Newbury Park, CA: Sage.

Cordova, F. (1983). *Filipinos: Forgotten Asian Americans.* Dubuque, IA: Kendall Hunt.

Espina, M. (1995). Readings on Filipinos in Louisiana. In P. G. Min (Ed.), *Asian Americans: Contemporary trends and issues.* Thousand Oaks, CA: Sage.

Fong, R. (1992). A history of Asian Americans. In S. M. Furuto et al. (Eds.), *Social work practice with Asian Americans.* Newbury Park, CA: Sage.

Glenn, E. K. (1988). Split household, small producer and dual wage earner: An analysis of Chinese-American family strategies. In C. H. Mindel et al. (Eds.), *Ethnic families in America* (3rd ed.), Englewood Cliffs, NJ: Prentice-Hall.

Hasia, J. (1988). Asian Americans in higher education and at work. In M. J. Justiz et al. (Eds.), *Minorities in higher education.* American Council on Education. Phoenix, AZ: Oryx Press.

Hess, B. B., Markson, E. W., & Stein, P. J. (1995). Racial and ethnic minorities: An overview. In P. S. Rothenberg (Ed.), *Race, class and gender in the United States: An integrated study.* (3rd ed.). New York: St. Martin's Press.

Ho, M. K. (1987). *Family therapy with ethnic minorities.* Newbury Park, CA: Sage.

Huang, L. J. (1981). The Chinese American family. In C. H. Mindel et al. (Eds.), *Ethnic families in America* (3rd ed.). Englewood Cliffs, NJ: Prentice-Hall.

Hurh, W. M., & Kim, K. C. (1995): Korean immigrants in America. In P. G. Min (Ed.), *Asian Americans: Contemporary trends and issues.* Thousand Oaks, CA: Sage.

Hurh, W. M., & Kim, K. C. (1995): Race relations paradigm and Korean-American research: A sociology of knowledge perspective. Quoted in In P. G. Min (Ed.), *Asian Americans: Contemporary trends and issues.* Thousand Oaks, CA: Sage.

Jensen, J. M. (1988). *Passage from India: Asian Indian immigrants in North America.* New Haven, CT: Yale University Press.

Kitano, H. H. L. (1969). *Japanese-Americans: The evaluation of a subculture.* Englewood Cliffs, NJ: Prentice-Hall.

Kitano, H., Yeung, Wai-Tsang, Chai, L., & Hatanaka, H. (1984). Asian American interracial marriage. *Journal of Marriage and the Family, 46*:179–190, February.

Kitano, H. H. L. (1988): Race relations. In C. H. Mindel et al. (Eds.), *Ethnic families in America.* (3rd ed.), Englewood Cliffs, NJ: Prentice-Hall.

Leong, F. T. L. (1986). Counseling and psychotherapy with Asian Americans: Review of the literature. *Journal of Counseling Psychology, 33*:196–206.

Leung, P., & Sakata, R. (1988). Asian Americans and rehabilitation: Some important variables *Journal of Applied Rehabilitation Counseling, 19*(4):16–20.

Min, P. G. (1995). Korean Americans. In P. G. Min (Ed.), *Asian Americans: Contemporary trends and issues.* Thousand Oaks, CA: Sage.

Miyamoto, F. (1988). Social solidarity among the Japanese in Seattle. In C. H. Mindel et al. (Eds.), *Ethnic families in America.* (3rd ed.). Englewood Cliffs, NJ: Prentice-Hall.

Nishi, S. M. (1995). Japanese Americans. In P. G. Min (Ed.), *Asian Americans: Contemporary trends and issues,* Thousand Oaks, CA: Sage.

Pido, L. L. L. (1995). The Filipinos in America. In P. G. Min (Ed.), *Asian Americans: Contemporary trends and Issues.* Thousand Oaks, CA: Sage.

Reitz, J. (1995). The survival of ethnic groups. In P. G. Min (Ed.), *Asian Americans: Contemporary trends and Issues.* Thousand Oaks, CA: Sage.

Sandermeyer, E. C. (1973). *The anti-Chinese movement in California* (2nd ed.). Urbana, IL: University of Illinois Press.

Sodowsky, G. R., Kwong-Liem, K. K., & Pannu, R. (1995). Ethnic identity of Asians in the United States. In J. G. Ponterotto et al. (Eds.), *Handbook of multicultural counseling.* Thousand Oaks, CA: Sage.

Sollenberger, R. T. (1988). Chinese-American child rearing practices and juvenile delinquency. In C. H. Mindel et al. (Eds.), *Ethnic families in America* (3rd ed.). Englewood Cliffs, NJ: Prentice-Hall.

Sue, D. W., & Sue, D. (1990). *Counseling the culturally different* (2nd ed.). New York: John Wiley and Sons.

Sue, D. W. (1994). Ethnic identity: The impact of two cultures on the psychological development of Asians in America. In Justiz et al. (Eds.), *Minorities in higher education.* American Council on Education. Phoenix, AZ: Oryx Press.

Suzuki, B. H. (1994). Higher education issues in the Asian American community. In Justiz et al. (Eds.), *Minorities in higher education.* American Council on Education. Phoenix, AZ: Oryx Press.

Toji, D. S., & Johnson, J. H. (1992). Asian and Pacific Islander American poverty: The working poor and the jobless poor. *Amerasia Journal, 18*(1):83–91.

Tsukada, M. (1988). Income parity through different paths: Chinese Americans, Japanese Americans and Caucasians in Hawaii. *Amerasia Journal, 14*(2):47–60.

Ueda, R. (1994). The Americanization and education of Japanese Americans. In Jutiz et al. (Eds.), *Minorities in higher education.* American Council on Education. Phoenix, AZ: Oryx Press.

U. S. Bureau of the Census. (1995). 1990 Census of population, general population characteristics, the United States. In P. G. Min (Ed.), *Asian Americans.* Thousand Oaks, CA: Sage.

U. S. Bureau of the Census. (1994). Asian and Pacific Islanders in the United States, 1990 census of population. In Justiz et al. (Eds.), *Minorities in higher education.* American Council on Education. Phoenix, AZ: Oryx Press.

Watanabe, C. (1973). Self-expression and the Asian-American experience. *Personnel and Guidance Journal, 51*:390–396.

Weiss, M. S. (1988). Selective acculturation and the dating process: The patterning of Chinese-Caucasian interracial dating. In C. H. Mindel et al. (Eds.), *Ethnic families in America* (3rd ed.). Englewood Cliffs, NJ: Prentice-Hall.

Wong, M. (1982). The cost of being Chinese, Japanese and Filipino in the United States, 1960, 1970, 1976. *Pacific Sociological Review, 5*:59–78.

Wong, M. G. (1995). Chinese Americans. In P. G. Min (Ed.), *Asian Americans: Contemporary trends and issues.* Thousand Oaks, CA: Sage.

Yanagisako, S. J. (1988). Transforming the past. In C. H. Mindel et al. (Eds.), *Ethnic families in America.* (3rd ed.). Englewood Cliffs, NJ: Prentice-Hall.

Yinger, S. (1995). Toward a theory of assimilation and dissemination. In P. G. Min (Ed.), *Asian Americans: Contemporary trends and issues.* Thousand Oaks, CA: Sage.

Suggested Readings

Gould, K. H. (1988). Asian and Pacific Islanders: Myth and reality. *National Association of Social Workers, 37*:142–147.

Ho, M. K. (1976). Social work with Asian Americans. *Social Casework, 57*:195–201.

Kibria, N. (1993). *Family tightrope: The changing lives of Vietnamese Americans.* Princeton, NJ: Princeton University Press.

Loo, C., Tong, B., & True, R. (1989). A bitter bean: Mental health status and attitudes in Chinatown. *Journal of Community Psychology, 17*:183–296.

Min, P. G. (Ed.). (1995). *Asian Americans: Contemporary trends and issues*. Thousand Oaks, CA: Sage.

Peterson, W. (1971). *Japanese Americans: Oppression and success*. New York: Random House.

Roland, A. (1988). *In search of self in India and Japan: Toward a cross-cultural psychology*. Princeton, NJ: Princeton University Press.

Schiller, B. (1989). *The economics of poverty and discrimination*. Englewood Cliffs, NJ: Prentice-Hall.

Sue, S., & Morishima, J. K. (1982). *The mental health of Asian Americans*. San Francisco: Jossey-Bass.

Wong, M. (1982). The cost of being Chinese, Japanese and Filipino in the United States, 1960, 1970, 1976. *Pacific Sociological Review, 5*:59–78.

Chapter 9

DISABILITY AND HISPANIC/LATINO AMERICANS

Chapter Outline
- Introduction
- Historical Background
- Social Issues
- Hispanic/Latino Americans and Disability
- Health Issues
- Economic Issues
- Employment Issues
- Educational Issues
- Family Dynamics
- Intervention Strategies
- Conclusion

Chapter Objectives
- Identify specific historical events that have impacted the lives of Mexican, Puerto Rican and Cuban Americans
- Identify the diversity of Hispanic/Latino Americans
- Identify the prevalence of disabilities among Hispanic/Latino Americans
- Identify social, educational and economical issues which impact the lives of Hispanic/Latino Americans
- Identify the impact the family has on Mexican, Puerto Rican, and Cuban American persons with disabilities
- Identify critical cultural information of which rehabilitation helping professionals must be aware.
- Provide suggestions with regard to ways of effectively working with Hispanic/Latino persons with disabilities.

Introduction

Terminology

As America has attempted to better attend to the needs of its ethnic and racial minorities, the federal government has attempted to classify the various groups. In the classification process, descriptive names have been attached. In most instances the groups being labeled have chosen to decide the name to which they feel most comfortable answering. In the case of African Americans, they have moved from colored to Negro to black to African American; likewise for Hispanics, there has been an evolution of names leading to the currently acceptable terminology of Hispanic/Latino. Terms that have been used are Chicano, Spanish-American, Spanish-Surname, Spanish-origin, and Spanish-speaking. Similar to the situation with the appropriate identity for African American, where not all persons of this group like to be called black or African American, there is not unanimity with regard to the most appropriate terminology to use in referring to Hispanic/Latino persons. The use of the terms Spanish-speaking or Spanish-Surname is misleading in that not all Hispanic/Latino persons have their origin as Spanish. This term tends to disregard the influence of Indian and African ancestry. The term Chicano, according to Marilyn and Carlos Molina (1994), "Grew out of the ethnic and ideological movements of young political activists during the 1960s and 1970s, particularly in the Southwest." They continue by emphasizing that these activists used the term Chicano to raise the awareness of the public to the depressed economic and political conditions that existed for persons of Mexican heritage. Since those activist days, the term has come to signify, for some, pride in their Mexican heritage. However, Munoz (1982) informs us that Chicano is used by some Mexican Americans to indicate racial pride and consciousness while it is rejected by others, particularly older Mexican Americans, who consider the term to be an insulting reference.

The author acknowledges that the term Hispanic/Latino is not without limitation in describing this particular population of people. However, Hispanic and Latino currently appear to be the most widely accepted terms to use. Hispanic recognizes the Spanish influence and Latino recognizes the origin of those from the Caribbean and Latin America.

Diversity

Implied in the discussion with regard to terminology is the fact that persons of Hispanic/Latino origin are not a homogeneous group. Some of the

Hispanic/Latino groups represented in the United States are: Mexican, Puerto Rican, Cuban, Dominican Republic, Costa Rican, Guatemalan, Honduran, Nicaraguan, Salvadoran, and Argentinean to mention a few. In this chapter, the three groups with the largest population, Mexican, Puerto Rican, and Cuban, will be discussed.

Historical Backgrounds

Mexicans

For approximately 200 years, Spain ruled Mexico, and during this period, a considerable portion of the United States, particularly the Southwest and West (Texas, California, Arizona, and New Mexico) were part of Mexico. During the Spanish colonization of Mexico, missions were established in California, Texas, and Arizona. According to McWilliams (1968), the mission system helped establish the Catholic church. The intermingling of the Spanish conquistadors, the Mexicans, and the indigenous Indians has created the racial mixture that we currently see among Mexican Americans. Additionally, the influence of African slaves can also be seen.

The Spanish colonization of Mexico ended in 1821 when Mexico achieved independence. Although their independence was gained, they continued to have conflicts with Euro-American settlers who wanted the land north of the Rio Grande River to be part of the United States. Perhaps the best known of these conflicts was when the Mexican General Santa Anna and his troops defeated a small group in a battle at the mission called the Alamo. Later that same year (1836), Sam Houston defeated Santa Anna at the battle of San Jacinto. As a result of this battle, Texas became independent of Mexico and later became part of the United States.

Battles between the U. S. and Mexico continued, culminating in the Mexican-American War, which ended with the Treaty of Guadalupe Hidalgo in which Mexico accepted the Rio Grande River as the Texas border. Additionally, Mexico sold parts of the Southwest and West to the United States. The acquisition of what is known as Texas, California, New Mexico and Arizona meant that a large number of persons of Mexican decent were living in the United States and it is from this foundation that many of the current Mexican American population originated.

Puerto Ricans

Puerto Rico became a territory of the United States as a result of the treaty signed ending the Spanish-American War in 1898. In 1900, the U. S.

Congress passed the Foraker Act which gave Puerto Ricans U. S. national status but not citizenship. Seventeen years later Congress passed the Jones Act which granted citizenship to the Puerto Rican people.

Because of their territorial status, and in 1917 citizenship status, Puerto Ricans have been able to enter and exit the United States with virtually no restrictions; however, the flow of Puerto Ricans into the United States appears to be tied closely to economic conditions on the Puerto Rican Islands. In other words, many have come to the States in search of a better life.

Cubans

The Spanish influence with regard to Cuba comes as a result of Spain's control of the island for over 300 years. Historians tell us that Spain's rule over Cuba, while in some cases economically beneficial to Cubans, was very domineering. The Spanish government maintained control over the government of Cuba, and made most of the important decisions by placing Spanish officials in most of the key Cuban governmental posts. This type of action on the part of the government of Spain is credited with developing within the Cuban people a mistrust of Colonial-type governments.

Jose Szapocznik and Roberto Hernandez' (1988) comments identify Africans and Chinese as also having a significant influence upon Cuban Culture.

In addition to the Spanish contributions to the formation of the Cuban national character, West Africa had a highly significant role in the molding of Cuban values and attitudes. The labor demands led to the massive importation of African slaves. It has been estimated that approximately one million slaves were transported to Cuba during the island's three and one-half centuries of slave trading. The vast majority, however, arrived during the last 100 years of this period to fulfill the increasing needs of the booming sugar industry. According to a census of Cuba's population conducted in 1846, the total slave population was 660,000 with an additional 220,000 free blacks and mulattoes. The white population, on the other hand, amounted to 565,000. After the decline of the slave trade following the enactment of the Emancipation Law of 1880, the demand for cheap labor was met by the importation of indentured servants from China, the arrival of a few thousand Indians from Mexico's Yucatan Peninsula and the continued Spanish immigration, largely from economically depressed Spain and the Canary Islands. After the blacks, the Chinese came to constitute Cuba's most important ethnic minority in the twentieth century.

The United States acquired Cuba after the Spanish-American War and occupied the country until 1902. Even after Cuba gained independence from the United States, the two countries maintained a close relationship until the Castro-led Cuban revolution took control of the government in 1959.

The immigration of Cubans to the United States has been in waves. McCoy and Gonzales (1985) inform us that the first wave came in the early 1900s resulting in approximately 79,000 Cubans of various economic and social backgrounds settling in the United States, with the majority locating in Florida. The second wave consisted of persons seeking exile from the Castro government. It is estimated that by 1973, there were 273,000 Cubans, primarily from the business and professional class, involved in this exodus. An estimate of 118,000 Cubans were part of the third wave of Cuban immigrants, many of whom left the island by boat. The majority of this group is considered unskilled. There continue to be groups of persons from Cuba seeking a home in the United States', most arrive in Florida having come on small and sometimes overcrowded boats. In working with persons who have come to the U. S. from Cuba, it is important to recognize the effect of arriving in waves or "wave effect." To be more precise, with regard to the first wave, those who are still alive obviously are elderly; however, a helping professional would be working with second, third, and fourth generations of decendants of those immigrants, thus various levels of acculturation come into play. There will be more discussion of this in the intervention strategies section of this chapter. An important matter to note with respect to the second wave is that these Cuban immigrants were generally well educated, had been high in the Cuban social society, had significant contact within the United States, and probably had reasonable economic resources, certainly more than any of the wave of immigrants that were to come after them. The third and subsequent waves have consisted of the economically, educationally, and socially poorer groups. There have been contentions that some persons in these groups have been those who have mental disabilities and/or are criminals. In attaching labels to this group, one should remember that in a dictatorial government such as the Castro regime, mental disability and criminal status for some may be applied for reasons that are different than why the U. S. would make similar labels.

Demographics

The 2004 U. S. Census Bureau report cites the overall Hispanic/Latino population at over 41 million. Additional demographic information of interest to helping professionals is that the Hispanic/Latino ethnic group is younger than the Euro-American group. Furthermore, the Hispanic/Latino group, in the 2000 U. S. Census, surpassed African Americans as the most populated ethnic/racial minority group in America. From a technical standpoint, Hispanic/Latino is not a racial minority; they are an ethnic minority group, since Hispanic/Latino persons can be of any racial background. This fact is simply a technicality and should not detract from the fact that they are a large minority group and will continue, in the twenty-first century, to increase in numbers.

Mexican Americans

As previously stated, Mexican Americans and persons of Mexican decent comprise approximately 60 percent of the Hispanic/Latino population in the United States. The majority of the Mexican American population lives in California, Texas, Arizona, and New Mexico.

Puerto Rican Americans

Approximately 10 percent of the Hispanic/Latino population is Puerto Rican. The majority of the population lives in New York with significant numbers in Illinois and New Jersey.

Cuban Americans

Of the three major Hispanic/Latino subgroups, Cubans have the smallest population less than five percent. Florida's Cuban population is by far the largest in the United States with the states of New Jersey, New York, and California also having significant populations of Cubans.

Social Issues

Poverty and Discrimination

With the exception of Cubans, the migration of Hispanic/Latinos to the United States has been an ebb and flow conditioned by the United States' need for cheap labor. For decades, Mexicans have been welcomed and encouraged to come to the states to help meet the labor demands of the country, only to find that they were equally unwelcome when the demand for their labor diminished. Similarly, Puerto Ricans have been attracted to the United States to meet some of the labor needs, especially in times when the Puerto Rican economy has had problems providing work for its willing population. Thus, poverty and discrimination have been major social problems, at least for Mexicans and Puerto Ricans. According to the United States

Commission on Civil Rights, "Both Mexicans and Puerto Ricans have been victims of economic and social discrimination and prejudice, it appears that Puerto Ricans have suffered even more intensely than any other group."

With regard to Cubans, since much of their entry into the United States has been in waves, there are considerable economic and social differences among the United States' Cuban population. The group of Cuban immigrants who came to America fleeing the Castro government were more affluent and well educated; therefore, they experienced fewer problems integrating into Euro-American society. Experiencing less discrimination and prejudice than many of the groups to follow has meant their social plight has been less traumatic.

Hispanic/Latino is not a racial group but an ethnic group. In fact, their composition as a group of people consists of members from all racial groups, thus their skin pigmentation ranges from white to black. Consequently, some human rights observers indicate that in America, the darker the skin pigmentation of a Hispanic/Latino, the more he/she is subject to experience various kinds of discrimination.

The proximity of the Mexican/American border makes for relatively easy access to the United States, resulting in considerable friction between Mexicans who have wanted to enter the United States seeking increased opportunities for themselves and their families and the United States government. A variety of opinions among United States citizens exist with regard to the entry of undocumented Mexicans. Some feel that they are in the U. S. illegally taking jobs and resources that should be reserved for U. S. citizens and others believe the U. S. should be compassionate and offer opportunities to those seeking to improve their lives. Of considerable concern to social and health care workers is the access, or in some cases lack thereof, of health and welfare services. It appears that the debate will continue well into the twenty-first century as to how much and what type of services can be provided to non-U. S. citizens; however, one important aspect with regard to disability was settled as it has been determined that non-U. S. citizens are protected by the Americans with Disabilities Act (ADA) from discrimination based on their status as a person with a disability.

Language Barrier

A major contributing factor to the high rate of poverty among some Hispanic/Latino groups and the prejudice and various forms of discrimination they experience is based upon communication barriers. The inability on the part of some Hispanic/Latinos to speak English and/or communicate effectively in English tends to cause them to become isolated in groups of persons who have similar limitations. Being unable to effectively communicate in the language of the dominant culture makes them easy targets for both discrimination and exploitation. To be more specific, they can easily be placed into unsafe work conditions, underpaid and overworked, as well as being forced to live in unsafe and unhealthy living environments.

The limited English communication skills, along with being undocumented creates problems of accessing and maintaining good health. More discussion with regard to this will occur in health issues.

Teen Pregnancy

Teenagers between the ages of 15 to 19 account for a high rate of Hispanic/Latino births. While this rate is not as high as African Americans, it does, however, represent a high rate of teenage pregnancies. Based upon a National Center for Health Statistics report, among the Hispanic/Latino subgroups, Mexicans are the highest followed by Puerto Ricans. Cubans have the lowest rate, of the three Hispanic/Latino groups.

HIV/AIDS

It is impossible to separate HIV/AIDS into either a social or health issue; it is in fact, both. It is a social issue because the sexual taboos about homosexuality and the barriers to communicating about sex between men and women thwart prevention efforts in Latino communities (Amaro, 1988). It is a health issue because Hispanic/Latinos are twice as likely to be affected by HIV than the general population.

More discussion of this problem will occur in the health issues section.

Hispanic/Latino Americans and Disabilities

It is estimated by the U. S. Bureau of the Census that persons of Hispanic/Latino origin have a lower (15.3%) rate of disabilities than Native American Indians and African Americans. For several reasons, the author has questions with regard to the accuracy of the Hispanic/Latino rates. First, the type of employment in which many Mexican Americans are engaged , i.e., farm labor, has the highest rate of accidents of any U. S. occupation. Second, many injuries that lead to disabilities go unreported by some undocumented Hispanic/Latino workers because of their fear of being removed from the United States. Third, there have been cases of employers not reporting accidents and not allowing the employees to report or seek medical care.

Health Issues

There are a number of health issues of major concern within the Hispanic/Latino communities, such as cancer, cardiovascular disease, diabetes, HIV/AIDS, and substance abuse. Each will be addressed briefly. However, Aida Giachello (1994) summarizes the single greatest problem Hispanic/Latino persons face in regard to health care is the lack of access to the health care system. She points out that "Latinos lack access to a broad array of health services, especially primary care." She continues by stating, "This lack results from financial, cultural and institutional barriers. Poor and uninsured Latinos confront high fees for both preventive and acute care, a lack of bilingual/bicultural services, long-time gaps between calling for an appointment and actually seeing a physician and long waits once they get to the clinic." She concluded her comments by saying these facts contribute to Hispanic/Latinos disproportionate use of more costly services such as hospital emergency rooms when symptoms of illness persist or when the illness has reached an advanced stage.

Valdez and associates (1993) research while dated the results remain true and serve as foundation for Giachello's comments with regard to lack of insurance being a major barrier to adequate access to health care for Hispanic/Latinos. Valdez found that 39 percent of Hispanic/Latinos under the age of 65 were uninsured. Giachello (1994) convincingly argues the problem of lack of insurance is related to employment status. To be more precise, uninsured Hispanic/Latinos are more likely to work in industries which lack insurance coverage or at best offer inadequate coverage and because of the low income associated with many of the jobs, their abilities to secure adequate health insurance is greatly diminished.

Aiuda Giachello (1994) adds to our understanding of uninsured Hispanic/Latinos by providing the following facts and statistics on uninsured by national origin, sex, and age.

> Insurance coverage varies among Latinos by national origin, with Central and south Americans and Mexicans being worst off. As reported by the National Council of La Raza (NCLR), 40% of persons from Central and South America were uninsured in 1990, as were 36% of those of Mexican origin. This compares with 24% of the Cuban population and 21% of other Latinos. The percentage of uninsured Puerto Ricans was the lowest (14%); perhaps owing to their higher levels of poverty and greater dependence on public assistance and medicaid coverage.

The lack of access to appropriate health care for Hispanic/Latinos causes health problems, such as the ones to be discussed, to become a major concern because they are often not attended until they reach advanced stages.

This along with inadequate primary and secondary prevention efforts and education often places many Hispanic/Latinos at risk for treatable conditions becoming lethal.

Smoking

The message that cigarette smoking is harmful has been clearly made by Surgeon General reports as well as other responsible health officials. Still, an alarming number of both youth and adults, particularly ethnic minorities, continue to engage in the harmful habit. There have been numerous claims (all denied by the tobacco industry) that the tobacco industry, in its advertising, has targeted ethnic and racial minorities, particularly the young and women. In other words, their advertising campaigns are designed to encourage them to begin and/or continue using tobacco products. Whether the industry is guilty of these charges, it can be debated that health educators have not done as effective of a job discouraging people from smoking as the tobacco groups have done encouraging people to smoke. Some researchers like Gerardo Marin and his colleagues (1995) convincingly argue that "Although cigarette smoking is the single most important preventable cause of death and disability in the United States, little has been done to develop culturally appropriate intervention for ethnic minority groups, particularly for Hispanics."

What this means is that there continues to be a high percentage of Hispanic/Latinos who smoke despite the health warnings and possible negative consequences. Also, it appears that the rate may increase in the future rather than decrease. Again, because of the risk to one's health with regard to possible death and disabilities, this fact becomes more and more alarming, especially since the negative aspects can be prevented by abstaining from cigarette smoking. Some of the many disabling conditions resulting from smoking are cancer and cardiovascular disease–two of the top ten causes of death regardless of racial or ethnic background.

Cancer

At the present time, the Hispanic/Latino population appears to contract cancer at the same rate as Euro-Americans. The most prevalent cancers among Hispanic/Latino males are cancers of the prostate, lung, and colon; most common among women are cancers of the breast, colon, and cervix.

Cardiovascular Disease

Although studies of the rate of cardiovascular diseases among Hispanic/Latinos are somewhat meager and limited, according to Doctor Eliseo Perez-Stable (1994), the data that does exist shows the incidence and prevalence of cardiovascular disease among Hispanic/Latino men in the United States is somewhat lower than for Euro-American males and African American males. No similar data appears to be available for Hispanic/Latino females.

Even though this health condition does not appear at this time to be more prevalent among Hispanic/Latinos than in the general population, there is cause for concern for two reasons: one, as previously stated, cardiovascular disease is one of the top ten causes of death of humankind; and two, lifestyles of some Hispanic/Latinos, particularly cigarette smoking and dietary habits which lead to obesity, if not decreased could very well trigger a dramatic increase in cardiovascular diseases among Hispanic/Latinos.

Diabetes

Diabetes ranks as one of the top ten causes of death of humans. In 1986, diabetes caused almost one million persons (of all races) to become totally disabled. Diabetes is a major health issue among Hispanic/Latinos. Henrietta Bernall and Eliseo Perez-Stable (1994) provide us with information which indicates that Hispanic/Latinos living in the United States have shown higher than expected prevalence of diabetes. Extracting information from a 1983-1984 Hispanic Health and Nutrition Examination survey (HHANES) report, the authors discovered that Mexicans between the ages of 20 to 74 years had two to three times the prevalence of diabetes than Euro-Americans and African Americans. In the same report, Puerto Ricans had a diagnosed rate of diabetes similar to Mexicans and they found the prevalence of diabetes to be higher for Puerto Ricans and Mexicans than for Cubans.

Human Immunodeficiency Virus (HIV) and Acquired Immunodeficiency Syndrome (AIDS)

Emilio Carrillo and Steven Uranga-McKane (1994) classify the rate of HIV infections and cases of AIDS among Hispanic/Latinos as an epidemic. They report that during 1990 to 1991, Hispanic/Latinos had the largest proportionate increase in AIDS cases of any ethnic/racial group in the United States. The researchers report that Hispanic/Latino women have been extremely hard hit by the epidemic. As evidence, at the end of 1992, 21 percent of women reporting AIDS cases to the Center for Disease Control were Hispanic/Latinos. As astonishing as this percentage is, the fact that 53% of the women reporting AIDS cases were African American is alarming.

Carrillo and Uranga-McKane (1994) further report that at the end of 1991, an estimated 18,500 children and adolescents had been orphaned by AIDS with more than 80 percent of those offspring being of African-American or Hispanic/Latino mothers. Finally, as a result of perinatal transmission of HIV from infected mothers, approximately 21 percent of children with AIDS are Hispanic/Latino children.

Social, economic, and cultural factors contribute to the magnitude of the problem; therefore, helping professionals and rehabilitation specialists must identify what these contributing factors are and devise ways of assisting those in need of help. Until appropriate attention is given to this epidemic it will continue to be a major health issue among Hispanic/Latino people.

Economic Issues

In 1982, Carillo made the observation that Hispanic/Latinos are overrepresented among the poor and he further observed that there is a significant discrepancy between the annual incomes of Hispanic/Latino and Euro-Americans. As Carlos and Marilyn Molina (1994) remind us, there is a danger in clustering all of the subgroups of Hispanic/Latinos into one category and with regard to review of economic conditions, the problem is that the overall or median family income for all Hispanic/Latino groups mask the depressed economic status of Puerto Ricans. Relatedly, it also does not adequately represent the higher level of family income representing the Cuban population.

The point to be made for the purpose of rehabilitation and other helping professionals when evaluating the economic condition of Hispanic/Latinos is to pay closer attention to the subgroup, rather than relying totally on the overall Hispanic/Latino group statistics.

Employment Issues

Whether one is employed and, if employed, the type of employment help determine one's earning potential which, in turn, has an impact upon one's socioeconomic status. Some of the reasons for the high rate of poverty among some Hispanic/Latinos are, as the Molinas describe, low wages, undereducation, increasing numbers of single heads of households, discrimination, and inadequate national attention being given to the socioeconomic conditions of Hispanic/Latinos.

Consistantly, the unemployment rate for Hispanic/Latinos has been at least double the national unemployment rate. In 1980 the unemployment rate for Hispanic/Latinos was 10 percent, while it was 5 percent for non-Hispanic/Latinos. According to the Children's Defense Fund (1990) in 1987, more than one-fourth of all Hispanic/Latino families earned incomes below the poverty level as compared to less than 10 percent of all non-Hispanic/Latino families, and Hispanic/Latinos in the work force were 50 percent more likely to be unemployed than non-Hispanic/Latinos. This trend has continued into the 1990s and probably will be the same in the first quarter of the twenty-first century.

As indicated, some reasons for the type and rate of employment can be attributed to discrimination; however, a portion has to be related to level of educational attainment.

Educational Issues

Perhaps the American Council on Education (1994) adequately summarizes the educational situation of many Hispanic/Latino youth with the following: "School statistics indicate that 43 percent of Hispanic students drop out of high school, and those who do graduate are not prepared for higher education." Other researchers, such as Johnson (1994), Orum (1986), and Howe (1987), place the dropout rate between 36 to 50 percent. Dropping out of school too frequently mobilizes events that have lifelong consequences, such as inability to secure gainful employment, low self-esteem, marital discord, and underemployment or unemployment.

Valencia (1989) lists several possible reasons for the poor academic success of some Hispanic/Latinos and the following are a select few: (1) racial and ethnic segregation in the schools, (2) language and cultural bias in school practices, (3) poor or low quality student-teacher interaction, (4) special education practices, and (5) absence of Hispanics in the teaching force.

Family Dynamics

Historical Perspective of Hispanic/Latino Families

Melba Sanchez-Ayendez's (1988) following remarks alert us to be cautious in attempting to describe a typical ethnic minority family such as Puerto Ricans: "In speaking of the traditional Puerto Rican family, one must realize that cultural traits are subject to variation by socioeconomic status, area of residence and even racial or age group." She continues by asserting, "the notion of a traditional family is mostly an idealized version, although one that allows for a starting point from which to make comparisons." This is very good advice and, with this admonition in mind, a discussion of Hispanic/Latino families will occur. In an attempt to avoid overgeneralization, the three major subgroups (Puerto Rican, Cuban American, and Mexican American) will be discussed separately.

Similar to American Indians, many people think of Hispanic/Latinos as a homogeneous group and, as already discussed, the ethnic groups of which Hispanic/Latinos is comprised are varied, some having similar cultural traits, but in most instances, there are considerable cultural differences among the various groups as well as significant differences within groups.

Historically, when describing Hispanic/Latino families, various authors have lumped all of the subgroups into one category and promoted stereotypical attributes as representing the composition of a typical or traditional Hispanic/Latino family. To be more specific, Hispanic/Latino families have been described as (1) male dominated, (2) extended family-oriented, (3) strictly adhered to old-world age and sex roles, (4) and the wife as a submissive partner. While certain aspects of these stereotypes exist within some families, however, by no standards are these the universal family structure of all Hispanic/Latino families. By reviewing the three major subgroups, a more realistic view of Hispanic/Latino families will come into focus.

Mexican Americans

The previously mentioned stereotypes of the Hispanic/Latino family is perhaps attached to the Mexican American family at least as much, if not more, than any of the other subgroups. Rosina Becerra (1988) believes these stereotypes have a foundation in facts. According to Becerra, the structure of the male being dominant, family protector and the female as the child-rearer and nurturer began as Mexicans lived in rural and isolated areas. Consequently, when the father was away, the elder son was expected to provide protection for the family. Relatedly, if the mother was absent, the elder female was responsible for overseeing the children as well as providing the cooking and cleaning aspect of family life. Thus, the stereotypical Hispanic/Latino family structure began as a method of survival.

Father Role. While the concept of machismo or complete male dominance is no longer the standard for many Mexican American males, they have, however, maintained their role as head of the household providing guidance and protection for the family. The point is that the dominating male who rules with an iron fist without regard to the feelings and needs of his wife and children is not accurate. Respect is a valued concept among Mexican Americans and within the family structure, it is a "two-way street." The male expects respect from his wife and children; likewise, he is expected to give proper respect to the feelings and needs of his family. Since approximately 80 percent of Mexican Americans live in urban areas, they have considerable contact with mainstream American life; therefore, they are influenced by the dominant culture's views. One of the influences is the expanding role of the female which requires that the male share family nurturing responsibilities with the female.

Mother Role. The idea of the Mexican American female as a totally submissive individual, accepting the husband's dominance, is as inaccurate as many of the other stereotypes already discussed. In the past, the female's role may have been submissive; however, today, her role within the family has evolved to the point she is able to express herself as an equal, especially since a significant number of Hispanic/Latino mothers are in the work force providing their earnings as part of the family's economy.

Family-Oriented. The Mexican American family, according to Murrillo (1971) offers emotional support and security to its members. The extended family concept is a major component of Mexican American family life. Extended family members provide valuable services such as financial support, babysitting, personal advice, and health care as well as emotional support. In summary, the extended family exists as an effective means of survival.

Today's Mexican American families, generally speaking, are larger than the other Hispanic/Latino subgroups. An important fact to remember is that members of large families are often supported by small incomes. Perhaps Becerra (1988) summarizes the modern Mexican American family best with these remarks:

> Today's modern Mexican American family can be characterized as having a disproportionate percentage of members in low socioeconomic status. They have lower incomes that support larger families. In part, these lower incomes are a result of higher levels of unemployment and lower paying jobs, which are partially explained by low educational attainment, which in turn creates a high proportion of family poverty.

Despite the adversity, some Mexican American families encounter the strong kinship bonds which serve as a powerful force in helping the family overcome the adversities. This is a point to be remembered by rehabilitation and other helping professionals.

Cuban Americans

According to Jose Szapocznik and Roberto Hernandez (1988), Cuban families are examples of Hispanic/Latino families who have deviated from the stereotypical extended family concept often ascribed to minority families. They contend that Cuban families have in recent years moved more toward a nuclear family orientation; they further point out that this transition did not occur only after Cubans had migrated to the United States, but began before many of them left Cuba in the 1959 exodus.

Husband and Wife Relations. Continuing to use the works of Szapocznik as a reference to the evolving Cuban family structure, he convincingly argues that as Cuban women entered the labor market in America and their earnings became essential to the household budget, they began to gain an increasingly stronger voice in the family affairs. As a result of the women exercising their rights within the home, the traditionally patriarchal family structure changed. Similar to Mexican Americans, the male dominance has decreased where there is more sharing of responsibilities and decision-making. Consequently, the young Cuban American families of the 1980s and 1990s are usually comprised of a husband and wife team which grew up in the United States, thus having fewer problems with the equality of males and females than perhaps their parents and grandparents.

Bicultural. The Cuban American families of this part of the twenty-first century are primarily bicultural, bicultural in the sense of being capable of adapting and successfully functioning within the dominant culture values of the United States as well as adhere to old country values. In older Cuban American families, bicultural adaptation occurs as the parents maintain Cuban mainland customs and values while the children who were born in the United States grow up interacting with the U. S. dominant cultural values. The ability of parents and children to successfully adjust to each other's viewpoints to a large degree determines how well the family functions as a unit. In most cases, these families become very skillful at communicating and negotiating in different cultural contexts which helps them to adjust to the larger American society.

Puerto Rican Americans

Family Structure. A modified version of the extended family exists in many Puerto Rican families, according to Mintz (1966), Bonilla (1958), Steward (1956), and Safa (1974). In this setting, the child-rearing responsibility is primarily the responsibility of the nuclear family. Even so, extended family members play an important role in many aspects of family life, particularly providing emotional support, personal advice and if needed, financial support. Bastida (1979) describes the relationship as interdependence which views the individual as being unable to do everything or do everything well and, therefore, in need of other's assistance.

Intervention

Acculturation

As illustrated in the beginning of this chapter, Hispanic/Latino Americans are among the most diverse group of people in the United States. With regard to acculturation, J. Manuel Casas and Melba Vasquez (1996) correctly emphasize that "individual Hispanics can be found at different levels of the acculturation process." The social issues section of this chapter sheds light on this point as the fact was discussed that some Cubans have had fewer problems adjusting to American life than Puerto Ricans and Mexicans because of the educational and economical resources they possessed when they enter the country. Even so, today the acculturation level of individual Cuban Americans varies considerably when one considers that most of the latest Cuban immigrants do not have the same educational and economical background as the earlier immigrants. Similarly, within groups, differences occur in the Mexican American and other Hispanic/Latino American populations; however, in this case, acculturation variations generally revolve around educational level and one's abilities or lack thereof to speak English. Additionally, Casas and Vasquez (1996) inform us that proximity or availability of inexpensive means of travel to the native homeland also influences level of acculturation. To be more specific, the easier it is for a person to keep in touch, especially physically involved with his native culture, the greater the chances he will maintain significant parts of his native culture. This, however, does not mean that the person will not take on significant portions of the dominant culture. It may mean the rate of acquiring the dominant culture traits will be slower (utilization of English, for example) and that the person will attempt to live in two cultural worlds. These are important facts that the rehabilitation helping professional would be wise to consider as she attempts to assess the acculturation level of Hispanic/Latino American clients.

Returning to the sage advice of J. Manuel Casas and Melba Vasquez, these comments proved somewhat of a capstone on thinking with respect to reason why assessing levels of acculturation of Hispanic/Latino Americans is important for the success of rehabilitation plans.

There is no way to understand and counsel a Hispanic client, or any client, without assessing cultural factors as well as the individual's experience of oppression.

• A Hispanic individual's culture, history, and experience with oppression cause variations in human behavior.

• As with all clients, counselors must develop the ability to see individual Hispanic clients as products of their unique life experiences and maintain a valid and realistic perspective on the differences between the counselor's and the client's cultural environments and the learning and conditioning that result from the cultural contexts.

• Acculturation is a major contributor to the dynamic, ever-changing aspect of the Hispanic population. The rate is faster for the younger generation and among Hispanics at the lower end of the socioeconomic spectrum; men who work outside the home acculturate more quickly than women who may find themselves working solely within the home.

Final comments with regard to assessment of levels of acculturation relate to the fact that the rehabilitation helping professional should as Olmedo (1979) remind us be aware of three major dimensions: (1) language, (2) socioeconomic status, and (3) culture-specific attitudes and value orientation. These factors can serve as a guide for the rehabilitation professional helper to begin his assessment.

Communication Style

Similar to Asian and Pacific Americans, Hispanic/Latino Americans' communication styles are a two-prong issue. One relates to style, verbal or nonverbal, quiet or aggressive in the approach to communicating and the second prong is type, English, non-English or bilingual.

With regard to the first prong style, the rehabilitation helping professional should not automatically interpret silence, or slowness to speak, as a sign of lack of intelligence, lack of understanding and/or lack of interest. Often silence denotes respect; respect shown to family, elders, and persons of authority is highly regarded. Being polite, letting others such as the counselor speak before one begins to speak is a trait that is emphasized in many Hispanic/Latino families. This may be an unfamiliar communication style for a helping professional who is accustomed to the aggressive, get-your-point-in-first Euro-American style.

When a rehabilitation helping professional encounters a person who has a conservative communication style, rather than make the previously mentioned assumptions, he perhaps will obtain better results by asking questions. Rather than have gaps in needed information and classifying the client as uncooperative, simply be direct and attempt to obtain the needed information by asking the appropriate questions. In some cases, the questions may also go unanswered and often this is the result of the second prong of the communication fork that is language. The Hispanic/Latino person may not understand English well enough to respond and/or may not speak English well enough to adequately explain himself. This type situation may be best solved by either referring the client to someone who speaks his language or having an interpreter assist.

Orlando Rivera and Rosonito Cespedes (1983) astutely point out that in the rehabilitation setting language and cultural barriers present a particular problem with regard to psychological testing. If the rehabilitation counselor is not sensitive to the level of English spoken and comprehension, having a Hispanic/Latino client take a test in English will in all probability provide inaccurate results and generally the errors of the results are to the detriment of the client. In most rehabilitation settings, many psychological and other tests are available in other languages such as Spanish; therefore, this problem will not occur if the counselor is sensitive to the client's needs. Rivera and Cespedes point out that professional helpers' sensitivity is needed in understanding cultural impact of psychological tests. They emphasize that the Hispanic client, particularly male clients, may not see the relevance of the test and tests that require manipulation of objects such as blocks may be viewed as child's play. To avoid this situation, the rehabilitation professional must take the appropriate time to explain the relevance of the test and for what purpose the results will be used.

Expectations

Whenever there are communication differences between the counselor and client, there are the increased chances of misunderstanding. Certainly no more important and potentially devastating misunderstanding can occur than in the area of the helping professions such as rehabilitation when there is a difference in expectations of the rehabilitation plan and process. Clearly stated goals and objectives provided both verbally and in print are essential. The use of an interpreter and/or referring the client to someone with whom he is better able to communicate may be necessary.

In most cases, rehabilitation plans will have input from the client and perhaps significant others, thus dependent upon the degree of involvement of the client and/or his significant others will help determine his understanding of expectations. The more the client is involved, the less likely there are gaps between the client and counselor's expectations. Conversely, less involvement increases the probability of incongruence in expectations. If there are concerns with regard to the lack of congruence in expectations, the counselor can ask the client to explain what he expects to happen in the rehabilitation process and what are the expected results from the process. In questioning the client, the rehabilitation helping professional must phrase the questions in both nonthreatening terms and tones as well as making sure they cannot be interpreted as questioning the client's intelligence.

Value Orientation

Orlando Rivera and Rosonito Cespedes (1983) list dignity, respect, personalism, a person's word (LaPalabra), and folk medicine as important values held by many persons of Hispanic/Latino backgrounds, of which rehabilitation helping professionals should be familiar.

Dignity, according to professors Rivera and Cespedes, is central to the person's self respect; it must be guarded, honored, and cannot be compromised. The person not only expects to be able to maintain his dignity in situations but also he feels he must respect the other person's sense of dignity. A very important point is made by the professors that rehabilitation professionals must take into consideration when working with Hispanic/Latino persons and that is the helping professional cannot expect the client to ask for, beg, or seek services at the expense of his dignity.

Respect is accorded to everyone, elders, adults, children, as well as strangers. As previously stated, the dignity of others is honored. The lesson for rehabilitation helping professions is, Hispanic/Latino American clients and/or significant others may refuse to answer sensitive questions, especially regarding someone else if the client and/or significant other feels the response will be disrespectful of others.

Personalism refers to the fact that many Hispanic/Latino persons prefer to work with agencies or organizations with which they are familiar. Likewise, they may be more comfortable working with someone with whom they are familiar. It is unrealistic to think that the rehabilitation helping professional is going to know every Hispanic/Latino person within his service area; however, familiarity does not always mean personal acquaintance. Familiarity can also mean reputation. By becoming acquainted with services, agencies, and organizations that have positive interaction with Hispanic/Latino individuals, the rehabilitation helping professional will establish a reputation of being a caring and trustworthy individual.

Rivera and Cespedes emphasize that many Hispanic/Latino persons do not negotiate with written contracts but through verbal contracts. In other words, their words are their bond. What a rehabilitation helping professional should gain from this is that without carefully explaining the "why's" and "what for's," many of the written documents that the client is asked to read and sign may be viewed by the client as a lack of trust.

The rehabilitation helping professional, when preparing to refer the client for medical evaluation should be aware that some Hispanic/Latino persons prefer folk medicine. This does not mean that the client should be sent to the person who assists with folk medicine for an evaluation; however, it does mean the counselor must be sensitive to the client's understanding of and involvement with modern medicine and the health care system. In other words, the process will not be as simple as referring the client to a physician. Persons whom the client trusts may need to be asked to help with conveying the need for the referral and resulting information.

With regard to the helping professions, J. Manuel Casas and Melba Vasquez (1996) offer the following advice in working with Hispanic/Latino American clients:

> Depending on level of acculturation, Hispanics often display a great concern for immediacy and the "here and now"; frequently attribute control to an external locus (causality replaced by luck, supernatural powers, and acts of God); favor an extended family support system (rather than a basic adherence to the nuclear family); often take a concrete, tangible approach to life (rather than an abstract, long-term outlook) may practice a unilateral communication pattern with authority figures that uses avoidance of eye contact, deference, and silence as signs of respect (as opposed to more self-assertive patterns); and may develop multilingual communication skills, using English, Spanish and "Spanglish" a hybrid of the two.

They conclude their comments with the following admonishment: "counselors must be aware of these culturally dictated traits just as they must avoid broad, all-encompassing generalizations." This is good advice that all rehabilitation helping professionals should use as part of their helping techniques.

Situational Control

To refresh, situational control refers to what influences, if any, the client believes exert control over his life. Previously, a reference was made to Casas and Vasquez' point that many Hispanic/Latino individuals attribute external controls such as luck, supernatural power, acts of God and family as having significant influences on their lives. The relevance of this information to the rehabilitation helping professional is that she may need to include family members, clergy, and even faith healers in the rehabilitation process. This may require the counselor to rethink and adapt her theoretical approach to working with clients. However, if it aids the rehabilitation process and helps the client, the success will have justified the effort.

Conclusion

Rehabilitation helping professionals must consider that even though Mexican Americans, Puerto Rican Americans, and Cuban Americans are classified as Hispanic/Latino, they come from very different backgrounds. In many instances the Spanish language may be the only link. In some parts of the United States, Mexicans and Mexican Americans face considerable discrimination and have been relegated to low-paying, dead-end jobs. In contrast, many Cuban Americans, especially those who came to the United States prior to 1959, were well educated, economically secure, and politically connected. Therefore, they have experienced less discrimination and have done better in employment and educational areas than either Mexican Americans or Puerto Rican Americans.

Rehabilitation helping professionals must consider the length of time the Hispanic/Latino persons have been residing in the United States and their level of acculturation. Additionally, language may be of concern in that English may be a second language for many Hispanic/Latino clients.

Finally, in working with some Hispanic/Latino clients, the rehabilitation helping professional may be well advised to explore the client's environment by visiting his/her community and talking with significant persons in the community. By doing so, he establishes his desire to be helpful as well as obtaining a better understanding of the client's culture.

Review Questions

1. Why is the U. S. Bureau of the census projecting a large increase in the U.S. Hispanic/Latino population?
2. Is the disability rate (percentage) among Hispanic/Latino Americans considered to be higher or lower than the rate for Euro-Americans?
3. Is the disability rate (percentage) among male Hispanic/Latino Americans higher or lower than female Hispanic Latino Americans?
4. What are five major health concerns of Hispanic/Latino Americans and what are their implications for rehabilitation helping professionals?
5. Of the three major Hispanic/Latino American groups, Cuban, Puerto Rican, and Mexican, which has the highest poverty rate and which has the lowest poverty rate?
6. Identify five reasons for poor academic success of some Hispanic/Latino Americans.
7. To successfully work with Mexican Americans, what are some cultural factors of which rehabilitation helping professionals must be aware?
8. To successfully work with Cuban Americans, what are some cultural factors of which rehabilitation helping professionals must be aware?
9. To successfully work with Puerto Rican Americans, what are some cultural factors of which rehabilitation helping professionals must be aware?
10. How can the concepts of respect and dignity influence the rehabilitation process?

Suggested Activities

1. Determine the number and/or percentage of Hispanic/Latino Americans living in your state.
2. Determine the percentage of your state's Hispanic/Latino population which has disabilities. Separate the population into the appropriate subgroups such as Mexican Americans, Cuban Americans, etc.
3. Determine the three most prevalent disabilities among Hispanic/Latino Americans in your state. You may wish to do this by sub-groups.
4. Conduct an informal interview of at least ten (10) Hispanic/Latino persons to determine which name they prefer–Hispanic, Latino, Spanish American, etc.
5. Make a list of five agencies and/or organizations in your state that specialize in working with Hispanic/Latino persons. The organizations do not have to be connected to disabilities. Summarize the services provided.

References

Ayndez-Sanchez, M. (1988). The Puerto Rican American family. In C. H. Mindel et al. (Eds.), *Ethnic families in America* (3rd ed.). Englewood Cliffs, NJ: Prentice-Hall.

Bastida, E. (1979). Family integration and adjustment to aging among Hispanic elders. In C. H. Mindel et al. (Eds.), *Ethnic families in America* (3rd ed.). Englewood Cliffs, NJ: Prentice-Hall.

Becerra, R. M. (1988). The Mexican American family. In C. H. Mindel et al. (Eds.), *Ethnic families in America* (3rd ed.). Englewood Cliffs, NJ: Prentice-Hall.

Bernall, H., & Perez-Stable, E. J. (1994). Diabetes mellitus. In M. Molina & C. Molina (Eds.), *Latino health in the U. S.: A growing challenge.* Washington D.C.: American Public Health Association.

Carillo, C. (1982). Changing norms of Hispanic families. In E. E. Jones & S. J. Korchin (Eds.), *Minority mental health.* New York: Praeger.

Carrillo, E., & Uranga-McKanne, S. (1994). HIV/AIDS. In M. Molina & S. Molina (Eds.), *Latino health in the U. S.: A growing challenge.* Washington D.C.: American Public Health Association.

Casas, J. M., & Vasquez, M. J. T. (1996). Counseling the Hispanic: A guiding framework for a diverse population. In P. B. Pedersen et al. (Eds.), *Counseling across cultures.* (4th ed.). Thousand Oaks, CA: Sage.

Centers for Disease Control. (1995). Human immunodeficiency virus infection in the United States. In A. M. Padilla (Ed.), Hispanic psychology. Thousand Oaks, CA: Sage.

Children's Defense Fund (1990). *Latino youth at a crossroads.* Washington, D.C.: Adolescent Pregnancy Prevention Clearinghouse, January/March.

Giachello, A. L. M. (1994). Issues of access and use. In M. Molina & C. Molina (Eds.), *Latino health in the U. S.: A growing challenge.* Washington D.C.: American Public Health Association.

Health, United States, 1990: National Center for Health Statistics, 1991, Hyattsville, MD, DHHS Publication PHS 91–1232.

Howe, H. H. (1987). 1980 high school sophomores from poverty backgrounds: Whites, blacks, Hispanics look at school and adult responsibilities. *The Research Bulletin, 1*(2):1–11, New York: Hispanic Policy Development Project.

Johnson, J. (1994). Hispanic dropout rate is put at 35%. In *Minorities in higher education.* American Council on Education. Phoenix, AZ: Oryx Press.

Justiz, M. J., Wilson, R., & Bjork, L. G. (1994). *Minorities in Higher Education.* Phoenix, AZ: American Council on Education.

Marin, G., Marin, B. V., Pérez-Stable, E. J., Sabogal, F., & Sabogal-Otero, R. (1995). Cultural differences in attitudes and expectancies between Hispanic and Non-Hispanic white smokers. In A. M. Padilla (Ed.), *Hispanic psychology: Critical issues in theory and research.* Thousand Oaks, CA: Sage.

Mays, V. M., Cochran, S., & Roberts, V. (1995). Heterosexual and AIDS. In A. M. Padilla (Ed.), *Hispanic psychology: Critical issues in theory and research.* Thousand Oaks, CA: Sage.

McCoy, C. B., & Gonzales, D. H. (1994). Cuban immigration and immigrants in Florida and the United States. Quoted in *Latino health in the U. S.: A. growing challenge.* Washington, D.C.: American Public Health Association.

McWilliams, C. (1968). *North from Mexico.* New York: Greenwood Press.

Molina-Aguirre, M. & Molina, C. (1994). Latino populations: Who are they? In M. Molina & C. Molina (Eds.), *Latino health in the U. S.: A growing challenge.* Washington, D.C.: American Public Health Association.

Munoz, R. F. (1990). The Spanish-speaking consumer and the community mental health center. In D. W. Sue & D. Sue (Eds.), *Counseling the culturally different.* New York: John Wiley and Sons.

Murrillo, N. (1988). The Mexican American family. In C. H. Mindel et al. (Eds.), *Ethnic families in America* (3rd ed.). Englewood Cliffs, NJ: Prentice-Hall.

National Center for Health Statistics. (1994). In M. Molina & C. Molina (Eds.), *Latino health in the U. S.: A growing challenge.* Washington D.C.: American Public Health Association.

Olmedo, E. L. (1996). Acculturation: A psychometric perspective. In P. B. Pedersen et al. (Eds.), *Counseling across cultures* (4th ed.). Thousand Oaks, CA: Sage.

Orum, L. S. (1986). *The education of Hispanics: Status and implications.* Washington, D.C.: National Council of LaRaza.

Pérez-Stable, E. J. (1994). Cardiovascular disease. In M. Molina & C. Molina (Eds.), *Latino health in the U. S.: A growing challenge.* Washington D.C.: American Public Health Association.

Rivera, O. A., & Cespedes, R. (1979). Rehabilitation counseling with disabled Hispanics. *Journal of Applied Rehabilitation Counseling, 14*(3):65–71.

Szapocznik, J., & Hernandez, R. (1988). The Cuban American family. In C. H. Mindel et al. (Eds.), *Ethnic families in America.* Englewood Cliffs, NJ: Prentice-Hall.

Valdez, R. B., Morgenstern, H., Brown, E. R., Wyn, R., Wang C., & Cumberland, W. (1994). Insuring Latinos against the cost of illness. In M. Molina & C. Molina (Eds.), *Latino health in the U. S.: A growing challenge.* Washington D.C.: American Public Health Association.

Valencia, R. R. (1994). For whom does the school bell toll? Chicano school failure and success: Research and policy agenda for the 1990s. In Justiz, M. J. et al. (Eds.), *Minorities in higher education.* American Council on Education. Phoenix, AZ: Oryx Press.

Suggested Readings

Bean, F., & Tienda, M. (1988). *The Hispanic population of the United States.* New York: Russell Sage.

Becerra, R. M. (1988). The Mexican-American family. In C. H. Mindel et al. (Eds.), *Ethnic families in America.* Englewood Cliffs, NJ: Prentice-Hall, pp. 141–159.

Chilman, C. S. (1993). Hispanic families in the United States: Research perspectives In H. P. McAdoo (Ed.), *Family ethnicity.* Newbury Park, CA: Sage, pp. 141–163.

Fitzpatrick, J. P. (1971). *Puerto Rican Americans.* Englewood Cliffs, NJ: Prentice-Hall, *Latino Youth at a Crossroads.* (1990). Washington, D.C.: Children's Defense Fund.

Padilla, A. O. (Ed.). (1995). *Hispanic psychology.* Thousand Oaks, CA: Sage.

Pedersen, P. B., Draguns, J. G., Lonner W. J., & Trimble, J. E. (Eds.). (1996). *Communicating across cultures* (4th ed.). Thousand Oaks, CA: Sage.

Rivera, O. A., & Cespedes, R. (1983). Rehabilitation counseling with disabled Hispanics. *Journal of Applied Rehabilitation Counseling, 14*(3), Fall.

Suarez, Z. E. (1993). Cuban Americans: From golden exiles to social undesirables. In H. P. McAdoo (Ed.), *Family ethnicity.* Newbury Park, CA: Sage, pp. 164–176.

Szapocznik, J., & Hernandez, R. (1988). The Cuban-American family: In C. H. Mindel et al. (Eds.), *Ethnic families in America.* Englewood Cliffs, NJ: Prentice-Hall, pp. 160–172.

Chapter 10

DISABILITY AND AMERICAN INDIANS

Chapter Outline
• Introduction
• Historical Perspective
• Social Issues Impacting American Indians
• American Indians and Disability
• Major Health Issues
• Employment Issues
• Economic Issues
• Family Dynamics
• Intervention Strategies
• Conclusion

Chapter Objectives
• Identify specific historical events which have impacted the lives of American Indians.
• Identify the diversity of American Indians
• Identify the prevalence of disabilities among American Indians
• Identify social, educational and economical issues which impact the lives of American Indians
• Identify how social, educational and economical issues impact the lives of American Indians with disabilities
• Identify the impact the family has on American Indians with disabilities
• Identify critical cultural information of which rehabilitation helping professionals must be aware
• Provide suggestions with regard to ways of effectively working with American Indians persons with disabilities.

Introduction

Most historians and anthropologists consider American Indians as the first people of what is now the United States of America, thus they are the Natives of America. At the time of Columbus' voyage to the western hemisphere, it is estimated that there were approximately 10 million Native Americans (Harjo, 1993). Robert John (1988) informs us that at the time of the Native Americans' first contact with Europeans, there were approximately 300 languages spoken, and Susan Harjo points out that Native Americans still maintain 300 separate languages and dialects even though the author notes they are not all the same 300 languages that existed at the time of Columbus.

Quite often, when we think of American Indians, we think of them as a single culture; however, to the contrary, there are over 500 tribes in America with approximately 300 of them being federally recognized (Porter, 1983). Instead of viewing American Indians as a homogeneous group, one must realize many American Indians tribes are nations. In other words, they are nations within a nation. Susan Harjo reminds us that Indian nations are inherently sovereign and have negotiated approximately 600 treaties with the U.S. government. Therefore, trying to assign a single culture to American Indians would be similar to assigning a single culture to North America. Just as one would be lumping Mexicans, American Indians, African Americans, and Canadians into one category, we make a similar mistake by trying to determine a common culture for all American Indian tribes.

Historical Background

In retrospect, at the time of first European contact, there were well over 300 tribes in America, each having its own form of government, living as what we might consider independent nations. As a result of this contact, the independence was to come to an end for most American Indian tribes. Richardson (1981) correctly points out that the American Indian population has been dramatically decreased as a result of two things—disease and war. By the end of the eighteenth century, the American Indian population had been decreased by at least 10 percent of the numbers that existed at the time of first contact. Relatedly, the American Indian population is increasing in that the 2004 census report placed the population at almost three million.

A large percentage of the decrease in population can be attributed to the European introduction of diseases such as diphtheria, smallpox, measles, chickenpox, influenza, scarlet fever, malaria, typhus, and typhoid fever. American Indians had no immunity to these diseases. The death toll from these diseases and others was so great that Susan Harjo has labeled it as one of the greatest natural catastrophes of all times.

The other major event that added to the decimation of the American Indian population was wars which generally were fought as a result of the

Europeans attempting to seize American Indians land. The process of taking Indian land not only impacted the number of American Indians, but also had an impact on their entire way of life. Despite numerous treaties and promises that assured Indians that their lands were safe from the encroachment of Euro-Americans, their land base has been significantly reduced. Their land was taken and generally they were forced to relocate to land which the United States government considered as unsuitable for Euro-American inhabitation.

Susan Harjo (1988) provides an excellent overview of what has happened to the American Indian's land base:

> The Indian land base has gone from 138 million acres in 1887 to approximately 50 million acres today. There are many reasons for land loss, including flooding for Corps of Engineer projects, creation of national monuments, taking of land for tax defaults and welfare payment, invalidation of wills, and Bureau of Indian Affairs (BIA) forced sales on the open market. The 1917 Allotment Act or Dawes Act alone resulted in the loss of more than half the Indian land. Of the 48 million acres left after the Allotment Act took its toll, 20 million acres were desert or semiarid and not suitable for cultivation. The federal government promised to irrigate these lands and "to make the deserts bloom." For most of these arid reservations, this promise remains unfulfilled.
>
> The Allotment Act allocated land on reservations that had been guaranteed by treaties. Every family head was to receive 160 acres and a single person 80 acres. The idea was that Indians should become farmers and thereby become more civilized. This notion of farming was not well received by many tribes and was particularly onerous to many Indians in the Great Plains. The land was to be held in trust for 25 years. Indians deemed "competent" by the federal government could end the trust status, own the land in fee simple, and become U. S. Citizens. Any land outside the allotted acreage was declared to be "excess" and sold to non-Indian settlers.

The relocation of American Indian is without a doubt one of the most shameful acts forced upon any group of people. Thousands of people were removed from places and ways of living that were familiar to them and forced to adjust to environments and surroundings that were unfamiliar. Additionally, many were required to adopt a new lifestyle that was foreign to them. Perhaps the most familiar acts of relocation to Americans is the "Trail of Tears" where the Cherokee people and other Indian tribes were moved from the Southeast area of the United States to Oklahoma. During this move, thousands of Indians died and many more suffered dehabilitating illness. While this forced march is the most often discussed relocation, there were many more. In fact, all of the "Five Civilized Tribes" (Cherokee, Creek, Chickasaw, Choctaw, and Seminole) as well as several others were relocated to what was titled Indian Territory, later to be named Oklahoma (meaning home of the red man).

The promise of an "Indian Land," where they would be free from further white encroachment ended in 1889 when parts of what is now Oklahoma were opened for non-Indian settlement. The frontier dash for free land further depleted the Indian's land base. In 1936, the Indian Reorganization Act was passed by the U. S. Congress and the result was the ending of the allotment policy, and as Susan Harjo points out, the Indian land base has remained relatively constant since that time.

As strange as it may seem today, America's first people were not considered citizens as the U. S. government was formed. During the previously mentioned allotment period, if the American Indian's land was held in "fee status," they were given citizenship. American Indian World War I veterans were granted citizenship by a law passed in 1919. Finally, in 1924, the Indian Citizenship Act was passed.

Assimilation

Susan Harjo (1988) identifies what she considers three major ways in which the goals of assimilation were to be programmed with American Indians: (1) Allowing Christian groups to establish their denominations on Indian land to convert Indians to Christianity, thus getting them to forsake their religious beliefs and practices and various religious ceremonies which to many of the Euro-Americans were paganistic. (2) Imposing an educational system upon the children that had as its primary objective to instill non-Indian values. This was done through a boarding school system which required the children to be separated from their parents for up to twelve years. The children were forbidden to speak their tribal language or practice any of the tribal traditions. Parents and relatives were not allowed to visit the children during the school year. The boarding school staff impressed upon the children that their tribal traditions were savage. Blanchard (1983) says these deplorable efforts were attempts to "civilize" the children. Scholars such as Lowrey (1983), Josephy (1982), Blanchard (1983), and Kleinfeld and Bloom (1977) feel that this experience, along with others, had a definite impact upon weakening the various American Indian cultures. Federal efforts were made to break up tribal land holdings and turn Indians into individual land owners, imposing taxes on their lands.

Again, I rely on the knowledge base of Susan Harjo to provide an explanation of the termination period.

> During the period from World War II to 1961, a series of disruptive assimilation efforts occurred to force Indians into the melting pot. This era is referred to as the "termination period." During the 1950s federal Indian policy involved the termination of the tribal-federal relationship with certain Indian govern-

ments, the liquidation of their estates, the transfer of federal responsibility and jurisdiction to states and the physical relocation of Indian people from reservations to urban areas. Termination legislation affected more than 100 tribes, bands and rancheros; some 12,000 individual Indians were disenfranchised, and 2.5 million acres of Indian land were removed from trust status.

It is abundantly clear that all of these efforts were to destroy the various cultures and instill a belief that the new ways were superior and better. The current conditions of some American Indian people is vivid and compelling evidence that many of these efforts were successful.

Recent laws such as Public Law 93-638, Indian Self-Determination and Educational Assistance Act, Indian Child Welfare Act, and the American Indian Religious Freedom Act are attempts by the U. S. government to allow American Indians to have the freedom to determine their own destinies.

Indian Self-Determination and Educational Assistance Act gives tribes the right to contract with the appropriate agencies to conduct and administer programs which are needed.

Indian Child Welfare Act forbid the removal of Indian children from their homes and placed with non-Indian families.

American Indian Religious Freedom Act protects Indians' rights to believe, express, and exercise the traditional religions of the American Indian, Eskimo, Aleut, and Native Hawaiians.

Social Issues

A major social issue for most American Indian tribes has been the regaining and/or maintenance of their cultures. If there is one common thread which weaves its way through all American Indian tribes, it is a belief in harmony with mind, body, spirit, and mother earth. Most American Indians view the earth as a living entity which has a spirit, thus, land is an important part of their cultural ways of life as is their spiritual and religious ceremonies. Several tribes have filed law suit in an attempt to regain land that was taken from them and opened for non-Indian settlement. Additionally, other tribes are engaged in discussion with the U. S. government over the ownership of Indian land on which the government has placed national monuments. Moreover, considerable concern exists among many tribes over the disturbance of sacred grounds, particularly the removal of Indian artifacts, including the bones of Indian ancestors.

Giving consideration to the facts presented in the historical background section, with regard to loss of land base, the efforts to destroy their religious beliefs and the attempt to degrade and remove other aspects of their culture by removing children from the home and placing them with non-Indian families and/or sending them to boarding schools, one can imagine the inner turmoil and confusion that many American Indians feel. Confusion is often heightened as American Indians engage in an emotional tug-of-war over the desires to maintain traditional values and the need to adjust to the dominant society values. The results of this emotional struggle tend to appear in some of the behaviors of American Indians, particularly in the form of substance abuse. Susan Harjo (1993) views substance abuse as the number one social issue among Indian people and alcohol-related diseases and accidents as the biggest killers of Indians. It is estimated that approximately nine percent of the American adult population experience significant drinking problems in contrast on some reservations the drinking problem is as high as 50 percent (Carpenter et al., 1985). Beauvis and LaBoueff (1985) feel that 80 to 90 percent of the problems Indian people have are related to abuse of alcohol and drugs.

Louise Sinclair (1987) provides a to-the-point summary of American Indian cultures and substance abuse:

> To be an adolescent and an Indian is to be in a state of crisis, of social and cultural confusion. The Indians belong to a cultural group that is undergoing its own identity crisis; Native people as a whole experience conflict and confusion, as they find themselves gradually immersed in white society. The pressure to conform to the way of life of the majority is great, yet the importance of the Native culture is equally great. The results of this conflict are saddening: drug and alcohol abuse affects as much as 70 percent of the Native population, and fatalities related to drug and alcohol occur more than three times as frequently to Natives as to the rest of the population.

Substance abuse appears to be the genesis of many problems Indian people encounter, including the high rate of accidents and homicides. Reasons for the high rate of substance abuse, particularly alcohol and drugs, will be explored. Also other issues which could be considered as social issues such as high unemployment rate, school dropout rate, and teen pregnancy will be discussed in other sections.

American Indians and Disabilities

While the total population of American Indians is set at approximately approximately one percent of the entire U. S. population, the rate of disabilities is disproportionately high, being estimated by some sources as high as 22 percent. Comparatively, the U. S. disability percentage considering all ethnic and racial groups is in the 19 percent range. The 20 percent rate of disability among the American Indian population makes their percentage not only higher than the national percentage, it is also higher than any other ethnic and racial groups.

American Indians, as a population of people, are younger than Euro-Americans as well as younger than the other major racial and ethnic groups. The median age for American Indians, in 2000 was approximately 28 years, whereas the median age for U. S. all races is approximately 36 years The American Indian population is a young population with the majority being in the child-bearing age; therefore, one may expect to see an increase in the future population statistics.

Given the fact that American Indians have a disproportionate rate of disabilities, the most logical question is, "Why?" At the risk of oversimplifying a complex question, perhaps the answer can be summarized by stating "lifestyle." In this situation, lifestyle is not intended to be negative or imply immoral behaviors but is intended to assert that the living conditions and the manner of life that society has forced upon many Native Americans places them "at risk" for various types of disabilities. To be more specific, many American Indians live on reservations and many of the reservations are in isolated locations with few chances for employment. Consequently, the boredom and lack of off-reservation socialization cause some to abuse alcohol which may lead to diseases such as cirrhosis of the liver and other liver diseases, automobile and other accidents, attempted suicide, and homicides. By no means do all disabilities occur on and to persons living on reservations. For American Indians on and off reservations, racism and discrimination cause stress and despair which can have similar results as the isolation and loneliness of the reservation. Additionally, the economic realities for many American Indians mean they have to live on minimal incomes; consequently many of the foods they consume have a high fat and caloric content. As will be discussed in health issues, American Indians have a high rate of obesity, which along with inappropriate dietary habits, is a major contributor to the development of diabetes. Relatedly, diabetes is a major contributor to blindness and the need for amputations. Also, diet and obesity are major causes of heart conditions as well as hypertension and this can lead to cerebrovascular diseases.

The obvious bad news is that American Indians rank high on many of the indices of poor health conditions; however, the good news is that these conditions are caused by lifestyle conditions that can be corrected by altering these lifestyle conditions. The author would like to point out that this is not an "Indian problem" but a national problem that will require cooperation and collaboration of Indians and the appropriate local, state, and federal governmental agencies and organizations. After all, American Indians did not create the problem of lifestyle in isolation; therefore, they should not be expected to solve all of the problems without appropriate assistance.

Major Health Issues

"On almost every indicator of morbidity, mortality, and quality of life, American Indians are substantially worse off than the dominant culture and as bad or worse off than other minorities." This observation was made by McCubbin and his associates (1993) as they attempted to provide a summary of the health conditions of Native Americans. They continued their observations with the following comments:

> Although the death rate for Native American infants is approximately equal to that for all races, postneonatal deaths and death from Sudden Infant Death Syndrome (SIDS) are nearly twice as common among Native Americans as in the general population. The prevalence of diabetes among Native Americans exceeds 20 percent in many tribes. The Native American death rate for alcoholism is four times higher than the national average. Alcoholism is also related to incidences of Fetal Alcohol Syndrome (FAS) six times greater than in the general population, to over 60 percent of cases of child abuse and neglect, to 75 percent of accidents and a homicide rate 60 percent higher than that of the general population. The suicide rates among various Native American tribes (also related to alcoholism) are three times the rates for general population.

In addition to the previously mentioned health issues, American Indians experience greater problems than the national average with: heart disease, accidents, cancer and diabetes. Moreover they have higher incidence rates, according to the Indian Health Service (1994), of tuberculosis (five times higher than the national average, alcoholism (43.5 times higher), homicide (71 times higher), suicide (54 times higher) and pneumonia/influenza (44 percent higher). At this point I will provide a brief discussion of several of the major health issues: alcoholism, fetal alcohol syndrome, diabetes, obesity, and drug use.

Alcoholism

According to Carpenter et al. (1985), alcohol abuse constitutes the single most significant health problem among American Indians. Excessive consumption of alcohol appears to be the norm among some American Indians and, unfortunately, this pattern of rapid and excessive drinking becomes part of adolescent American Indians who begin to drink in peer groups where drinking may be sanctioned. Recent evidence indicates that problem drinking is quite prevalent among adolescents and younger Indian children.

The fact that there is a high rate of alcoholism among American Indians should in no way be considered as low moral standards and a lack of self-control. There are some major contributing factors that have caused many American Indians to become dependent upon alcohol. (1) Poverty—In a message to the United States Congress in 1970, President Richard M. Nixon described Native Americans as "the most deprived and most isolated minority group in our nation." Indian reservations have been described as "America's third world" and American Indians have described themselves as "beggars in our land." Some public health officials contend that the depth of poverty among American Indians is reflected in that American Indian's homes were five times more likely to be lacking plumbing and nearly fourteen times more likely to be without sewage disposal than other homes in America. Reservation life—Approximately half of the American Indian population lives on reservations and, according to Beauvis and LaBoueff (1988), poverty and its attendant ills of poor nutrition, poor health, and inadequate housing and transportation are still a way of life on most reservations. It is postulated that these conditions, coupled with the isolation of many reservations, lead to chronic stress which put many American Indians in a vulnerable position when confronted with opportunities to use alcohol and/or drugs. Allen Cheadle and associates (1994) support Fred Beauvis and his associate's position with these comments, "Reasons for the high levels of alcohol abuse among Indians on reservations have been attributed to the poverty and hopelessness associated with reservation life and with problems of adapting traditional Indian values to a culture that is predominantly white with contrasting values." (3) Peer pressure—The combination of pressure from one's peers "to be social," and the lack of anyone discouraging the use of alcohol leads many adults and, more particular, adolescents down the path toward excessive drinking.

As destructive as excessive alcohol consumption is, it can be a double disaster for females, particularly those within the child-bearing ages. The consumption of alcohol affects both the female and her unborn child. This condition is called Fetal Alcohol Syndrome (FAS).

Fetal Alcohol Syndrome

The consumption of alcohol while pregnant has been known to be a danger to babies for many centuries. In Judges 13:7, the Bible states, "Behold, thou shalt conceive and bear a son: and now drink no wine or strong drink." Alcohol consumed during pregnancy reaches the fetus in a very short time; thus, as Streissguth et al. (1988) correctly contend, "Prenatal exposure to alcohol can damage the baby and have profound and lasting affects on its development."

The National Organization on Mental Retardation (1992) explains that Fetal Alcohol Syndrome refers to a group of physical and mental birth defects resulting from a woman drinking alcohol during pregnancy. Fetal Alcohol Syndrome, according to Masis and May (1991), is the leading known cause of mental retardation. Other symptoms can include organ dysfunction, growth deficiencies before and after birth, central nervous dysfunction resulting in learning disabilities and lower intelligence, and physical malformation in the face and cranial areas (Streissguth, LaDue, Randels, 1988). In addition, children may experience behavioral and mental problems which may progress into adulthood.

Again, the National Organization on Mental Retardation provides valuable information with regard to how alcohol affects the development of the fetus. It is believed that alcohol may affect the way cells grow and arrange themselves as they multiply, altering tissue growth in the part of the fetus that is developing at the time of exposure. The brain is particularly sensitive to alcohol which diminishes the development of cells.

Frequently, children born with Fetal Alcohol Syndrome have low birth weight. As the infant grows, it is not uncommon for various symptoms to develop, such as muscle problems, bone and joint problems, genital defects, and heart defects.

Other less obvious symptoms such as mental retardation and developmental delays may also occur. Frequently, social adaptions are difficult for persons with Fetal Alcohol Syndrome. Studies have shown that persons with Fetal Alcohol Syndrome have long-term disabilities enduring into adolescence and adulthood. Perhaps the most handicapping long-term disability is poor adaptive behavior. In addition to endangering their children, American Indian women who drink alcohol to an excess are at risk for advanced liver disease, decreased life expectancy, and because of depression, are at risk to be involved in domestic violence.

As a result of the various problems associated with excessive drinking and the high rate of alcoholism among American Indians, tribal leaders and public health official have declared alcoholism the number one health problem. The magnitude of the problem has promoted some Indians to say that alcoholism is a form of genocide.

Diabetes

Health complications from diabetes makes it the sixth leading cause of death among American Indians (Healthy People 2000). Relatedly, the prevalence rate for diabetes in American Indians is higher than any of the other ethnic minority groups–African Americans, Hispanic/Latino Americans, and Asian and Pacific Americans.

A deficiency in the body's ability to produce insulin is a simplified definition of diabetes. Bogardus and Lillioja (1992) explains that diabetes is classified into two categories: insulin-dependent diabetes mellitus (IDDM) and noninsulin-dependent diabetes mellitus (NIDDM). They further point out that there are approximately ten million people in the United States who are considered diabetic. Noninsulin-dependent diabetes appears to be the most prevalent form of diabetes, comprising approximately 90 percent of the cases.

The noninsulin-dependent diabetes is the most prevalent form among American Indians (Orchard et al., 1992). As there is significant cultural and ethnic diversity among American Indian tribes, there are wide variations in the prevalence of diabetes among American Indians. As an example, the Pima Indians have the highest reported prevalence rate of Noninsulin-dependent diabetes in the world, as high as 50 percent of those 35 years of age and older (Sugarman et al., 1993); whereas, according to Newman (1992), Alaska Natives have the lowest rates in America, only half that of the United States population all races and ethnic groups. A major reason for the difference appears to be difference in lifestyles, particularly dietary habits.

Both forms of diabetes, insulin-dependent (Type I) and noninsulin-dependent (Type II) can and do cause disabilities such as amputees (neuropathy), blindness (retinopathy), cardiovascular disease (CVD), and End Stage Renal Disease (nephropathy).

Amputations–Persons with diabetes are at significant risk for lower extremity amputations; such procedures are 15 times more common among persons with diabetes. Persons with diabetes account for approximately 50,000 (50%) of all nontraumatic amputations performed in the United States.

Blindness–Diabetes mellitus is a major cause of blindness in the United States and is the leading cause of new blindness in working-aged Americans. Diabetic retinopathy accounts for approximately 12 percent of new cases of blindness each year in the United States. Persons who have diabetes are 25 times more at risk for blindness than the general population. It is projected that, if untreated, 70 percent of American Indians persons with diabetes will develop retinopathy which may lead to more serious visual problems.

Cardiovascular Disease–Diabetes may lead to cardiovascular disease which is the leading cause of morbidity and mortality among persons with diabetes. The annual risk for death or disability from cardiovascular disease is two to three times greater for persons with diabetes than for persons without diabetes. Additionally, persons with diabetes are at risk for cerebrovascular disease and for coronary artery disease at a rate that is two to three times greater than the general population.

One of the suspected contributing causal factors for development of diabetes is obesity. In many cases, obesity is a result of lifestyle, thus is preventable.

Obesity

Welty (1991) reminds us that American Indian have experienced an epidemic of diabetes, increasing rates of cardiovascular disease and hypertension, and poor survival rates for breast cancer—all partially attributed to the increasing prevalence of obesity over the past generation. Further comments by Welty indicate that obesity may be a contributing factor to gallstones, arthritis, and to adverse outcomes of pregnancy. Additionally, research points to obesity as one of the most common risk factors predisposing persons to certain cancers, as well as osteoarthritis.

Broussard (1991) provides us with some very revealing and informative facts and statistics with regard to obesity and American Indians.

> In the United States, the greatest incident of obesity is found among minority women of low socioeconomic status. In 1987 it was estimated that the prevalence of obesity in Native American males older than 18 years of age was 13.7 percent compared with the U. S. rate of 9.1 percent for males. The prevalence for Native American females was 16.5 percent compared with the U. S. rate of 8.2 percent for females. Obesity rates in Native American adolescents and preschool children are higher than the respective rates for U. S. all races combined.

In summary, according to Barbara Erickson (1993), obesity is more prevalent in American Indians than in the U. S. population in practically all age groups. Adult American Indian men and women are significantly more overweight than the comparable U. S. population. Obesity rates in Native American adolescents and preschool children are higher than the respective rate for U. S. all-races combined. The rates of obesity differ among the various tribal regions. A possible explanation is that their cultures have undergone significant changes over the past half century and as a consequence, their lifestyles and diets have changed. Studies indicate that factors shown to influence the development and maintenance of obesity include lack of physical activity, diet, ethnicity, income, education, and genetic susceptibility.

Drug Use

Rhoades and associates reported in 1988 that drug use is well established among Indian fourth to sixth graders, with 26 percent having tried marijuana. Continuing with the report, it indicated more than 50 percent have tried marijuana by the time they enter the seventh grade. Consequently, by the eighth grade, 63 percent have tried marijuana and 46 percent can be classified as users, and almost seven percent were listed as daily users. These statistics are of the good news, bad news variety. The bad news is that there appears to be a significant number of American Indian youth who experiment with drugs, particularly marijuana. However, the good news is that only a small percentage become daily users.

There appears to be a higher rate of drug use among reservation youth than the American Indian youth living off reservations (Beauvis 1992). One possible reason is again the isolation and poor living conditions found on some reservations.

While the statistics regarding drug use are cause for concern, one should not lose sight that more American Indian youth do not use drugs on a daily basis than those who do use them; therefore, an appropriate intervention would be to mobilize those who abstain and have them work with the users in an effort to convince them to become drug free. As Beauvis and LaBoueff postulate, "Among younger children, at least, there is practically no use if friends do not encourage drug use and if friends would actively try to prevent one from using drugs."

Providers of Health Care Services

Medicine Men. Long before we had primary care physicians and managed care, medicine men provided the health care for American Indians. Through the use of herbs, spiritual and religious ceremonies, as well as many other methods, the medicine man provided for the health needs of his people. During the period of assimilation where the U. S. government and others were attempting to strip Native American people of their culture, one of the things that was almost lost was the tradition of the medicine man. Fortunately, some of the traditions were retained; consequently, some American Indians rely to some degree upon the efforts and knowledge of the medicine man. There are those who question the effectiveness of these practices; however, as with any healing process, it is aided by faith.

Indian Health Services. As Hershman and Campion (1985) accurately state, today's Native Americans are faced with many chronic health problems. Because of the migration and changing ways of life, many of the traditional ways of diagnosing and treating illnesses have been lost. They continue by stating that despite the changes, Indian people are more receptive to modern medicine; however, some will resort to the medicine man or other traditional medicine if a cure is not forthcoming. Relatedly, the Indian Health Service is the agency designated to provide health care to American Indians.

A student in one of the author's classes made the following astute analysis regarding the way many American Indians handle their personal health:

Typically, the Native American lives in circumstances where habitual lifestyles develop. Proportionately, health is a concern. Untreated illness is commonplace. From self-diagnosing and self-medicating to self-care these become patterns of response.

One buys time with these methods. Eventually, conditions develop leading to a severely compromised health status. A true state of emergency occurs and the individual becomes a patient. (Theresa Prairie Chief, 1993)

Historical Background of Indian Health Service

In 1954, Public Health Service took over the Bureau of Indian Affair's role of providing Indian health care. To help determine some of the health needs and concerns and to become prepared to deliver health care to American Indians, in 1957, a comprehensive health survey was conducted. The results were stunning in that there were significant statistical differences existing relative to other populations in the United States. Virtually all comparisons were undesirable.

Not until 1976 were issues created by the study addressed. The Indian Health Care Improvement Act was formulated to provide corrections to the disparities. Because of inadequate funding, some of the problems remained to be corrected. In 1988, reauthorization of the act gave the Indian Health Service agency status within the Public Health Service.

Most knowledgeable observers of American Indian affairs acknowledge that the Indian Health Service needs additional funding and more efficient management to better serve the health requirements of American Indian people. Therefore, it will take a collective effort of Indian and concerned non-Indian people to improve the health services available to Indian people which will dramatically improve the health of the American Indian population.

Employment Issues

Traditionally, American Indians have had a much higher rate of unemployment than most other races and ethnic groups. One of the reasons for the high unemployment rate is that there are not many job opportunities on reservations and since some reservations are in remote areas, traveling to a job site outside of the reservation boundaries becomes challenging, especially if one has limited transportation options. Similar to African American youth, American Indian youth unemployment is double the Euro-American youth unemployment rate.

In discussing problems of American Indians frequently the issue of Indian reservations, their remoteness and lack of opportunities become points for discussion. Too frequently, this discussion is slanted because it is felt that those living on reservations are disadvantaged. While this may be true in some and perhaps many aspects, one has also to realize approximately 50 percent of American Indians do not live on reservations. Consequently, their employment possibilities are enhanced. The point is that part of the reason for high unemployment rates for American Indians is prejudice against Indians. Until the nation effectively addresses the problem of employment discrimination based upon ethnicity, American Indians and African Americans will continue to have unemployment rates that are double and triple that of their Euro-American counterparts.

Economic Issues

Some tribes and their members are improving economically, especially since they have become involved in gaming (bingo, lotto, pull tabs, casinos, etc.). Additionally and more prevalent than gaming, many tribes have developed various industries such as ownership of hotels, motels, plant nurseries, and convenience stores, to mention a few. Obviously, this is a giant step forward in that it produces revenue and provides employment for Indian people.

A final point is that there are some misperceptions concerning American Indians and money. First, it is not true that by virtue of being an Indian one automatically receives a check from the government. Some American Indians receive checks for oil, mineral and/or grazing leases on land that the U.S. government holds in trust for them or their tribe. Second, American Indians do not pay taxes similar to other American citizens. The misperceptions perhaps come from the fact that Indians do not pay federal income taxes on income from trust lands held for them by the United States, nor do they pay state income taxes on income earned on an Indian reservation. Third, being an Indian does not constitute a tuition-free college education.

American Indians receive very few special economic concessions. The ones they do receive are more than justified given the extent of the resources they had to give to the government, which some would say was taken and/or stolen from them.

Family Dynamics

Historical Perspective of American Indian Families

Because of the diversity among American Indian tribes, over 500 different tribes each having its own cultural background, it is with extreme difficulty one encounters in attempting to describe American Indian families. In reality, it is impossible to condense American Indian family characteristics into a neat concise overview. Deloria (1969) attempts to dispel the myth of American Indians as a homogeneous group with these terse comments, "People can tell just by looking at us what we want, what should be done to help us, how we feel and what a real Indian is like."

The stereotyping of Indian people perhaps began with and continues through the media. The image of American Indian family life is that of the tribal leaders sitting around a fire making decisions for all the tribal people, thus the idea is that Indian family life was dictated to and controlled by the tribal leaders and elders. When the image magnified beyond the tribal fire and counsel activities to the family unit, it was projected as the male-dominated family where the father was the hunter and provider and the female's roles were subordinate to the male. No doubt in some tribes, this is a fairly accurate view of family life; however, in other tribes, this is quite distorted in that women were not totally subservient to the males. The point is that it is difficult at best to portray American Indian family life in a homogeneous fashion.

As already discussed, as American Indian people encountered European immigrants, the Europeans attempted to destroy the American Indian's cultures and "civilize" them. One of the ways was to remove the children from their homes and send them to boarding schools where they were educated in the "white man's ways."

> Susan Shown Harjo (1993) effectively describes the intent of the boarding schools: The establishment of boarding schools for children was a deliberate attempt to disrupt traditional child-rearing practices. Children were forcibly removed from their homes for up to 12 years, and parents and other relatives were not allowed to visit the children during the school year. Children were taught that their traditions were savage and immoral. There are many accounts of parents in this century camping outside the gates of boarding schools to get a glimpse of their children.

Harjo continues by pointing out other impacts the boarding school systems have had on the American Indian family dynamics in that most grandparents and many current Indian parents are the product of boarding and other governmental schools. She contends that for those who spent a considerable portion of their formative years in the schools away from their families, they have very little in the way of family rearing role models. Harjo concludes her comments by explaining that in past years there have been attempts to recover from past experiences and reestablish traditional Indian family values. These values, according to Harjo, include extended family concept. She believes the extended family identification is central to citizens of Indian nations.

Mother Role

As is true in most segments of American societies, the mother's role in Native American families is one of nurturing the young; however, there is evidence that in the past several years, this role has expanded toward becoming coresponsibile with the male (again levels of acculturation come into play in this matter). American Indian women tend to be employed at approximately the same percentage as males and there is increasing numbers of female-headed households.

Father Role

The idea of the male as the primary provider within any family, regardless of race or ethnicity, is no longer a realistic view of family life in America. American Indian males, similar to African American males, experience considerable difficulties in securing and maintaining gainful employment. (This is evident by the high rate of unemployment among American Indian males.) Therefore, the roles of American Indian males are beginning to be restructured. As the American Indian females are sharing provider responsibilities, the males are beginning to share in the nurturing and household.

Intervention

In the section on African American intervention, we began by discussing Cross' Black Identity Model as a method of determining the stage at which African Americans were with regard to their acceptance of their racial identity. As was discussed in the historical background of this chapter, American Indians have experience numerous attempts at degrading and destroying their heritages and cultures. Sandra Choney and her associates (1995) convincingly argue that it is more appropriate to consider American Indians' levels of acculturation rather than attempt to develop a theory or model of Indian identity. Their primary reason for taking this position is that because of the diversity among American Indians with regard to their tribal affiliations, American Indians derive their cultural base more from tribal association than from any concept of "Indianness." They further point out that the fact there is no homogeneous world view complicates the determination of a single description of Indianness or racial identity and makes its use as a defining concept problematic. Consequently, Choney et al. believe that attempts to explain American Indians through racial identity does more harm than good in that it has the potential of perpetuating the stereotypical thinking of American Indians as a homogeneous group of people. Conclusively, they urge helpers to assess American Indian clients on the basis of levels of acculturation.

Levels of Acculturation

In assessing level of acculturation of American Indians, determining tribal affiliation, and whether the person originates and/or lives in a rural, urban, or reservation area are necessary.

Once tribal affiliation is determined, the helper should determine the following:

1. Does the person participate in tribal activities?
2. What type of tribal activities does the person participate?
3. What are some of the customs and beliefs of the tribe?
4. How does the person feel with regard to the customs and beliefs?
5. What is the tribal language?
6. Does the person speak the language?
7. When does the person speak the language?
8. Does anyone in the family (including extended family) speak the language?
9. Which language is spoken the most in the home and at tribal events, English or tribal language?
10. What does being an Indian mean to him?

It is also helpful to determine the type of schooling, whether the person attended a missionary school, tribal school, and/or traditional American school. Additional information that helps determine level of acculturation is asking questions with regard to how and with whom the person socializes, as well as the types of entertainment in which the person engages.

Initially, the rehabilitation professional helper will be able to determine some aspects of level of acculturation by the way the person is dressed, speech patterns, and mannerisms. A word of caution is appropriate at this point in that the helper should not expect all traditional American Indians to enter his office wearing moccasins, buckskin pants and shirt, beads, and speak in the movie stereotype manner. However, if the person appears in a three-piece suit, it is an indication his level of acculturation is high. Even so, it is not uncommon for American Indians to live in two worlds: during week days, they function as a nontraditional American Indian; however, on the weekends, they become more involved in traditional tribal customs. The best and really the only way for the helper to know is to ask the person how does he view himself?

The point for determining rural, urban or reservation background provides information with regard to lifestyle and opportunities. This information can be used to help determine level of acculturation but also can be used by the helper to determine resources available to be used in the rehabilitation process.

William Martin, Jr., and his colleagues (1988), reporting from a survey of Vocational Rehabilitation counselors who work with American Indians, identified the following barriers in delivering rehabilitation services to American Indians living on reservations:

1. Lack of understanding cultural differences
2. Transportation problems
3. Lack of employment opportunities
4. Lack of commitment to Vocational Rehabilitation goals
5. Language barriers, and
6. Substance abuse problems.

Communication Style

In reading books that discuss culture of minority groups, quite frequently these documents state that American Indians value silence, thus they tend to be more nonverbal than verbal. Often to the amazement of a professional helper, he encounters a very articulate American Indian. The point being made is that this is a generalization that the rehabilitation professional cannot afford to become trapped into believing. American Indians' communication styles and abilities have the same range as Euro-Americans.

The stereotype of American Indians as nonverbal is an interesting myth because the reality is that the history of most American Indian tribes is based in oral communication. To be more specific, most American Indian history has been transferred from generation to generation orally; therefore, many American Indians are great storytellers. One suspects this myth of the nonverbal American Indian began because their communication styles were different than Euro-Americans, thus rather than acknowledging the differences, American Indians were tagged as nonverbal.

Similar to other ethnic minorities, in a helping relationship, American Indians may be very "guarded" with their information and release small bits at any given time. The reason for this is that they are very suspicious of giving information to "officials" in that in the past this receipt of such information by government officials and missionaries was used against them. In fact, in some cases they lost their land and children from officials knowing too much of their business.

Another fact which the rehabilitation helper should be aware is that some American Indians, similar to African Americans, are often very good at reading body language. This is not a generalization because the reason for this is simple; for a group of people who were restricted in their communication and interaction with Euro-Americans, they learned to read body language to determine fact from fiction when dealing with Euro-Americans. This means that the rehabilitation helping professional must be very aware of his body language and insure that what he communicates verbally is congruent with what his body is communicating.

The final point with regard to communication style is that the rehabilitation helping professional should assess the communication style of the American Indian client and develop the rehabilitation efforts within that style rather than attempting to change the style, unless communication is an aspect of the rehabilitation plan.

Expectations

Realizing that the clients' level of understanding with regard to the rehabilitation process will vary depending upon prior experiences with the mental health process as well as prior experiences with illness and disability, the rehabilitation helping professional must determine what the American Indian client expects from the rehabilitation helping process. The rehabilitation helping professional will be aided in his process of helping if he becomes familiar with the Indian Health Service which is a unique setting that is not available to other ethnic minorities (see the section on Indian Health Services in this chapter). The rehabilitation professional should also be aware that there are varying opinions held by American Indians with regard to the usefulness of the Indian Health Service. Additionally, the clients' expectations may in fact have been influenced (good or bad) by previous experiences with this health service agency. Moreover, the helper should be aware of the faith or lack thereof the American Indian client places in the medicine man. The helpers' efforts may be disregarded by the client if he believes the medicine man can help and further believes the rehabilitation helping professional's work is contrary to what has been prescribed by the medicine man. The helping professional would be wise in this type of situation to include the medicine man in the rehabilitation process.

The final point with regard to expectations is made via the following recommendation offered by Sandra Choney and her colleagues (1995):

1. Some Native Americans, particularly those with more traditional beliefs about health, may respond better to treatment if traditional healers are involved.

2. The use of the extended family can have a positive therapeutic outcome. The counselor, however, should be aware that using the Indian family will be somewhat different than when working with non-Indians. Sessions may occur outside the clinic or office setting. The Indian family may be less motivated to engage in "talk therapy" and more willing to be active agents of change.

3. Differences in communication styles, perceptions of trustworthiness, gender role definitions, medicine and social support networks including family relationships all provide major considerations when undertaking problem identification and treatment planning for Native American clients.

4. Caution must be taken when using standardized tests to assess Native Americans. Life experiences, cognitive structure, use of nonstandard English, differences in epistemologies and economic hardship characterize the lives of many Indian people.

Value Orientation

Similar to the other minority groups discussed in this book, knowledge of history, traditions, and customs, along with asking appropriate questions, will aid the rehabilitation professional helper in identifying some of the client's values. The professional helper should be accepting of these values and whenever possible use them in the rehabilitation plan rather than attempting to force the client to change his values to conform to those that are most comfortable for the professional helper. Additionally, the helper can improve his chances of success with an American Indian client if he will recognize that quite often the client is attempting to live in two cultures—one the dominant society culture, and two, his tribal culture. The professional helper should be sensitive to this and assist the client with this balancing act. In some instances, the most difficult part of this balancing act, especially for a younger American Indian, is remaining connected to his family, particularly the parents who may be more traditionally oriented than he. Some behavioral science specialists in American Indian affairs suggest that the helper can provide support to the client by encouraging him to maintain those things in his culture that have endured over the ages but also learn to adapt to the new techniques and technology of the dominant culture.

Situational Control

Family, religious beliefs and activities, as well as social environment may be more influential in the lives of some American Indians than in the lives of many Euro-Americans. Depending upon the tribe, religious beliefs dictate tribal members' response to illness, disease, and disabilities. Religious activities, medicine men, and church elders may exert considerable influence, especially for American Indians who are traditional in their beliefs. Family and family elders also will provide advice and counsel to some American Indian clients. The rehabilitation professional helper in these instances may need to include these significant influences in the rehabilitation process.

Conclusion

With over 500 tribes, many of which are sovereign nations and many having their own language, American Indians are among the most diverse group of people in the United States. Many attempts have been made by both governmental and non-governmental entities to strip the various tribes and their people of their culture. Boarding schools, forced relocations to unfamiliar environments, as well as attempts to force tribes to not speak their native language are but a few of the things that were done to force American Indians to abandon their ways of life and adapt the Euro-American standards. Even today, some American Indian tribes engage in dialogue with the United States government, attempting to regain land and other property taken from them. Some mental health professionals indicate that the stress of dealing with day-to-day discrimination as well as the isolation and lack of resources that are available on reservations has contributed to the epidemic of alcoholism prevalent among some American Indians. It should be noted that alcoholism occurs at high rates among American Indians who do not live on reservations; therefore, alcoholism is not a reservation problem. Reservation life appears to be a contributing factor.

Alcoholism too frequently is the major contributing factor to accidents and violence. These situations, as well as the emotional problems caused by excessive drinking, are issues rehabilitation helping professionals will encounter when working with some American Indians. Pregnant American Indian women who drink to an excess also risk having babies who suffer from fetal alcohol syndrome.

Noninsulin diabetes also is a major problem among many American Indians. Rehabilitation helping professionals need to be aware of the effects of diabetes, which include amputations and blindness, and other impact upon their American Indian clients.

Unemployment and underemployment creates problems for some American Indians with regard to their abilities to provide safe living environments for their families. Also because of the types of jobs in which many are employed, they are at risk of injuries which may lead to disabilities.

All of these previously mentioned factors have resulted in American Indians having the highest rate of disabilities of any ethnic and/or racial group in America.

Review Questions

1. What were some of the methods used by Euro-Americans to acculturate American Indians?
2. Why should American Indians be considered a diverse group of people?
3. What is the prevalence of disabilities among American Indians?
4. What is a reason for a disproportionate rate of disabilities among American Indians?
5. What are some of the major health problems among American Indians?
6. What are some of the obstacles a rehabilitation helping professional may encounter with regard to working with an American Indian client who lives on a reservation?
7. What impact(s) may occur if you were working with a American Indian who utilizes the services of a Medicine Man?
8. In a helping relationship what are some of the reasons an American Indian may limit his verbal communication?
9. What do you believe are important and relevant cultural factors of American Indians in the rehabilitation process?

Suggested Activities

1. Determine the number and/or percentage of American Indians living in your state.
2. Determine how many tribes are represented in your state.
3. Determine whether your state has reservations. If yes, visit at least two and observe and make notes with regard to the following: living conditions, employment opportunities, educational opportunities and language commonly spoken on the reservation.
4. Determine the percentage of your state's American Indian population which have disabilities.
5. Determine the five leading causes of disabilities among your state's American Indian population.
6. Make a list of five agencies and/or organizations in your state that specialize in assisting American Indians. These organizations do not have to be connected with disabilities. Also summarize the services provided.

References

Bailey, L. (1997). Diabetes as a disability in the Native American population. Unpublished paper, University of Oklahoma Health Sciences Center, Oklahoma City, OK.

Beauvis, F., & LaBoueff, S. (1985). Drug and alcohol abuse interventions in American Indian communities. *International Journal of Addictions, 20*(1):139–171, January.

Beauvais, F. (1992). Comparison of drug use rates for reservation Indians, non-reservation Indians and Anglo youth. *American Indian and Alaska native Mental Health Research, 5*(1):13–31.

Blanchard, E. L. (1983) (1990). In D. W. Sue & D. Sue, *Counseling the culturally different* (2nd ed.). New York: John Wiley and Sons.

Bogardus, C., & Lillioja, S. (1992). Pima Indians as a model to study the genetics of NIDOM. *Journal of Cellular Biochemistry, 48*(40):337–343.

Carpenter, R. Lyons, C., & Miller, W. (1985). Peer-managed self-control program for prevention of alcohol abuse in American Indian high school students: A pilot evaluation study. *International Journal of the Addictions, 20*(2):299–310, February.

Cheadle, A., Pearson, D., Wagner, E., & Psaty, B. (1994). Relationship between socioeconomic status, health status, and lifestyle practices of American Indians: Evidence from a plains reservation population. *Public Health Reports, 109*(3):405–413.

Choney, S. K., Berryhill–Paapke, E., & Robbins, R. R. (1995). The acculturation of American Indians: Developing frameworks for research and practice. In J. G. Ponterotto et al. (Eds.), *Handbook of multicultural counseling.* Thousand Oaks, CA: Sage.

Cunningham, P. J., & Altman, B. M. (1993). The use of ambulatory care services by American Indians with disabilities. *Medical Care, 31*(7):600–616, July.

Deloria, V. (1969). *Custer died for your sins: An Indian manifesto.* New York: Macmillan.

Erickson, B. (1993). Obesity in Native Americans. Unpublished paper, University of Oklahoma Health Sciences Center, Oklahoma City, OK.

Harjo, S. S. (1993). The American Indian experience. In H. P. McAdoo (Ed.), *Family ethnicity.* Newbury Park, CA: Sage.

Hershman, M. J., & Campion, K. M. (1985). American Indian medicine. *The Royal Society of Medicine, 78*:432–434.

Indian Health Service (1996). Trends in Indian Health. U. S. Department of Health and Human Services, Washington, D.C., p. 68.

Indian Health Service (1996). Trends in Indian Health. U. S. Department of Health and Human Services, Washington, D.C., p. 33.

John, R. (1988). The Native American family. In C. H. Mindel et al. (Eds.), *Ethnic Families in America* (3rd ed.). Englewood Cliffs, NJ: Prentice-Hall.

Josephy, A. M. (1982). *Now that the buffalo's gone: A study of today's American Indians.* New York: Knopf.

Kleinfield, J., & Bloom, J. (1977). Boarding schools: Effects on the mental health of Eskimo adolescents. *American Journal of Psychiatry, 134*:411–417.

Lewis, C. (1970). *Indian families of the northwest coast: The impact of change.* Chicago: University of Chicago Press.

Lowrey, L. (1983). Bridging a culture in counseling. *Journal of Applied Rehabilitation Counseling, 14*:69–73.

Martin, Jr., W. E. Frank, L. W., Minkler, S., & Johnson, M. (1988). A survey of vocational rehabilitation counselors who work with American Indians. *Journal of Applied Rehabilitation Counseling, 19*(4):29–34.

Masis, K. B., & May, P. A. (1991). A comprehensive local program for the prevention of fetal alcohol syndrome. *Public Health Reports, 106*(5):484–489.

McCubbin, H. I., Thompson, E. A., Thompson, A. I., McCubbin, M. A., & Kaston,
A. J. (1993). Culture, ethnicity and the family: Critical factors in childhood chronic illnesses and disabilities. *Pediatrics, 91*:1063–70, May.

National Organization on Mental Retardation (1992). *Facts about alcohol use during
pregnancy*, The Arc.

Newman, B. (1993). Diabetes camp for adults. *The IHS Primary Care Provider,
18*(1):3–7.

Orchard, T. J. LaPorte, R. E., & Dorman, J. S. (1992). Diabetes. In J. M. & R. D.
Wallace (Eds.), *Public health and preventive medicine*. Norwalk, CT: Appleton and
Lange, pp. 873–883.

Porter, F. W. (1988). In C. H. Mindel et al. (Eds.), *Ethnic families in America* (3rd ed.).
Englewood Cliffs, NJ: Prentice-Hall.

Prairie Chief, T. (1993). *U. S. health care of Native Americans: The impossibility is the reality.* Unpublished paper, University of Oklahoma Health Sciences Center,
Oklahoma City, OK.

Redhorse, J. G. (1978). Family behavior of urban American Indians. *Social Work,
59*(2):67–72.

Rhoades, E. Mason, R. Eddy, P. Smith, E., & Burns, T. (1988). The Indian Health
Services approach to alcoholism among American Indians and Alaska Natives.
Public Health Reports, 103(6):621–627, November.

Richardson, E. H. (1981). In D. W. Sue & D. Sue, *Counseling the culturally different* (2nd
ed.). New York: John Wiley and Sons.

Sinclair, L. (1987). Native adolescents in crisis. *Canadian Nurse, 83*(8):28–29,
September.

Streissguth, A. P., LaDue, R. A., & Randels, S. P. (1988). A manual on adolescents
and adults with fetal alcohol syndrome with special reference to American
Indians. *Indian Health Service*, Contract #240–83–0035.

Sugarman, J. R. Gilbert, T. J., & Weiss, N. S. (1992). Prevalence of disabilities and
impaired glucose tolerance among Navajo Indians. *Diabetes Care, 15*(1):114–120.

U. S. Department of Health and Human Services. *Healthy People 2000* (DHHS
Publication No. PHS 91–50213). Washington, D.C.: U. S. Government Printing
Office.

Wagner, J. K. (1976). The role of intermarriage in the acculturation of selected urban
American women. *Anthropologica, 18*(2):215–229.

Welty, T. (1991). Health implications of obesity in American Indians and Alaska
Natives. *American Journal of Clinical Nutrition, 53*(6 Suppl.).

Suggested Readings

Dauphinais, P., Dauphinais, L., & Rowe, W. (1981). Effects of race and communication style on Indian perceptions of counselor effectiveness. *Counselor Education and
Supervision, 21*:72–80.

Dauphinais, P. (1993). Boarding schools: Fond memories of anguish and heartache. *Focus, 1*:11–12.

DuFrene, P., & Coleman, V. (1992). Counseling Native Americans: Guidelines for group process. *Journal for Specialists in Group Work, 17*:229–234.

Harjo, S. S. (1993). The American Indian experience. In H. N. McAdoo, *Family ethnicity: Strength in diversity.* Newbury Park, CA: Sage, pp. 199–207.

John, R. (1988). The Native American family. In C. H. Mindel et al. (Eds.), *Ethnic families in America: Patterns and variations,* (3rd ed.). Englewood Cliffs, NJ: Prentice-Hall, pp. 325–363.

Chapter 11

DISABILITY AND WOMEN

Chapter Outline
- Societal Attitudes Toward Women
- Employment Status
- Sexism
- Impact of Disabilities on Women
- Feminine Role
- Marriage and Family
- Economic Status of Women
- Violence Against Women with Disabilities
- Intervention Strategies
- Conclusion

Chapter Objectives
- To identify some of the ways in which women are discriminated
- To identify the prevalence of disabilities among women with disabilities
- To identify some of the impacts a disability has on women

Societal Attitudes Toward Women

Past

The fact that women in the United States only gained the right to vote in 1920 speaks volumes to the past treatment of women in America. The fact that they were not allowed to vote is sufficient proof that women have been victims of discrimination; however, this is only one example of the oppression women have experienced. Giving consideration to the fact that for many years, married women were treated as property of their husbands–in many cases they could not make debts or conclude business transactions without the approval of their spouse.

Despite the subjugated treatment of women, history is replete with examples of women working with their spouses to accomplish remarkable things such as building homes in the wilderness, and establishing communities, schools, hospitals and other facilities that added to the community structure. Regardless of their accomplishments and contributions to the building of America as it currently exists, women were considered the "weaker sex," and in this context, early American society (as well as most other nations) treated women as not being equal to men. In addition to the perceived inherent weakness, women were considered fragile, unable not only to match the physical prowess of men, but also overly sensitive and unable to withstand the pressures of leadership. Given the fact women are the child bearers, it was felt that their natural role in life was nurturing. Nurturing not only consisted of caring for the children; additionally, it included caring for the home and the husband. Therefore, the "pedestal" upon which many women, particularly Euro-American women, were placed, some social scientists as well as feminists have described as being built to help the males maintain their dominance over women. In other words, by characterizing women as the ones who must have the protection of males and by describing the nurturing role as one that could only be done by or at least best be accomplished by females, women were kept in an inferior and dependent condition in relationship to males.

Present

At approximately 51 percent of the United States population, women numerically are not a minority; however, because of continued discrimination by males, women are considered in the same classification as ethnic minorities. Considerable progress with regard to civil rights has been made, particularly in the past thirty years. Women have increasingly moved from being unpaid laborers in the home to being paid employees in businesses and industries. Currently, women constitute over 45 percent of all U. S. workers. Whereas in previous years, if Euro-American women worked outside the home it was considered a reflection on her spouse's inability to adequately provide for the family. Today that attitude has been softened considerably since over 60 percent of Euro-American women are employed outside the home. Likewise, over 57 percent of African American women and over 50 percent of Hispanic/Latino women also work outside the home.

Part of the reason for changing attitudes with respect to the role of women is the changes in the U. S. economic situation. Today, in the majority of families, two wage earners are necessary to provide the standard of living many Americans demand. Additionally and perhaps more important has been that many women have demanded equal treatment.

Employment Status

While women have made gains with regard to equality there remain vestiges of the male dominance. This may be best seen in the U. S. labor force and how women are clustered in certain jobs, particularly the lower paying jobs, while males enjoy better access to higher paying jobs, particularly executive positions. Paula Rothenberg (1995) provides proof with the following 1992 labor force statistics relating to women.

- Women were 99.0% of all secretaries
- Women were 93.5% of all registered nurses
- Women were 98.8% of all preschool and kindergarten teachers
- Women were 89.0% of all telephone operators
- Women were 73.2% of all teachers (excluding college and universities), and
- Women were 86.6% of all data entry operators.

Contrast that information with the following which represents higher paying and more prestigious jobs:

- Women were 8.7% of all engineers
- Women were 30.3% of all lawyers and judges, and
- Women were 26.2% of all physicians.

In addition to not being paid at the same rate as men for the same or similar jobs, women also indicate that they are discriminated against when competing with men for promotions. Many women believe that they are not given an equal chance at higher paying and more prestigious jobs as their male counterparts. This glass ceiling effect is the same complaint that ethnic and racial minorities lodge as they compete with Euro-American males for promotions.

Sexism

Henderson (1994) defines sexism as the process of assigning life roles according to gender. As previously demonstrated, women in the labor force have been traditionally assigned specific roles and in many instances these roles are subordinant to males. As sexism is a reality in America, one must ask, "How and why does it exist?" George Henderson (1994) argues that sexism begins in the family and is perpetuated and supported by the manner in which males and females are socialized. He further believes that the behaviors associated with sexism are so deeply ingrained into our minds that sexist behaviors are generally unconscious. Sexism is a two-way street; both sexes practice the behaviors that lends itself to sexism. Similar to racism, sexism is motivated by power, prejudice, and prestige. The use of one's gender to gain an advantage is just as unfair as the use of one's race to place oneself in a more advantageous position. Perhaps the ultimate discrimination occurs when one combines one's race and gender to afford him/herself a position of privilege.

Women are not immune from discriminating within their own gender. To be more specific, there appears to be a pecking order with Euro-American females at the top, next women of color, and at the lowest are women with disabilities, regardless of racial background. Since women with disabilities occupy a declined position within the female hierarchy, this is an indication that they perhaps experience some unique problems related to the fact they have a disability. Next we will look at the impact of disabilities on women.

Impact of Disabilities on Women

As stated, women experience disabilities at a greater rate than men. Also, with the exception of American Indian women, females of the other major U. S. racial and ethnic groups have a higher percentage of disabilities than males.

The following provides a brief example of the magnitude of disabilities among women:

• Of those with work-related disabilities in the 16-64 age group, 50 percent are women.

• Of the work-related disabilities which are classified as severe, 55 percent are women.

• Of the severely disabled women, 34 percent are African Americans or of Hispanic/Latino origin.

These facts related to work-related disabilities. Adrienne Asch and Michelle Fine (1988) estimate that approximately one-sixth of the U. S. female population has a disability. Regardless of the source, in almost all accounting of rate of disability among Americans, women have the highest rate. Knowing this certainly has value–perhaps of greater value is the impact disabilities have on women.

Feminine Role

The degree to which a disability impacts one's ability to meet society's prescribed female role often plays a major role in the development and maintenance of a healthy self-esteem. Since the early 1970s, physical fitness has been emphasized. No doubt this emphasis has been good for most citizens in that healthier lifestyles have been promoted, i.e., better diets, no smoking, and regular exercise as well as reduction of emotional stress. Various types of diets appear almost monthly, new exercise devices appear at about the same rate as diets, and a variety of "experts" write books and articles all with the expressed purpose of developing the ideal American man or woman. With regard to women, the image goes beyond the perfect body but also includes an unrealistic view of facial beauty. The multitude of beauty products as well as the increased use of plastic surgery are sufficient proof as to the extent some will go in attempting to attain the all-American girl or woman image.

Women with disabilities glean facts and images from the same media as women without disabilities and realize that to a great extent society's judgment of them as attractive or unattractive persons depends upon how close they can approximate the previously mentioned image of the American female. The more severe the disability, generally the more the person deviates from the societal norm of beauty. Thus, a female who has a missing limb, cerebral palsy, or some type of facial disfigurement generally will find it difficult to be accepted as a beautiful person. Deborah Kent (1988), a female with a visual impairment, provides an excellent summarization of the impact of being a female with a disability:

> I can't remember a time when I wasn't aware that I was different from most other people, and that my differentness was a judgment against me. By the dawn of adolescence I had absorbed enough innuendoes to suspect that, no matter what social graces I managed to cultivate, no matter how I dressed or wore my hair, I would never be the kind of girl boys wanted to flirt with or ask on dates. My reading heightened my apprehensions about the future. In books, it seemed the only way a woman could be fulfilled was through the love of a man and the only women worthy of that love were lithe and lovely, unblemished, and physically perfect. The smallest flaw–an uneven gait, a malformed hand, a squint was enough to disqualify a woman from romance, from all hope of happiness. If even a trifling imperfection could loom as such an insurmountable obstacle to fulfillment, what chance was there for a girl who was totally blind and I was?

Deborah Kent's self-disclosure reflects the difficulties often experienced by females with a disability as they are maturing into adults and the difficulties associated with fulfilling the adult role.

Marriage and Family

In some instances, parents overprotect a child who has a disability. This is particularly true of female children. The result of the overprotection quite often is that the child with a disability has difficulty establishing reasonable interaction with members of the opposite sex. It is a proven fact that prejudice and stereotyping gain a foothold as a result of lack of interaction between individuals and groups of individuals. As one adds these misperceptions of females with disabilities with the males evaluating their attractiveness with the aforementioned societal standards, females with disabilities too frequently experience difficulties in establishing meaningful and lasting romantic relationships. To add to the problems of females establishing relationships with the opposite sex that may lead to marriage, frequently nondisabled persons view females with disabilities, particularly those who are visible and/or severe, as asexual, devoid of the normal sexual feelings and urges that most humans experience. While this perception is generally not intended to be malicious it never-the-less has the effect of being a devastating blow to one's self-esteem. When a woman with a disability marries, some people think it is unrealistic for her to have children. The general thought pattern is that persons with disabilities cannot produce a nondisabled child. One only has to remember that in the not-too-distant past, mentally retarded males and females were sterilized to "keep them from reproducing persons similar to themselves."

In addition to the feeling of producing a defective child, there also is the belief that women with disabilities will be unable to adequately care for their offspring. Of course, many of these fears are unfounded and based upon ignorance of what persons with disabilities are capable of doing. Adrienne Asch and Michelle Fine (1988) convincingly argue that women with disabilities have been ignored in studies and research which if conducted would shed light and be very revealing with regard to the needs of women with disabilities and their abilities as well. They explain their position with these comments.

> Women with disabilities traditionally have been ignored not only by those concerned about disabilities but also by those examining women's experiences. The popular view of women with disabilities has been one mixed with repugnance. Perceiving disabled women as childlike, helpless and victimized, nondisabled feminists have severed them from the sisterhood in an effort to advance more powerful, competent and appealing female icons.

According to Asch and Fine, not only have social scientists been negligent in researching and discussing women with disabilities' needs but also women's rights groups have backed away from including them in their manifestoes. The exclusion of women with disabilities, according to Asch and Fine, is deliberate because some of the feminist groups believe women with disabilities not only do not add anything to their cause but in fact detract from their efforts. The following statement, which the authors indicate was made by a feminist academician, speaks clearly to this question, "Why study women with disabilities? They reinforce traditional stereotypes of women being dependent, passive and needy."

Economic Status of Women

Women are in general paid less than men for similar work. Additionally, women have been stereotyped and cluster in certain types of jobs and, in general, these jobs are at the lower end of the pay scale, while males, particular Euro-American males, enjoy open access to the higher paying jobs. This information provides a vivid reminder how women, particularly minority women, are discriminated with regard to their incomes when compared to Euro-American males with similar or even less education and/or training. As deplorable as these facts are, they are even more shocking when a disability is added to the status of a woman. Asch and Fine (1988) state that "disabled men and women are poorer than those without disabilities. Again, disabled women are at the bottom of the ladder, with black disabled women having less income than any other race/gender/disability category."

It is reasonable to expect that a person with a disability who is unable to work will not have a monthly income equal to those who are employed full time; therefore, the fact that women unable to work have a median monthly family income that is 40 percent less than nondisabled females who work full time is not shocking. However, according to Mitchell LaPlante and his associates (1996), the fact that 36 percent of women with disabilities who are unable to work live in poverty does produce waves of shock.

Violence Against Women with Disabilities

A growing concern among rehabilitation helping professionals is violent acts committed against women who have disabilities. Experts in the areas of disabilities and women studies point out that women with disabilities are vulnerable to violence because they are often isolated by society—unable to access needed services. Too frequently, they live in poverty and their disabilities may create mobility and communication problems. Additionally, if a woman has a mental, emotional, and/or severe disability such as cerebral palsy, society tends to discredit her feelings and even disbelieves her when she reports acts of violence, particularly rape.

Because of the nature of some disabilities, women are often unable to escape or defend themselves. Mobility and communication problems place them in extremely difficult situations to provide effective resistance.

Frequently attackers are persons whom the woman with a disability knows, such as parents, siblings, caregivers, and even husbands. These persons know how easily it is to violate the woman with a disability. They also know that in most cases the violence is never reported because the attacker has either threatened to discontinue assistance or she is made to believe officials are unlikely to believe her. Unfortunately, because of feelings of shame, guilt, and/or fear of further isolation or abandonment, women with disabilities endure abusive situations. Sadly, in some instances, their only escape is either death or psychologically retreating into a world in which they feel safe.

Intervention Strategies

It appears clear, at least to this author, that in addition to providing basic rehabilitation services that will assist women with disabilities to engage in a productive life, there is a tremendous need for rehabilitation helping professionals, social workers, psychologists, and educators to advocate with and for women with disabilities.

Conclusion

It is shameful that women with disabilities are forced into positions where they are isolated and totally dependent on others, thus making them easy targets for uncaring and demented family members, friends, and caregivers. The helping professional must not allow himself/herself to continue to see women with disabilities as the ward of their family. As a nation, America has made considerable progress in accepting women as equal to men. No longer do we view wives as the property of their husbands and no longer are men free to treat wives in any manner they desire. Even though these changes have been made with regard to our view of nondisabled women, some women with disabilities continue to be at best indentured servants to their husbands and family. We continue to think that the woman with a disability is incapable of taking care of her needs or express her needs and perhaps know what her needs are; therefore, our society is willing to place women with disabilities in positions that require them to be subservient to their families.

As one considers that women experience disabilities at a greater rate than men, the issue of women with disabilities' rights are of significant importance. These women should not be separated from their families unless it is an abusive setting; however, needed resources should be made accessible and available. Their income should be equal to their male counterparts and economic assistance programs should provide enough so that they are not totally dependent upon their families for needs.

Finally, as helping professionals work with women with disabilities they must remember the ethnic/racial background will impact how women view the world as well as the opportunities that are available to them. The helping professional must keep in mind that for some women with disabilities, society views them as having three strikes against them, gender, disability, and race.

Review Questions

1. Define sexism.
2. Who has the highest rate of disabilities, men or women?
3. Why are women with disabilities vulnerable to violence?
4. Who are the most frequent abusers of women with disabilities?

Suggested Activities

1. Visit a battered women's center and determine how accessible it is for women with a mobility disability.
2. If your college or university has a women's study program, see if they have a course or courses with regard to women with disabilities.
3. Check with the most available social work and/or counseling programs to determine if they have any courses relevant to women with disabilities.
4. Check with your state vocational rehabilitation agency to determine the percentage or number of women with disabilities in your state. If available, obtain the types of disabilities.
5. Interview at least five women with disabilities and obtain their perspectives on being a woman with a disability. Make sure that you pick persons who represent a variety of disabilities.

References

Fine, M., & Asch, A. (Eds.). (1988). *Women with disabilities.* Philadelphia: Temple University Press.

Henderson, G. (1994). *Cultural diversity in the workplace: Issues and strategies.* Connecticut: Praeger Press.

Kent, D. (1988). In search of a heroine: Images of women with disabilities in fiction and drama. In M. Fine & A. Asch (Eds.), *Women with disablities.* Philadelphia: Temple University Press.

National Committee on Pay Equity (1995). The wage gap: Myths and facts. In P. S. Rothenberg (Ed.), *Race, class and gender in the United States* (3rd ed.). New York: St. Martin's Press.

Rothenberg, P. S. (Ed.). (1995). *Race, class and gender in the United States: An integrated study* (3rd ed.). New York: St. Martin's Press.

Suggested Readings

Asch, A. (1984). The experience of disability: A challenge for psychology. *American Psychologist, 39*(5):529–536.

Goffman, E. (1963). *Stigma: Notes on the management of spoiled identity.* Englewood Cliffs, NJ: Prentice-Hall.

Stone, D. A. (1984). *The disabled state.* Philadelphia: Temple University Press.

Chapter 12

DISABILITY AND ELDERLY

Chapter Outline
- Introduction
- African American Elderly
- Asian and Pacific American Elderly
- Hispanic/Latino American Elderly
- American Indian Elderly
- Conclusion

Chapter Objectives
- To identify significant facts with regard to African American elderly and the implications for the helping professional
- To identify significant facts with regard to Asian and Pacific American elderly and the implications for the helping professional
- To identify significant facts with regard to Hispanic/Latino American elderly and the implications for the helping professional
- To identify significant facts with regard to American Indian elderly and the implications for the helping professional

Introduction

Defining what is considered elderly in America appears to be difficult. Some suggest that "old age" begins at age 50 while the majority of experts in the field of aging view age 65 as the defining point for the elderly. The lack of agreement with regard to what constitutes an elderly person emphasizes that in many instances aging is a state of mind. There is no question that aging involves physiological and psychological changes; however, there are persons who have been alive for over 60 years and have fewer physiological deficits than someone half their age. Relatedly, it would not be difficult to identify persons who are 60 years of age who have been rendered by the aging process physically and/or mentally incapable of carrying out normal activities of daily living. In general terms, it is true that as one grows older he or she experiences decreased abilities to function at previous levels of activity and often experiences pain and soreness from performing activities that were formerly done with little effort and no side effects. However, the rate at which one ages varies from person to person which accounts for the 60-year-old man being able to function at a higher level than his 30-year-old junior.

The elderly population is one of the fastest growing groups in America. The following narrative of aging in America, provided by Deborah L. Best and John E. Williams (1996), gives us a glimpse of how the elderly population has grown in America.

> In 1790 when the USA was just 14 years old, the official census began and has been conducted every 10 years ever since. At the time of the first census, barely 2% of the population of the USA was over the age 65, and that number had grown to only 4 percent by 1900 (Kalish, 1982). As of 1990 more than 35 million persons, or almost 16% of the population of the USA was 65 years of age or older. (Hoffman, 1991)

Those persons born in the late 1940s and early 1950s are thinking seriously about retirement and their soon-to-be status of senior citizen. Consequently, America will experience increasing numbers of persons reaching the senior citizen status. This will undoubtedly influence many facets of American life. As one analyzes the population aging in America, we realize that with a large number of Americans approaching senior citizen status, tremendous political influence will be seen with this population base. Therefore, more laws and policies favorable to the needs of this population will be placed at the top of the American agenda. A second factor to consider is that the majority of the economic wealth will be concentrated within this group; therefore, business will begin to pay more attention to the wants, desires, and needs of this group. In summary, this group will exert considerable influence in America during the twenty-first century.

As stated before, even though aging can be a state of mind for some, the reality exists that as we grow older, our bodies begin to show the effects of years of use and, in some cases, abuse. By virtue of the increase of persons reaching age 65, and considering the normal aging process, it is within reason to state that rehabilitation helping professionals will encounter an increased number of persons who are considered elderly. The rehabilitation helping professional must purge from her mind many of the stereotypes of elderly persons, such as unproductive, fragile, uncooperative, and desiring to be young again. Instead, she must see them as a diverse group to be viewed also from their cultural base. Because they are now considered "old" does not mean they shed their skin and suddenly become a member of a neutral ethnic/racial group–the elderly. With this in mind, let's look at the elderly from the perspective of the ethnic/racial group membership.

The author would like to request the reader to review the previous chapters on ethnic/racial minorities because the reader must view the elderly person in the context of their cultural background.

African American Elderly

In 1971, the Committee on Aging in the Group for the Advancement of Psychiatry issued the following statement that summarizes what it means to be an elderly African American:

> Being black and aged frequently means the piling up of life problems associated with each characteristic. The black aged often have less education, less income, smaller or no social security income, less adequate medical service, and fewer family supports than the aged in general. . . .Racism and "ageism" may be combined to prevent the black aged from getting needed services of all types.

It is often from this background that rehabilitation helping professionals must begin their work with elderly African American clients. Additional information of which a helper must be aware is that while many groups reach retirement age, they either retire, semi-retire, or begin a second career. Many African American elderly persons must continue working far beyond the initial time they could retire. In many cases, due to economic reasons, they must continue working even though their health care provider(s) advise against it. Rose C. Gibson (1987) identifies the employment patterns of elderly African Americans and provides the answer to why the elderly black person must work even though working may react negatively to their health status.

> The level and source of income for blacks in old age have also been affected by their lifetime work experiences. Restriction to jobs characterized by instability, low earnings, and few benefits are directly related to low levels of retirement pensions and Social Security benefits. Therefore, the income packages of older blacks, compared to other groups, contain a greater proportion of money from their own work and non-retirement sources.

In addition to inadequate retirement incomes, some African American elderly must continue to work to support grandchildren. An unfortunate result of violence, teen pregnancy and substance abuse has resulted in an increasing number of elderly rearing their second and sometimes third set of children. Many African American families have a strong philosophical viewpoint that there are no unwanted children in the family; therefore, children who become "parentless" are frequently informally adopted by grandparents or other close relatives or family friends.

Implication for the rehabilitation helping professional: the previously mentioned factors have been pointed out because the rehabilitation helping professional must be aware that in many cases his elderly African American client has few skills, poor educational background, minimum income, and maximum needs. Many times these needs require immediate attention; therefore, long-term planning should not be of immediate concern to the helper. The professional helper should become aware of the immediate needs of his client. The helper can be of tremendous benefit to the African American client by identifying resources and assisting the client to access the resources by helping cut through some of the "red tape" that too frequently is associated with various agencies and organizations. The rehabilitation helping professional can assist the client by linking them with support groups which may help by being a social outlet. Additionally, the professional helper can assist by counseling the client(s) to recognize that there is nothing wrong with needing and receiving help. Often African American clients feel guilt about requesting help, they sometimes feel it displays their weakness and failures. In most instances, they are embarrassed about having to ask for help. Despite the stereotype of African Americans as "dole hogs," most would prefer not to receive help; however, circumstances often dictate otherwise.

The rehabilitation helping professional must become aware of the environment in which the person lives. Becoming acquainted with the client's religious beliefs, family support, formal and informal social activities, and the client's crisis-meeting resources will be invaluable information.

Asian and Pacific American Elderly

Kenneth Sakauye (1990) reminds us that unlike African American elderly, "For most Asian Pacific subgroups the culture of poverty is not the primary factor underlying differences. The impact of ethnicity and culture may be more important." Therefore, we will look at Asian Pacific American elderly from the vantage of Chinese Americans, Japanese Americans, Korean Americans, and Filipino Americans.

Chinese American Elderly

As discussed in Chapter 8, Chinese values promote the concept of family power flowing through the father to the eldest son. Likewise, it is the responsibility of the son to provide for the elderly parents. As more and more generations of Chinese Americans are born and reared in the United States, the more acculturated they have become; therefore, according to Huang (1981), there has been a lessening of this responsibility concept. This is not to imply that the Chinese elderly are abandoned by their children, but there is not the strict adherence to the old tradition. It is not uncommon for the Chinese elderly to continue to live in their ethnic community, whereas their offspring have moved to the suburbs.

Implications for the rehabilitation helping professional: It is important for the helper to be aware of the generation to which the Chinese elderly belong as well as how much does he/she follow the old traditions. It is also helpful to determine the kind of social, emotional, and economical support the person has.

Japanese American Elderly

Because of the experience of the internment campus, it is important to understand the generation of the Japanese American. Scholars have pointed out that many Japanese who were placed in these camps refuse to talk about their experiences. Holding in feelings and emotions of this magnitude that would be generated by such an experience has to have an effect on the rehabilitation process. While it may be difficult, if not impossible, to get them to express their thoughts and feelings with regard to the incident, it is imperative that the professional helper be cognizant that feelings and emotions exist and they are having an impact.

The helper should be aware that the Japanese elderly have experienced situations that were hurtful, embarrassing, and cruel. On the other hand, the younger generation did not experience the event but may have been told stories of the camps by their elders. The younger generation will be more acculturated, having moved away from some of the old Japanese traditions. A combination of the emotions associated with the indignities suffered in the campus, plus a feeling of stepping away from traditions can cause emotional stress in the Japanese elderly. The helper must be prepared to deal with this stress, regardless of whether it is verbalized by the Japanese elderly client.

Filipino American Elderly

Paul Kim (1990) speaks of three cultural characteristics cherished among Filipino American elderly of which the rehabilitation helping professional should be aware: respect, social structure, and shame. Respect is extended to everyone, including children, parents, and the elderly. According to Kim, those who are to be respected receive special treatment in Filipino society. Social structure refers to good relationships, or avoidance of disagreements or conflict. Shame relates to an inner fear of being left exposed, unprotected, and unaccepted.

Implication for the rehabilitation helping professional: The helping professional would be well advised to keep these guiding principles in mind, particularly respect and shame, as he works with Filipino elderly clients. First, respect is a two-way street. The Filipino culture has considerable respect for authority, and the helping professional will be viewed as an authority figure. Therefore, this client may expect direct advice and answers rather than the exploratory, "How do you feel about this," or "How does that make you feel." On the other side, the helper must show respect to all clients; however, he must be aware of the importance this culture places upon respect and may view expressions of disapproval on the part of the professional helper as disrespecting him as a person. Consequently, the professional helper must make sure that when disagreeing with the client, he does it in a manner that does not invoke feelings of disrespect. The professional helper must not exclude the elderly Filipino client when executing the rehabilitation plan. One might ask how a plan can be executed without including the client? It is not uncommon when working with a person who has a disability, especially an older person, to talk to his family or caregiver rather than address questions and comments directly to the client.

Korean American Elderly

Paul Kim offers the following:

Unlike the Japanese elderly who maintain a strong informal support network among their cohort group members, the Korean elderly appears to be independent, too proud to ask for help from others outside their immediate family. They seem most concerned about their traditional values, (face saving) and tend to internalize their problems. They are highly competitive even among their family members, and thus the mutual support system is much weaker than that of other Asian groups.

Implications for the rehabilitation helping professional: The professional helper, similar to working with Filipino Americans, must make sure that he does not do anything that will shame the elderly Korean client. Additionally, the helper must not force the client into a "corner," he should always be allowed to "save face." To be more specific, sometimes when a counselor encounters a client who has difficulty committing to things and/or making a decision, the counselor will set the situation where he has to make a commitment. To a Korean American elderly person, this may be viewed as a situation that is embarrassing.

Hispanic/Latino American Elderly

The best estimates indicate a population of over 40 million Hispanic/Latinos residing in the United States. The Hispanic/Latino population is relatively young; however, it also indicates that in the next 20 to 30 years there will be increasing numbers of persons who are of Hispanic/Latino decent becoming elderly.

Mexican American Elderly

With the current generation of elderly and those about to numerically become elderly, several issues are of paramount concern to helping professionals working with Mexican American elderly. One in particular is the language barrier. Additional isolation becomes a problem for many Hispanic/Latinos as they are unable to communicate as their circle of friends will begin to decrease due to death, moving, etc.

Implication for the rehabilitation helping professional: The language barrier presents an obvious communication problem for a helping professional who is unable to effectively communicate in the client's primary language, and likewise the client has difficulties expressing himself/herself in English. In such cases, referral to a Spanish-speaking helping professional is appropriate or seek an interpreter. In some instances either one of these solutions may not be available. At this point, the use of family members as interpreters would be advised. The professional helper may be surprised to see a young child who speaks English assisting an elder because the elderly client's older children may not speak English well or their employment keeps them from attending their parent's appointment. The professional helper may need to consider contacting the elderly client "after hours" when English-speaking family or friends are available. Additionally, the helper should become aware of community resources such as clubs, churches, and other civic organizations that are willing to assist.

Puerto Rican American Elderly

Jose Cuellar (1990) discusses the importance of the family in Hispanic/Latino persons' lives. This is particularly relevant to a helping professional who plans to work with Puerto Rican Americans in that many families remain very close to their parents—especially as they age.

> Most Mexicans, Cubans, Puerto Ricans and other Hispanics place a great deal of value on their family relations. Attempts to instill a sense of family pride and obligation begin early in a person's life and are nurtured throughout. Most Hispanics are socialized to believe that the needs or welfare of the family, as a whole or other individual family members, particularly the very young or very old, should take precedence over one's own needs. These children and older adults alike are often reminded that during good times or bad, la familia comes first.

Implications for the rehabilitation helping professional: The professional helper should be able to use the very strong commitment to the family as an advantage to the elderly in the rehabilitation process. Therefore, keeping family members involved and informed is of major importance. This does not mean the family should make decisions for the client when he/she is capable of making decisions, but it implies that both the professional helper and the client should probably consult frequently with family members.

Cuban American Elderly

As discussed in the Cuban American section of Chapter 9, Cubans came to the United States in waves. The second group represented a better educated and more economically affluent group than the later groups. This implies that many of the elderly from the second group will have fewer problems with English and will have the economic resources to access appropriate health care services when needed. The reverse is likely for later groups coming to America.

Implications for the rehabilitation helping professional: Since the second group of Cuban elderly have possessed adequate resources, they will be easier to work with, especially if the helping professional will remember cultural values. The subsequent groups of Cuban American elderly may present more of a challenge because of language barriers and inadequate resources. Since many of this latter group will be cut off from their family and other support networks in Cuba, many of this group will rely on their Cuban community support system. The rehabilitation helper must work to keep them connected to this system. This means the professional helper must be knowledgeable of the system(s).

American Indian Elderly

With the magnitude of the health problems American Indians face throughout their lives, it is conceivable that those who reach an advanced age will have considerable health and physical difficulties. Alcoholism, accidents, emotional stress, and diabetes are some of the health factors that contribute toward their quality of life, or perhaps better stated–decrease their quality of life. Also influencing quality of life are educational levels and language barriers, in that some elders speak their tribal language and use English secondary.

There are over 500 American Indian tribes; many have their own language which creates considerable cultural diversity within this group. E. Daniel Edwards and Margie Egbert-Edwards (1990) list the following values they believe can be generalized to the majority of American Indian groups:

1. Appreciation of individuality with emphasis upon the individual's right to freedom, autonomy and respect.
2. Group consensus in tribal/village decision making.
3. Respect for all living things.
4. Appreciation, respect and reverence for the land.
5. Feelings of hospitality toward friends, family, clans people, tribe men, and respectful visitors.
6. An expectation that tribal/village members will bring honor and respect to families, clans, and tribes. Bringing shame or dishonor to self or tribe is negatively reinforced.
7. A belief in a supreme being and life after death. Indian religion is the dominant influence for traditional Indian people.

Implications for the rehabilitation helping professional: The professional helper should be aware that many American Indian elders believe in all or some of the previously mentioned concepts and they have guided their lives to some extent. Therefore, the helper should work within and respect these values as he/she works with the elderly. Additionally, the professional helper must be aware that in most American Indian tribes, the elders are very highly respected. They may no longer be involved in day-to-day decision making with regard to issues affecting the tribe, but their wisdom and counsel is respected by tribal leaders.

Finally, the professional helper must be cognizant that the tribe has considerable influence on the members' lives; therefore, the helper should become familiar with tribal customs and beliefs, particularly as they relate to treatment of the elderly.

Conclusion

Speaking of the elderly in general, there are many concerns facing them. Diminishing physical ability and slowing of mental function are often the major changes that are associated with growing older. However, things such as isolation, abuse by family members and caregivers, loss of life-long friends, or decreasing freedoms such as driving a car or taking vacations are situations that elderly persons encounter.

When we are very young, we feel that time passes too slowly, it seems like an eternity from one Christmas to the next; when we become an adult, we think we do not have enough time to do all things we need to; then, when we become elderly, we realize that we truly are running out of time. The reality of life is about time and how we use it. As helping professionals, the most important accomplishment in working with elderly, or aged clients, is to help them make the best use of their time.

Review Questions

1. Why will "baby boomers" (persons born in the late 1940s and early 1950s) have a major impact upon American society when they reach retirement age?
2. What are some of the stereotypes of older persons?
3. What are some issues faced by African American elderly?
4. Is the culture of poverty a major issue facing most Asian and Pacific American elderly?
5. What are some issues faced by Hispanic/Latino elderly?
6. What are some of the health problems often encountered by American Indian elderly?
7. Name five cultural traits believed to be common among American Indians.
8. How will understanding the importance of these cultural traits impact the helper-helpee relationship?

Suggested Activities

1. Visit a nursing home, a senior citizens center, and a retirement center. Observe the services of each. Compare the goals and objectives among the three.

2. Discuss with a vocational rehabilitation counselor the types of services rehabilitation agencies provide for the elderly.
3. Contact the American Association of Retired Persons to determine the benefits of joining this association.
4. Interview at least five persons 10-14 years of age and ask them their perceptions of being an elderly person. Ask at what age does one become elderly.
5. Interview at least five persons 21-26 years of age to determine their views of aging and what they think life will be like for them when they become elderly. Ask at what age does one become elderly.
6. Interview at least five persons over 64 years of age to determine if they view themselves as elderly. Ask their views on growing older.

References

Best, D. L. & Williams, J. E. (1996). Anticipation of aging: A cross-cultural examination of young adults' view of growing old. In J. Pandey et al. (Eds.), *Asian contributions to cross-cultural psychology*. New Delhi: Sage.

Committee on Aging of the Group for the Advancement of Psychiatry. (1971). Quoted in *Minority aging*. Washington, D.C.: U. S. Department of Health and Human Services.

Cuellar, J. B. (1990). Hispanic American aging: Geriatric education curriculum development for selected health professionals. In *Minority aging*. Washington, D.C.: U. S. Department of Health and Human Services.

Edwards, E. D., & Egbert-Edwards, M. (1990). Family care and the Native American elderly. In *Minority aging*. Washington, D.C.: U. S. Department of Health and Human Services.

Gibson, R. C. (1987). Reconceptualizating retirement for black Americans. Quoted in *Minority aging*. Washington, D.C.: U. S. Department of Health and Human Services.

Huang, I. J. (1981). The Chinese American family. Quoted in *Minority aging*. Washington, D.C.: U. S. Department of Health and Human Services.

Kim, P. K. H. (1990). Asian-American families and the elderly. In *Minority aging*. Washington, D.C.: U. S. Department of Health and Human Services.

Sakauye, K. (1990). Differential diagnosis, medication, treatment and outcomes: Asian Americdan elderly. In *Minority aging*. Washington, D.C.: U. S. Department of Health and Human Services.

Suggested Readings

Brody, E. (1985). *Mental and physical health practices of older people*. New York: Springer.

Folstein, M. S., Anthony, J. C., & Parhad, I. The meaning of cognitive impairment in the elderly. *Journal of the American Geriatric Society, 33*:228–235.

Ho, M. K. (1987). *Family therapy with ethnic minorities.* Newbury Park, CA: Sage.

Jackson, J. S., Newton, P., Ostfield, A., Savage, D., & Schneider, E. L. (1988). *The black American elderly.* New York: Springer.

Part Four
HELPING

Chapter 13

THE HELPING RELATIONSHIP

Chapter Outline
- Introduction
- Understanding Self
    Personal inventory
- Tips for Increasing Cultural Sensitivity
- Understanding Human Behavior
    Psychological influences
    Social influences
    Integrative concept
    Cultural influences
- Conclusion
    Psychological talk therapy with persons with disabilities

Chapter Objectives
- Introduce a method of self-analysis
- Offer tips for increasing cultural sensitivity
- Provide information with regard to various influences on human behavior

Introduction

To be an effective helper, a person must have a good understanding of him or herself (his/her beliefs, attitudes, and motivations), and must have a good understanding of human behavior. In this chapter, both of these elements will be discussed.

Understanding Self

Understanding self in the context of this chapter is referring to things one should do to become culturally sensitive. The reader should notice that the author is not saying become culturally competent. Being culturally compe-

267

tent implies one is knowledgeable of the various cultures he encounters and competent to deal with various cultural issues that may arise. It is the author's opinion that no one can become totally culturally competent. There are too many aspects of culture for anyone to become competent in all aspects of culture. The best one can expect with regard to cultural competence is to become aware of one's own attitudes regarding various cultures which he/she encounters, either directly or indirectly, and try to ensure that the foundation of these attitudes is not prejudice, bigotry, myths, and irrational thinking. Given the variety and complexity of cultures, the helping professional striving to become culturally sensitive must be aware of the fact that he/she will eventually make mistakes in interacting with persons of different cultural persuasions. As long as they are honest mistakes not intended to be malicious, they should be treated as learning experiences, mistakes not to be repeated.

Personal Inventory

Unless we are specifically challenged to do so, rarely do we question our belief system. Questions such as what are some of my basic beliefs and what is the foundation of those beliefs are rarely confronted. Although this type of self-examination would help us to become more sensitive with regard to our interactions with others, it is understandable that this kind of self soul searching does not occur on a routine basis. However, as a helping professional, this type of self-examination is essential, because one's views with regard to human nature influence how one interacts with clients/patients. The following exercise is designed to prompt the reader to examine his/her beliefs with regard to human nature. The reader is asked to write on a piece of paper his/her response to each question. Do not simply answer the question yes or no; defend your answer. The implications for the rehabilitation and other helping professionals are (1) a better understanding of what the reader believes causes humans to react as they do and (2) an awareness of one's beliefs and how they affect interaction with others. The questions of this self-inventory to be addressed are:
  • What is the nature of humans?
  • Do individuals have innate drives to do good deeds?
  • Are individuals evil and have to be guided toward appropriate behavior?
  • Are humans selfish, primarily concerned with their own survival?
  • Do individuals strive to create a balance in their lives (in this context balance means striving to be of benefit and comfort to others as well as striving for self satisfaction)?

• What is your view of human development? (What has the greatest influence on human personality development?)

  • Nature or
  • Nurture or
  • Combination

• What roles does past behavior play with regard to human personality development?

  • Do past events affect present behavior?
  • Do you believe that humans repress certain events and feelings associated with those events? If the answer is yes, how do these repressed feeling affect present and future behavior?

• What are the basic goals of humans?

  • Survival
  • Happiness
  • Service to humanity
  • Ecological balance (harmony between self and environment)
  • Greed (accumulation of personal wealth)
  • Spiritual

• In your opinion, what should the basic goals of humans be?
• Based upon your cultural background, what constitutes normal and socially acceptable human behavior?
• How is the previously mentioned normal and socially acceptable human behavior fostered?
• Based upon your cultural background, what constitutes abnormal or socially unacceptable human behavior?
• What are some of the reasons persons develop unacceptable human behavior?
• In situations where the environment (prejudice, oppression, paternalism, etc.) contributes to abnormal and/or socially unacceptable behavior, what responsibility, if any, does the individual with the problem bear?
• How is behavior changed?
• What are some of the techniques you would use to aid in behavioral change?

Tips for Increasing Cultural Sensitivity

Accept Others as Equals

There has been considerable commentary on the destructive nature of ethnocentrism. As previously stated, there is nothing wrong with having pride in one's culture; however, problems arise when we view our culture as being superior to others. When we view things that are different as being inferior and worthy of either elimination or not the same courtesy and considerations as our culture, then we cross the line from being proud and patriotic to being bigots and suppressors of human rights. Mature individuals not only accept differences, they also celebrate the opportunities that accrue from learning about something new. Personal growth occurs when we open our minds and hearts to accepting and learning from new experiences. If we view new and different experiences from this view point, we will have accepted others and their differences as equal to our own culture.

Expand Comfort Zones

Most people prefer to think of themselves as open-minded and recognize that, generally speaking, there are various points of view to virtually all issues. Despite their declaration of accepting differences, the real truth is that most people blanket themselves with beliefs, attitudes, and opinions which they rarely change; thus the aggregate of these personal views become their comfort zone. All humans have comfort zones and we rarely like to venture beyond them. When we are faced with new experiences, too often, we subconsciously view them as a threat to our emotional equilibrium and reject the differences, because to consider them presents the possibility of having to change or move beyond our comfort zone. To be culturally sensitive, one must learn to expand the comfort zone and take in new information, ideas, and ways of viewing life.

Recognize That There Are Only A Few Absolute Truths

Change is the first law of the universe. To live means things are constantly changing. As the decades and millenniums pass, we gain new information about our surroundings and this information helps explode long-held erroneous beliefs. At one time in human history, we accepted as absolute truth that the world was flat, and that the sun revolved around the earth. Even today we accept irrational views with regard to our fellow human beings as being absolute truths. Women are the weaker sex; certain minorities are evil, lazy, and dishonest; and persons with disabilities need protecting are only a few of these views. To be culturally sensitive, one has to recognize that stereotyping of individuals, and stereotyping of beliefs are some of the most debilitating things we can do to another human being. One must recognize that there are few absolute truths in this world. If one is religious, the fact that there is a God perhaps is the only absolute truth, and for those who do not believe in a supreme being, perhaps change is the only absolute truth.

In the helping profession, truth is an elusive concept. Truth in this context is not whether the client or patient is being honest; rather, it means what is right or correct. For an individual, there can be several truths. Likewise, what is good for one individual is not always correct for someone else with a similar cultural background. Some may say that this is stating the obvious, but is the obvious really being stated? Unfortunately, don't we tend to group people together, and based upon what is believed to be common characteristics, we treat them the same?

Understanding Human Behavior

Introduction

Does having a disability cause a person to feel and/or act differently than other persons with problems that create stress? Is the stress that may be created by having a disability different than other forms of stress? Does a person with a disability confront psychological issues differently than a nondisabled person? Are there unique psychological, social, and environmental factors encountered by a person with a disability, thus warranting different psychological treatments than that provided to nondisabled persons? From a psychological standpoint, are all disabilities the same in that they cause similar feelings and create similar reactions within persons with disabilities; therefore, the person should be treated differently than the nondisabled client? Or is disability one element in adjusting to stress and/or trauma? These and many other similar questions have been debated since the 1940s (perhaps longer) in an attempt to determine the most effective methods of assisting persons with disabilities in the rehabilitation process. Add to these questions the variables of race, ethnicity, gender, and age and we began to wonder if a new psychology of minority disability is in order. The answer is no; however, the variables of disability and ethnicity have to be given more consideration in the application of psychological intervention. Why is there a need to consider all of these variables with regard to their impact upon the rehabilitation process? Franklin C. Shontz (1984), in the following statements, provides a clear and concise answer to this question.

Rehabilitation maintains a long standing interest in improving its understanding of human behavior. In part, this interest derives from the need to assure that the expense and effort of rehabilitation do not go to waste because of patients' poor psychological adjustments to their physical conditions. Assumptions about the causes of human behavior directly influence patient-staff interactions; therefore it is important that rehabilitation professionals be sensitive to current thinking on the subject. (p. 119)

Several attempts have been made toward establishing a rehabilitation psychology and psychology of disabilities. In this effort, major debates have occurred with regard to what has the most influence on the behavior, feelings and attitudes of persons with disabilities. A result of these debates, three viewpoints have emerged: (1) those that believe **psychological, internal mental factors** such as motivation, ones image of his/her body, depression resulting from having a disability, mourning the loss of functions and defense mechanisms, to mention a few, have the greatest impact; (2) **sociological factors**, such as attitude and environmental barriers, have been promoted as the major influence on persons with disabilities; and (3) what some have called the **integrative concept**, which put forth the belief that a combination of **psychological** and **social factors** is responsible for psychosocial aspects of disabilities. This author is adding to the integrative concept, **cultural factors** as major contributors that **must** be taken into consideration when working with persons with disabilities. In this section, the three major psychological schools of thought, psychodynamic, humanistic, and behavioral, including examples of each, will be discussed. Relevance of these schools of thought for individual and family counseling with regard to meeting the needs of persons with disabilities and cultural minorities also are discussed. These variables must be considered when attempting to work with any client/patient for the helping process to be successful. A brief discussion of each of the rehabilitation concepts will be provided, followed by an explanation of the components of psychological therapies. The component explanation is important for the understanding of Chapter 14, "Review of Individual Counseling Therapies," and Chapter 15, "Reviews of Family Counseling Therapies."

Psychological Influences

As rehabilitation and other helping professionals have worked with persons with disabilities to provide comprehensive rehabilitation plans, considerable thought, over the past several decades, has been given to the internal factors which impact the degree to which persons with disabilities adjust to their disabilities and to the role these internal factors play in the rehabilitation plans. Some of the significant influences that have been studied include: **motivation, body image,** and **defense mechanisms**.

Motivation–One of the earlier beliefs with regard to the rehabilitation of persons with disabilities was that with high levels of motivation, the chances increased for a successful outcome. At first glance, this appears to be a reasonable and sound assumption. Certainly being positively motivated to accomplish tasks increases one's chances of being successful; however, a major problem with the motivation theory of earlier rehabilitation specialists and other helping professionals was their almost total reliance on the lack of positive motivation by the client to explain the lack of success of a rehabilitation plan. In other words, if the person with a disability did not progress in the rehabilitation program as expected, too often the patient was accused of not being sufficiently motivated. Little consideration was given to whether the rehabilitation plan was realistic and adequate for the needs of the person with the disability. Furthermore, very little consideration was given to social and environmental factors which the patient may encounter that could impact the successful implementation of the rehabilitation plan. Additionally, these specialists occasionally failed to consider that a patient could be motivated in ways that did not enhance chances of success. To be more specific, in past years, and unfortunately in too many cases today, some patients were expected to assume the **sick role**, whereby they were passive participants in the medical and rehabilitation process. The medical and rehabilitation staff expected them to accept the treatments without questioning why the use of that approach as opposed to any other treatments. Also, in reality, many patients expected this type of handling of their rehabilitation plans. They took the position that the professionals knew what was best; therefore, they should accept without question any treatment and therapy prescribed. Related to this belief, patients sometimes received rewards for being sick, such as attention being given to them and being relieved of responsibilities by medical staff as well as their family and friends. Also, in some cases, financial benefits were received for being incapacitated. Perhaps Franklin Shontz (1984) best summarized the mistakes made by rehabilitation and helping professionals with regard to their early assumptions of patient motivation:

> In actual practice, few patients truly lacked motivation; the problem was not usually a deficiency of psychological energy, but a blocking of misdirection of it. A patient who rebels against treatment is obviously strongly motivated from a treatment point of view; the important question is why the patient's motives fail to correspond to those of the treatment staff. (pp. 120–121)

Body Image–is the belief that how one views her body and the extent that one accepts her body will influence one's concept of herself as a person with a disability. The body image theory with regard to persons with disabilities follows along the line of thinking that the more one's body deviates from the accepted norm, the more difficulties the person will have in accepting himself as a viable productive person.

The body image theoretical concept is attributed to Paul Schilder. Richard Duval (1982) offers the following explanation of Schilder's thinking.

> The basic notion in this theory is that thoughts, feelings and attitudes about oneself are largely determined by the perception of one's own body. This body perception or body image is itself, a result of the non-verbal cues (e.g. behavior and body language) of others and one's own physical status (size, beauty) and abilities. The body image is much like a self-concept; it is hypothesized to influence both internal mental processes and external social behavior.
>
> From this orientation, the psychology of disability is explained by the effect of disability on the body image. Loss of physical ability is theorized to damage or lower the acceptability of the body image. As a result, both attitudes toward oneself and others are changed. Depression, denial and anger are seen as the natural results of loss of acceptability of body image. (p. 180)

There is no doubt that regardless of whether one is nondisabled or a person with a disability, he will be affected by his perception of his body. At one time, most professional helpers would have assumed that the view would be negative; however, today with increased emphasis on **disability pride**, one's image of her body perhaps does not have as much of an negative impact as in previous years. Disability pride is encouraging all people to view disability as one component of their lives, not consuming all aspects of the same.

Defense mechanisms–Another early assumption regarding the psychological influence of a disability was application of defense mechanisms, by persons with disabilities, as means of adjusting to a disability. Many defense mechanisms identified by rehabilitation specialist and other helping professionals have been extracted from the works of Sigmund Freud as he outlined them in his psychoanalytic theory. Defense mechanisms are described in more details in Chapter 14. Additionally, some have taken the position that persons with disabilities go through the stages of adjusting to having a disability as persons experience who go through the process of grieving. In fact, they go further to say that the person with a disability is mourning the loss of a body part or the loss of certain functions.

Social Influences

In the 1960s, the school of thought began to shift from thinking that the major influence on how a person with a disability adjusted to the disability was internal or mental influences to considering societal or environmental influences. Talcott Parson (1958) set forth a conceptual construct with regard to illness and disability, by relating the sick role to social influences. James McDaniel (1969) provides the following points regarding Parson's concepts and they are:

1. Role is an individual's performance of various differentiated tasks within his own social system.
2. Illness or disability produces incapacity and therefore limits or inhibits the performance of accustomed tasks.
3. Health, conversely, represents a state of optimum capacity for the performance of valued tasks.
4. Likewise, rehabilitation operationally refers to any treatment or services, which is designed to restore or at least optimize the person's capacity for appropriate role performance.
5. Illness or disability, furthermore, disrupts the role patterns of the family and it's permanence back to a reorganization of the fundamental social system of the family. (pp. 9–10)

In summary, Parsons is saying that society has certain role expectations of persons who are ill and/or have a disability and one role is to be incapacitated or dependent. It is the role expectations that influence the behavior of persons with a disability and the perception of the nondisabled of persons with a disability.

In the 1970s and 1980s, which has been referred to as the **Disability Rights Movement Era**, considerable emphasis was placed on and attention given to social and environmental barriers that created stumbling blocks for persons with disabilities. Attention was given to attitudinal barriers such as societal stereotyping of persons with disabilities and employers' inaccurate beliefs about persons with disabilities being unable to be gainful and productive employees. Also considerable attention was directed toward physical barriers that persons with disabilities faced, such as stairs, inaccessible restrooms, and lack of elevators, to mention only a few. The disability rights movement tended to support the contention that social factors were major influences with regard to a person with a disability's adjustment to her disability.

Integrative Concept

Most rehabilitation specialists and other helping professionals recognize that one cannot either scientifically or empirically support the claim that internal/mental factors have the greatest influences on a person's reaction to his disability. Likewise, one cannot prove that the greatest influence can be attributed to social/environmental factors. Most will agree that it is a combination of internal/mental and social/environmental factors. Related to this discussion, one engages in a fruitless exercise if he attempts to identify one factor as having greater influence than the other as they relate to the universe of disabilities.

It is my contention that the influence of a disability on an individual is just that, "an individual situation," and to generalize to the universe of disabilities produces inaccurate information. Therefore, as one works with an individual with a disability, she will find that factors, internal/mental and social/environmental, are influencing the person's adjustment and she probably will further discover that one factor is influencing more than the other. The point being made is that this is an individual situation and the amount of influence will vary by individual.

This point of view should not be interpreted to mean, from a psychological therapeutic standpoint, persons with a disability should only be counseled on a one-to-one basis; in fact, most forms of counseling, individual and group as well as family counseling, can be effective. Chapter 14 will provide a brief overview of some psychological counseling therapies that can and are used in counseling multicultural persons with disabilities. Chapter 15 will discuss selected family therapies that can be used to counsel families of multicultural persons with disabilities.

Cultural Influences

In the process of attempting to identify the most relevant factors influencing the adjustment to having a disability, one glaring omission is evident. The omission is culture. In the 1980s, and perhaps earlier, psychological helping professionals began to give more attention to the impact that culture has on persons' willingness to be engaged in the psychological helping process. Additionally, they looked at the impact that culture had on the outcome of the helping process of those who participated in this form of psychological assistance. The results of these inspections were that culture can be a pivotal factor in working with persons from ethnic/racial backgrounds.

Even considering the integrative and social factor concepts, little has been done in the field of disability study to consider cultural factors in the rehabilitation process. In the process of attempting to make the point that social factors play a major role in the rehabilitation of persons with disabilities, the role of cultural was inadequately studied, if at all. Unfortunately, then and today, the prevailing model for studying and applying treatment for personal, emotional, and psychological problems is the Euro-American middle class male model. Although more effort is being made in attempting to better understand ethnic and racial factors in the helping process; too many helping professionals continue to ignore culture as an important variable and continue to work with their clients/patients as though they are all the same–having similar life experiences and being motivated by the same life factors.

Since the common sense fact is acknowledged that the helping professional cannot possibly know all there is to know about the myriad of cultural factors, one might ask what is wrong with treating all client's/patients the same? To answer this hypothetical question, one has to realize that the clients/patient's culture is not going to change because we have helping methods that may be adequate for many other clients. Thus, to use a metaphor, we will be attempting to fit a square peg in a round hole. The helping professional must take into consideration cultural factors that help shape the person's life. Some of these factors can have a profound effect upon the client's perception and reception of being helped. Provided as an example, one's religious beliefs may influence the extent the client involves himself in the helping process. Based upon religious doctrine, the person may not believe in either medical or psychological intervention. The person, because of cultural influences, may utilize the help of medicine men or some other form of help, frequently called alternative medicine. More obvious influences may be lack of education, and lack of adequate employment which impacts the ability to carry adequate health insurance as well as impede the ability to purchase rehabilitation aids necessary to continue the rehabilitation plan.

With regard to talk therapy, culture, as has been discussed in previous chapters, may influence one's perception of what talk therapy is and its relevance to the person's life situation. The point being made is that there has been inadequate attention given to the impact that culture has and will have in the helping relationship. With regard to the role of talk therapy in the rehabilitation process, therapies discussed in Chapters 14 and 15, along with others not discussed are adequate to meet the needs of ethnic/racial minorities, if the counselor/therapist is cognizant of and diligent in considering culture as a factor that will influence the outcome of the helping relationship.

Conclusion

Psychological Talk Therapy with Persons with Disabilities

Aspects of psychological theories can provide guidance with regard to personality development and human behavior which can offer clues to reasons why clients/patients react in certain ways to their life situations and efforts to provide adjustment assistance. The study of psychological therapies in this book is not provided to imply that everyone who has a disability also has a mental illness associated with the adjustment to the disability. In some cases, this may be true; however, in the majority of cases, this is not the reality. The reality, however, is that many problems persons with disabilities experience are not the result of poor personal adjustment to their disability; rather, the problems are often the result of societal influences. To be more specific, negative attitudes possessed by family, friends, and other associates projected onto the person with a disability may cause the person to have problems adjusting to life situations. A reasonable analogy is psychological problems that may be created by a racial ethnic minority person being discriminated against in employment and kept at low levels of employment while nonminorities with lesser experience and talent are promoted. The emotional problems this person experiences are not because he dislikes being a racial/ethnic minority; rather, the problem is the result of discrimination and unfair treatment. Likewise, persons with disabilities who are qualified for gainful employment but denied such employment because of either the ignorance or unwillingness of the employer to hire persons with disabilities may experience emotional problems not because they dislike or hate themselves because of having a disability, instead their problems are the result of attitudinal barriers. Regardless of the reason, the emotional problem exists and talk therapies can help persons with disabilities with their life situations. Expressed in other terms, components of talk therapies offer explanations of human behavior and some of the techniques contained therein can be beneficial in assisting persons with disabilities adjust to their life situations. Therefore, a major advantage of psychological talk therapies is the explanation of factors which influence human behavior and the fact that they offer techniques designed to assist with adjustment to troubling life situations.

Review Questions

1. What does expand your comfort zone mean to you?
2. What does the term "sick role" mean?
3. What are some of the pitfalls in attempting to determine a person's motivation for following through with rehabilitation plans?
4. What are some of the impacts of one's perception of his/her body upon self-concept and self-esteem?
5. What are some of the impacts culture may have upon the rehabilitation process?

Suggested Activities

1. List some of the things that you consider to be "absolute truths" and identify information that offer a different view than your own. After this review, think about whether your original belief continues to represent an absolute truth.
2. List some of the things you will need to do to expand your comfort zone.
3. List some of your psychological defense mechanisms.

References

Eisenberg, M., Giggins, C., & Duval, R. (Eds.). (1982). *Disabled people as second-class citizens.* New York: Springer

McDaniel, J. W. (1969). *Physical disability and human behavior.* New York: Pergamon.

Parsons, T. (1958). Definitions of health and illness in the light of American values and social structures. In J. W. McDaniel, *Physical disability and human behavior.* New York: Pergamon.

Shontz, F. C. (1984). Psychological adjustment to physical disability: Trends in theories. In R. P. Marinelli & A. E. Dell Orto, *The psychological and social impact of physical disability* (2nd ed.). New York: Springer.

Suggested Readings

Adams, M. V. (1996). *The multicultural imagination.* New York: Routledge.

Adler, A. (1959). *Understanding human nature.* New York: Premier Books.

Brammer, L. M., & MacDonald, G. (2003). *The helping relationship: Process and skills.* Boston: Allyn and Bacon.

Egan, G. (1994). *The skilled helper.* CA: Brooks/Cole

Horney, K. (1942). *Self-analysis.* New York: W.W. Norton.

Marinelli, R. P., & Dell Orto, A. E. (Eds.). (1984). *The psychological and social impact of physical disability.* New York: Springer.

McDaniel, J. W. (1969). *Physical disability and human behavior.* New York: Pergamon.

Okun, B. F. (2002). *Effective helping: Interviewing and counseling techniques.* United States: Brooks/Cole.

Reik, T. (1948). *Listening with the third ear.* New York: Farrar and Strauss.

Wrigtht, B. A. (1983). *Physical disability: A psychosocial approach.* New York: Harper & Row.

Chapter 14

BRIEF REVIEW OF SELECTED INDIVIDUAL COUNSELING THERAPIES

Chapter Outline
- Introduction
- Psychological Therapies
- Components of Psychotherapy
- Psychoanalytic Therapy
- Person-Centered Therapy
- Adlerian Therapy
- Gestalt Therapy
- Behavior Therapy

Chapter Objectives
- Identify the three major forces in psychological talk therapy
- Identify and discuss the components of psychotherapy
- Provide a brief discussion of psychoanalytic therapy and some of the implications for multicultural persons with disabilities
- Provide a brief discussion of person-centered therapy and some of the implications for multicultural persons with disabilities
- Provide a brief discussion of Adlerian therapy and some of the implications for multicultural persons with disabilities
- Provide a brief discussion of gestalt therapy and some of the implications for multicultural persons with disabilities
- Provide a brief discussion of behavior therapy and some of the implications for multicultural persons with disabilities

Introduction

This overview does not cover counseling process; rather, it explains relevant parts of selected theories. Additionally, only selected individual counseling therapies are included. Group counseling is excluded, not because it is not important; however, the justification for not including group counseling is that all of the theories that are explained are also used in group counseling. Techniques will vary for group counseling; however, this discussion is not oriented to techniques.

The reader should be aware that the following discussion does not provide a complete explanation of any of the therapies. Instead the intent is to provide a summary of the theoretical foundation of the therapies as well as some of the goals of the therapy and techniques used. Moreover it should be mentioned that very few contemporary therapist conduct their therapy in precisely the way the originator(s) designed or envisioned the therapy. Stated in other terms, contemporary therapists have added to and in some cases deviated from the original techniques of the therapy; however, most remain true to the original philosophical belief as well as the overall goals of the therapy. Additionally, the reader should be aware that no attempt is being made to indicate that contemporary therapists strictly adhere to one therapy or therapeutic belief. The fact is, many, if not most, use an eclectic approach when engaging in a therapeutic helping approach. The helper engages in searching through the helping tool bag attempting to identify the appropriate approach that will offer the best opportunity for a successful helping relationship. Finally, each therapy will be discussed from a multicultural standpoint; however, no attempt is being made to say any particular therapy is best for a particular ethnic, racial, or gender group. The overall goal of this section is to inform and educate the reader with regard to some therapies that are in use today.

Psychological Therapies

Currently there are over three hundred psychological therapies; however, most therapies can be classified into one of three basic schools of thought: **(1.) psychodynamic, (2.) behavioral,** and **(3.) humanistic.**

Psychodynamic–The basic tenet of this school of thought is that past events that are held in our subconscious affect current behavior; therefore, an effective way of helping a client/patient is to assist him/her with regard to understanding him/her subconscious and how information stored there is impacting current behavior.

Behavioral–This school of thought believes in observation and assessment of conscious behavior so that an appropriate treatment can be applied to either strengthen or extinguish the behavior.

Humanism–Therapies within this school of thought are often called growth therapies. A major belief of humanism is that everyone has the potential for psychological and emotional growth; therefore, a primary belief is that everyone has the potential to solve his/her own problems.

Components of Psychotherapy

Most therapies have at least four components which I will identify as: **philosophical element, developmental element, structural element,** and **process element.** The **philosophical element** component explains the theoretical foundation of the therapy. In most cases, the theoretical foundation is based upon experiences, or revelations of the founder(s) or major contributors of the therapy. The second component is the **developmental element**, which attempts to explain what constitutes normal and abnormal behavioral development. The third component is the **structural element**. This component identifies the goals of the therapy. The fourth component is the **process element**, which outline techniques used in the therapy. It is easier to understand a therapy by dividing the therapy into these components. Therefore, the following therapies discussed in this chapter: **psychoanalytic, cognitive behavioral, person centered, Adlerian,** and **gestalt,** as well as the family counseling therapies discussed in Chapter 15, will be presented in this manner.

Psychoanalytic Therapy

Brief Outline of Elements of Psychoanalytic Therapy

Philosophical Elements (theoretical foundation)

1. Human behavior is driven by instinctual urges, primarily seeking pleasure and attempting to avoid pain.
2. Unconscious repressed material provides a major influence on current behavior.
3. Defense mechanisms are developed as we attempt to avoid pain, and these defense mechanisms can create psychological and emotional problems.

Developmental Elements (concepts central to human development)

1. Id, ego, and superego.
2. Unconscious material.
3. Anxiety.
4. Ego defense mechanisms.
5. Psychosexual development.

Structural Elements (goals)

1. Modification of behavior by bringing the unconscious to consciousness
2. Strengthen the ego.

Process Elements (some techniques)

1. Free association.
2. Analyzing client's thoughts, behavior, dreams, and defense mechanisms
3. Interpretation of client's thoughts, behavior, and dreams as well as interpretation of other aspects of the client's life.

Introduction

Arguably the grandfather of all contemporary psychological therapies is psychoanalytic therapy. This statement is being made not because the author thinks this therapy is the best or better than the other therapies; however, the statement reflects the influence its creator, Sigmund Freud, has had on the field of psychotherapy. Virtually all current psychological therapies have been influenced one way or another, by Freud and his theoretical concepts that serve as the foundation for psychoanalytic therapy. Some are strongly influenced by Freud's concept that unconscious material serves as the bedrock foundation for current behavior. Others reject this notion and have developed their therapeutic foundation as the opposite of Freud's belief. Many psychologists, psychiatrists, and counselors acknowledge that the unconscious does exist and can influence present behavior; they, however, proclaim that the client's perceptions of his/her current life situation are more important than an understanding of past events. These and various other ways represent how Freud and his psychoanalytic therapy have had a profound influence on psychological therapies and the psychological helping process.

Theoretical Foundation of Psychoanalytic Therapy

Psychoanalytic therapy is a member of the psychodynamic school of thought. Sigmund Freud is the founder and has had the most profound influence on the development of this therapy. Freud believed that as humans we have a basic desire to avoid pain and increase pleasure in our lives. Since the world is not a utopia, where every thing we encounter is pleasant and pleasurable, sometimes when we encounter things that create pain and or stress, in our effort to avoid some of the unpleasant aspects of life, we develop psychological defenses such as suppression, projection, sublimation, and regression, to mention only four mechanisms. Often because these defense mechanisms are deployed, psychological and emotional problems are developed. The result of some of these defense mechanisms is that information is stored in our subconscious, which is either not readily available to our immediate recall or too painful to handle; therefore, the information becomes repressed. According to Freud, this repressed or unconscious material in turn influences current behavior.

Human Development

Some of the key concepts that influence human development, from the viewpoint of psychoanalytic theory, are personality development (id, ego, and superego), unconscious material, anxiety, ego defense mechanisms, and psychosexual stages of development.

Personality Development. Sigmund Freud put forth the concept that the human personality has three basic components: **Id**, which has as its primary goal satisfying instinctual needs. Thus the id is our primitive side. **Superego** represents the moralistic side of our personality. With regard to the superego, things are right or wrong, black or white, and rarely are shades of gray considered. The **ego** is the balance between the id and the superego.

A further explanation of the three components can be provided by looking at the human personality on a continuum, the id on one end and the superego on the other end, with the ego in the middle, giving a sense of balance to our personality. When we examine the id and the superego, it becomes quite clear that it would be very difficult to constantly live at either end of the continuum. In a civilized society, we cannot constantly do only those things that make us feel good; we have to consider the laws of the society in which we live as well as have concerns with regard to the rights of others. On the other end of the continuum, life events do not always provide a perfect clear path of correctness, as our superego prefers. There generally is more than one rightness, thus the ego mediates between the two extremes and helps us function appropriately within societal guidelines as well as help maintain our sanity. Although Freud did not state the importance of the ego in this manner, one can see how an unchecked id can lead to antisocial behavior and an unmediated superego could cause emotional and mental problems trying to live with an uncompromising belief system.

Unconscious material. A core belief of Freudians, with regard to personality development, is that the unconscious stores all of our experiences and memories; thus, when we repress material in our subconscious, the information influences our present behavior. Therefore, it is imperative when emotional and or psychological problems occur, the therapist/counselor must help the client/patient understand the connection between the unconscious and current behavior.

Anxiety. Freud recognized the obvious, which is that everyone throughout life experiences anxiety. Freud identified three types of anxiety: **reality anxiety**, which is the fear of danger from the external world; **neurotic anxiety**, the fear that our instincts will get out of control and cause us to do things for which we will be punished; and **moral anxiety**, is the fear of our own conscious, which means we develop feelings of anxiety when we act contrary to our moral beliefs (Corey, 2005).

Ego-defense mechanisms. When anxieties get out of control, we develop defenses such as **denial, rationalization, repression, projection** and **regression** to mention only a few. The previously mentioned defense mechanisms are only a few defensive actions we take to protect ourselves from pain. Some may be conscious reactions and others are unconscious reactions; however, most, if not all, are in some ways distortion of reality.

Psychosexual stages of development. Freud identified what he considered to be five stages of personality development: *oral stage* (first year of life); this stage centers around the child's relationship with the mother. To be more specific, the closeness or lack thereof that develops between the mother and the child, during the first year of the child's life, has an impact upon how the personality develops. Inadequate adjustment at this stage may, according to psychoanalytic theory, set into motion later life personality problems such as mistrust of others and fear of intimate relationships (Corey, 1994).

Anal stage (ages 1–3). Arlow (2005) explains the anal phase in the following manner. "During the anal phase, interest in the bodily processes with regard to smelling, touching, and playing with feces is paramount. The disgust displayed by those who train the child and the shame the child is made to feel may contribute to a lowered sense of self-esteem. In reaction, the child may respond by stubborn assertiveness, control rebelliousness, and the determination to be in control" (p. 28). A logical inference with regard to this stage of personality development is that the manner in which parents discipline their children can have an impact upon personality development (Corey, 2005).

Phallic stage (ages 3–6): This stage is characterized by incestuous desires of the child toward the parent of the opposite sex. The reaction of the child's significant others toward these desires may set the tone for later life attitudes with regard to the person's sexual attitudes (Corey, 2005).

Latency stage (ages 6–12): Previous to this stage, the child has directed most of his/her attention to family members; however, during this stage of personality development, the child begins to show interest in socialization and forming interests outside of the home. The psychological implications for this stage relate to how the significant others in the child's life react to these efforts of independence. At this stage, the child wants more independence; however, at the same time, he needs the reassurance of the safety and comforts of the home and his significant others. How this attempt at semi-independence is handled by significant others can have an impact upon the child's ability to interact socially.

Genital stage (ages 12 to death). Freud believed that from adolescent through the rest of our lives we seek loving and satisfactory relationships; therefore, he did not develop additional stages.

For a detailed discussion of Freud's psychosexual stages of personality development the reader is referred to two excellent books: Gerald Corey's *Theory and Practice of Counseling and Psychotherapy* (Seventh Edition) (2005) and Raymond J. Corsini and Danny Wedding's edited book *Current Psychotherapies* (Seventh Edition) (2005).

Psychoanalytic Goals

There are a number of goals; however, two of the primary goals are (1) to bring the unconscious to consciousness so that the client will better understand the basis for some of her feelings, behaviors and other actions related to the situation(s) at hand; (2) to strengthen the client's ego so that her behavior is congruent with reality rather than being driven by instinctual urges.

Psychoanalytic Techniques

Gerald Corey (2005) has suggested that there are six basic techniques of psychoanalytic therapy; however, I have modified them to five and they are: (1) **maintaining the analytic framework;** this refers to establishing and maintaining a consistent style and pattern of procedural activities related to conducting therapy such as starting and ending sessions on time. (2) **Free association;** the client is encouraged to discuss without censorship whatever comes to his/her mind. It is believed through this technique clients disclose hidden information that may be influencing current situations. (3) **Dream analysis;** as the name implies, it is the analysis of dreams, as psychoanalytic followers believe that dreams expose what is in the unconscious. (4) **Interpretation;** this refers to interpretation of the discussion that results from free association and interpretation of dreams as well as other information that may emerge from talk therapy. (5) **Analysis of defense mechanisms;** the analysis deals with how and why these defense mechanisms are being used.

Implication for Multicultural Persons with Disabilities

Advantage: The fact that some persons with disabilities are the recipients of discrimination, albeit in many cases paternalistic, is well documented. Additionally, as well documented is the fact that persons of color, women, and elder persons with disabilities also have been the victims of discrimination, because of their gender, age, and or race and ethnicity. Because of the multiple ways multicultural persons with disabilities are discriminated and the resulting feeling that they are helpless to protect themselves, some may tend to suppress their feelings of being a victim of society's wrath. As a result of this suppression of feeling, some persons may develop emotional problems, and others may become angry and exhibit antisocial behavior. Psychoanalytic therapy, with its emphasis on exploring the unconscious and strengthening the ego, can be a good choice to deal with some of the hidden feelings and underlying causes of behavior. This therapeutic approach can be of benefit to multicultural persons with disabilities with regard to helping them develop a better understanding of their feelings. Psychoanalytic therapy can be beneficial for persons with some mental and/or personality disorders such as bipolar disorder, disorders caused by anxiety, and some forms of depression, to mention only three. Psychoanalytic therapy can also be beneficial with regard to assisting clients understand some of the defense mechanisms they may be using to deal with unconscious and hidden feelings.

Disadvantage: Delving into the unconscious and attempting to uncover underlying causes of present feelings and behavior as well as identifying and understanding defense mechanisms can take considerable time. Time that the multicultural client with a disability cannot afford to spend on therapy or perhaps is unwilling to devote to long-term talk therapy.

As previously discussed, attitudes of others with regard to what persons with disabilities can and should be able to do tend to be the greatest obstacle that they have to overcome. Because of the limitations society places upon persons with disabilities, quite often the most immediate needs of many persons with disabilities are appropriate education, skilled contemporary training, and employment that helps support their dignity and their families; long-term talk therapy such as psychoanalytic therapy can be a disadvantage for persons with disabilities because it does not meet the immediate needs of the person. Another disadvantage with psychoanalytic therapy, which also relates to being time consuming, is the fact that uncovering suppressed information can initially create more emotional problems. The material that has been suppressed has been stored away in the subconscious for a reason. Generally speaking, the reason is the information is too emotionally sensitive for the client to handle. Bringing this type of information to the forefront of one's awareness can be very emotionally disturbing. Because of this fact additional time will be needed to help the client sort through feelings and emotions. Again this becomes time consuming and expensive, if the client is paying a fee for service. Finally, for many racial/ethnic minorities, all psychological talk therapies are intimidating. Many think of these therapies as being for "crazy" persons, and none of the talk therapies are more associated with this conception as psychoanalytic therapy.

Dependent upon their mental and cognitive abilities, persons with mental retardation may not be good candidates for psychoanalytic therapy. This is true for most talk therapies.

Person-Centered Therapy

Brief Outline of the Elements of Person-Centered Therapy

Philosophical Elements (theoretical foundation)

1. People have the ability to understand and solve their own problems.
2. The counselor does not have all of the answers.
3. The role of the counselor is to establish an environment conducive to the client solving his problems.

Developmental Elements (concept central to human development)

There are a number of concepts set forth by Carl Rogers; the following represent six of the basic ones:
1. The client is the center of his/her world.
2. The client's perception is his reality and this is to what he reacts.
3. The goal of behavior is to satisfy the client's needs as he perceives them.
4. Part of what the client perceives becomes incorporated into his self.
5. The self is developed through one's perceptual field and interaction with his environment.
6. Humans behave in ways that are consistent with one's concept of self.

Structural Elements (goals)

1. Assist the client in his/her growth process.
2. Be empathic.
3. Be congruent.
4. Provide unconditional positive regard.

Process Elements (techniques)

Rogers did not emphasize techniques as one normally think of techniques of counseling. He emphasized counselor qualities and skills; therefore, the counselor is the technique. In essence, the skills of the counselor are the techniques.

Introduction

One of the best known therapies of the humanistic school of thought is person centered; the major contributor is Carl Rogers. This therapy under the development and direction of Rogers has gone through an evolution; first being called nondirective, based in part on the major way the therapy sessions were conducted. Next the name was changed to client-centered to reflect the emphasis on the client not the technique. The current evolution has occurred as a result of Carl Rogers expanding the use of his therapy beyond clients into the educational and business setting, thus the name person-centered.

Theoretical Foundation of Person Centered Therapy

Person-centered therapy is a humanist therapy and as such believes strongly in the growth potential of humans. To be more specific, person-centered therapy believes that unless persons have conditions that severely limit their cognitive abilities, they are capable of understanding and solving their own problems. In the case of persons with severe physical limitations, but not severely limited from a cognitive standpoint, he/she has the capabilities to orchestrate the elements necessary to affect a solution to the problem(s). Therefore the key ingredient in the client counselor interaction is the client. According to the Rogerian approach, the counselor should help establish an environment conducive to the client realizing his/her growth potential.

Human Development

Person-centered therapy takes a phenomenological approach to personality development in that Carl Rogers emphasized that the client's perception is his reality and this is what he acts upon. Therefore, to understand the client, the counselor must know something about how the client views his environment. This is very important because, from the person-centered viewpoint, the client's self-esteem is developed in part by what the client perceives to be real.

Goals of Person-Centered Therapy

Some of the goals of person-centered therapy are to assist the clients in their growth process; help the clients get to know themselves, to listen to the client being fully present at the session; to view the world as the clients view the world, and to encourage the following characteristics in the client: openness to experiences, self-trust, internal source of evaluation, and willingness to continue growing (Corey, 1986).

Techniques of Person-Centered Therapy

As previously stated, the counselor and his/her skills are in essence the techniques. Some of the major skills the counselor must possess to be successful are: **congruence/genuineness, unconditional positive regard,** and **empathy**. Raskin and Rogers (2005) explain what these terms mean. **Congruence** refers to the correspondence between the thoughts and the behavior of the therapist; thus, genuineness describes this characteristic. **Empathy** is the process whereby the therapist gets close to the client's meanings and feelings, developing an ever deepening relationship based on respect for and understanding of the client. **Unconditional positive regard** is represented by the therapist experiencing and exhibiting nonjudgmental accepting attitude toward whatever the client is at that moment (pp. 131, 144–145).

From the person-centered therapy viewpoint, it is important for the counselor to immerse herself in the client's feelings because the closer she can get with regard to being empathic, the better chance she will have at helping the client clarify his thinking, feelings, and behavior.

Implications for Multicultural Persons with Disabilities

Advantages: The fact that person-centered therapy primarily concentrates on the present rather than delving in the past lends this therapy to shorter time frames than psychodynamic therapies which concentrate on unconscious material. Person-centered therapy can be adapted to a brief therapy format and be conducted in a few sessions, or conducted in short terms such as all day or weekend format. This could benefit those clients that either do not have the time for longer sessions or have issues which need immediate attention.

The emotional support and closeness of person-centered counselors can be an advantage in establishing rapport with clients who have been traditionally disenfranchised from the mainstream of society. Assuming that the counselor is able to engage the clients in discussing their feelings, the fact that the counselor is basically nondirective and nonintrusive can also be an advantage in that multicultural clients with disabilities who have distrust for authority may feel less threaten by the person-centered counselor's style of interaction. Another advantage is in the fact that person-centered therapy is existentially based; thus a central tenet of this therapy is that the client/patient has within him/herself the ability to understand the problem(s) being confronted; therefore, she has the ability to develop answers to the problems. The key in person-centered therapy is the relationship between the client/patient and the counselor. Because the counselor provides encouragement and support, the client will be able to develop a reasonable solution to problems confronting her.

Disadvantages: The nondirective approach can be both an advantage and a disadvantage. The disadvantages relate to the fact that some ethnic and racial individuals prefer a direct approach; they view the counselor as an authority figure and they expect him to provide direction and answers to their issues. Talk, in their opinion, does not solve many problems; rather, action contains the answers to their problems. Having a person basically clarifying what they are saying or in their view repeating what they have already said is, in their opinions, an ineffective way to resolve issues of significant magnitude. In fact, these clients may view the counselor as being manipulative, especially since they view, based upon past experience, persons of authority as being manipulative. To overcome this disadvantage, the counselor must do a through job of explaining the philosophy of person-centered therapy and the unique role the counselor plays in the therapy.

Adlerian Therapy

Brief outline of the elements of Adlerian therapy

Philosophical Elements: (theoretical foundation)

1. Human nature is to be goal oriented.
2. Humans begin life with an feeling of inferiority.
3. Humans work toward superiority.
4. Humans have and make choices in their lives.
5. Adlerian therapy is present and future oriented.

Developmental Elements (concepts of human development)

1. Humans work toward an ideal self.
2. Life goals impact development.

3. Birth order may effect personality development.
4. Social interest impacts personality development.

Structural Elements (goals)

1. Assist client to clarify life goals.
2. Assist clients in moving toward ideal self.
3. Assist clients to become reeducated.

Process Elements (techniques)

1. Assist.
2. Assess.
3. Reeducate.

Introduction

Adlerian therapy, or individual therapy as it was called by its creator Alfred Adler, is also part of the humanistic therapy school of thought. Alfred Alder was a colleague of Sigmund Freud and at one point in his career was a follower of psychoanalytic therapy. Alder disagreed with the deterministic philosophy of psychoanalytic therapy which promoted the idea that humans are driven by their instinctual urges and desires and behavior is basically controlled by unconscious material. Alder began to promote the idea that humans have choices and make life choice; thus he developed Adlerian therapy as a present and future-oriented therapy.

Philosophical Elements

Adlerian therapy is a humanistic therapy which champions the philosophy that behavior occurs in a social context and to accurately understand the behavior of humans, the therapist must be aware of the client's phenomenological viewpoints. According to Adlerian theory, early in life, around age six, humans begin to develop a personal view of their **ideal self**. To be more specific, the young child begins to formulate in his mind what an ideal world would be when he is grown. In this process of developing a mental image of an ideal self, the person realizes that he is not the person he would like to become. This realization in Adlerian terminology is called a state of **inferiority**. In Adlerian terminology inferiority, does not denote a negative condition; rather, it identifies a state of realization that one is not what he wants to be and therefore he has to grow as a human entity to become the ideal self. Stated more succulently, inferiority means an opportunity to grow and to become creative.

Human Development

Because the person recognizes that he is in an inferior position, the person begins to develop **life goals** which hopefully will lead to a position of **superiority**. Again it should be noted that superiority is not used by Adler to denote being better than another person; rather, it identifies the fact that the person is striving toward the ideal self.

The movement toward the ideal self is an indication that from the Adlerian point of view, human behavior is goal orientated. As Adlerian followers state the person is moving from a **felt minus** (inferior) to a **felt plus** (superior).

Adler posited that children's psychological development, in part, is based upon their birth order within the family. Stated in other expressions, the experiences that one has based upon the relationship with siblings and parents have an impact upon psychological development and these relationships are affected by the birth order within the family.

Goals

From a therapeutic point of view, it is important for the counselor to identify and understand the client's ideal self and the person's life goal, because the person's beliefs, ideas, and motivation are driven and connected to his attempt to move toward the ideal self. According to Mosak (2005), individuals with psychopathology are discouraged rather than sick.

Another way of viewing the philosophy of moving from a felt minus to a felt plus is that as humans our life style is determined by our efforts to reach our ideal self. Therefore, our behavior is based upon conscious awareness rather than unconscious motivation. Additionally, life is not predetermined; rather, life is dynamic and we have choices. This therapy recognizes that environmental factors and events may influence behavior and limit our choices; however, we are free to make choices, which will ultimately determine the direction of our lives. Therefore, it is important that the counselor view and understand the client within the system of which she is part.

One of the most important concepts of Adlerian therapy is that all behavior occurs in a social context and because of this fact, we must engage in social interaction. Alfred Adler taught that we must successfully master three universal life tasks: **building friendships (social task), establish intimacy**

(love-marriage task), and **contribute to society (occupational task)** (Corey, 2005, p. 99).

With regard to social usefulness, according to Corey (2005), "social interest is the central indication of mental health. Those with social interest tend to direct their social strivings toward the healthy and socially useful side of life. Stated in other terms, persons with good mental and emotional development direct their social interaction in ways that benefit society rather than being selfish and directing their interaction in ways that primarily benefit their own well-being. Individual psychology rests on a central belief that our happiness and success are largely related to this social connectedness. Those who lack this community feeling become discouraged and end up on the useless side of life (Corey, 2005, p. 99).

Techniques

In looking at techniques, we must revisit some of the key concepts of Adlerian therapy, namely the ideas that as humans we develop early in life a mental picture of our ideal self and we develop our life style in search of that ideal self. Also, good mental health, in part, is predicated upon our social interactions within our environment. Therefore, one way of developing problems is to become selfish in our social interactions and either lose track of our ideal self or deviate from a good and reasonable pathway toward our ideal self. Taking this information into consideration, one of the techniques that the therapist must use is to help **reeducate** the client back to a correct pathway. In this reeducation process, additional techniques are used, such as **assisting** the client to understand his/her ideal self, and to help them **assess** where things went wrong and how to get back on a pathway that will provide a reasonable chance of reaching the ideal self.

Implications for Multicultural Persons with Disabilities

Advantages: Similar to other humanistic-oriented therapies, Adlerian therapy believes in the growth potential of clients. Additionally, this therapy does not view clients as being sick; rather, it takes the position that clients need to be reeducated. These positive approaches are good news for persons who are either rejected by society or blamed by society for their life situations. The approach of not blaming the victim helps the therapist gain the trust of the multicultural client. This method of interacting with clients who have low self esteem is especially productive.

Disadvantages: For a person with a disability, the ideal self may take on a meaning different than what Alfred Adler had in mind. Stated another way, a person with a disability that has physical limitations may view ideal self as the body perfect image; therefore, developing a life style striving for the impossible can be emotionally disastrous. Adlerian therapists probably will state that reeducation toward more realistic goals would be appropriate. This is true, but the point being made is the concepts of ideal self and life style may create some difficulties for the counselor trying to fit this therapy into working with persons with disabilities. Likewise, the concept of social interaction can be problematic. The theory uses the concept of social interaction from the viewpoint of the client choosing to interact with society and selecting the manner in which he develops this relationship with his environment. This may fit reasonably well for persons from the dominate culture in the United States; however, for multicultural persons with disabilities, the reverse too often tends to be true. To be more specific, multicultural persons with disabilities' involvement in the dominate culture society tends to be predicated upon the dominate culture allowing the involvement. Additionally, the involvement, when allowed, tends to have limitations. Again, the point being made is that this concept takes on a different meaning for multicultural persons with disabilities. Finally, as is the case with any talk therapy, participation is predicated upon the person's cognitive abilities. For persons with severe cognitive limitations this therapy may be unproductive.

Gestalt Therapy

Brief Outline of the Elements of Gestalt Therapy

Philosophical Elements (theoretical foundation)

1. Existential concept.
2. Phenomenological concept.
3. Field theory.
4. Emphasis on here-and-now.
5. Awareness.

Development Elements (concepts central to human development)

1. Psychological growth is dependent upon effective contact with one's environment.
2. Self-regulation impacts growth.
3. Self-awareness impacts growth.

Structural Elements (goals)

1. Assist clients to gain awareness of environment and self.
2. Assist clients to gain awareness of their resistance to effective contact.
3. Assist clients in becoming responsible for their own actions.

Process Elements (techniques)

1. Any technique that therapist can devise that assists the client in making effective contact.
2. Focusing.
3. Enactment.
4. Mental experiments.
5. Guided fantasy and imaging.
6. Body awareness and loosening.
7. Integrating.

Introduction

Frederick (Fritz) Perls and his wife Laura are considered the major contributors to gestalt therapy. Fritz Perls was trained as a psychiatrist and he began his psychological practice as a psychoanalyst. He later rejected the psychoanalytic view that the unconscious and instinctive urges are the major determinants of behavior. Thus, he began to formulate his theory which focused on the client's awareness of his/her here-and-now feelings. From this philosophical approach, gestalt therapy was developed. The key word in gestalt therapy is **awareness**. To be more specific, the emphasis is on what the client is feeling, thinking, and experiencing at that moment or in the **here-and-now**. An important thing to remember with regard to awareness in the here-and-now is that the feelings one is experiencing are not static; they change. In the therapeutic process, the therapist is an active participant in that she may also identify what she is experiencing and feeling with regard to the client's issues in the here-and-now. The therapist is encouraged to be creative with regard to techniques used to assist the client bring forth the awareness of his feelings and what he is experiencing. It is through awareness and interaction with the therapist assisting in clarification of the awareness that the client is able to better understand issues he has and make appropriate changes.

Theoretical Foundation

Gestalt therapy is part of the humanistic school of psychotherapy. There are a number of concepts which serve as foundation for this therapy: **phe-**

nomenology, existentialism, and **field theory**. The phenomenology contribution to the therapy emphasizes one's perceptions of life events. Existential philosophy makes its contribution by highlighting the fact that humans have growth potential and is constantly in the process of change. Field theory's contribution to gestalt therapy relates to its emphasis on the understanding that a person's beliefs, actions, and feeling have to be viewed in the context of one's environment. What all of this means is that a client has to be evaluated based upon her perceptions, feelings, and reactions to those perceptions and feelings at the current moment. As humans, we are in a state of constant change; therefore, our perceptual environment also is constantly changing.

Development Element

Self-awareness. From the view point of gestalt therapy, self-awareness refers to the client becoming aware of his feelings and reactions to those feelings he is experiencing in the moment. Growth occurs when we are in touch (**effective contact**) with emerging (here-and-now) feelings. Too often we avoid making effective contact with our feelings; According to Polster and Polster (1973), we exhibit one or more of five types of resistance to making effective contact with our environment, and this impedes our psychological and emotional growth. The five types of resistance are **introjection, projection, retroflection, deflection,** and **confluence. Introjection** occurs when we let others think for us rather than think for our selves. Stated another way, we allow others to make decisions for us. **Projection** is a denial of our feelings; we project onto others our feeling rather than own them as our beliefs and attitudes. **Retroflection** refers to internalization of feelings. **Deflection** means not allowing others to know our real self. **Confluence** refers to blending in to avoid conflict. One can easily see how any one of these defense mechanisms can inhibit one from making effective contact with his/her environment.

Gestalt therapy emphasizes the point that as humans we have the ability to correct ourselves, change directions of our lives when we are not functioning in productive ways. This is called self-regulation. Stated in other terms, when our lives are out of equilibrium, we have the ability to correct ourselves.

Goals

Since the key concept of gestalt therapy is **awareness**, it is logical that the goals of the therapy revolve around this concept. One goal is to assist the client in gaining awareness of her environment and how she is interacting and reacting to that environment. Another goal is to assist the client in gaining awareness with regard to ways she is resisting effective contact with her environment, and related to this goal is the role of the therapist to assist the client in becoming responsible for her own actions, rather than use mechanisms of resistance described in the human development section.

Techniques

Gestalt therapy does not have a set menu of techniques to be used by its therapist. Gestalt therapists are encouraged to be creative and develop and use any technique that will accomplish the previously mentioned goals as well as other goals not mentioned. The following techniques (in gestalt therapy, techniques are referred to as **experiments**) are extracted from the excellent writings of Corsini and Wedding (2005, pp. 321–324) and are provided as an example of techniques that have been used.

Focusing: The therapist helps clarify what is important by helping the patient focus his or her awareness.

Enactment: The patient is asked to experiment with putting feelings or thoughts into action. This may be as simple as encouraging the patient to "say it to the person" or might be enacted using role playing, psychodrama, or empty chair technique.

Mental Experiments: This involves visualizing an experience in the here and now.

Body Awareness: Awareness of body activities, observation of breathing and body posture are two examples of body awareness.

Loosening and Integrating: This technique is used to help break down rigid thinking with the goal of getting the patient to consider other alternatives. Loosening techniques such as fantasy, imagination, or experimenting with the opposite of what is believed are examples.

Implications for Multicultural Persons with Disabilities

Advantages: When we encounter difficulties in life, it is not uncommon to blame others for our misfortunes; also we tend to blame others for the roadblocks, real or perceived, that we are experiencing. While it may be true that others are contributing to some of the issues we are experiencing, rarely does blaming solve many of these problems. Often blaming begets more problems which generates more blaming, thus the vicious cycle continues without the problem being effectively solved. The goal of assisting the client to become aware of his or her feelings and reaction to those feelings in that moment can be a definite advantage to those persons who have problems that may be increased by external influences. Making the client aware of the reality that he is responsible for his own behavior and that he has the ultimate control over his feelings can give some measure of comfort to the client. This perhaps, in a different way, has been the motivating factor in the disability rights movement.

Another advantage is keeping the client focused on the present, not what has happened in the past, because little, if anything; can be done about the past; however, the client does have control of the present. Finally, the closeness or collaboration of the therapist with the client is a strong point of Gestalt therapy. For clients who want and need to feel that the therapist is actively involved in securing solutions to issues, Gestalt therapy can provide this assurance.

Disadvantages: Unfortunately, there is some level of comfort in blaming others for our problems, thus insisting that the client avoid this type of resistance to effective contact with one's environment can cause resentment of the counselor. The counselor must be prepared for this reactions and be able to deal with the same. Similarly, keeping the client in the here-and-now can also create resentment which may cause the client to want termination of the session. Perhaps a greater disadvantage is the tendency of clients who feel they need immediate action and solutions to their issues; therefore, they may perceive dealing with feelings in the moment as being nonsense and ineffective.

Behavior Therapy

Brief outline of elements of behavior therapy

Philosophical Elements (theoretical foundation)

1. A major impact upon human behavior is how the environmental influences are perceived and how the individual interprets these influences.
2. How a person perceives, interprets, and assigns meaning to events determines how he/she will react.
3. Individuals have an impact upon their behavior because of the ability to think.

Developmental Elements (concepts central to human development)

1. How we think and interpret events helps shape our behavior.
2. Faulty thinking or interpretation leads to inadequate responses to life situations.

Structural Elements (some goals)

1. Collaborative empiricism.
2. Guided discover.
3. Client providing self-therapy.

Process Elements (some techniques)

1. Identification and testing of beliefs.
2. Exploration of origin of beliefs.
3. Teaching client to be self therapist.

Introduction

For a therapeutic tool to remain viable, it must adjust its theory and techniques to incorporate the latest discoveries relevant to the understanding of what motivates human behavior. The generic term of behavior therapy is no exception and in fact is a very good example of the evolutionary nature of some psychological therapies. As one views the various significant contributors to the field of behavior therapy, the evolution and expansion of the field become quite apparent. Significant contributors such as Ivan Pavlov, B. F. Skinner, Arnold Lazarus, Albert Bandura, Albert Ellis, Aaron Beck, Joseph Wolpe, and others have made contributions and in the process of making those contributions have added new dimensions to the concept of how human behavior is developed and altered. As an example, Aaron Beck introduced principles of learning theory to behavioral therapy which has led to the development of **cognitive behavior therapy** and Albert Ellis introduced the concept of human's irrational thinking as a major factor affecting how humans behave, thus creating **rational emotive behavior therapy**.

This discussion of behavioral therapy, as is true for the discussion of the other previously mentioned therapies, is not constructed to train therapists; rather it is developed to help the reader understand what behavior therapy is, so that he/she can become knowledgeable of how the therapy may be of benefit in his/her assisting minorities with disabilities. Behavioral therapy will be discussed with regard to its origin and further discussion will relate to the evolution/expansion of behavior therapy into cognitive behavior therapy.

Theoretical Foundation

The foundation for behavior therapy is **classical conditioning** and **operant conditioning**. The Russian physiologist Ivan Pavlov is credited with being the first to demonstrate classical conditioning. Pavlov demonstrated that in classical conditioning, when an unconditioned stimulus such as food produces an unconditioned response such as salivation and is associated with a conditioned stimulus such as the ring of a bell, if the paring is repeated often enough, the conditioned stimulus will alone produce the unconditioned response.

The concept of **operant conditioning** can be credited to the Harvard-educated psychologist B. F. Skinner. Skinner postulated that behavior that is positively reinforced will be repeated; conversely, behavior, that is punished or ignored will be eliminated. Michael Nichols and Richard Schwartz (1995) offer an explanation of how operant conditioning works in a clinical setting.

> The operant conditioner carefully observes target behavior and then quantifies its frequency and rate. Then to complete a functional analysis of the behavior, the experimenter or clinician notes the consequences of the behavior to determine the contingencies of reinforcement. For example, someone interested in a child's temper tantrums would begin by observing when they occurred and what the consequences were. A typical finding might be that the parents gave in if the tantrums were prolonged. Thus the parents would be discovered to have been reinforcing the very behavior they least wanted. To eliminate the tantrums, they would be taught to ignore or punish them. Moreover they would be told that giving in even occasionally would maintain the tantrum because behavior that is partially or intimately reinforced is the most difficult to extinguish. (p. 322)

As one may observe, the original function of behavior therapy (classical and operant conditioning) treated human behavior as significantly devoid of the influence of the process of thought. Expressed another way, behavior occurres as a result of stimulus and its continuation or elimination is predicated upon reinforcement or lack thereof.

Albert Bandura made a significant contribution to the concept of what affects human behavior as he utilized principles of learning theory to help explain how behavior is changed. According to Gerald Corey (2005), Bandura posited that "behavior is influenced by stimulus events, by external reinforcement and by cognitive mediational experiences" (p. 230). G.

Terence Wilson (2005) explains Bandura's contribution in the following way: "In social-cognitive approach, the influence of environmental events on behavior is largely determined by cognitive process governing how environmental influences are perceived and how the individual interpreted them. Psychological functioning, according to this view, involves a reciprocal interaction among three interlocking sets of influences: behavior, cognitive processes, and environmental factors" (p. 203).

In addition to Bandura, Aaron Beck introduced cognition into the area of behavior therapy. Aaron Beck and Marjorie Weishaar (2005) provide the following concise explanation of the underlying concept of cognitive behavior therapy: "The cognitive system deals with the way that individuals perceive, interpret, and assign meaning to events" (p. 238). With the addition of cognition to the theory of human behavior therapy there is the recognition that we have the capability to affect our environment, thus we have significant impact upon our behaviors.

Behavior therapy has progressed from solely classical and operational condition influenced to including principles of social learning theory and cognitive approaches to learning as basis for understanding human behavior. As Gerald Corey (2005) explains, there are few traditional behavior therapists practicing today. He continues his analysis of the area of behavior therapy by pointing out that, "cognitive behavior therapy along with social learning theory, now represents the mainstream of contemporary behavior therapy" (p. 230).

Developmental Element

Cognitive behavior therapy views human behavior as being predicated upon how we think; to be more specific, how we interpret our environment. Therefore, psychological problems occur as a result of faulty thinking or interpretation. Aaron Beck postulated that psychological problems occur because we place incorrect interpretation on events that impact our lives. He further believes that often these interpretations are not based in reality. According to Weishaar (1993), "The theoretical assumptions of cognitive therapy are (1) that people's internal communication is accessible to introspection, (2) that clients' beliefs have highly personal meaning, and (3) that these meanings can be discovered by the client rather than being taught or interpreted by the therapist" (p. 283).

Each person has a unique way of taking in and interpreting information and it is the manner in which we process information that impacts our daily lives that helps determine the direction of our behavior. From a cognitive behavior therapy perspective, persons who have psychological problems often have flawed interpretation of some or perhaps all of the information they receive. Frequently these individuals develop a thought process that interprets information and situations in a negative manner. These interpretations often cause the person to doubt his abilities to be successful. Therefore, one of the things that must be done is for the client to recognize his/her flawed or negative thinking and with the collaboration of the therapist develop more balanced thinking.

Goals

The therapist in collaboration with the client may establish specific goals that relate to the client's unique problem(s) and life situation; however, the overarching goals of cognitive behavior therapy can be classified into two broad goals. (1) Conduct **collaborative empiricism**. Expressed in other terms, collaborative empiricism means a collaborative effort between the therapist and the client with regard to exploring the person's beliefs and identifying any dysfunctional interpretation of these beliefs and attempting to modify them. Gerald Corey (2005) provides further explanation of this point with these comments: "Therefore most cognitive behavior therapists have the general goal of teaching clients how to separate the evaluation of their behavior from the evaluation of themselves–their essence and their totality–and how to accept themselves in spite of their imperfections" (p. 276). (2) Conducting what Beck and Weishaar call **guided discover**. Guided discover means discovering the origin of the persons dysfunctional thinking. The cognitive therapist emphasizes **client self-discover**. From the therapist's vantage point, it is important that the client learn the origin of his dysfunctional thinking and interpretation of events and how these variable are impacting his life situation and ability to effectively function. It is equally important that the client learn to conduct his own therapy within his environment.

Techniques

As is the case with goals, each therapist adjusts her techniques to the uniqueness of the client's situation; however, the overall goals are:

1. Identify and test the person's beliefs.
2. Explore the origin of the person's beliefs.
3. Correct the beliefs if they fail an empirical or logical test or problem solving (Beck & Weishaar, 2005).
4. Teach the client to conduct her therapy within her own environment.

Implications for Multicultural Persons with Disabilities

Advantages: Because cognitive behavior therapy targets specific behavior such as those associated with phobias and because the therapy concentrates on specific behaviors associated with disorders such as anxiety, to mention only two, it can be an effective treatment for some disabilities. According to Aaron T. Beck and Marjorie E. Weishaar (2005), various psychopathological conditions such as anxiety disorders, depressive disorders mania, paranoid states, and obsessive-compulsive neuroses are treatable by using cognitive behavior therapy. One reason why cognitive behavior therapy can be effective is the fact the therapist concentrates on understanding and identifying faulty thinking, or as Beck and Weishaar state: "A specific bias affects how the person incorporates new information. Thus a depressed person has a negative bias, including a negative view of self, world and future. In anxiety, there is a systematic bias of danger. In paranoid conditions the dominant shift is toward indiscriminate attributions of abuse or interference and in mania the shift is toward exaggerated interpretations of personal gain" (p. 239).

It is the ways the person perceives his/her life situation that contribute to abnormal behavior. The cognitive behavior therapist and the client select areas of thinking to work toward changing, hopefully altering inappropriate or unwanted behavior. One of the strengths of cognitive behavior therapy and any behavior therapy is the fact that it is designed to be replicated. Stated another way, the treatment is established in a scientific manner so that the effectiveness or lack thereof can be measured. Thus, there will be very little guessing as to the impact, at least short term. An additional strength is that the treatment is designed to be conducted by the client within his daily environment. This is a strength, especially if the client is diligent with regard to conducting his therapy and a weakness if not. Thus a major advantage is that it has the potential of empowering the client and building his self-esteem, once he realizes he has control over his life

The fact that cognitive behavior therapy does not rely on uncovering subconscious feelings can be both an advantage and a disadvantage. The disadvantage will be discussed in the next section. The advantages of not concentrating on subconscious feelings are (1) it makes this therapy less time intensive and (2) the understanding curve of the client is less impacted. Expressed in other terms, the client does not have to devote time to understanding and buying into how past events and perhaps events of which she has very little memory are impacting her current life situation and (3) not delving into past subconscious experiences can be less painful than dealing with thoughts and attitudes that are at surface level, even though these thoughts maybe faulty.

Disadvantages: A major disadvantage with cognitive behavior therapy is the same as discussed with the other therapies: the ability of the client to understand his problems and some of the impacts on his life activities. In the case of cognitive therapy this disadvantage is magnified since much significance is placed upon identification and treatment of faulty thinking. With regard to persons with disabilities, where one's cognitive abilities are significantly impaired, the use of this therapy may not be effective. In the case of severe mental retardation, traditional behavioral therapy that primarily uses classical and operant conditioning has a better chance of being effective than cognitive behavior therapy.

In many cases, the most effective approach will be to work with the family and/or significant caregivers. Thus, behavioral family therapy will be the treatment of choice.

Another disadvantage is whether the client is willing to take charge of conducting his own therapy. As previously mentioned, behavior therapy including cognitive behavior therapy emphasizes the client eventually conducting his own therapy within his environment. Certainly, this disadvantage is not unique to persons with disabilities.

The disadvantage of not dealing with unconscious feeling and instead concentrating on the present is the fact that the client may not ever develop an in-depth understanding of the origin of his problems. Some would argue that by not having this deeper understanding of the problem, the client is prone to repeat the dysfunctional behavior. The behaviorist could counter with the response that knowing the origin of the problem is fine, but this knowledge does not solve the problem. The solution is what is being done to deal with the current behavior.

Conclusion

At the beginning of this section, the question of whether a different set of psychological therapies should apply to persons with disabilities and multicultural persons with disabilities was presented. As stated then, the answer was no and continues to be the same. In this chapter, I have given a very brief overview of some, but not all, of the most commonly used psychological therapies and I have attempted to point out the strengths and weakness of these therapies with regard to working with the previously mentioned clients. One of the points to be made is that if as a professional helper one becomes culturally sensitive, most contemporary therapies can be effective.

Review Questions

1. What are the three major forces in psychological talk therapy?
2. Explain what the philosophical element component of psychotherapy means?

3. Explain what the structural element component means?
4. What do the terms Id, Ego and Superego mean from the psychoanalytic therapy viewpoint?
5. What are the psychoanalytic psychosexual stages of development?
6. Who was Carl Rogers?
7. What do the following person-centered terms mean: congruence/genuineness, unconditional positive regard, and empathy?
8. Who was Alfred Adler?
9. What do the following terms from Adlerian therapy mean: inferiority, superiority, and life style?
10. In gestalt therapy, what does the term "awareness" mean?
11. To which of the three major forces in psychological therapy does gestalt therapy belong?
12. In gestalt therapy, are clients' feelings, thinking and experiences considered from the subconscious or here-and-now point of view?
13. What are the basic foundations for behavior therapy?
14. What does the term cognitive behavior therapy mean?
15. With regard to behavior therapy, is the client a passive participant or and active participant?

Suggested Activities

1. Contact several rehabilitation counselors and ask them the types of counseling and techniques they prefer and why.
2. Contact several social workers and ask them the types of counseling and techniques they prefer and why.

REFERENCES

Arlow, J. (2005). Psychoanalysis. In R. J. Corsini & D. Wedding, *Current Psychotherapies* (7th ed.). United States: Brooks/Cole.

Beck, A. T., & Weishaar, M. (2005). Cognitive therapies. In R. J. Corsini & D. Wedding, *Current psychotherapies* (7th ed.). United States: Brooks/Cole.

Corey, G. (2005). *Theory and practice of counseling & psychotherapy* (7th ed.). United States: Brooks/Cole.

Corsini, R. J., & Wedding, D. (2005). *Current psychotherapies* (7th ed.). United States: Brooks/Cole.

Mosak, H. H. (2005). Adlerian therapy. Quoted in Corsini, R. J., & Wedding, D. *Current Psychotherapies* (7th ed.). United States: Brooks/Cole.

Nichols, M. P., & Schwartz, R. C. (1993). *Family counseling: Concepts and Methods* (4th ed.). Boston: Allyn and Bacon.

Polster, E., & Polster, M. (2005). Gestalt therapy integrated. Quoted in G. Corey, *Theory and practice of counseling psychotherapies* (7th ed.). United States: Brooks/Cole.

Raskin, N. J., & Rogers, C. R. (2005). Person centered therapy. In R. J. Corsini & D. Wedding, *Current psychotherapies* (7th ed.). United States: Brooks/Cole.

Wilson, G. T. (2005). Behavior therapy. In R. J. Corsini & D. Wedding, *Current psychotherapies* (7th ed.). United States: Brooks/Cole.

SUGGESTED READINGS

Adler, A. (1959). *Understanding human nature.* New York: Premier Books.

Bandura, A. (1977). *Social learning theory.* Englewood Cliffs. NJ: Prentice-Hall.

Beck, A. T., Freeman, A., & Davis, D. D. (2003). *Cognitive therapy of personality disorders.* New York: Plenum.

Bugental, J. F. T. (1963). Humanistic psychology. A new breakthrough. *American Psychologist, 18,* 563–567.

Corey, G. (2005). *Theory and practice of counseling & psychotherapy.* United States: Brooks/Cole.

Corsini, R. J., & Wedding, D. (Eds.). (2005). *Current psychotherapies* (7th ed.). United States: Brooks/Cole.

Ellis, A., & Dryden, W. (1997). *The practice of rational emotive behavior therapy.* New York: Springer

Mitchell, S. A., & Black, M. J. (1995). *Freud and beyond: A history of modern psychoanalytic thought.* New York: Basic Books.

Rogers, C. R. (1951). *Client-centered therapy.* Boston: Houghton Mifflin.

Chapter 15

BRIEF REVIEW OF SELECTED FAMILY COUNSELING THERAPIES

Chapter Outline
• Introduction
• Family Counseling and Disabilities
• Experiential Family Therapy
• Structural Family Therapy
• Behavioral Family Therapy
• Psychoanalytic Family Therapy

Chapter Objectives
• Discuss some of the benefits of family counseling as a rehabilitation tool
• Discuss components of experiential family therapy and some of the implications for multicultural persons with disabilities
• Discuss components of structural family therapy and some of the implications for multicultural persons with disabilities
• Discuss components of behavioral family therapy and some of the implications for multicultural persons with disabilities
• Discuss components of psychoanalytic family therapy and some of the implications for multicultural persons with disabilities

Introduction

Family counseling as a professional therapy began in the 1950s; prior to that time, most counseling which related to family issues were conducted in individual sessions. Although there are a variety of family counseling therapies, generally speaking, family counseling is based upon the following principles and most family therapies have these principles in common, although they may dress them up with different names. The basic principles are:

1. Family counseling concentrates upon the family's communication patterns, not only what is being said, but also how it is being said.

2. Family counseling looks at how families attempt to solve problems.

3. Family counseling looks at what have been the family's experiences with regard to handling difficult situations.

4. Family counseling looks at the power structure of the family, how decisions are made and by whom.

5. Family counseling looks at who talks with whom within the family and under what circumstances.

6. Family counseling, generally speaking, views the family as a system, and members of the family as subsystems.

By assessing a family's communication styles and patterns of interacting, the therapist, generally speaking, can gain valuable insight into family dynamics that may be hindering the family with regard to being a positively focused family. Another basic concept of family counseling is that when a family has problems, all of the members of the family have responsibility with regard to the solution of the situation. Expressed in other terms, all members of the family are part of the problem; therefore, all should be part of the solutions.

Family Counseling and Disabilities

Family counseling may benefit families with a member who has a disability deal with problems of adjusting to some family issues which may be amplified by the disability. Depending upon the nature of the disability, family members may become the primary caregiver of the individual; thus in some instances, issues of demands upon family members' time may become paramount concerns. Help may be required to deal with stress, frustration, and anxiety. Guilt feelings may be experienced by some family members as they entertain thoughts of what life would be like without the family member with the disability. Tension between the husband and wife may increase as they attempt to provide care and attention to a loved one with a disability. In addition, the cumulative affect on some family members may be depression. It should be pointed out that some or all of these reactions occur to families as they encounter stressful and/or traumatic situations; therefore, family counseling can be as natural for families with a member who has a disability as for any family.

Given the fact that disabilities are one of life's conditions, there is no one type of family therapy or counseling that is best for the universe of disabilities. Similarly, there is no one therapy that is best for ethnic or racial minority families. In selecting a family therapist/counselor, family members should base their decision, with regard to type of family counseling on the therapeutic philosophy, goals, techniques, and experience of the therapist.

To help the reader better understand family counseling, the following family therapies will be summarized: **structural family therapy, experiential family therapy, psychoanalytic family therapy** and **behavioral family therapy**. One should keep in mind that the following discussions represent a brief overview and that these therapies consist of more than is being presented here. Additionally, how these therapies are applied will vary according to the individual therapist's professional judgment. The reader is encouraged to seek additional information with regard to the therapy or therapies which are of particular interest. See the suggested reading section of this chapter for additional readings.

As was discussed in Chapter 14, the intent of this chapter is not to teach family counseling process; rather, the goal of this chapter is to acquaint the reader with the composition and goals of each discussed therapy as well as how each therapy attempts to achieve its stated goals. It is believed, by this author, that by increasing professionals and caregivers understanding of these facts, they will be better able to assist persons with disabilities, even if the assistance is through referrals. Also, the author would like to acknowledge that some information in this chapter is adapted from the excellent work of Michael P.Nichols and Richard C. Schwartz and recommends their book, *Family Therapy: Concepts and Methods*. Finally, as is the case with the individual therapies previously presented, there are additional family therapies that are good; thus their omission is based upon limitation of space rather than lack of worth.

Experiential Family Therapy

Introduction

Experiential family therapy derives a great deal of its psychological foundation from the humanistic school of thought. As previously discussed in previous chapters, humanism emphasizes the point that humans have within themselves the potential for growth. Likewise, experiential family therapist emphasizes individual growth potential over the growth of the family as a unit. Many family therapies also promote the idea of human growth potential; however, most view the family as a system and growth in part comes through family growth. The psychological footing of experiential family therapy is based upon the individual feeling free to experience her feelings and having the freedom within the family to express those feelings. The emphasis is on immediate or here-and-now experiences.

Philosophical Element (Theoretical Foundation)

Experiential purests proclaim that there is no theoretical foundation, and argue that therapy is constrained by theory; consequently, therapy should be creative and spontaneous; therefore, some of the characteristics of experiential therapists are their openness and spontaneous interaction with the family members. As Nichols and Schwartz (1995) point out, no theory is in fact a theory and some of the basic premises are: (1) individual awareness of one's own feelings; (2) expression of those feelings; (3) self-fulfillment; and (4) effective communication with family members. The essence of the theoretical foundation is each family member understanding their own feelings and being able to express those feelings.

Developmental Element (Human Development)

Experiential family therapists believe that healthy family members are ones who feel free to be in touch with their feelings and also have the freedom to express these feelings within the family. Additionally, they believe that society, in general, and families specifically, attempt to control the expression of feelings, thus the family members often suppress the feelings which can lead to dysfunction within the family. From the standpoint of experiential family therapists' belief, a major cause of family problems is family members' denial of impulses and suppression of feelings. Thus avoidance of true feelings contributes to dysfunction within a family. Growth occurs when family controls are not excessive. Functional families are characterized by being supportive and encouraging a range of expressions.

The therapist role is to teach the family members, by example, to be open, creative, and spontaneous. Although this freedom of expression by family members may create some stress within the family, this stress will lead to the individual's and the family's growth.

Structural Element (Goals)

Stated succulently, three of the major goals are (1) individual growth, rather than family growth; (2) development of individual family members' sensitivity to their own needs and learning to share those needs within the family; and (3) improvement of individual family member's self-esteem.

Process Element (Techniques)

Somewhat similar to person-centered therapy, the personality of the therapist is considered the most important technique. To be more specific, the therapist's abilities to be open, creative, and spontaneous become a model for the family members to pattern their actions.

Because of the spontaneous nature of the therapy, each counselor/therapist is free to develop and employ her own techniques; however, some of the techniques that have been used are:

Family Sculpturing: The technique used is to ask each member of the family to arrange the other members in a family setting based upon the arranging member perception of how the others fit within the family. The arrangement of the family members provides the counselor/therapist with valuable information with regard to family dynamics, at least from the prospective of the arranger.

Family Art Therapy: Based upon the same philosophy as family sculpturing of determining family dynamics from the way pictures are drawn and the arrangement of family members, depicted in the drawings of the family member, the counselor/therapist gains insight into how the artist views the family, its members, and how he/she fits within the family.

Puppet Interview: This technique is primarily used with children to gain insight into their feelings with regard to their roles within the family structure. With the aid of puppets, the child uses role playing to reveal family dynamics. From a rehabilitation helping perspective, this can be an excellent tool for working with not only children, but also working with persons who have retarded mental capabilities.

In summary, experiential family therapy emphasizes the belief that family issues can be best resolved and/or avoided by each individual being free to experience and express his/her feelings. Family problems occur as a result of the family restricting the feelings and expression of the same. Thus a functioning family is one that allows and encourages openness of its members.

A major role that the counselor can play is to be open, spontaneous, and creative; and by being this way, he encourages family members to react in a similar manner. Therefore, the counselor/therapist is the best technique.

Implications for Rehabilitation

Advantages: Two of the major hurdles persons with disabilities have to overcome are the attitudes of others and paternalist views of significant others toward their abilities to adequately function in society and within the family structure. Experiential family therapy's foundational concept of promoting individual family member growth can be a significant advantage for family members with disabilities. Working with the family to get them to recognize and honor the need for each family member to be able to grow psychologically and emotionally independent of other family members can be an avenue of freedom that many persons with disabilities do not often enjoy. Getting family member to recognize the importance of allowing their member with a disability the space and opportunities to express himself is vital to good emotional adjustment. This concept can also be a liberating experience for the nondisabled family members in that it can decrease stress that builds within a family as they deal with the pressures of being a caregiver. Oftentimes the stress is self-induced as a result of being overprotective. The theoretical foundation of experiential family therapy fits well with the philosophy of the disability rights movement of persons with disabilities taking charge of their lives and making decisions for themselves.

Disadvantages: A hallmark technique of this therapy is spontaneity. Often a by-product of spontaneous action is lack of structure. Persons seeking help frequently need a great deal of structure to help them make sense of their situation. Families with a member who has a disability may need considerable structure to help deal with some of the emotions being experienced. The goal of getting family members to openly express their feelings and thoughts can be a double-edge instrument; on one side, it allows each member an opportunity to extricate him/herself from feelings and emotions which are suffocating them. However, on the other side, the release of these feeling can cause more distress and may cause hurt feeling among other family members. Of course, a skilled helping professionals can help deal with this situation.

Structural Family Therapy

Introduction

Given the emphasis on the growth of the family and its members, this therapy has major components of humanism and also has components of behavioralism in that one goal is to alter family behavior. One of the major contributors to the development of this therapy is Salvador Minuchin who emphasized that family units have structure and by observing this structure, the counselor/therapist can develop a map of treatment (plan of treatment). Minuchin postulated that family structure consist of unspoken rules proscribing, who does what, when things are done, how things are done, and how the family members interact with each other.

Philosophical Element (Theoretical Foundation)

Three constructs which are often associated with structural family therapy are: **structure, subsystems,** and **boundaries**.

Family Structure: According to this theory, each family has rules by which the family operates. These rules include, but are not limited to, a hierarchy of authority which determines who is responsible for making major decisions, who determines child rearing practices, etc. The structural family counselor/therapist, by becoming aware of these rules and how they are applied within the family, is able to gain valuable insight into the family dynamics.

Subsystems: According to structural family therapy, each individual family member is a subsystem and each subsystem may join with another subsystem to form a larger subsystem or subgroup. Additionally, each subsystem may form subsystem alliances. As an example, the father and mother may join together to establish family rules; the father and the daughter may develop a subsystem with regard to sharing information and exclude the mother and other siblings from the information sharing. Expressed in other terms, at various times a family member may form an alliance with another family member to further his/her agenda. These alliances are fluid, in that they may be formed at different times with different family member depending upon the objectives of those forming the alliances. By observing these various subsystems, the counselor/therapist can gain valuable information with regard to the structures of the family, thus aiding in developing the map for treatment.

Boundaries: According to Nichols and Schwartz (1995), "boundaries are invisible barriers that surround individuals and subsystems, regulating the amount of contact with others. Boundaries serve to protect the autonomy of the family and its subsystems" (p. 214).

Structural family therapist refers to family members as being **disengaged** or **enmeshed**. **Disengagement** means the individuals have become isolated from one or more family members. An example of disengagement would be a father of a child who has a disability who emotionally has difficulty accepting the child's life situation, thus he withdraws from any significant interaction with the child. **Enmeshed** refers to a smothering attachment to one or more family members. An example of this behavior is the father overprotecting the previously mentioned child.

Developmental Element (Human Development)

A key to being a functional family is the ability to adopt to change. To be alive is to be in the process of change; therefore, a family encounters numerous situation, which call for adaptation. As partners enter into a marriage, each bring into the union preconceived ideas of what a marriage is, additionally; each brings experiences from his/her family of origin which influences their perceptions of his/her union. In most instances, the perceptions are somewhat different; therefore, the two partners must learn to adjust and compromise for the union to be a successful marriage. This becomes particularly true when children enter the family; again each parent has ideas of child rearing. Generally speaking, they were developed from the experiences of their family of origin.

Structural family counselor/therapist emphasizes the point that families will experience stress as a result of dealing with change. However, a functional family will learn to accommodate change and set appropriate boundaries. This is an important point for counseling families with a person or persons with a disability in that change, and in some cases stress, may be the order of the day. The counselor/therapist must work with the family to adjust to these changes and learn to manage the stress that may be associated with these changes.

Structural Element (Goals)

Nichols and Schwartz remind us that the goals of therapy will be directed by the needs of the family (p. 224). However, some broad based goals are to (1) alter family structure so the family can solve its problems, (2) modify the family's functioning so that family members can solve their own problems, and (3) create an effective hierarchical structure.

Process Element (Techniques)

Some of the terminology used by structural therapists identifies several of the technique used, and they are **joining and accommodating, working with interaction, diagnosing, highlighting and modifying, interactions,** and **boundary making**. A brief explanation of each will follow.

Joining and accommodating refers to the counselor joining the family for the purpose of assisting them in working through family issues. The counselor/therapist becomes more than a therapeutic observer, but becomes actively involved in family therapeutic discussions. This may not be the role that family member perceive for the counselor; in fact, they may view the joining as intrusive, thus moving them beyond their comfort level. In the process of joining the family, the counselor/therapist has to become aware of the possibility of anxiety being built within the family thus leading to defenselessness. To avoid this problem from occurring, the counselor must become acquainted with each family member as an individual. Stated in other terms, the counselor must establish rapport with each family member.

Working with interaction refers to the observation of family dynamics. The key word is observation. The structural family therapist takes the approach that he must observe the behavior and interaction of family members rather than rely on what they say, because families, generally speaking, describe themselves as they perceive themselves, which may not be the way they really are.

Diagnosing, from the structural family therapist point of view, should occur early, preferably in the first session, before the counselor becomes too familiar with the family. From the view point of structural family therapy, if diagnosis occurs after the counselor has become familiar with the family, he may overlook important facts.

Highlighting and modifying interactions relates to how the therapist makes the family aware of its patterns and structures as well as assisting them with modification of the same. Two examples of how highlighting is accomplished are (1) by using the volume of the voice to emphasize relevant points, this is called affective intensity and (2) by repetition; repeating themes that emphasize things that are being done correctly, rather than dwelling on errors or mistakes.

Boundary making is intervention of the therapist to help realign boundaries. Dysfunctional families are characterized by rigid boundaries, thus realignment is necessary.

In summary, structural family therapy looks at the structures of the family and the patterns of interaction of family members; the counselor/therapist looks for disengagement and enmeshed family interaction. With enmeshed families the goal is to differentiate individuals and subsystems by strengthening the boundaries around them. With regard to disengaged families, the goal is to increase the interaction by making boundaries more permeable (Nichols & Schwartz, 1995, p. 224).

Implications for Rehabilitation

Advantages: A cornerstone of structural family therapy is identifying and understanding family structure. The fact that all families have structure is true but is not always evident to each family member. Too often family member go about their daily activities without recognizing how they are interacting with each other. Family members continue with their daily lives without recognizing the fact that members have become disengaged or enmeshed and the implications of these actions. This therapy helps bring into focus family characteristics and their implications. By being aware of the family structure, family members can realize an opportunity to become more effective communicators and more appreciative of each other's space and feelings. Also by recognizing family structure, family members may become aware of interaction that serves as stumbling blocks to their member with a disability. An additional benefit of this therapy is its emphasis on change. One of the most difficult things for any family to do is change its mode of daily operations. Rules, both spoken and unspoken, tend to be followed as though they were anchored in cement. An outside observer can serve as the source of helping the family to recognize the need for change.

Disadvantages: The level of counselor involvement within this therapy can foster dependency. To affect the necessary level of understanding to get the family to recognize the need for change, some times the therapist must join the family. Joining the family means that the counselor gets directly involved with the family interaction and this level of involvement could lead to the family members either resenting the counselor and viewing him as an intruder or they could become dependent upon the helper to direct their thinking and activities.

Behavioral Family Therapy

Introduction

The reader is referred to the individual behavioral therapy section of this chapter, where there is a detailed discussion of what behavioral therapy is and identification of major contributors to the therapy. Of course, a major difference in family therapy is the direction toward families rather than individuals.

Behavioral family therapy is different from most other family therapies in that its foundation is based on classical and operant conditioning. To be more specific, behavior which is targeted to be modified is identified in operational terms, specifically the frequency or rate of occurrence, and those behaviors which are targeted to keep are positively reinforced and those that are to be extinguished are ignored or in some manner negatively reinforced.

Philosophical Element (Theoretical Foundation)

As was mentioned in the explanation of individual behavioral therapy, the basic foundation of the therapy is built upon several sources: classical conditioning, operant conditioning, learning theory, social learning theory, and cognitive behavior theory. The hallmark of behavioral therapy is assessing a problem in measurable terms (frequency and rate of occurrence) and applying reinforcement to either strengthen or eliminate the consequence of the behavior. Reinforcers come in two categories: (1) positive reinforcement which is rewarding the desired behavior to strengthen its reoccurrence; and (2) negative reinforcement, which is designed to eliminate or lessen the undesirable behavior.

Development Element (Human Development)

Behavioral family therapists take a very pragmatic view of human psychological development. They look at what is happening behaviorally within the family and give little if any attention to things that have happened in the past that other therapists might consider as being the root cause of the behavior. The behavioral therapist would say that sure past behavior impacts present behavior; however, this knowledge does not eliminate the behavior. Since behavioral family therapists concentrate on behavior, a very simplified way of explaining normal and abnormal family behavioral development is that good family development has a maximum of desirable or positive behavior experiences and a minimum of unpleasant or destructive behavioral experience. Abnormal family behavioral development would be the reverse. It should be noted that some behavioral therapists use an eclectic approach and may look at past behavior as well as current behavior.

Behavioral family therapists point out the common sense fact that no family always experiences positive and uplifting experiences; true to human nature, all families experience stress and trauma at some points in their relationships. How families adjust to these troubled experiences, in part, determines a family's well-being. Healthy families are able to effectively communicate, and are able to engage in effective problem solving.

Structural Element (Goals)

The goals of behavioral family therapy are very straightforward, and they are modification of behavior patterns to alleviate the presenting symptoms; elimination of undesirable behavior; increasing positive behavior as defined by the family; effective communication and problem solving.

Process Element (Techniques)

As previously stated, the goals of behavioral therapy are straightforward and so are the techniques. There are basically three techniques: assessment of behavior, measurement of the frequency of occurrence of the behavior, and application of the treatment to strengthen the desired behavior(s) or weaken and/or eliminate the unwanted behavior(s).

Implication for Rehabilitation

Advantages: With regard to application to the rehabilitation process, behavioral therapy has been proven to be effective in treating some of the behaviors associated with alcoholism, mental retardation, psychosis, phobias, and speech disorders, to mention a few. It should be emphasized that neither behavioral family therapy nor any other psychological therapy cures mental retardation, alcoholism, or psychosis, but it can be effective in modifying some of the behavior resulting from these disabilities. Behavior therapy also can be effective with regard to helping family members with codependency and other behaviors related to living with a person who has some of the previously mentioned disabilities.

Disadvantages: As discussed in the section on individual behavior therapy (Chapter 14) a major problem is getting the family member to continue to conduct their therapy away from the therapist.

Psychoanalytic Family Therapy

Introduction

Psychoanalytic family therapy is a psychodynamic theory, which in simplified terms means the belief that human problems result from suppressed or unconscious feelings that may have come from past events such as suppression (defense mechanism) of biological urges such as sex drives. A major goal of the therapist is to help the client gain insight into these issues and by doing so, efforts can be taken to effectively deal with the same.

Philosophical Element (Theoretical Foundation)

As previously stated, the foundation of psychoanalytic therapy is the recognition and interpretation of unconscious desires and defenses against them. Psychoanalytic therapy is based upon the precepts of Sigmund Freud. Two of the basic elements of his theory are referred to as, **drive psychology** and **self psychology**. **Drive psychology** refers to biological drives such as sexual and human urges such as aggression. Mental conflict may have occurred when as a child we became aware that the expression of these impulses would lead to punishment. Thus, we have a tendency to suppress or move these urges to the unconscious; in effect, what we have done is develop defenses against the display of these impulses. **Self psychology** relates to the human need for appreciation and recognition. As a child, to the extent our parents show or do not show appreciation of us determines the extent we grow-up craving appreciation. Since all humans crave appreciation, the key becomes how we display this need.

Psychoanalytic therapy was originally developed for use in individual or one-on-one therapy and because of the intensity of its efforts to uncover and deal with individual human dynamics, it may be difficult to understand how this approach can be used in family therapy. Individual psychoanalytic therapy focuses on intrapsychic structure, personal drives, impulses, and urges; whereas family therapy involves interpersonal interaction; to be more specific, social interactions. The theory that brings these two approaches together is called **object relation theory**. Again I rely on Nichols' and Schwartz's expert and excellent explanation of object relation theory: "Our present relationship to people is based upon expectations formed by early experiences. The residue of these early relationships leaves internal objects (mental images of self and others and our relationship with others). Additionally, the unconscious remnants of those internal objects form the core of the person" (pp. 247–248).

Developmental Element (Human Development)

From the psychoanalytic family counselor/therapist standpoint, normal or abnormal development begins with the parents. In fact, the parents' abilities to provide a secure and nurturing environment depend upon how secure they feel. One can begin to see the pattern of human psychological development unfold. Parents' feelings of security, to a major degree, depend upon their interactions with their parents and their parent's security upon their interactions and so on. In essence, parents pass to their offspring remnants of their interactions with their parents. A major question unanswered is how is the chain of either positive or negative interactions broken?

In psychoanalytic family therapy, the mother plays a prominent role in child development. If the mother is a loving individual and feels secure in her psychological being, the child will develop good internal object relations. Because of the mother's secure feeling of herself, she does not unnecessarily cling onto the child, which makes the process of the child differentiating himself from his parents, particularly his mother, easier. If this separation occurs without considerable difficulty, the child is able to begin the development of a secure self-identity. Stated succinctly, the key to good family relationships, according to psychoanalytic family therapy is the development of good object relationships. Abnormal development is the result of a faulty object relationship development.

Structural Element (Goals)

Since the basic theory of the psychoanalytic approach is to focus on unconscious material, the primary goal is to remove the unconscious restrictions that the family members possess. Additionally, the goal is to strengthen the ego so that behavior is based in reality rather than being controlled by instinctual cravings.

Process Element (Techniques)

There are four basic techniques in psychoanalytic family therapy: **listening, empathy, interpretation** and **maintaining analytic neutrality**. With regard to **listening**, all therapies recognize the importance of effective listening; however, psychoanalytic family therapy places a great deal of emphasis on listening because it helps avoid the therapist interrupting the client's discussion of his problems. Psychoanalysts place a great deal of emphasis upon free-flowing spontaneous conversation. It is their belief that this type of conversation yields tremendous information.

Empathy refers to being able to place oneself in the situation of the client and as much as possible experience what the client is feeling. As is true with listening, it is important for the counselor/therapist not to allow the empathy to hinder the spontaneity of the clients.

Through attentive listening and analyzing what the family members are saying, the counselor is able to **interpret** to the clients what their actions and behaviors mean.

Analytic neutrality means not taking sides with regard to family dynamics.

In summary, the connection between individual psychoanalytic therapy and family psychoanalytic therapy is object relations theory. Object relation theory emphasizes the point that present relationships to people are predicated upon expectations from early in life. Normal family development depends to a large extent upon the relationship the child has with his/her parents, particularly the mother. The more secure the parents are in their own personal being, the greater the chances are that the children will make good psychological adjustments. If parents are psychologically secure within themselves, the greater the chances are that the children will be able to establish a secure self-identity. When as children we are unable to develop secure self-identities, we suppress some of our feelings and develop other defense mechanisms to deal with these unconscious urges. Psychoanalytic family therapy is designed to assist the family in recognizing these unconscious urges and deal effectively with them.

Implications for Rehabilitation

Advantage: The depth to which psychoanalytic therapy goes can help the family to recognize areas of their lives together as a family which need strengthening. Also, this depth of understanding suppressed feeling and defensive mechanisms can be beneficial with regard to developing a better understanding of one's behavior.

Disadvantage: Basically, the same as individual psychoanalytic therapy, time consuming, expensive, and uncovering feelings that may be difficult for the family to handle.

Review Questions

1. What are the six (6) basic principles of family counseling discussed in this chapter?
2. What are some of the benefits of family counseling with families of persons with disabilities?
3. Why does experiential family therapy claim that it does not have a theoretical foundation?
4. What are the three (3) goals for experiential family therapy discussed in this chapter?
5. What is "family sculpturing"?
6. With regard to structural family therapy what does the term "subsystems" mean?
7. What do the terms "enmeshed and disengaged" mean?
8. What are some of the advantages and disadvantages of the technique of joining and accommodating?
9. What are the philosophical foundations upon which cognitive behavior therapy is based?
10. What role does object relation theory play in psychoanalytic family therapy?
11. What are the four (4) basic techniques in psychoanalytic family therapy discussed in this chapter?
12. What are some of the advantages and disadvantages of the use of psychoanalytic family therapy with families of persons with disabilities?

Suggested Activities

1. Contact several family counselors who work with families of persons with disabilities and ascertain the techniques they use in their counseling.
2. Contact several family counselors and ask them about the benefits of family counseling with families of persons with disabilities.
3. Contact several family counselors and ask them to what extent they involve the person with a disability when they are working with the family.

4. Contact several family counselors and ask them to what extent they involve the person with a disability if he/she has severe cognitive limitations, when they are working with the family.

References

Nichols, M. P., & Schwartz, R. C. (2001). *Family counseling concepts and methods* (5th. ed.). Boston: Allyn and Bacon.

Nichols, M. P., & Schwartz, R. C. (1995). *Family counseling concept and methods* (4th ed.). Boston: Alyn and Bacon.

Suggested Readings

Epstein, N., Schlesinger, E. E., & Dryden, W. (1988). *Cognitive-behavioral therapy with families.* New York: Brunner/Mazel.

Falloon, I. R. H. (1988). *Handbook of behavioral family therapy.* New York: Guilford Press.

Hoffman, L. (1981). *Foundations of family therapy.* New York: Basic Books.

Jefferson, C. (1978). Some notes on the use of family sculpture in therapy. *Family Process, 17:* 69–76.

Kaslow, F. W. (1980). History of family therapy in the United States: A kaleidoscopic overview. *Marriage and Family Review, 3:*77–111.

Minuchin, S., & Nichols, M. P. (1993). *Family healing.* New York: The Free Press.

Perls, F. S. (1961). *Gestalt therapy verbatim.* Lafayette. CA: Real People Press.

Rogers, C. R. (1951). *Client-centered therapy.* Boston: Houghton Mifflin.

Satir, V. M. (1964). *Conjoint family therapy.* Palo Alto, CA: Science and Behavior Books.

Scharff, D. (1989). *The foundations of object relations family therapy.* New York: Jason Aronson.

Chapter 16

CONCLUSION

Chapter Outline
• Final Statements

Chapter Objectives
• To provide brief final comments

Final Statements

In most societies, some group or groups become dominant; this is to be expected. Generally, this is considered leadership and there is nothing wrong as long as the dominant group does not impose its will, values, lifestyle, beliefs, etc. on the subordinate groups to the point it suppresses the subordinate groups' values, lifestyles, and beliefs.

Americans have begun to realize the destructive nature of one culture totally dominating all others; therefore, the nation has begun to value cultural diversity. In 1954, after many years of segregated public schooling, the United States Supreme Court's ruling in Brown vs. the Topeka Board of Education struck down the old Plessy vs. Ferguson decision that solidified the doctrine of separate but equal facilities. This ruling made it illegal to conduct segregated public school systems. After having limited effects on creating cultural diversity, Congress passed and President Lyndon Johnson signed into law the Civil Rights Act of 1964 making it illegal to discriminate against anyone based upon their race, creed, color, or gender.

There is no doubt that the Civil Rights Act of 1964 created more opportunities for minorities and women than had previously existed. However, the act fell considerably short of creating a society where diversity is valued. Additionally, the act did very little for persons with disabilities. It is true that a person of color or a female with a disability received some protection through the 1964 Civil Rights Act with respect to their civil rights as a minority or woman. Unfortunately, it did not protect these same people from acts of discrimination based upon their disability.

This type of protection for persons with disabilities became a reality in a limited way with the enactment of the 1973 Rehabilitation Act and in a comprehensive manner with the passage and enactment of the 1990 Americans With Disabilities Act (ADA). *The Americans With Disabilities Act Handbook*, published by the Equal Employment Opportunity Commission and the United States Department of Justice, clearly enunicates the aim of the ADA:

> The ADA is a federal antidiscrimination statute designed to remove barriers which prevent qualified individuals with disabilities from enjoying the same employment opportunities that are available to persons without disabilities.
>
> Like the Civil Rights Act of 1964 that prohibits discrimination on the basis of race, color, religion, national origin and sex, the ADA seeks to ensure access to equal employment opportunities based on merit. It does not guarantee equal results, establish quotas, or require preferences favoring individuals with disabilities over those without disabilities. The ADA thus establishes a process in which the employer must assess a disabled individual's ability to perform the essential functions of the specific job held or desired. The ADA does not relieve a disabled employee or applicant from the obligation to perform the essential functions of the job.

From this statement, it is clear that the ADA's primary function is to eliminate discrimination based upon disability, not provide the person with a disability an advantage. With this in mind it is incumbent that rehabilitation helping professionals, as well as others working with persons with disabilities, insure that their clients/patients are rehabilitated and well prepared to compete with nondisabled persons for jobs. In the past, part of the reason some rehabilitation plans were unsuccessful was that they did not take into consideration cultural differences. In other words, all clients were treated the same and to add further difficulties, all clients were judged by Euro-American standards. To enhance the chances of carrying out a successful rehabilitation plan, today's helping professional must be aware of the client's culture from the standpoint of his/her race, gender, and disability. To concentrate on one characteristic without considering all others decreases the chances of success. Whereas, considering all aspects of the client's culture increases the chances of success.

NAME INDEX

SUBJECT INDEX